CLYMER®

HONDA

CB750 SOHC FOURS • 1969-1978

The world's finest publisher of mechanical how-to manuals

CLYMER®

P.O. Box 12901, Overland Park, Kansas 66282-2901

FIRST EDITION
First Printing December, 1971

SECOND EDITION
Updated to include 1972 models
First Printing April, 1972

THIRD EDITION
Updated to include 1973 models
First Printing June, 1973

FOURTH EDITION
Updated to include 1974 models
First Printing August, 1974

FIFTH EDITION
Updated by Jim Combs to include 1975-1976 models
First Printing August, 1976

SIXTH EDITION
Updated by Brick Price to include 1977 models
First Printing August, 1977

SEVENTH EDITION
Updated by Mike Bishop to include 1978 models
First Printing December, 1978

EIGHTH EDITION
First Printing January, 1980
Second Printing February, 1982
Third Printing February, 1983
Fourth Printing August, 1983
Fifth Printing March, 1984
Sixth Printing February, 1985
Seventh Printing October, 1985
Eighth Printing August, 1986
Ninth Printing November, 1986
Tenth Printing January, 1988
Eleventh Printing November, 1988
Twelfth Printing April, 1990
Thirteenth Printing February, 1991
Fourteenth Printing January, 1992
Fifteenth Printing October, 1992
Sixteenth Printing April, 1994
Seventeenth Printing July, 1995
Eighteenth Printing November, 1995
Nineteenth Printing January, 1997
Twentieth Printing May, 1998
Twenty-first Printing September, 1999
Twenty-second Printing January 2001
Twenty-third Printing July, 2002
Twenty-fourth Printing December, 2003
Twenty-fifth Printing January, 2005
Twenty-sixth Printing January, 2010

Printed in U.S.A.

ISBN-10: 0-89287-167-9

ISBN-13: 978-0-89287-167-4

TECHNICAL ASSISTANCE: Kolbe Honda, Woodland Hills, California.

COVER: Photography and 1978 CB750F by Mark Dickinson. Special thanks to the Vintage Japanese Motorcycle Club at www.vjmc.org.

TOOLS AND EQUIPMENT: K & L Supply Co. at www.klsupply.com.

CLYMER®

Publisher Ron Rogers

EDITORIAL

Editorial Director
James Grooms

Editor
Steven Thomas

Associate Editor
Rick Arens

Authors
Michael Morlan
George Parise
Ed Scott
Ron Wright

Technical Illustrators
Steve Amos
Errol McCarthy
Mitzi McCarthy
Bob Meyer

SALES

Sales Manager
Matt Tusken

CUSTOMER SERVICE

Customer Service Manager
Terri Cannon

Customer Service Account Specialist
Courtney Hollars

Customer Service Representatives
Dinah Bunnell
April LeBlond
Suzanne Myers
Sherry Rudkin

PRODUCTION

Group Production Manager
Dylan Goodwin

Production Manager
Greg Araujo

Production Editors
Holly McComas
Adriane Roberts

Associate Production Editor
Kendra Lueckert

Graphic Designer
Jason Hale

P.O. Box 12901, Overland Park, KS 66282-2901 • 800-262-1954 • 913-967-1719

More information available at *clymer.com*

CONTENTS

QUICK REFERENCE DATA

BREAKER GAP ADJUSTERS AND TIMING PLATE SCREWS

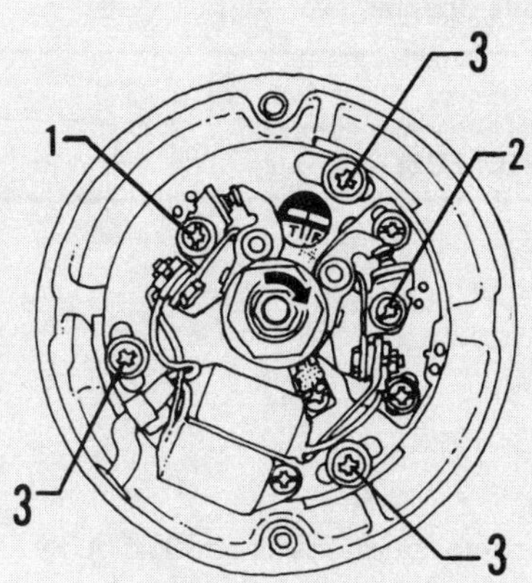

1. Lock screw, No. 1 and 4 points
2. Lock screw, No. 2 and 3 points
3. Timing plate screw

SYNCHRONIZING ADJUSTERS

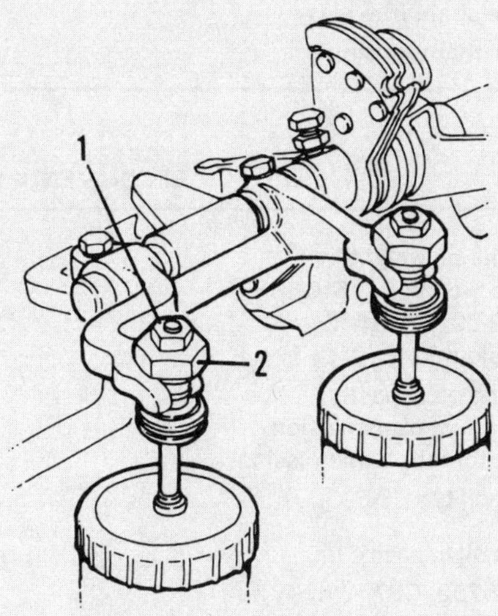

1. Locknut 2. Adjuster

ENGINE TUNE-UP SPECIFICATIONS

Valve clearance (cold)	
Intake (rear)	0.002 in. (0.05mm)
Exhaust (front)	0.003 in. (0.08mm)
Spark plug gap	0.024-0.028 in. (6-7mm)
Ignition point gap	0.012-0.016 in. (0.3-0.4mm)
Ignition timing	"F" mark @ 850-900 rpm or at rest 23.5-26.5° in advance of the "F" mark @ 2,500 rpm
Dwell	92-98° (2-cylinder scale) or 46-49° (4-cylinder scale)
Carburetor	
Float level	1.023 in. (26mm)
Air screw	Counterclockwise from seat one complete turn
Idle adjustment screw	850-900 rpm
Vacuum gauge reading	8 in. of vacuum

SPARK PLUG APPLICATION

Brand	Hot	Standard	Cold
Champion	——	A8Y-MC	R-6
NGK	D7ES	D8ES	D10E
Bosch	X260T2	X300T2	X320T2
Autolite	HG2	HG1	——

ADJUSTMENTS

Throttle cable free play	0.04-0.05 in. (1-2mm)
Throttle lever free play	Approximately 10-15°
Clutch cable free play	0.4-0.8 in. (10-20mm) at lever tip
Rear brake lever free play (drum brake)	0.75-1.25 in. (20-30mm)
Drive chain free play	0.75-1.0 in. (20-25mm)
Cam chain tensioner	See Chapter Two

RECOMMENDED LUBRICANTS AND FUEL

Engine oil weight*	
Above 59°F (15°C)	SAE 30, SAE 30W, or SAE 10W-40
32-59°F (0-15°C)	SAE 20 or SAE 20W
Below 32°F (0°C)	SAE 10W
Engine oil capacity	
Manual transmission	3 qt. (2.7 liter)
Automatic transmission	4.2 qt. (4 liter)
Fork oil type	SAE 10W-30 or automatic transmission fluid (ATF) 10W or 20W fork oil**
Fork oil capacity	
CB750, CB750 K1-K2	6.9-7.1 oz. (207-213 cc)
CB750 K3-K6, CB750A	5.3-5.4 0z. (160-162 cc)
Drive chain	Special chain lubricant
Cables	Powdered graphite or SAE 30W oil
Bearings	High-temperature bearing grease
Grease fittings	White grease
Hydraulic brake fluid	DOT 3
Breaker point cam	Cam grease
Fuel	85-95 octane (Research method)

*Must be rated "for API service SE." **Do not use engine oil.

ENGINE TORQUES

Tightening Point	Ft.-lb.	Cmkg
Crankcase and crankcase covers	5-8	70-110
Cylinder head	15	200
Nuts*		
Bolts	6-9	80-120
Carburetor insulator-to-cylinder head	5-8	70-110
Cam sprocket	12-15	160-200
Alternator rotor	22-29	300-400
Primary drive gear	22-29	300-400
Tappet adjusting nut	5-8	70-110
Upper and lower crankcases	15-19	220-260
Cylinder head cover	5-8	70-110
Clutch center	29-33	400-450
Connecting rod	14-15	200-220

*(Apply oil to the nuts before tightening.)

FRAME TORQUES

Tightening Point	Ft.-lb.	Cmkg
Steering stem nut	58-87	800-1,200
Fork top bridge to front forks	13-17	180-230
Handlebar holder	13-17	180-230
Front fork bottom bridge to front forks	13-17	180-230
Spokes		
Front wheel	1.9-2.2	25-30
Rear wheel	1.5-1.9	20-25
Swing arm pivot bolt	40-51	550-700
Front axle nut	33-40	450-550
Front fork axle holder	13-17	180-230
Engine hanger bolt	22-29	300-400
Rear axle nut	58-72	800-1,000
Final driven sprocket	29-36	400-500
Brake arm	6-7	80-100
Front and rear brake torque links	13-17	180-230
Rear suspension	22-29	300-400
Footpeg	33-40	450-550
Gearshift pedal and kick arm	6-7	80-100

2
1
3
4
T
F
1-4

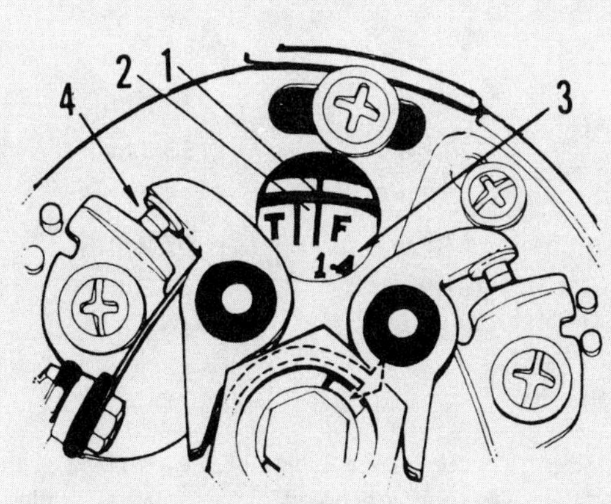

TIMING MARKS

1. Index mark
2. "F" (fire) mark
3. Cylinder number
4. 1-4 cylinder breaker points

CARBURETOR ADJUSTMENT

IDLE AIR SCREW

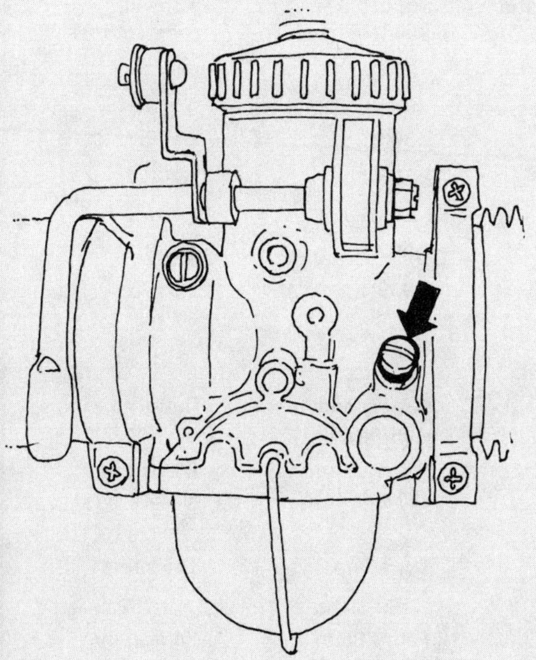

Index mark
T-mark

0.04-0.08 in.
(1-2mm)
Cable
adjuster
Cable
adjuster
locknut

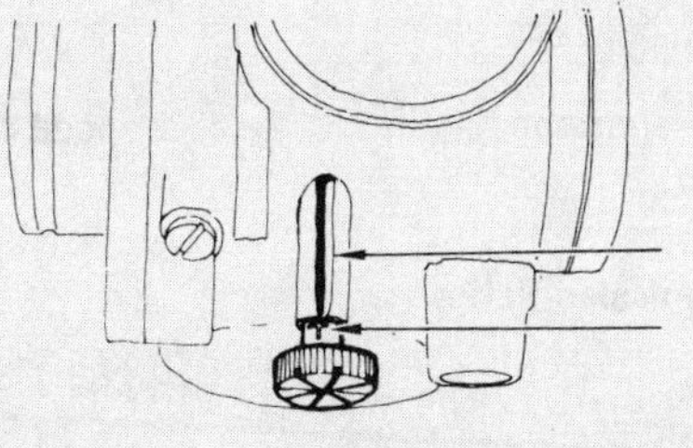

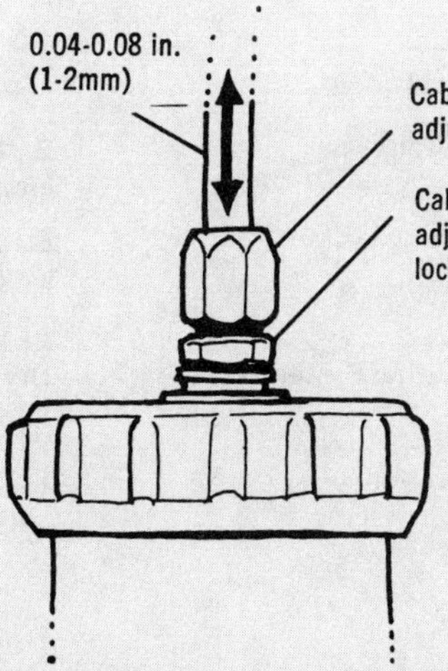

DIMENSIONS AND GENERAL SPECIFICATIONS

	CB750A	CB750 K1-K8	CB750F
Dimensions			
Overall length	88.6 in.	85.0 in.	86.6 in.
Overall width	34.1 in.	34.8 in.	33.9 in.
Overall height	46.7 in.	45.5 in.	45.0 in.
Wheelbase	58.3 in.	57.3 in.	57.9 in.
Seat height	32.3 in.	31.9 in.	31.9 in.
Dry weight	531 lb.	480 lb.	499 lb.
Engine			
Type	4 stroke, 4 cylinder sohc, air cooled	4-stroke, 4-cylinder, sohc, air cooled	4-stroke, 4-cylinder, sohc, air cooled
Displacement (cc/cu. in.)	736cc/44.93	736/44.93	736/44.93
Compression ratio	8.6:1	9.0.1	9.2:1
Bore and stroke			
Millimeters	61 x 63	61 x 63	61 x 63
Inches	2.401 x 2.480	2.401 x 2.480	2.401 x 2.480
Drive Train			
Clutch		Wet, multi-plate	Wet, multi-plate
Transmission	2-speed automatic	5-speed, constant mesh	5-speed, constant mesh
Transmission Ratios			
1st	2.263:1	2.500:1	2.500:1
2nd	1.520:1	1.708:1	1.708:1
3rd		1.333:1	1.333:1
4th		1.097:1	1.133:1
5th		0.939:1	0.969:1
Electrical			
Ignition	Battery and ignition coil	Battery and ignition coil	Battery and ignition coil
Starting system	Electric and kickstarter	Electric and kickstarter	Electric and kickstarter
Lubrication System	Dry sump	Dry sump	Dry sump
Carburetion	Four 24mm carburetors	Four 28mm carburetors	Four 28mm carburetors
Brakes			
Front	Disc	Disc	Disc
Rear	Drum	Drum	Disc

CLYMER®

HONDA

CB750 SOHC FOURS • 1969-1978

INTRODUCTION

This book provides maintenance, troubleshooting, and repair information for the Honda CB750 series of 4-cylinder motorcycles.

Although Honda discontinued the CB750K series after the 1975 K5, the same basic bike was re-introduced in 1976 as the CB750. To avoid confusion with the early CB750, in this book the 1976 model will be referred to as the CB750 K6, or simply "K6."

All models use the same basic 736cc engine, and all use either a 5-speed manual or the 2-speed Hondamatic transmission. All models through the CB750A use similar 4-pipe exhaust and muffler systems, but the CB750F model uses a 4-in-1 exhaust and muffler system. Other minor differences exist between the various models. A majority of the procedures contained in this book, however, are common to all models. Exceptions are noted.

Where repairs are practical for the owner/mechanic, complete procedures are given. Equally important, difficult jobs are pointed out. Such operations are usually more economically performed by a dealer or independent repair shop.

A shop manual is a reference. You want to be able to find information fast. As in all Clymer books, this one is designed with this in mind. All chapters are thumb tabbed. Important items are extensively indexed at the rear of the book. Finally, all the most frequently used specifications and capacities are summarized on the *Quick Reference* pages at the front of the book.

Keep the book handy. It will help you to better understand your bike, lower repair and maintenance costs, and generally improve your satisfaction with your motorcycle.

CHAPTER ONE

GENERAL INFORMATION

The troubleshooting, maintenance, tune-up, and step-by-step repair procedures in this book are written specifically for the owner and home mechanic. The text is accompanied by helpful photos and diagrams to make the job as clear and correct as possible.

Troubleshooting, maintenance, tune-up, and repair are not difficult if you know what to do and what tools and equipment to use. Anyone of average intelligence, with some mechanical ability, and not afraid to get their hands dirty can perform most of the procedures in this book.

In some cases, a repair job may require tools or skills not reasonably expected of the home mechanic. These procedures are noted in each chapter and it is recommended that you take the job to your dealer, a competent mechanic, or a machine shop.

MANUAL ORGANIZATION

This chapter provides general information, safety and service hints. Also included are lists of recommended shop and emergency tools as well as a brief description of troubleshooting and tune-up equipment.

Chapter Two provides methods and suggestions for quick and accurate diagnosis and repair of problems. Troubleshooting procedures discuss typical symptoms and logical methods to pinpoint the trouble.

Chapter Three explains all periodic lubrication and routine maintenance necessary to keep your motorcycle running well. Chapter Three also includes recommended tune-up procedures, eliminating the need to constantly consult chapters on the various subassemblies.

Subsequent chapters cover specific systems such as the engine, transmission, and electrical system. Each of these chapters provides disassembly, inspection, repair, and assembly procedures in a simple step-by-step format. If a repair is impractical for the home mechanic it is indicated. In these cases it is usually faster and less expensive to have the repairs made by a dealer or competent repair shop. Essential specifications are included in the appropriate chapters.

When special tools are required to perform a task included in this manual, the tools are illustrated. It may be possible to borrow or rent these tools. The inventive mechanic may also be able to find a suitable substitute in his tool box, or to fabricate one.

The terms NOTE, CAUTION, and WARNING have specific meanings in this manual. A NOTE provides additional or explanatory information. A

CAUTION is used to emphasize areas where equipment damage could result if proper precautions are not taken. A WARNING is used to stress those areas where personal injury or death could result from negligence, in addition to possible mechanical damage.

SERVICE HINTS

Time, effort, and frustration will be saved and possible injury will be prevented if you observe the following practices.

Most of the service procedures covered are straightforward and can be performed by anyone reasonably handy with tools. It is suggested, however, that you consider your own capabilities carefully before attempting any operation involving major disassembly of the engine.

Some operations, for example, require the use of a press. It would be wiser to have these performed by a shop equipped for such work, rather than to try to do the job yourself with makeshift equipment. Other procedures require precision measurements. Unless you have the skills and equipment required, it would be better to have a qualified repair shop make the measurements for you.

Repairs go much faster and easier if the parts that will be worked on are clean before you begin. There are special cleaners for washing the engine and related parts. Brush or spray on the cleaning solution, let stand, then rinse it away with a garden hose. Clean all oily or greasy parts with cleaning solvent as you remove them.

WARNING

Never use gasoline as a cleaning agent. It presents an extreme fire hazard. Be sure to work in a well-ventilated area when using cleaning solvent. Keep a fire extinguisher, rated for gasoline fires, handy in any case.

Much of the labor charge for repairs made by dealers is for the removal and disassembly of other parts to reach the defective unit. It is frequently possible to perform the preliminary operations yourself and then take the defective unit in to the dealer for repair, at considerable savings.

Once you have decided to tackle the job yourself, make sure you locate the appropriate section in this manual, and read it entirely. Study the illustrations and text until you have a good idea of what is involved in completing the job satisfactorily. If special tools are required, make arrangements to get them before you start. Also, purchase any known defective parts prior to starting on the procedure. It is frustrating and time-consuming to get partially into a job and then be unable to complete it.

Simple wiring checks can be easily made at home, but knowledge of electronics is almost a necessity for performing tests with complicated electronic testing gear.

During disassembly of parts keep a few general cautions in mind. Force is rarely needed to get things apart. If parts are a tight fit, like a bearing in a case, there is usually a tool designed to separate them. Never use a screwdriver to pry apart parts with machined surfaces such as cylinder head or crankcase halves. You will mar the surfaces and end up with leaks.

Make diagrams wherever similar-appearing parts are found. You may think you can remember where everything came from — but mistakes are costly. There is also the possibility you may get sidetracked and not return to work for days or even weeks — in which interval, carefully laid out parts may have become disturbed.

Tag all similar internal parts for location, and mark all mating parts for position. Record number and thickness of any shims as they are removed. Small parts such as bolts can be identified by placing them in plastic sandwich bags that are sealed and labeled with masking tape.

Wiring should be tagged with masking tape and marked as each wire is removed. Again, do not rely on memory alone.

Disconnect battery ground cable before working near electrical connections and before disconnecting wires. Never run the engine with the battery disconnected; the alternator could be seriously damaged.

Protect finished surfaces from physical damage or corrosion. Keep gasoline and brake fluid off painted surfaces.

Frozen or very tight bolts and screws can often be loosened by soaking with penetrating oil like Liquid Wrench or WD-40, then sharply striking the bolt head a few times with a hammer and punch (or screwdriver for screws). Avoid heat unless absolutely necessary, since it may melt, warp, or remove the temper from many parts.

Avoid flames or sparks when working near a charging battery or flammable liquids, such as gasoline.

No parts, except those assembled with a press fit, require unusual force during assembly. If a part is hard to remove or install, find out why before proceeding.

Cover all openings after removing parts to keep dirt, small tools, etc., from falling in.

When assembling two parts, start all fasteners, then tighten evenly.

Wiring connections and brake shoes, drums, pads, and discs and contact surfaces in dry clutches should be kept clean and free of grease and oil.

When assembling parts, be sure all shims and washers are replaced exactly as they came out.

Whenever a rotating part butts against a stationary part, look for a shim or washer. Use new gaskets if there is any doubt about the condition of old ones. Generally, you should apply gasket cement to one mating surface only, so the parts may be easily disassembled in the future. A thin coat of oil on gaskets helps them seal effectively.

Heavy grease can be used to hold small parts in place if they tend to fall out during assembly. However, keep grease and oil away from electrical, clutch, and brake components.

High spots may be sanded off a piston with sandpaper, but emery cloth and oil do a much more professional job.

Carburetors are best cleaned by disassembling them and soaking the parts in a commercial carburetor cleaner. Never soak gaskets and rubber parts in these cleaners. Never use wire to clean out jets and air passages; they are easily damaged. Use compressed air to blow out the carburetor, but only if the float has been removed first.

Take your time and do the job right. Do not forget that a newly rebuilt engine must be broken in the same as a new one. Refer to your owner's manual for the proper break-in procedures.

SAFETY FIRST

Professional mechanics can work for years and never sustain a serious injury. If you observe a few rules of common sense and safety, you can enjoy many safe hours servicing your motorcycle. You could hurt yourself or damage the motorcycle if you ignore these rules.

1. Never use gasoline as a cleaning solvent.
2. Never smoke or use a torch in the vicinity of flammable liquids such as cleaning solvent in open containers.
3. Never smoke or use a torch in an area where batteries are being charged. Highly explosive hydrogen gas is formed during the charging process.
4. Use the proper sized wrenches to avoid damage to nuts and injury to yourself.
5. When loosening a tight or stuck nut, be guided by what would happen if the wrench should slip. Protect yourself accordingly.
6. Keep your work area clean and uncluttered.
7. Wear safety goggles during all operations involving drilling, grinding, or use of a cold chisel.
8. Never use worn tools.
9. Keep a fire extinguisher handy and be sure it is rated for gasoline (Class B) and electrical (Class C) fires.

EXPENDABLE SUPPLIES

Certain expendable supplies are necessary. These include grease, oil, gasket cement, wiping rags, cleaning solvent, and distilled water. Also, special locking compounds, silicone lubricants, and engine and carburetor cleaners may be useful. Cleaning solvent is available at most service stations and distilled water for the battery is available at supermarkets.

SHOP TOOLS

For complete servicing and repair you will need an assortment of ordinary hand tools (**Figure 1**).

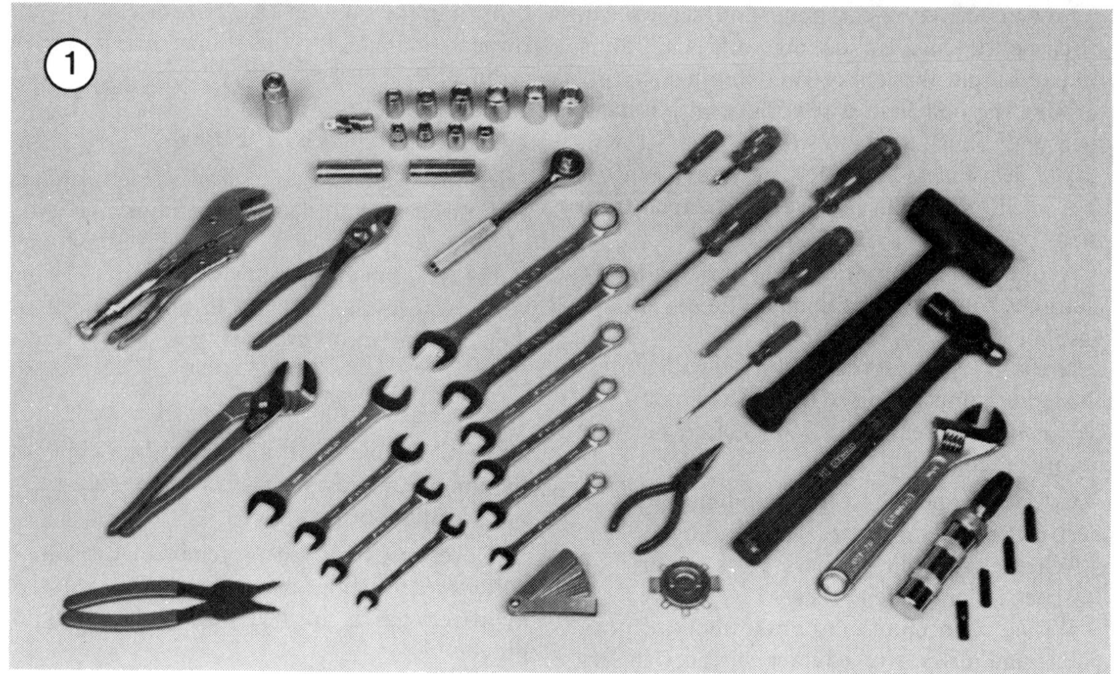

As a minimum, these include:

a. Combination wrenches
b. Sockets
c. Plastic mallet
d. Small hammer
e. Impact driver
f. Snap ring pliers
g. Gas pliers
h. Phillips screwdrivers
i. Slot (common) screwdrivers
j. Feeler gauges
k. Spark plug gauge
l. Spark plug wrench

Special tools required are shown in the chapters covering the particular repair in which they are used.

Engine tune-up and troubleshooting procedures require other special tools and equipment. These are described in detail in the following sections.

EMERGENCY TOOL KITS

Highway

A small emergency tool kit kept on the bike is handy for road emergencies which otherwise could leave you stranded. The tools and spares listed below and shown in **Figure 2** will let you handle most roadside repairs.

a. Motorcycle tool kit (original equipment)
b. Impact driver
c. Silver waterproof sealing tape (duct tape)
d. Hose clamps (3 sizes)
e. Silicone sealer
f. Lock 'N' Seal
g. Flashlight
h. Tire patch kit
i. Tire irons
j. Plastic pint bottle (for oil)
k. Waterless hand cleaner
l. Rags for clean up

Off-Road

A few simple tools and aids carried on the motorcycle can mean the difference between walking or riding back to camp or to where repairs can be made. See **Figure 3**.

A few essential spare parts carried in your truck or van can prevent a day or weekend of trail riding from being spoiled. See **Figure 4**.

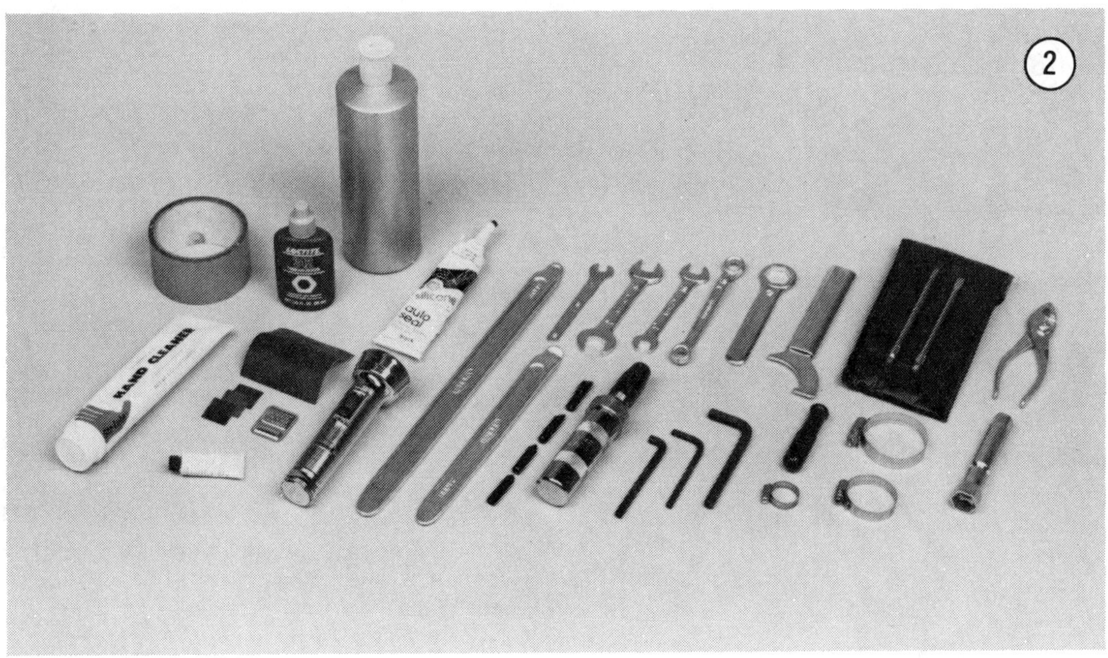

On the Motorcycle

a. Motorcycle tool kit (original equipment)
b. Drive chain master link
c. Tow line
d. Spark plug
e. Spark plug wrench
f. Shifter lever
g. Clutch/brake lever
h. Silver waterproof sealing tape (duct tape)
i. Loctite Lock 'N' Seal

In the Truck

a. Control cables (throttle, clutch, brake)
b. Silicone sealer
c. Tire patch kit
d. Tire irons
e. Tire pump
f. Impact driver
g. Oil

WARNING
Tools and spares should be carried on the motorcycle — not in clothing where a simple fall could result in serious injury from a sharp tool.

TROUBLESHOOTING AND TUNE-UP EQUIPMENT

Voltmeter, Ohmmeter, and Ammeter

For testing the ignition or electrical system, a good voltmeter is required. For motorcycle use, an instrument covering 0-20 volts is satisfactory. One which also has a 0-2 volt scale is necessary for testing relays, points, or individual contacts where voltage drops are much smaller. Accuracy should be ± ½ volt.

An ohmmeter measures electrical resistance. This instrument is useful for checking continuity (open and short circuits), and testing fuses and lights.

The ammeter measures electrical current. Ammeters for motorcycle use should cover 0-50 amperes and 0-250 amperes. These are useful for checking battery charging and starting current.

Several inexpensive VOM's (volt-ohm-milliammeter) combine all three instruments into one which fits easily in any tool box. See **Figure 5**. However, the ammeter ranges are usually too small for motorcycle work.

Hydrometer

The hydrometer gives a useful indication of battery condition and charge by measuring the

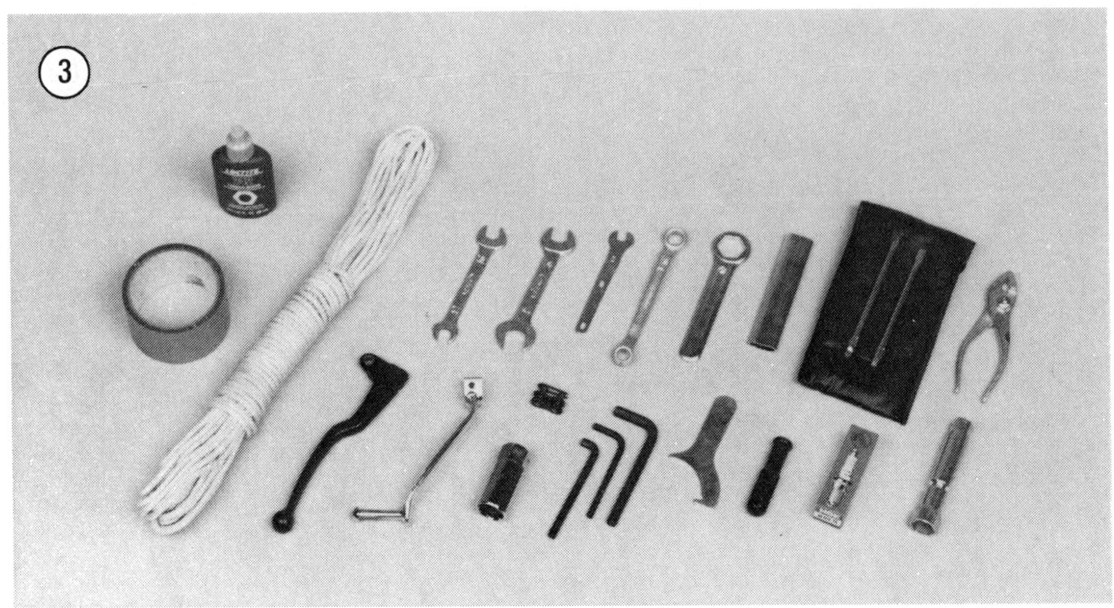

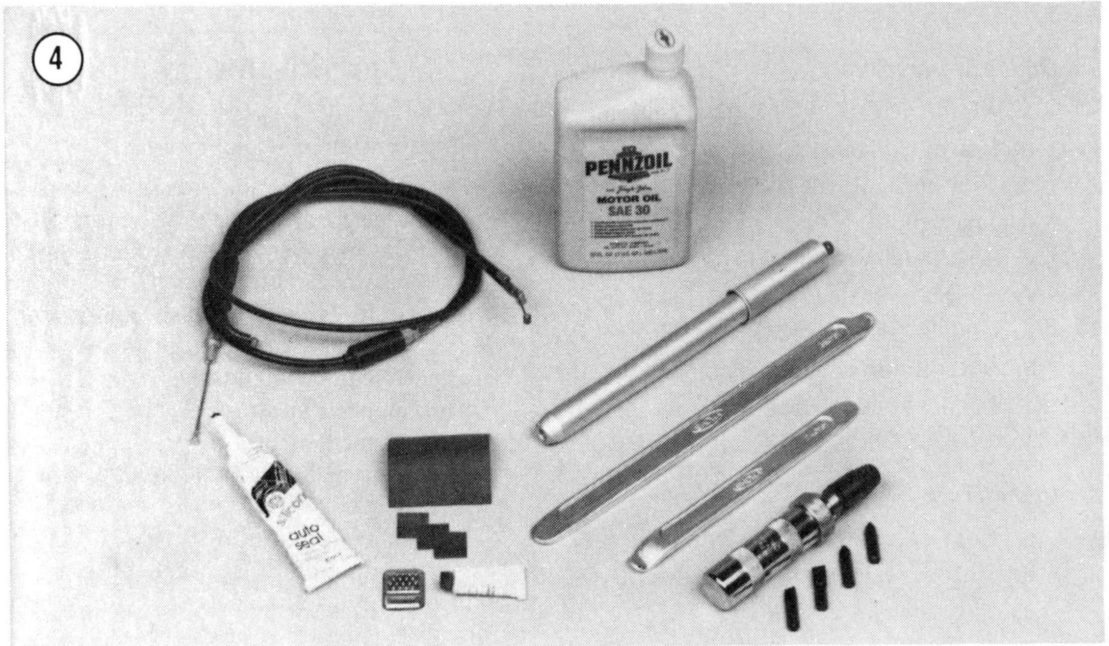

specific gravity of the electrolyte in each cell. See **Figure 6**. Complete details on use and interpretation of readings are provided in the electrical chapter.

Compression Tester

The compression tester measures the compression pressure built up in each cylinder. The results, when properly interpreted, can indicate general cylinder, ring, and valve condition. See **Figure 7**. Extension lines are available for hard-to-reach cylinders.

Dwell Meter (Contact Breaker Point Ignition Only)

A dwell meter measures the distance in degrees of cam rotation that the breaker points remain closed while the engine is running. Since

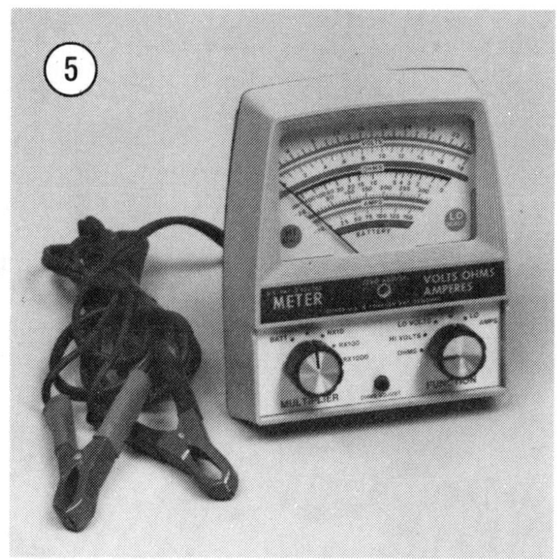

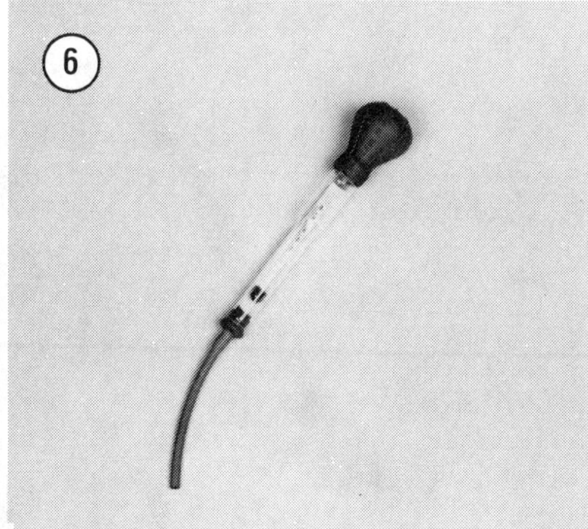

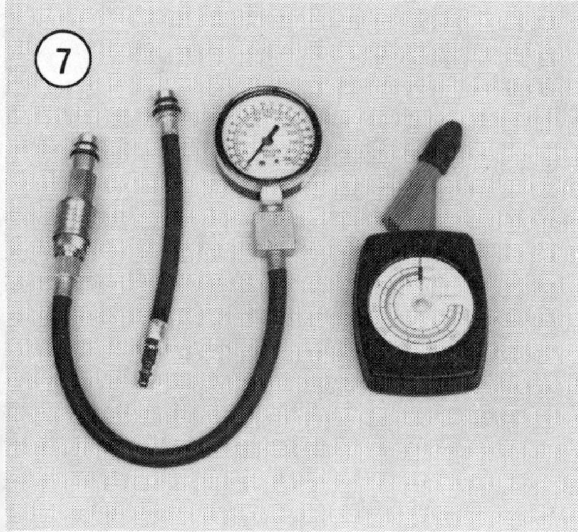

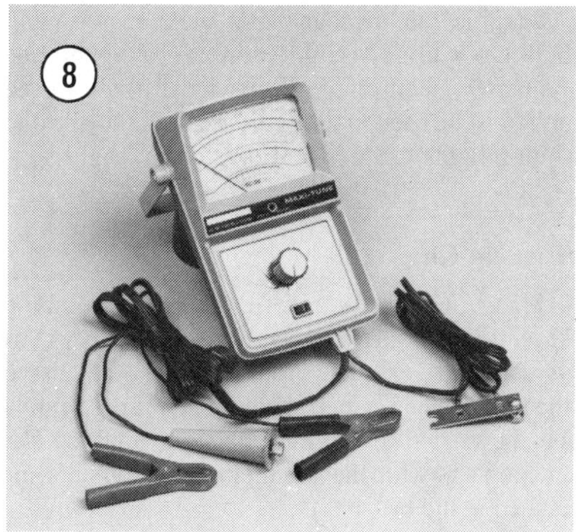

this angle is determined by breaker point gap, dwell angle is an accurate indication of breaker point gap.

Many tachometers intended for tuning and testing incorporate a dwell meter as well. See **Figure 8**. Follow the manufacturer's instructions to measure dwell.

Tachometer

A tachometer is necessary for tuning. See **Figure 8**. Ignition timing and carburetor adjustments must be performed at the specified idle speed. The best instrument for this purpose is one with a low range of 0-1,000 or 0-2,000 rpm for setting idle, and a high range of 0-4,000 or more for setting ignition timing at 3,000 rpm. Extended range (0-6,000 or 0-8,000 rpm) instruments lack accuracy at lower speeds. The instrument should be capable of detecting changes of 25 rpm on the low range.

> NOTE: *The motorcycle's tachometer is not accurate enough for correct idle adjustment.*

Strobe Timing Light

This instrument is necessary for tuning, as it permits very accurate ignition timing. The light flashes at precisely the same instant that No. 1 cylinder fires, at which time the timing marks on the engine should align. Refer to Chapter Three for exact location of the timing marks for your engine.

Suitable lights range from inexpensive neon bulb types to powerful xenon strobe lights. See **Figure 9**. Neon timing lights are difficult to see and must be used in dimly lit areas. Xenon strobe timing lights can be used outside in bright sunlight.

Tune-up Kits

Many manufacturers offer kits that combine several useful instruments. Some come in a convenient carry case and are usually less expensive than purchasing one instrument at a time. **Figure 10** shows one of the kits that is available. The prices vary with the number of instruments included in the kit.

Manometer (Carburetor Synchronizer)

A manometer is essential for accurately synchronizing carburetors on multi-cylinder engines. The instrument detects intake pressure differences between carburetors and permits them to be adjusted equally. Suitable manometers are available from motorcycle shop and aftermarket suppliers. See **Figure 11**.

Fire Extinguisher

A fire extinguisher is a necessity when working on a vehicle. It should be rated for both *Class B* (flammable liquids – gasoline, oil, paint, etc.) and *Class C* (electrical – wiring, etc.) type fires. It should always be kept within reach. See **Figure 12**.

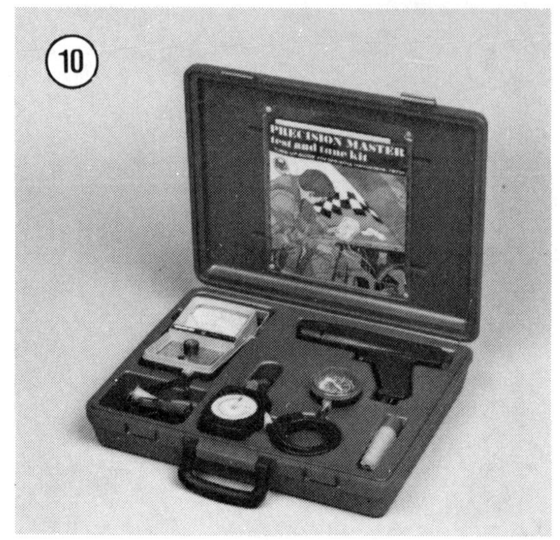

10

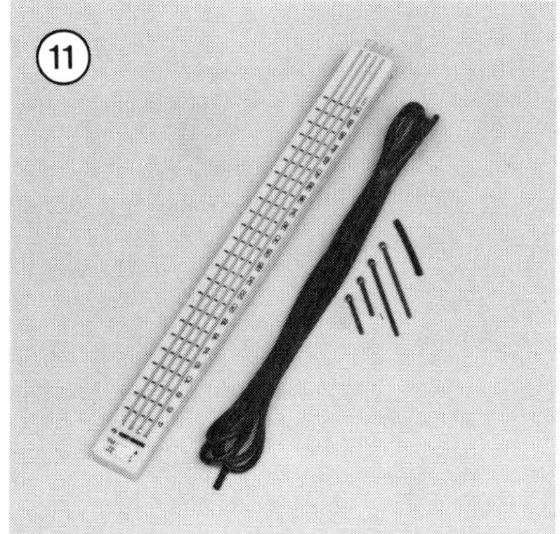
11

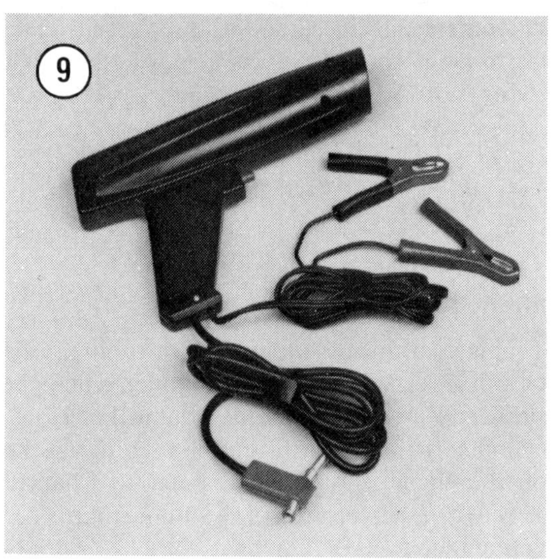
9

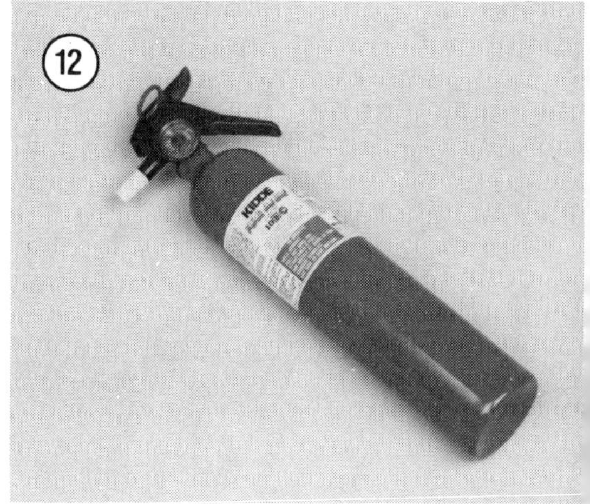

12

CHAPTER TWO

2

TROUBLESHOOTING

Troubleshooting motorcycle problems is relatively simple. To be effective and efficient, however, it must be done in a logical step-by-step manner. If it is not, a great deal of time may be wasted, good parts may be replaced unnecessarily, and the true problem may never be uncovered.

Always begin by defining the symptoms as closely as possible. Then, analyze the symptoms carefully so that you can make an intelligent guess at the probable cause. Next, test the probable cause and attempt to verify it; if it's not at fault, analyze the symptoms once again, this time eliminating the first probable cause. Continue on in this manner, a step at a time, until the problem is solved.

At first, this approach may seem to be time consuming, but you will soon discover that it's not nearly so wasteful as a hit-or-miss method that may never solve the problem. And just as important, the methodical approach to troubleshooting ensures that only those parts that are defective will be replaced.

The troubleshooting procedures in this chapter analyze typical symptoms and show logical methods for isolating and correcting trouble. They are not, however, the only methods; there may be several approaches to a given problem, but all good troubleshooting methods have one thing in common — a logical, systematic approach.

ENGINE

The entire engine must be considered when trouble arises that is experienced as poor performance or failure to start. The engine is more than a combustion chamber, piston, and crankshaft; it also includes a fuel delivery system, an ignition system, and an exhaust system.

Before beginning to troubleshoot any engine problems, it's important to understand an engine's operating requirements. First, it must have a correctly metered mixture of gasoline and air (**Figure 1**). Second, it must have an air-tight combustion chamber in which the mixture can be compressed. And finally, it requires a precisely timed spark to ignite the compressed mixture. If one or more is missing, the engine won't run, and if just one is deficient, the engine will run poorly at best.

Of the three requirements, the precisely timed spark — provided by the ignition system — is most likely to be the culprit, with gas/air mixture (carburetion) second, and poor compression the least likely.

STARTING DIFFICULTIES

Hard starting is probably the most common motorcycle ailment, with a wide range of problems likely. Before delving into a reluctant or non-starter, first determine what has changed

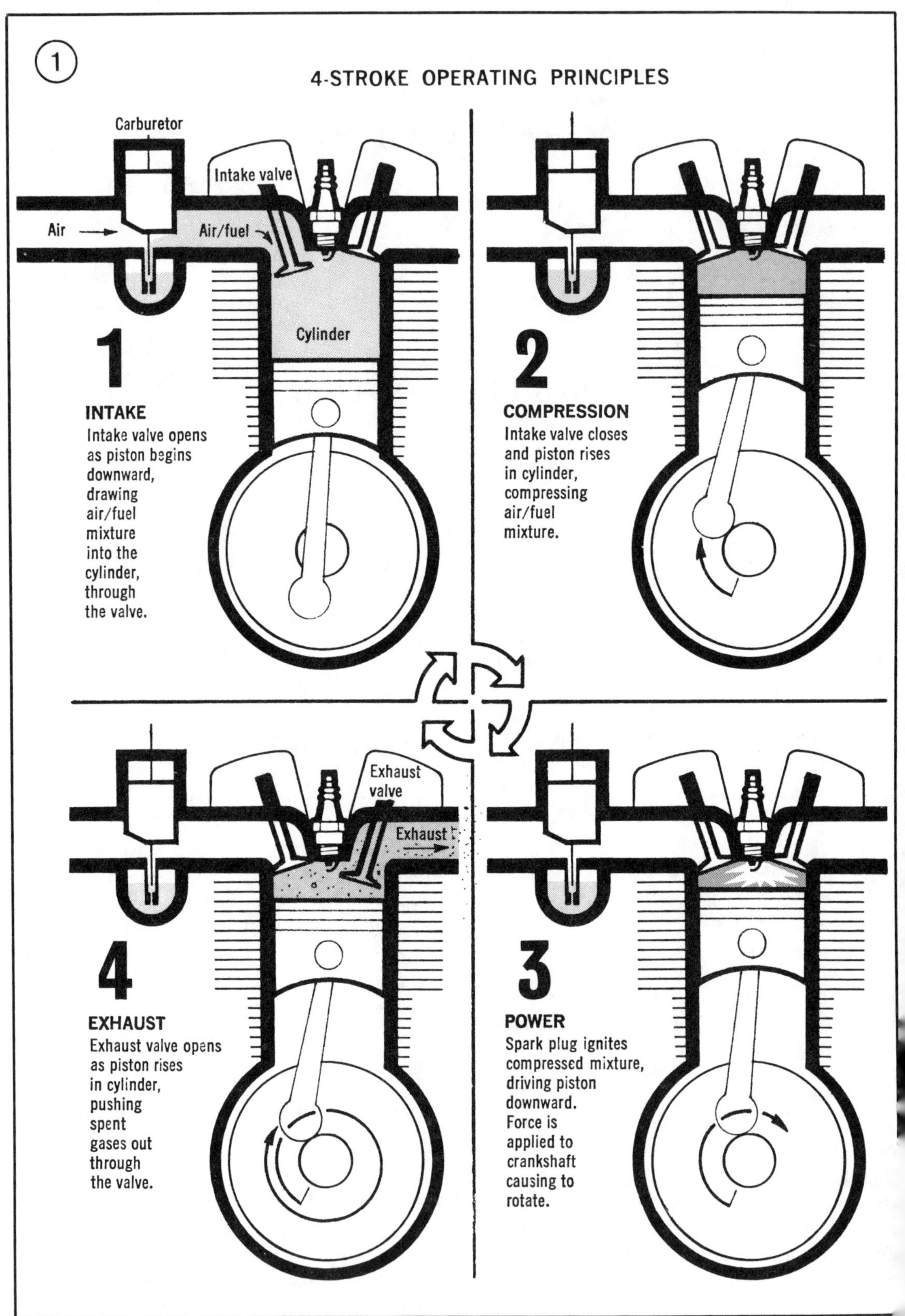
1
4-STROKE OPERATING PRINCIPLES
Carburetor
Intake valve
Air
Air/fuel
Cylinder
1
INTAKE
Intake valve opens as piston begins downward, drawing air/fuel mixture into the cylinder, through the valve.
2
COMPRESSION
Intake valve closes and piston rises in cylinder, compressing air/fuel mixture.
Exhaust valve
Exhaust
4
EXHAUST
Exhaust valve opens as piston rises in cylinder, pushing spent gases out through the valve.
3
POWER
Spark plug ignites compressed mixture, driving piston downward. Force is applied to crankshaft causing to rotate.

since the motorcycle last started easily. For instance, was the weather dry then and is it wet now? Has the motorcycle been sitting in the garage for a long time? Has it been ridden many miles since it was last fueled?

Has starting become increasingly more difficult? This alone could indicate a number of things that may be wrong but is usually associated with normal wear of ignition and engine components.

While it's not always possible to diagnose trouble simply from a change of conditions, this information can be helpful and at some future time may uncover a recurring problem.

Fuel Delivery

Although it is the second most likely cause of trouble, fuel delivery should be checked first simply because it is the easiest.

First, check the tank to make sure there is fuel in it. Then, disconnect the fuel hose at the carburetor, open the valve and check for flow (**Figure 2**). If fuel does not flow freely make sure the tank vent is clear. Next, check for blockage in the line or valve. Remove the valve and clean it as described in the fuel system chapter.

If fuel flows from the hose, reconnect it and remove the float bowl from the carburetor, open the valve and check for flow through the float needle valve. If it does not flow freely when the float is extended and then shut off when the flow is gently raised, clean the carburetor as described in the fuel system chapter.

When fuel delivery is satisfactory, go on to the ignition system.

Ignition

Remove the spark plug from the cylinder and check its condition. The appearance of the plug is a good indication of what's happening in the combustion chamber; for instance, if the plug is wet with gas, it's likely that engine is flooded. Compare the spark plug to **Figure 3**. Make certain the spark plug heat range is correct. A "cold" plug makes starting difficult.

After checking the spark plug, reconnect it to the high-tension lead and lay it on the cylinder head so it makes good contact (**Figure 4**). Then, with the ignition switched on, crank the engine several times and watch for a spark across the plug electrodes. A fat, blue spark should be visible. If there is no spark, or if the spark is weak, substitute a good plug for the old one and check again. If the spark has improved, the old plug is faulty. If there was no change, keep looking.

Make sure the ignition switch is not shorted to ground. Remove the spark plug cap from the end of the high-tension lead and hold the exposed end of the lead about ⅛ inch from the cylinder head. Crank the engine and watch for a spark arcing from the lead to the head. If it's satisfactory, the connection between the lead and the cap was faulty. If the spark hasn't improved, check the coil wire connections.

If the spark is still weak, remove the ignition cover and remove any dirt or moisture from the points or sensor. Check the point or air gap against the specifications in the *Quick Reference Data* at the beginning of the book.

If spark is still not satisfactory, a more serious problem exists than can be corrected with simple adjustments. Refer to the electrical system chapter for detailed information for correcting major ignition problems.

Compression

Compression — or the lack of it — is the least likely cause of starting trouble. However, if compression is unsatisfactory, more than a simple adjustment is required to correct it (see the engine chapter).

An accurate compression check reveals a lot about the condition of the engine. To perform this test you need a compression gauge (see Chapter One). The engine should be at operating temperature for a fully accurate test, but even a cold test will reveal if the starting problem is compression.

Remove the spark plug and screw in a compression gauge (**Figure 5**). With assistance, hold the throttle wide open and crank the engine several times, until the gauge ceases to rise. Normal compression should be 130-160 psi, but a reading as low as 100 psi is usually sufficient for the engine to start. If the reading is much lower than normal, remove the gauge and pour about a tablespoon of oil into the cylinder.

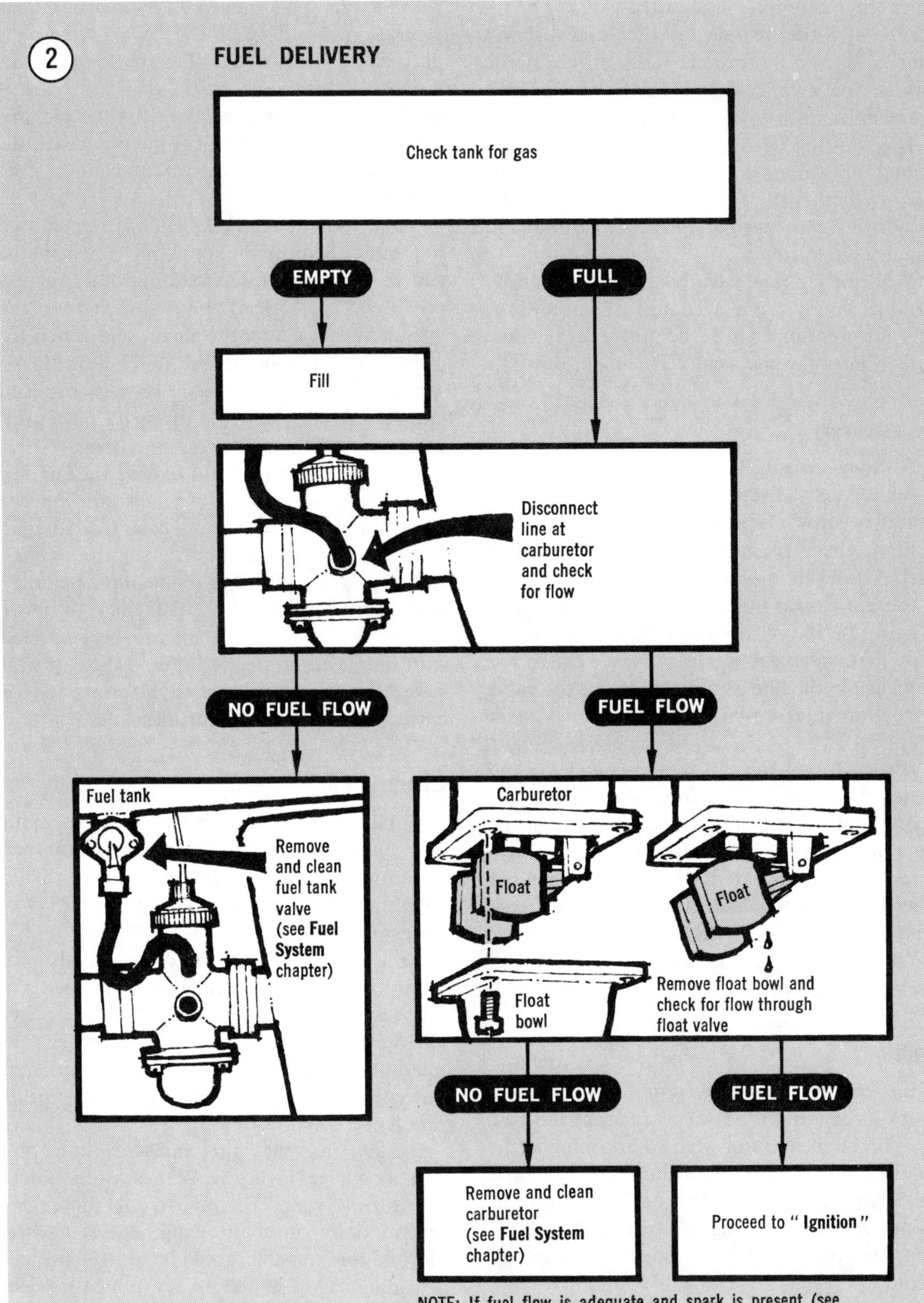

NOTE: If fuel flow is adequate and spark is present (see **Ignition** which follows), increase fuel ratio with idle screw.

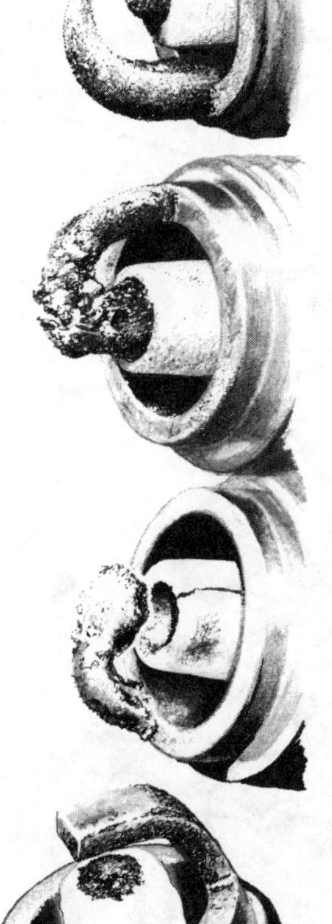

NORMAL
- Appearance—Firing tip has deposits of light gray to light tan.
- Can be cleaned, regapped and reused.

CARBON FOULED
- Appearance—Dull, dry black with fluffy carbon deposits on the insulator tip, electrode and exposed shell.
- Caused by—Fuel/air mixture too rich, plug heat range too cold, weak ignition system, dirty air cleaner, faulty automatic choke or excessive idling.
- Can be cleaned, regapped and reused.

OIL FOULED
- Appearance—Wet black deposits on insulator and exposed shell.
- Caused by—Excessive oil entering the combustion chamber through worn rings, pistons, valve guides or bearings.
- Replace with new plugs (use a hotter plug if engine is not repaired).

LEAD FOULED
- Appearance — Yellow insulator deposits (may sometimes be dark gray, black or tan in color) on the insulator tip.
- Caused by—Highly leaded gasoline.
- Replace with new plugs.

LEAD FOULED
- Appearance—Yellow glazed deposits indicating melted lead deposits due to hard acceleration.
- Caused by—Highly leaded gasoline.
- Replace with new plugs.

OIL AND LEAD FOULED
- Appearance—Glazed yellow deposits with a slight brownish tint on the insulator tip and ground electrode.
- Replace with new plugs.

FUEL ADDITIVE RESIDUE
- Appearance — Brown colored hardened ash deposits on the insulator tip and ground electrode.
- Caused by—Fuel and/or oil additives.
- Replace with new plugs.

WORN
- Appearance — Severely worn or eroded electrodes.
- Caused by—Normal wear or unusual oil and/or fuel additives.
- Replace with new plugs.

PREIGNITION
- Appearance — Melted ground electrode.
- Caused by—Overadvanced ignition timing, inoperative ignition advance mechanism, too low of a fuel octane rating, lean fuel/air mixture or carbon deposits in combustion chamber.

PREIGNITION
- Appearance—Melted center electrode.
- Caused by—Abnormal combustion due to overadvanced ignition timing or incorrect advance, too low of a fuel octane rating, lean fuel/air mixture, or carbon deposits in combustion chamber.
- Correct engine problem and replace with new plugs.

INCORRECT HEAT RANGE
- Appearance—Melted center electrode and white blistered insulator tip.
- Caused by—Incorrect plug heat range selection.
- Replace with new plugs.

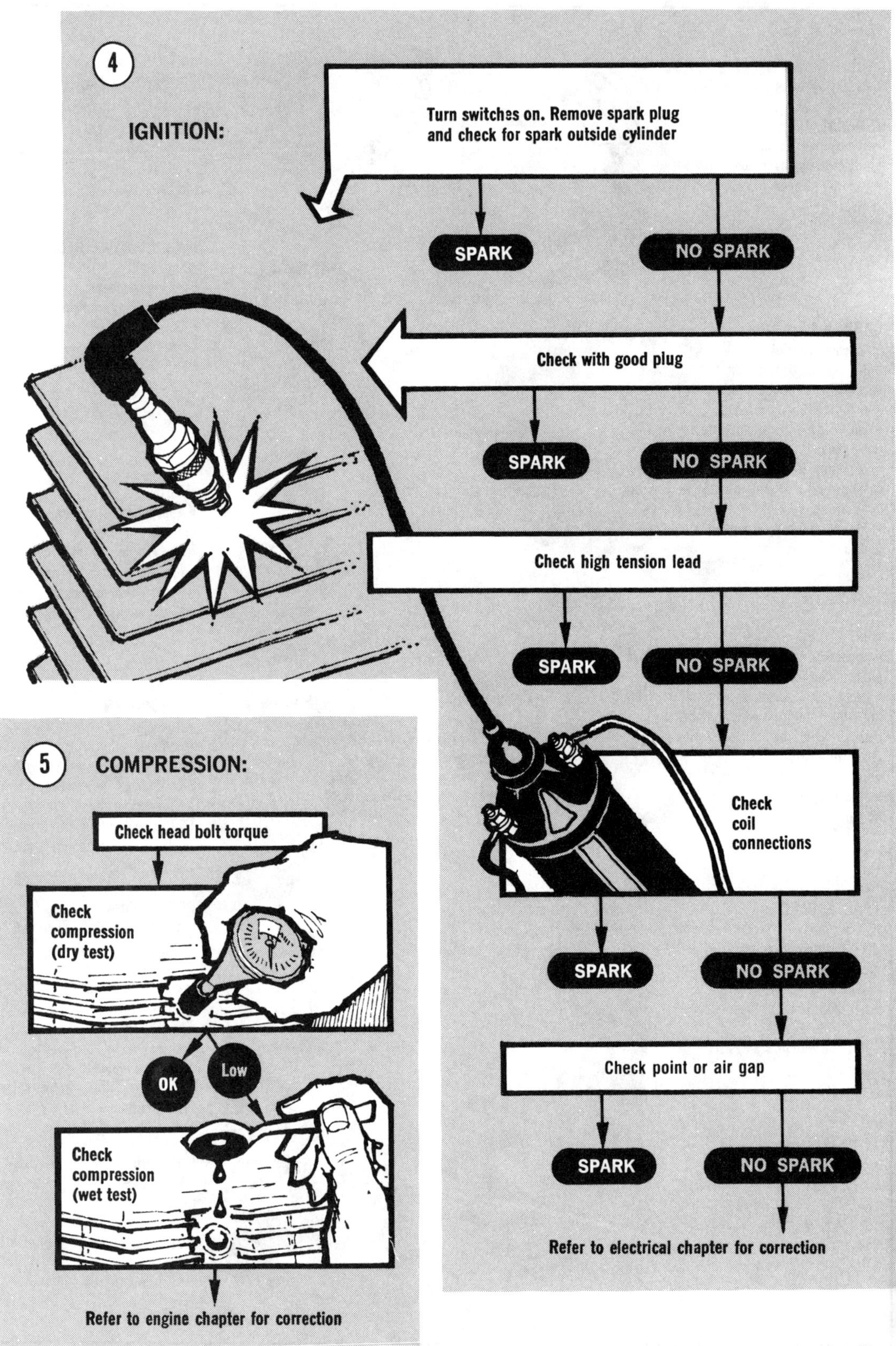
4
IGNITION:
Turn switches on. Remove spark plug and check for spark outside cylinder
SPARK
NO SPARK
Check with good plug
SPARK
NO SPARK
Check high tension lead
SPARK
NO SPARK
Check coil connections
SPARK
NO SPARK
Check point or air gap
SPARK
NO SPARK
Refer to electrical chapter for correction
5
COMPRESSION:
Check head bolt torque
Check compression (dry test)
OK
Low
Check compression (wet test)
Refer to engine chapter for correction

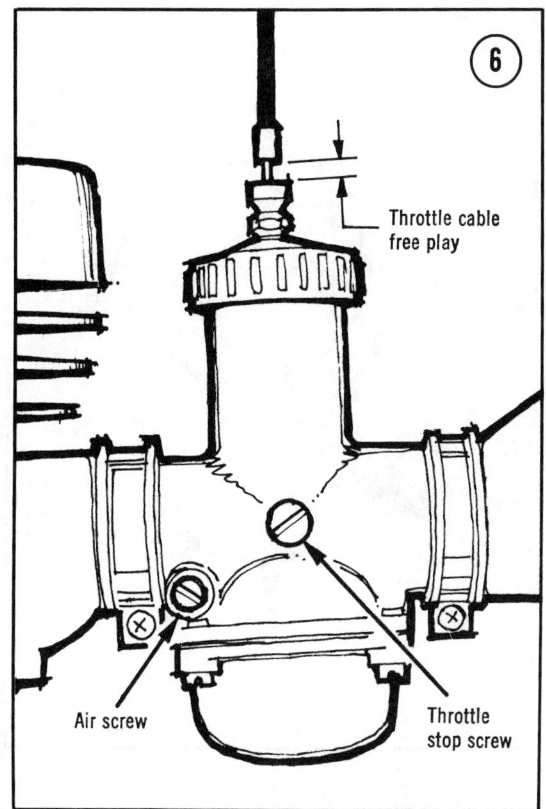

Crank the engine several times to distribute the oil and test the compression once again. If it is now significantly higher, the rings and bore are worn. If the compression did not change, the valves are not seating correctly. Adjust the valves and check again. If the compression is still low, refer to the engine chapter.

NOTE: *Low compression indicates a developing problem. The condition causing it should be corrected as soon as possible.*

POOR PERFORMANCE

Poor engine performance can be caused by any of a number of things related to carburetion, ignition, and the condition of the sliding and rotating components in the engine. In addition, components such as brakes, clutch, and transmission can cause problems that seem to be related to engine performance, even when the engine is in top running condition.

Poor Idling

Idling that is erratic, too high, or too low is most often caused by incorrect adjustment of the carburetor idle circuit. Also, a dirty air filter or an obstructed fuel tank vent can affect idle speed. Incorrect ignition timing or worn or faulty ignition components are also good possibilities.

First, make sure the air filter is clean and correctly installed. Then, adjust the throttle cable free play, the throttle stop screw, and the idle mixture air screw (**Figure 6**) as described in the routine maintenance chapter.

If idling is still poor, check the carburetor and manifold mounts for leaks; with the engine warmed up and running, spray WD-40 or a similar light lube around the flanges and joints of the carburetor and manifold (**Figure 7**). Listen for changes in engine speed. If a leak is present, the idle speed will drop as the lube "plugs" the leak and then pick up again as it is drawn into the engine. Tighten the nuts and clamps and test again. If a leak persists, check for a damaged gasket or a pinhole in the manifold. Minor leaks in manifold hoses can be repaired with silicone sealer, but if cracks or holes are extensive, the manifold should be replaced.

A worn throttle slide may cause erratic running and idling, but this is likely only after many thousands of miles of use. To check, remove the carburetor top and feel for back and forth movement of the slide in the bore; it should be barely perceptible. Inspect the slide for large worn areas and replace it if it is less than perfect (**Figure 8**).

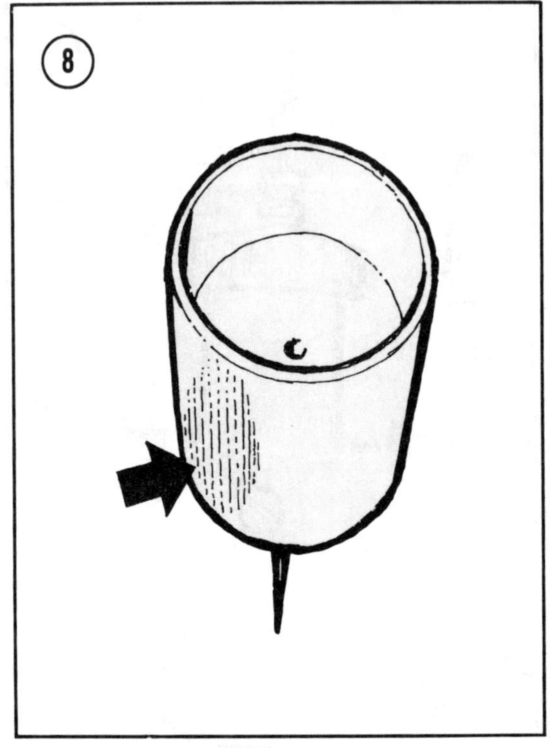

8

If the fuel system is satisfactory, check ignition timing and breaker point gap (air gap in electronic ignition). Check the condition of the system components as well. Ignition-caused idling problems such as erratic running can be the fault of marginal components. See the electrical system chapter for appropriate tests.

Rough Running or Misfiring

Misfiring (see **Figure 9**) is usually caused by an ignition problem. First, check all ignition connections (**Figure 10**). They should be clean, dry, and tight. Don't forget the kill switch; a loose connection can create an intermittent short.

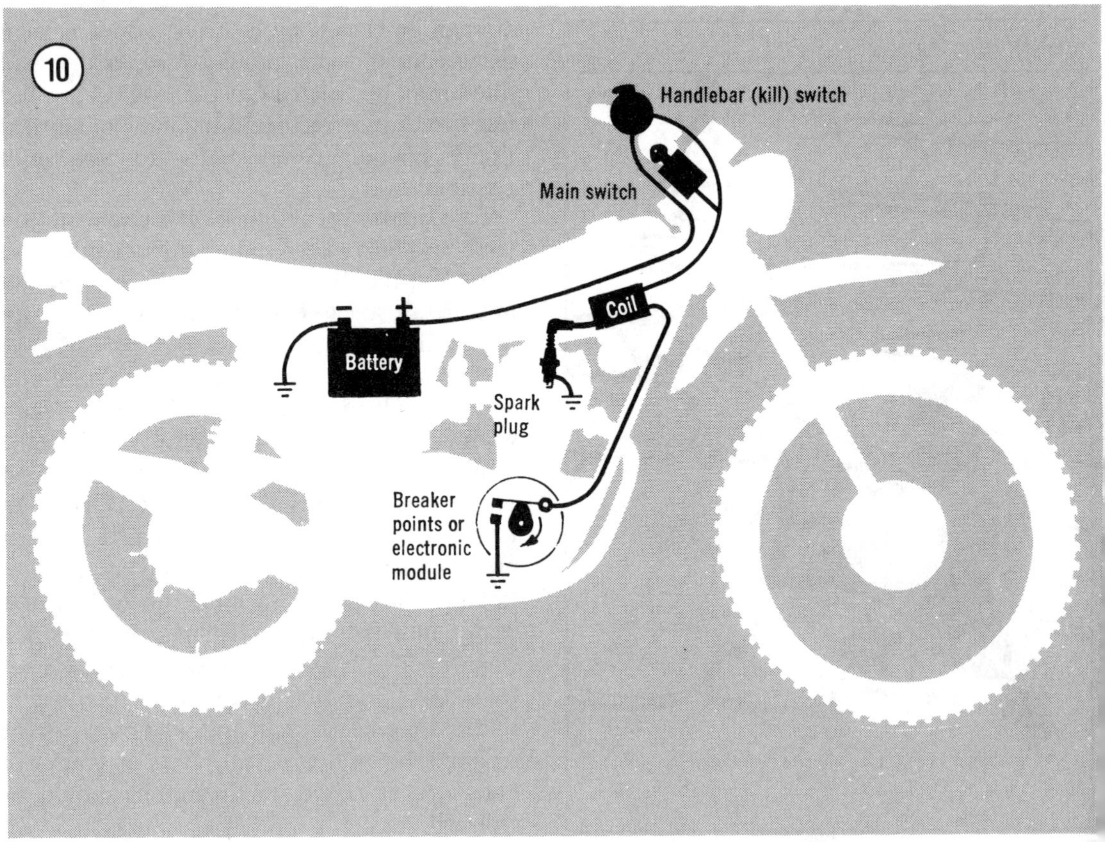

10

ENGINE RUNS ROUGH AND MISFIRES

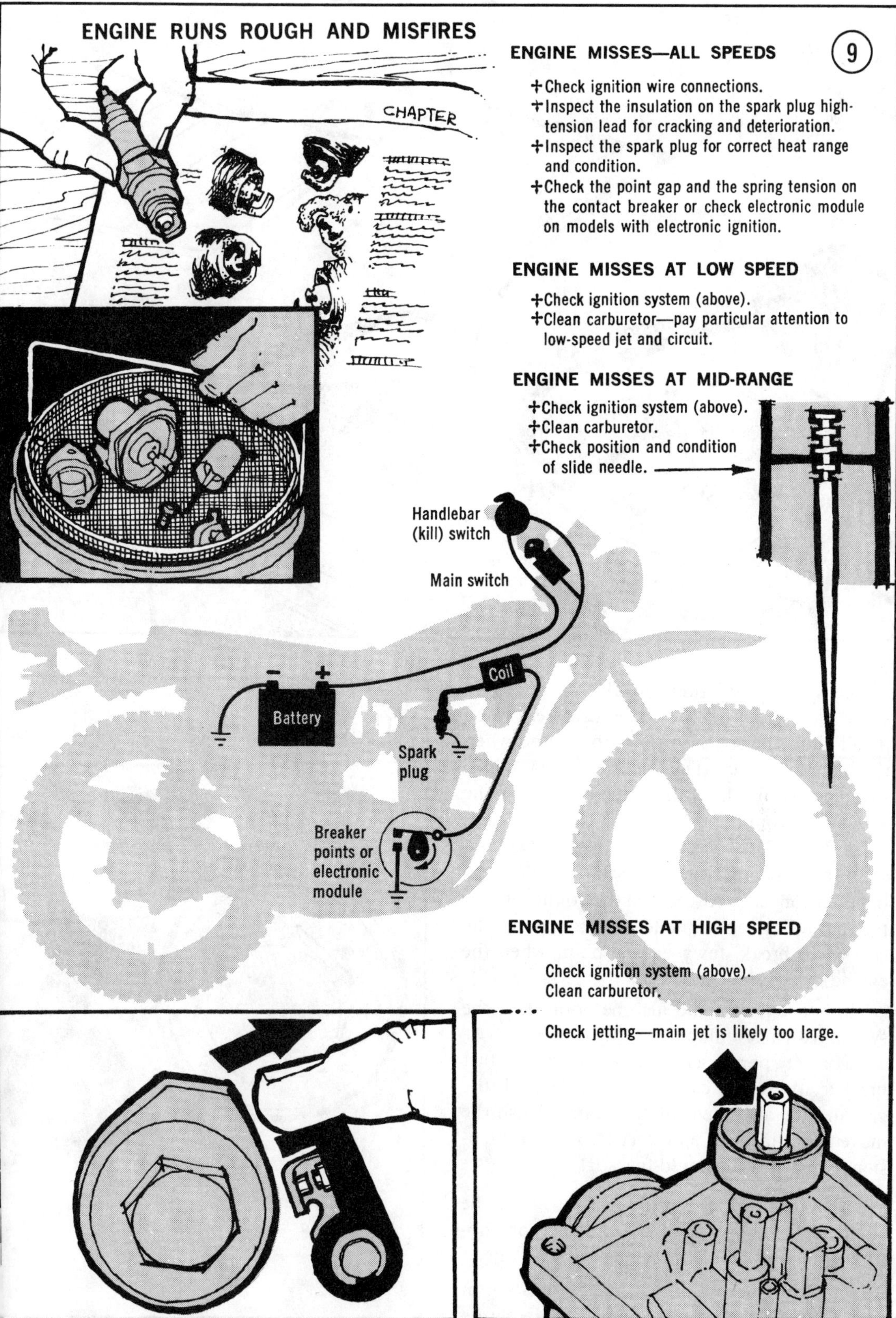

ENGINE MISSES—ALL SPEEDS (9)

- Check ignition wire connections.
- Inspect the insulation on the spark plug high-tension lead for cracking and deterioration.
- Inspect the spark plug for correct heat range and condition.
- Check the point gap and the spring tension on the contact breaker or check electronic module on models with electronic ignition.

ENGINE MISSES AT LOW SPEED

- Check ignition system (above).
- Clean carburetor—pay particular attention to low-speed jet and circuit.

ENGINE MISSES AT MID-RANGE

- Check ignition system (above).
- Clean carburetor.
- Check position and condition of slide needle.

ENGINE MISSES AT HIGH SPEED

Check ignition system (above).
Clean carburetor.
Check jetting—main jet is likely too large.

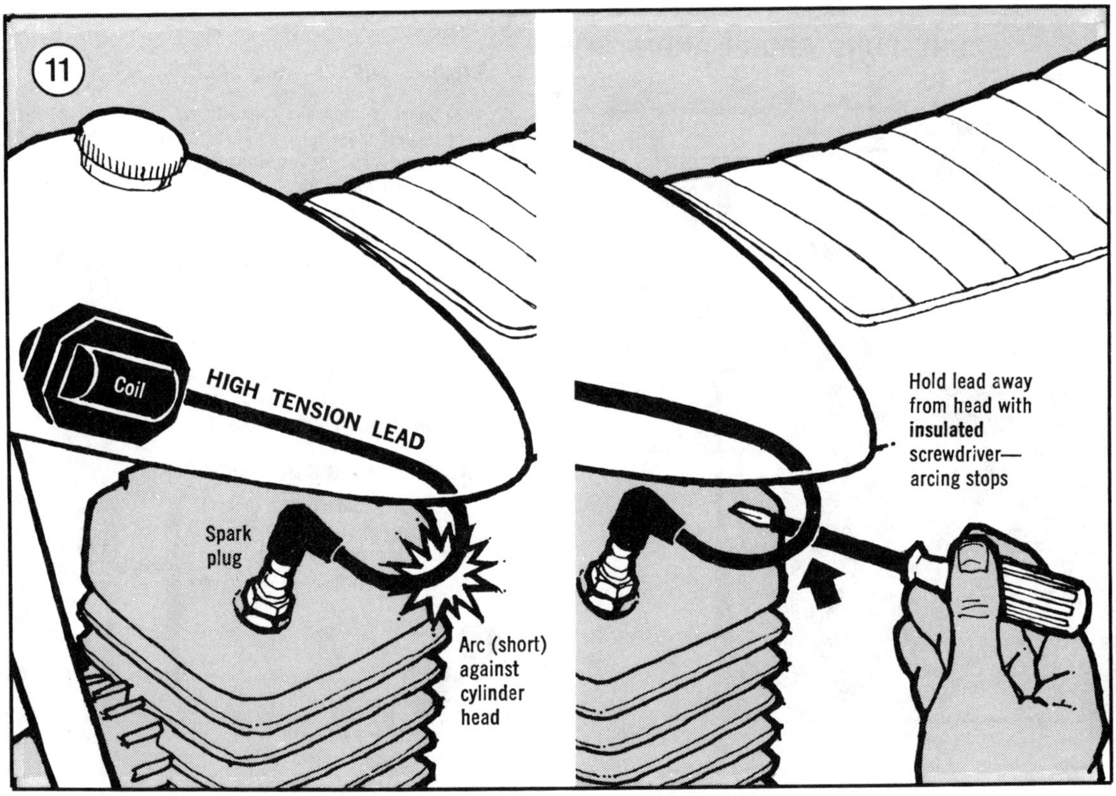

Check the insulation on the high-tension spark plug lead. If it is cracked or deteriorated it will allow the spark to short to ground when the engine is revved. This is easily seen at night. If arcing occurs, hold the affected area of the wire away from the metal to which it is arcing, using an insulated screwdriver **(Figure 11)**, and see if the misfiring ceases. If it does, replace the high-tension lead. Also check the connection of the spark plug cap to the lead. If it is poor, the spark will break down at this point when the engine speed is increased.

The spark plug could also be poor. Test the system with a new plug.

Incorrect point gap or a weak contact breaker spring can cause misfiring. Check the gap and the alignment of the points. Push the moveable arm back and check for spring tension **(Figure 12)**. It should feel stiff.

On models with electronic ignition, have the electronic module tested by a dealer or substitute a known good unit for a suspected one.

If misfiring occurs only at a certain point in engine speed, the problem may very likely be

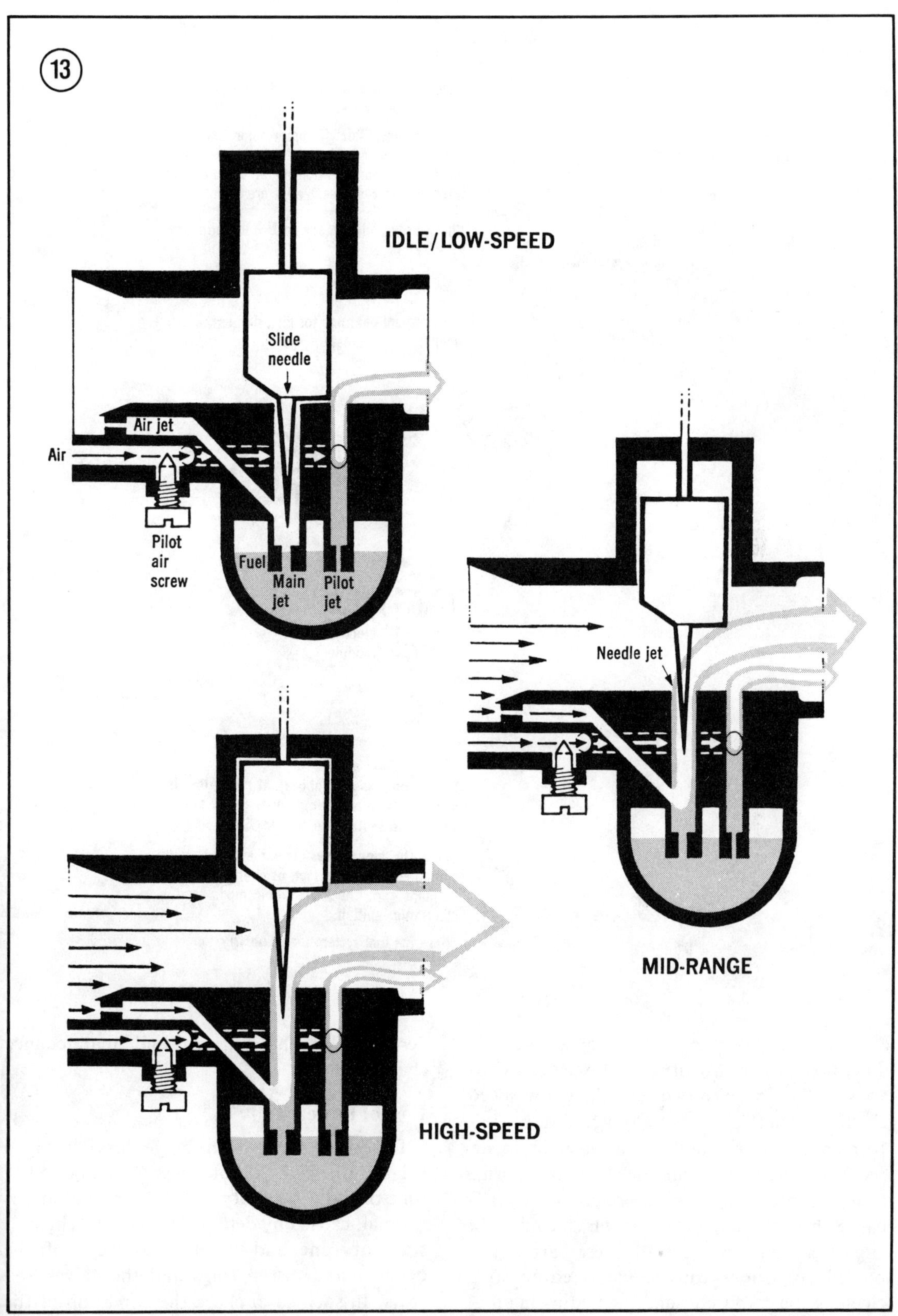
13
IDLE/LOW-SPEED
Slide needle
Air jet
Air
Pilot air screw
Fuel
Main jet
Pilot jet
Needle jet
MID-RANGE
HIGH-SPEED

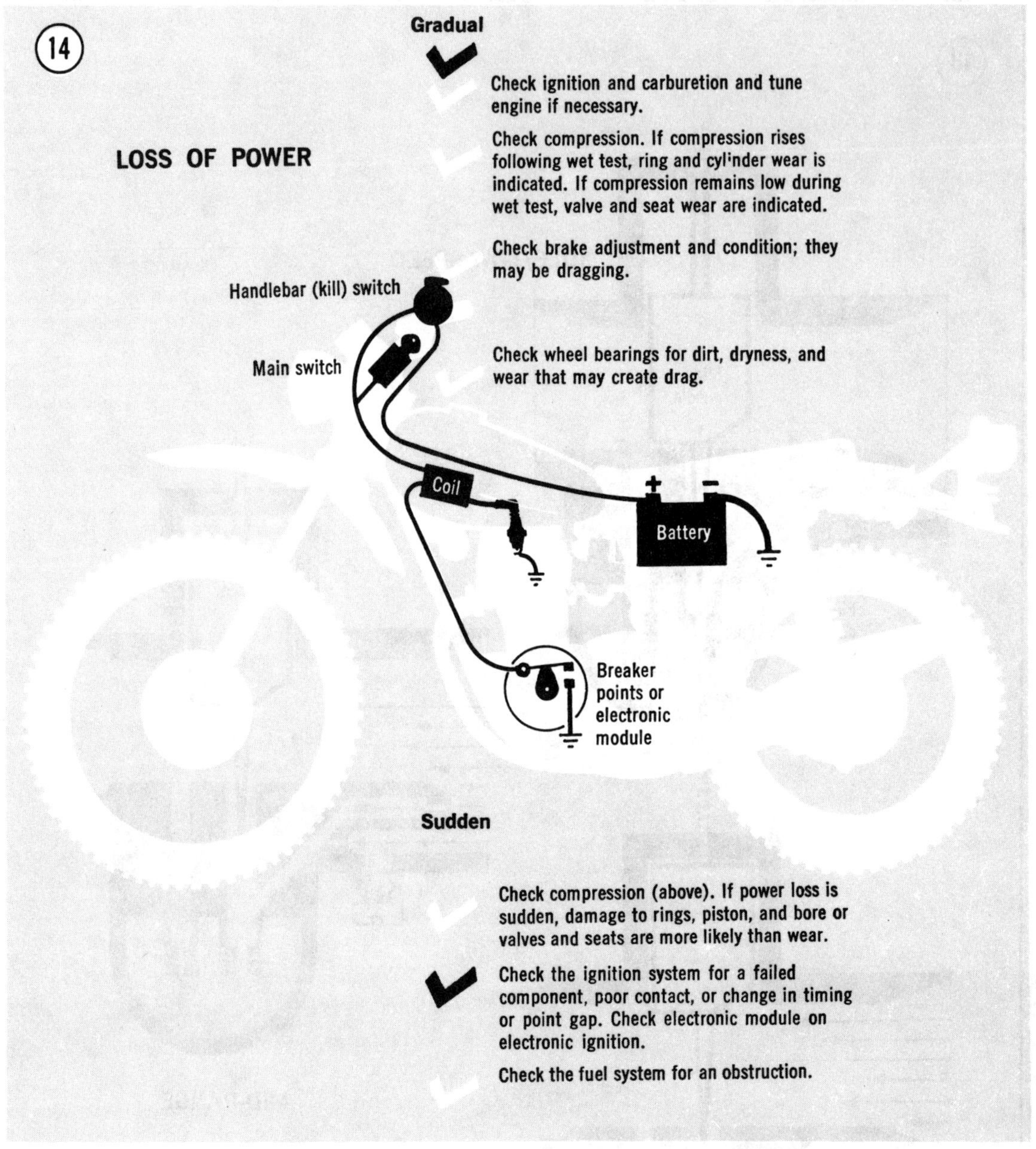

carburetion. Poor performance at idle is described earlier. Misfiring at low speed (just above idle) can be caused by a dirty low-speed circuit or jet (**Figure 13**). Poor midrange performance is attributable to a worn or incorrectly adjusted needle and needle jet. Misfiring at high speed (if not ignition related) is usually caused by a too-large main jet which causes the engine to run rich. Any of these carburetor-related conditions can be corrected by first cleaning the carburetor and then adjusting it as described in the tune-up and maintenance chapter.

Loss of Power

First determine how the power loss developed (**Figure 14**). Did it decline over a long period of time or did it drop abruptly? A gradual loss is normal, caused by deterioration of the engine's state of tune and the normal wear of the cylinder and piston rings and the valves and seats. In such case, check the condition of the

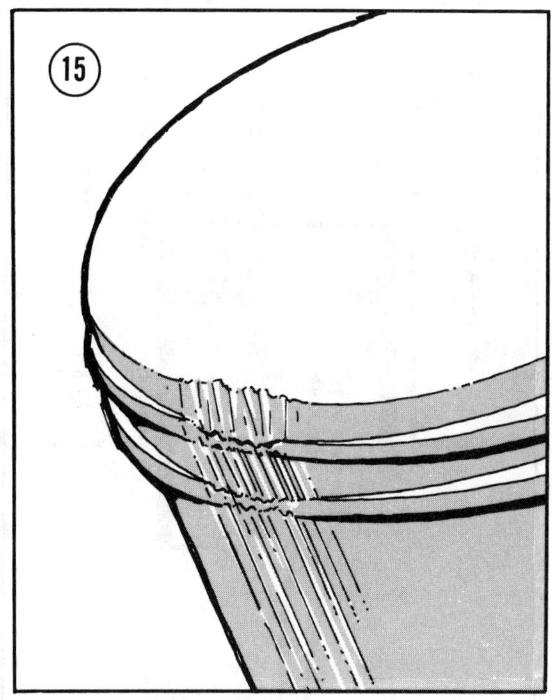

ignition and carburetion and measure the compression as described earlier.

A sudden power loss may be caused by a failed ignition component, obstruction in the fuel system, damaged valve or seat, or a broken piston ring or damaged piston (**Figure 15**).

If the engine is in good shape and tune, check the brake adjustment. If the brakes are dragging, they will consume considerable power. Also check the wheel bearings. If they are dry, extremely dirty, or badly worn they can create considerable drag.

Engine Runs Hot

A modern motorcycle engine, in good mechanical condition, correctly tuned, and operated as it was intended, will rarely experience overheating problems. However, out-of-spec conditions can create severe overheating that may result in serious engine damage. Refer to **Figure 16**.

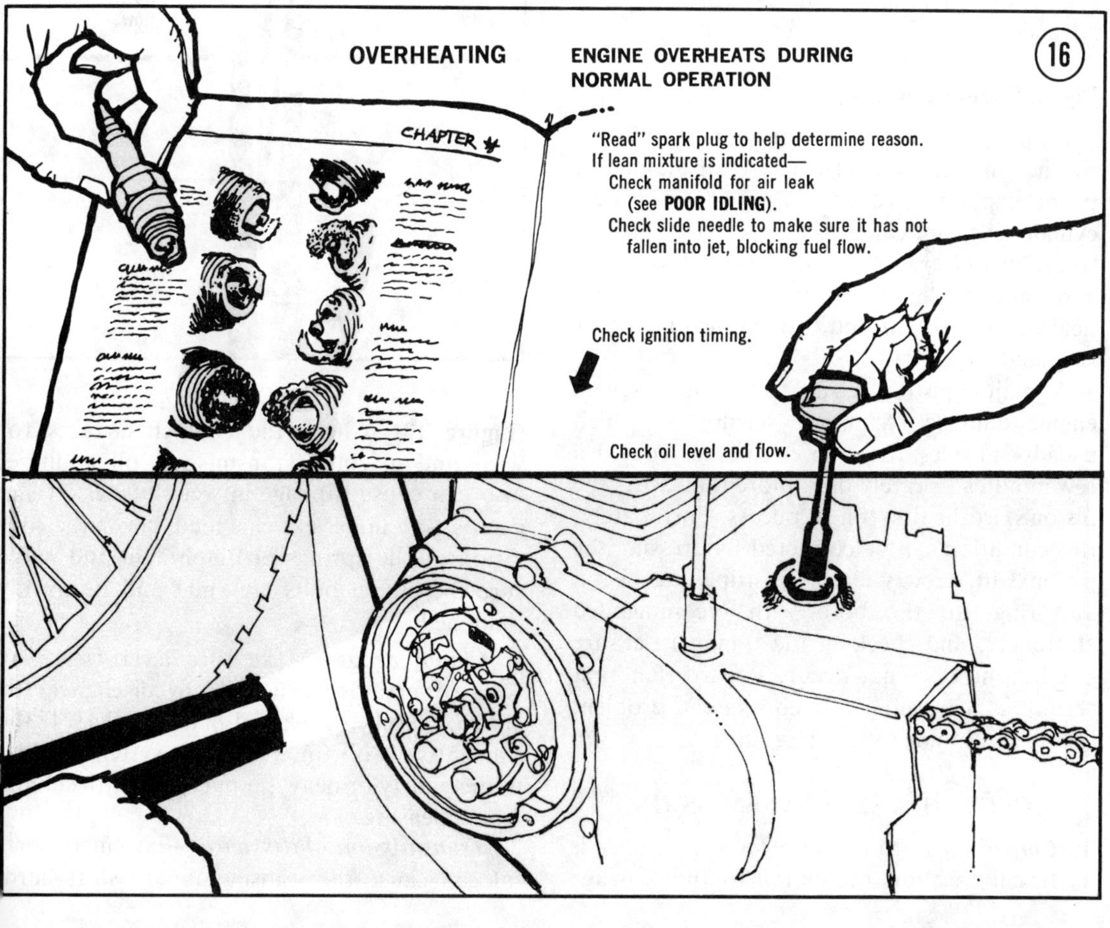

16

OVERHEATING

ENGINE OVERHEATS DURING NORMAL OPERATION

"Read" spark plug to help determine reason.
If lean mixture is indicated—
Check manifold for air leak (see **POOR IDLING**).
Check slide needle to make sure it has not fallen into jet, blocking fuel flow.

Check ignition timing.

Check oil level and flow.

CHAPTER 4

Overheating is difficult to detect unless it is extreme, in which case it will usually be apparent as excessive heat radiating from the engine, accompanied by the smell of hot oil and sharp, snapping noises when the engine is first shut off and begins to cool.

Unless the motorcycle is operated under sustained high load or is allowed to idle for long periods of time, overheating is usually the result of an internal problem. Most often it's caused by a too-lean fuel mixture.

Remove the spark plug and compare it to **Figure 3**. If a too-lean condition is indicated, check for leaks in the intake manifold (see *Poor Idling*). The carburetor jetting may be incorrect but this is unlikely if the overheating problem has just developed (unless, of course, the engine was jetted for high altitude and is now being run near sea level). Check the slide needle in the carburetor to make sure it hasn't come loose and is restricting the flow of gas through the main jet and needle jet (**Figure 17**).

Check the ignition timing; extremes of either advance or retard can cause overheating.

Piston Seizure and Damage

Piston seizure is a common result of overheating (see above) because an aluminum piston expands at a greater rate than a steel cylinder. Seizure can also be caused by piston-to-cylinder clearance that is too small; ring end gap that is too small; insufficient oil; spark plug heat range too hot; and broken piston ring or ring land.

A major piston seizure can cause severe engine damage. A minor seizure — which usually subsides after the engine has cooled a few minutes — rarely does more than scuff the piston skirt the first time it occurs. Fortunately, this condition can be corrected by dressing the piston with crocus cloth, refitting the piston and rings to the bore with recommended clearances, and checking the timing to ensure overheating does not occur. Regard that first seizure as a warning and correct the problem before continuing to run the engine.

CLUTCH AND TRANSMISSION

1. *Clutch slips*—Make sure lever free play is sufficient to allow the clutch to fully engage

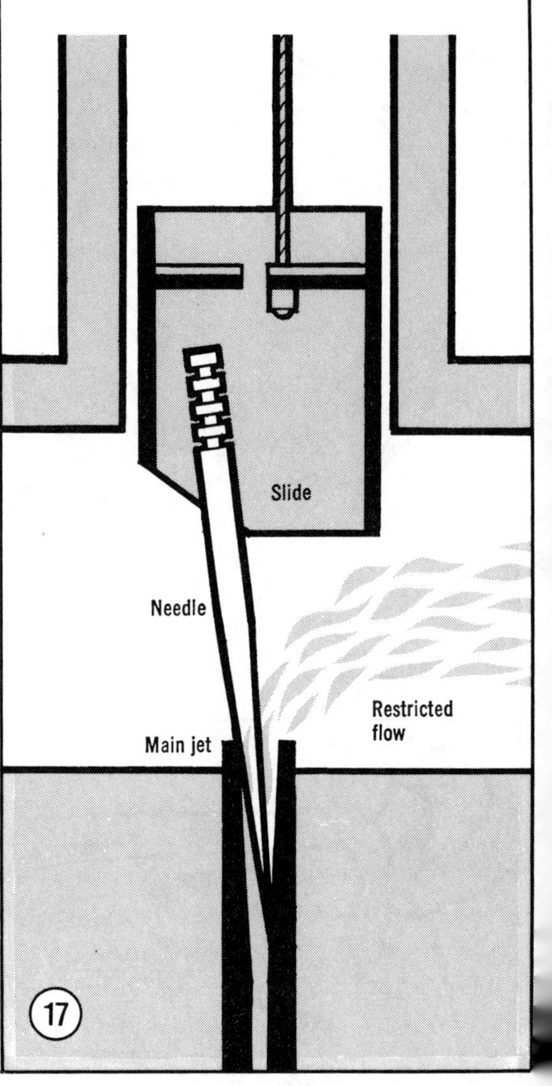

(**Figure 18**). Check the contact surfaces for wear and glazing. Transmission oil additives also can cause slippage in wet clutches. If slip occurs only under extreme load, check the condition of the springs or diaphragm and make sure the clutch bolts are snug and uniformly tightened.

2. *Clutch drags*—Make sure lever free play isn't so great that it fails to disengage the clutch. Check for warped plates or disc. If the transmission oil (in wet clutch systems) is extremely dirty or heavy, it may inhibit the clutch from releasing.

3. *Transmission shifts hard*—Extremely dirty oil can cause the transmission to shift hard

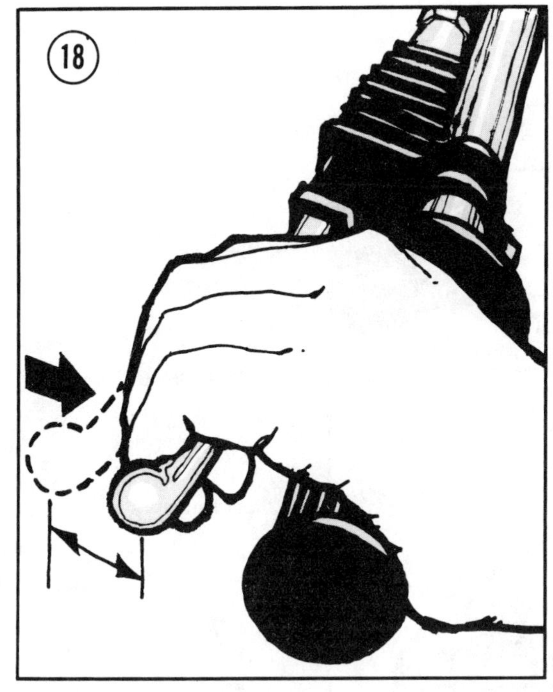

Check the selector shaft for bending (**Figure 19**). Inspect the shifter and gearsets for wear and damage.

4. ***Transmission slips out of gear***—This can be caused by worn engagement dogs or a worn or damaged shifter (**Figure 20**). The overshift travel on the selector may be misadjusted.

5. ***Transmission is noisy***—Noises usually indicate the absence of lubrication or wear and damage to gears, bearings, or shims. It's a good idea to disassemble the transmission and carefully inspect it when noise first occurs.

DRIVE TRAIN

Drive train problems (outlined in **Figure 21**) arise from normal wear and incorrect maintenance.

CHASSIS

Chassis problems are outlined in **Figure 22**.

1. ***Motorcycle pulls to one side***—Check for loose suspension components, axles, steering

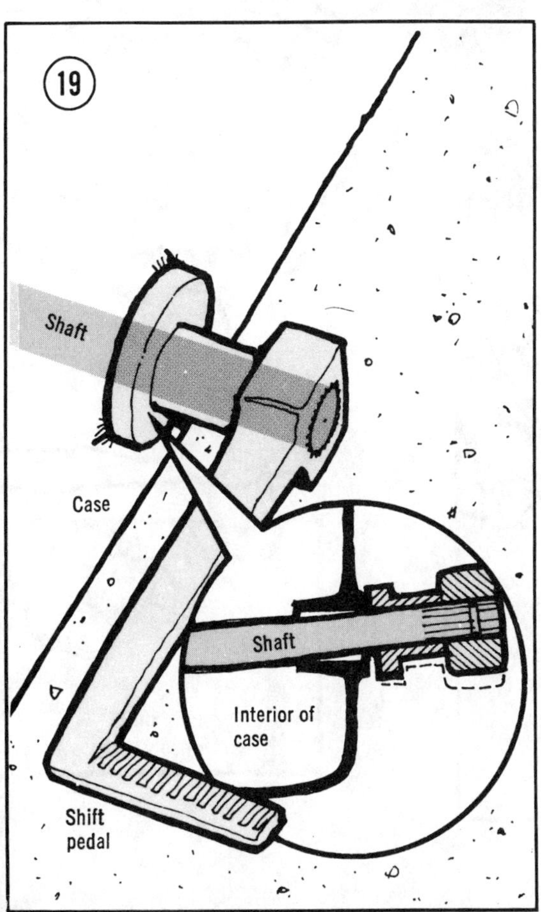

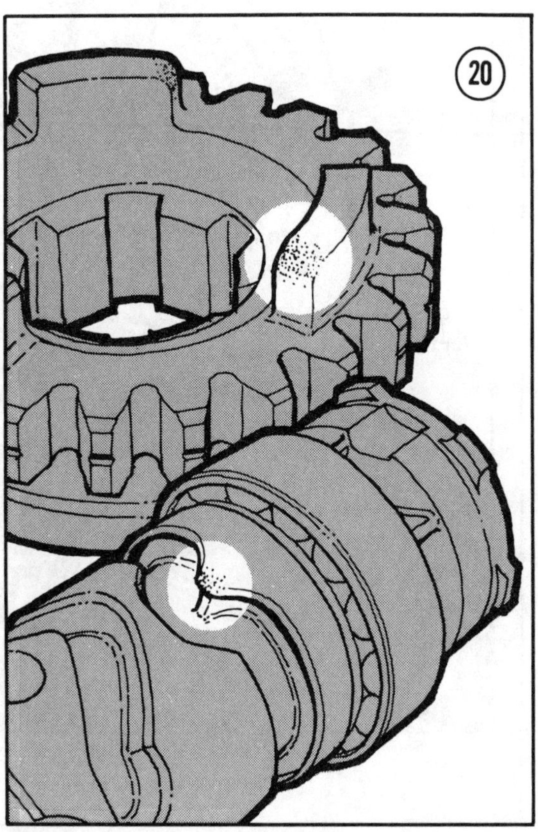

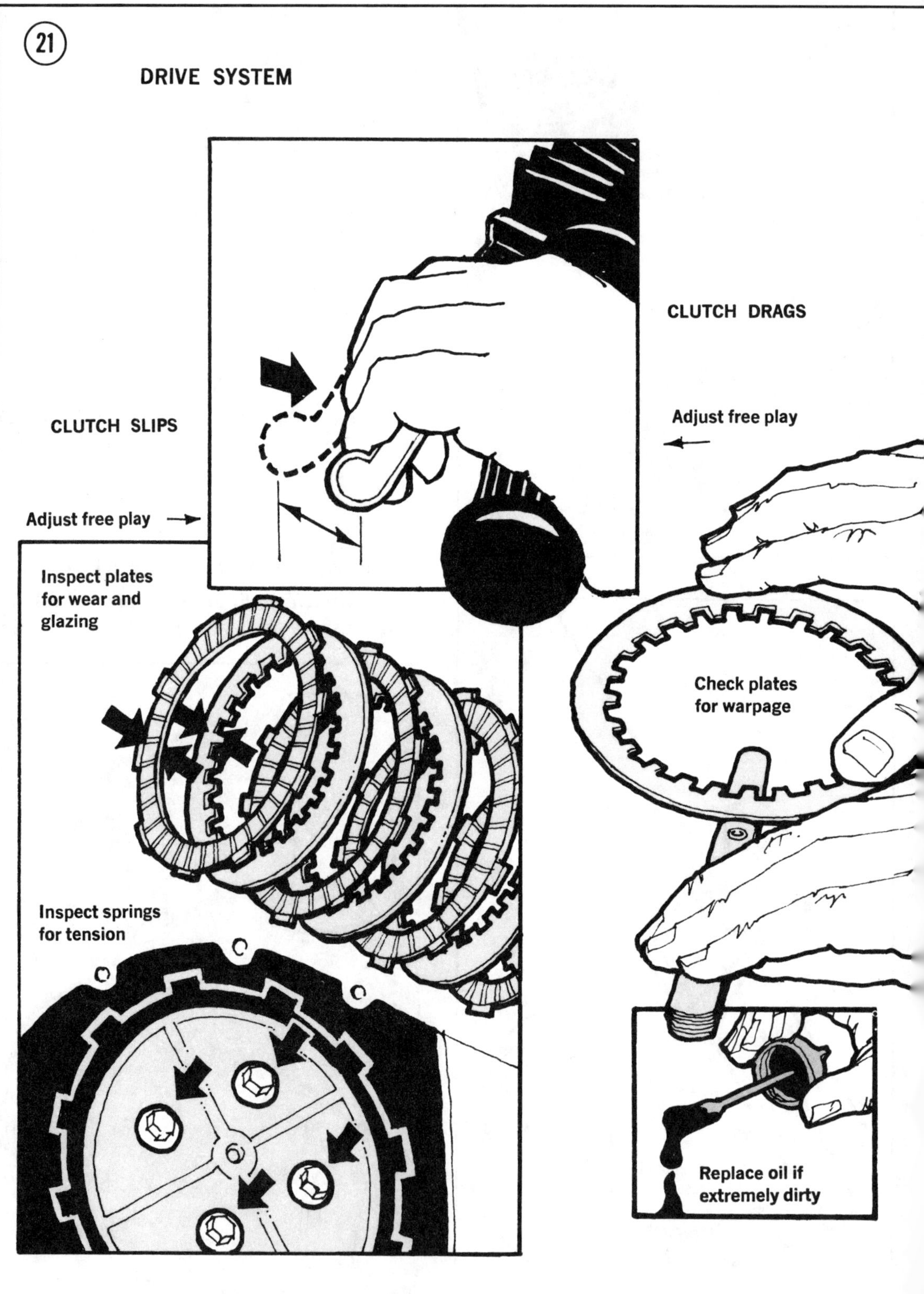
21
DRIVE SYSTEM
CLUTCH DRAGS
Adjust free play
CLUTCH SLIPS
Adjust free play
Inspect plates
for wear and
glazing
Check plates
for warpage
Inspect springs
for tension
Replace oil if
extremely dirty

TRANSMISSION SHIFTS HARD

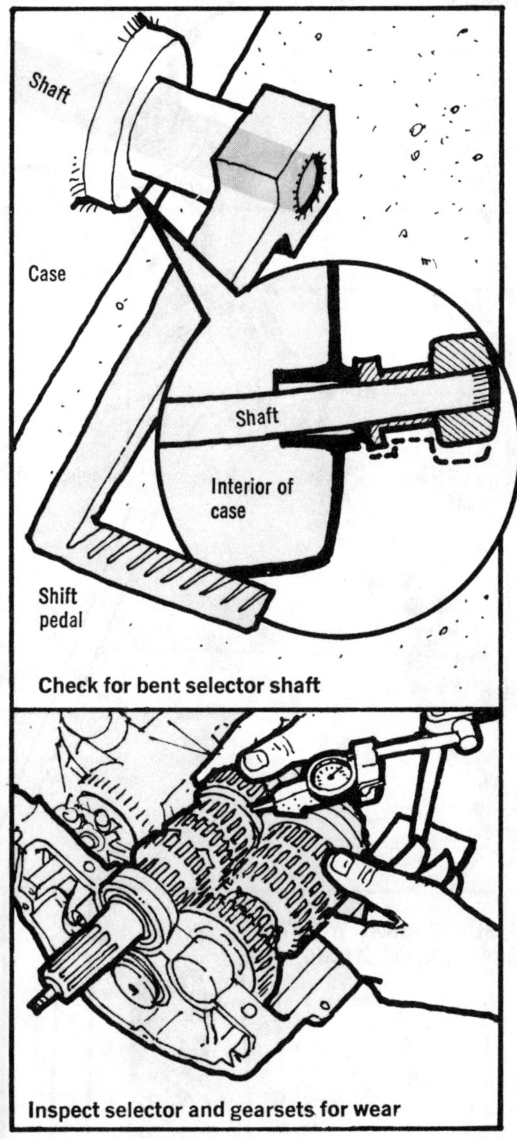

Check for bent selector shaft

Inspect selector and gearsets for wear

TRANSMISSION SLIPS OUT OF GEAR

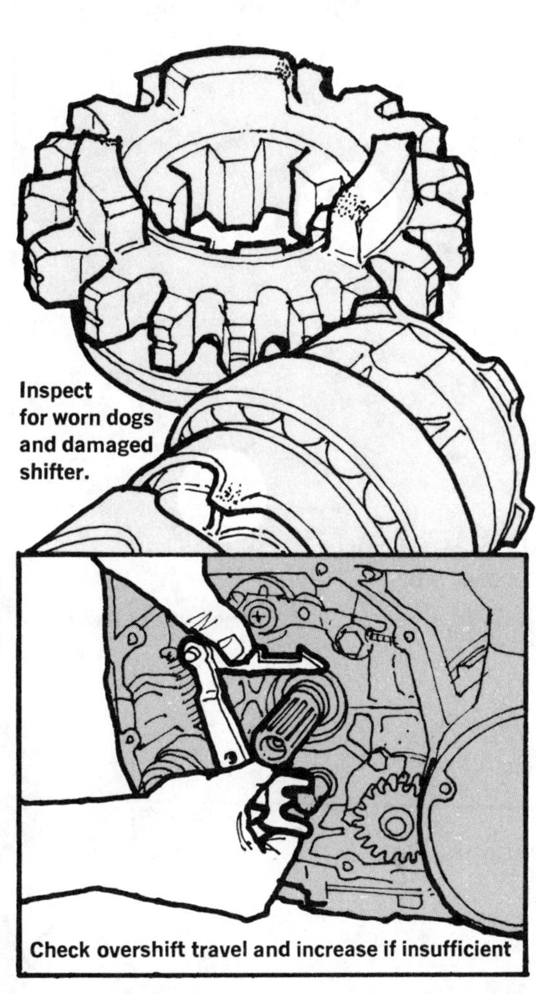

Check overshift travel and increase if insufficient

TRANSMISSION IS NOISY

Check oil level

Disassemble and inspect (see Transmission chapter)

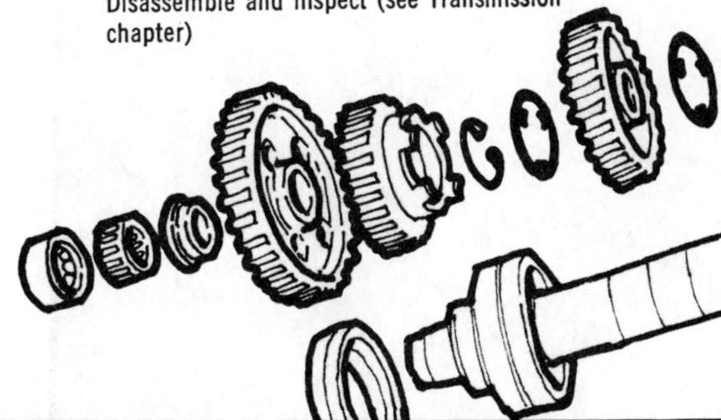

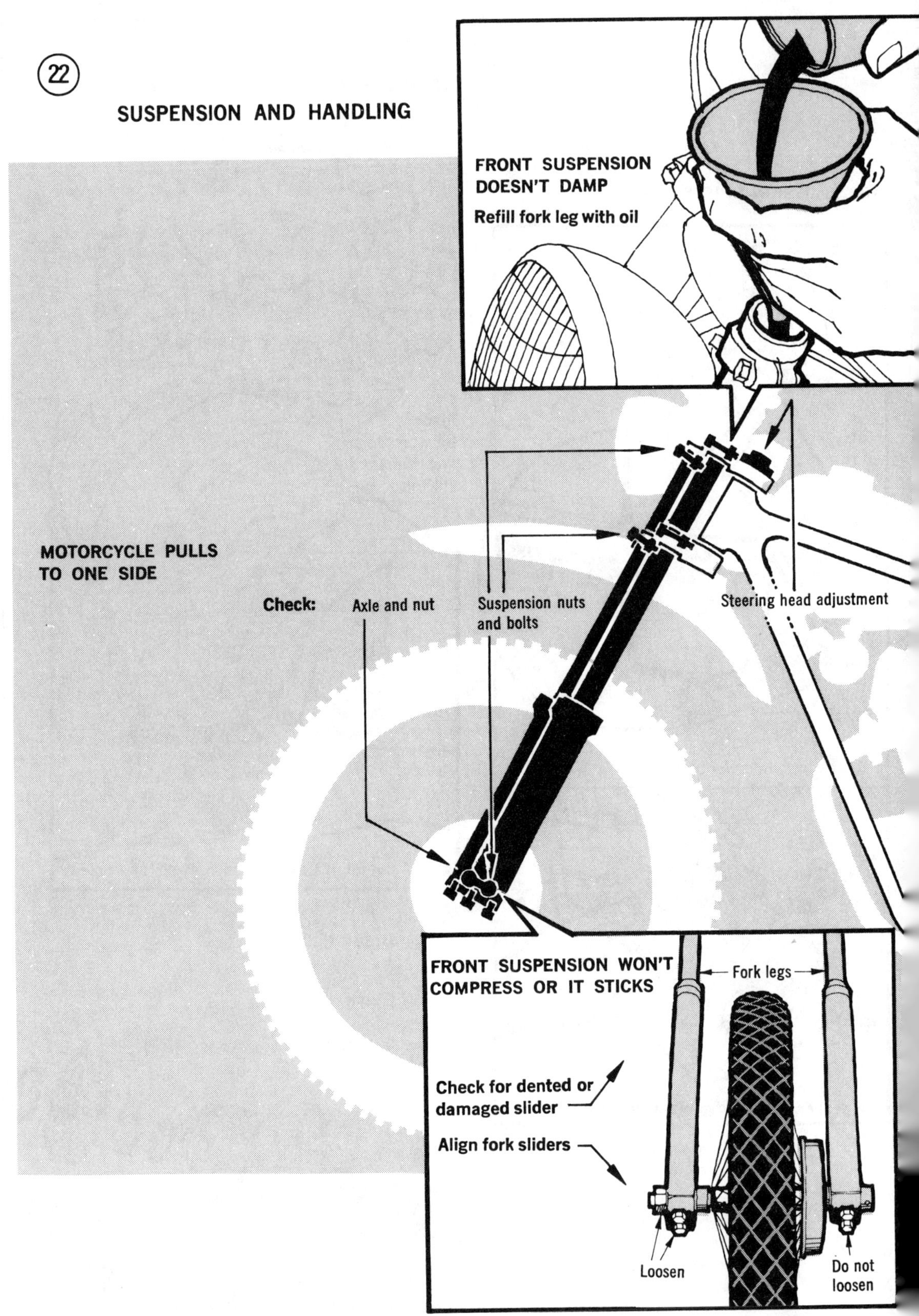
22
SUSPENSION AND HANDLING
FRONT SUSPENSION DOESN'T DAMP
Refill fork leg with oil
MOTORCYCLE PULLS TO ONE SIDE
Check:
Axle and nut
Suspension nuts and bolts
Steering head adjustment
FRONT SUSPENSION WON'T COMPRESS OR IT STICKS
Fork legs
Check for dented or damaged slider
Align fork sliders
Loosen
Do not loosen

Slider
Replace seals if fork legs are oily

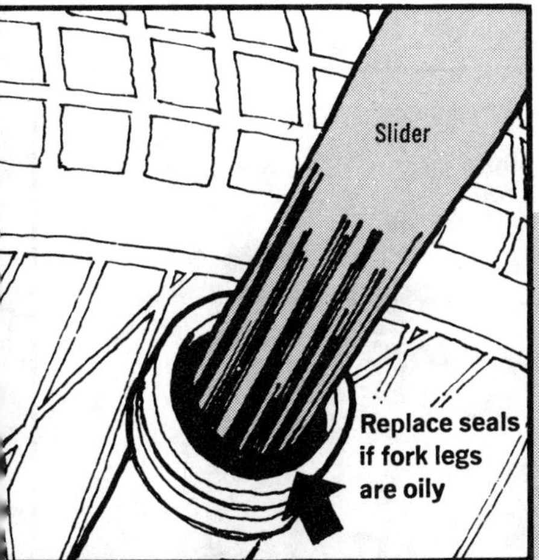

SUSPENSION AND HANDLING CONTINUED

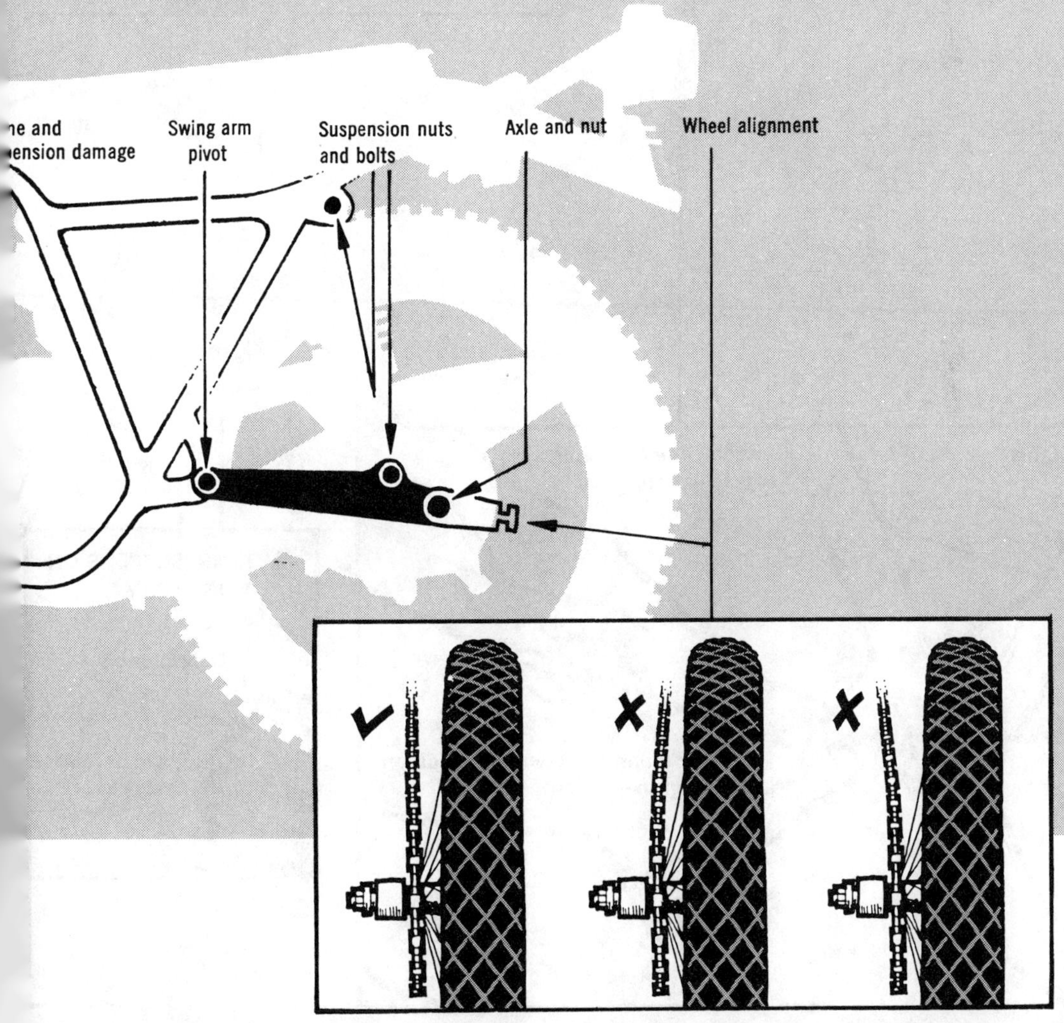

ne and
ension damage
Swing arm pivot
Suspension nuts and bolts
Axle and nut
Wheel alignment

SUSPENSION AND HANDLING CONTINUED

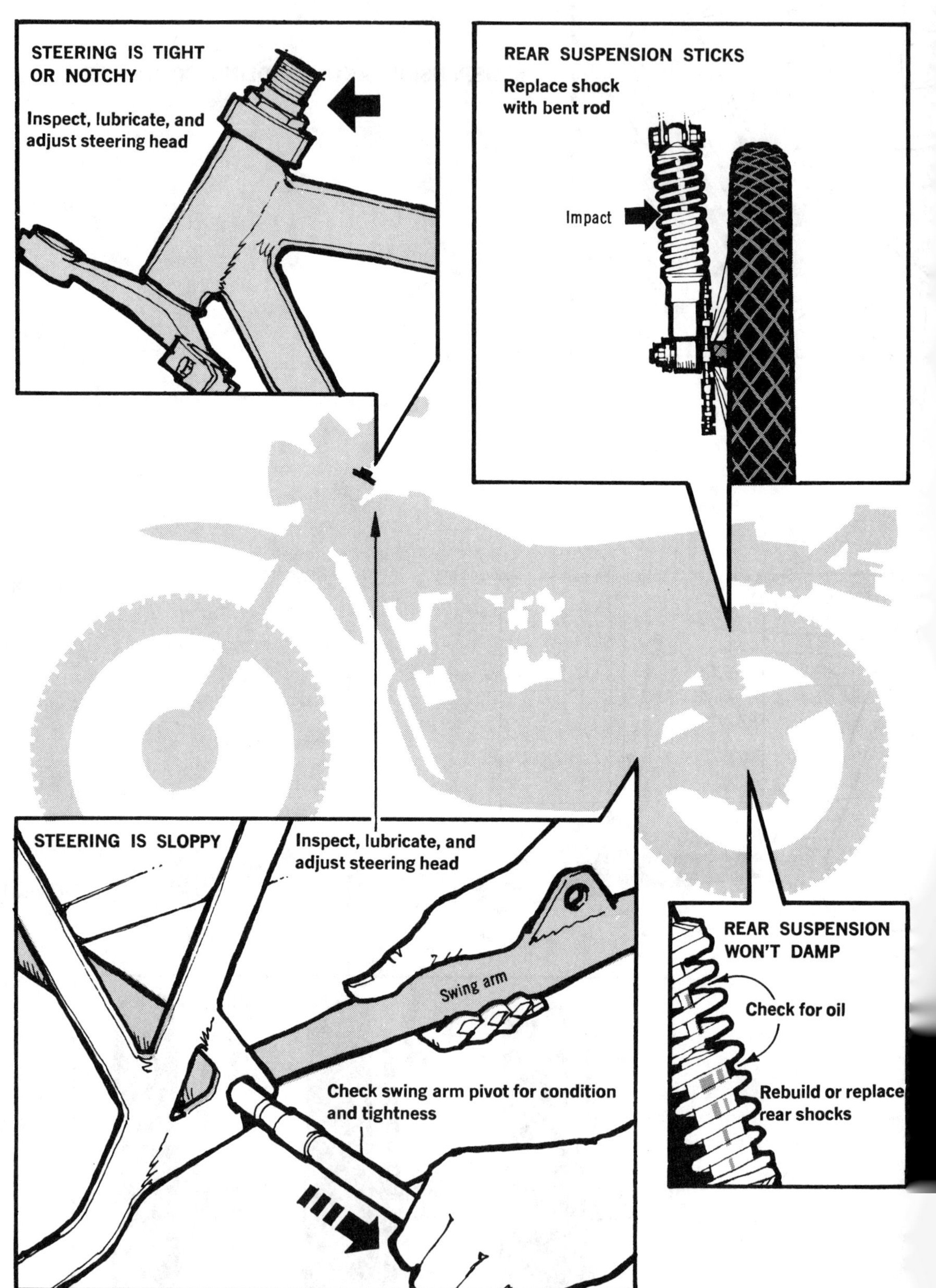

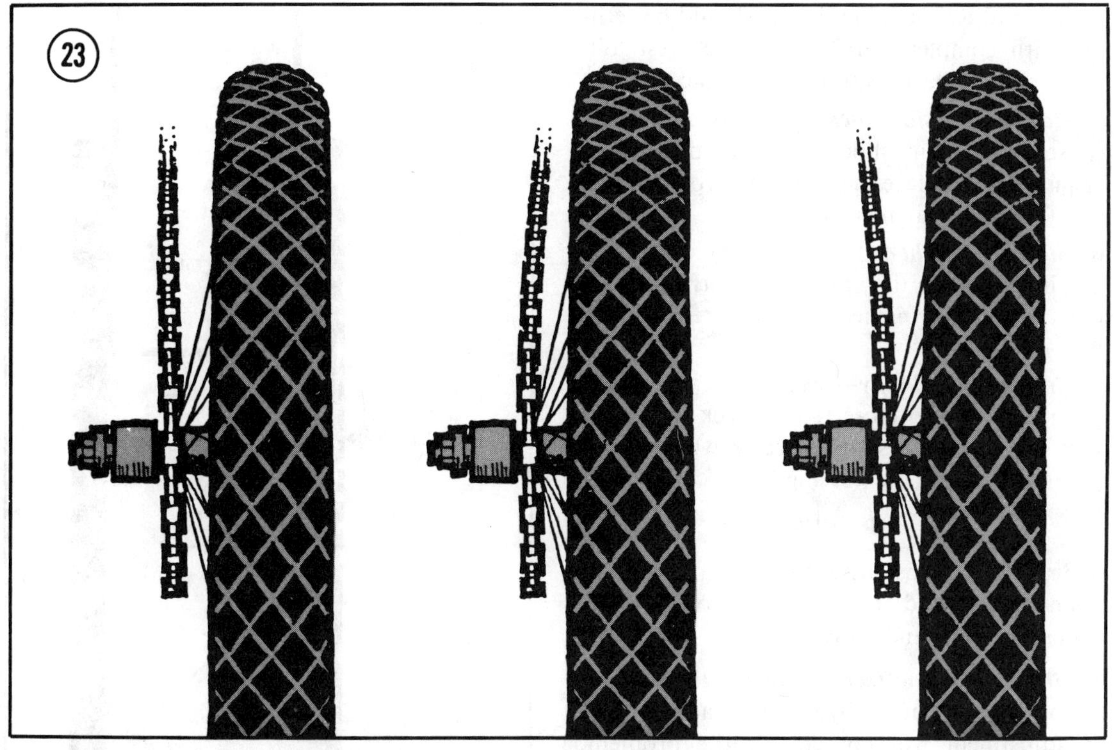

head, swing arm pivot. Check wheel alignment **(Figure 23)**. Check for damage to the frame and suspension components.

2. ***Front suspension doesn't damp***—This is most often caused by a lack of damping oil in the fork legs. If the upper fork tubes are exceptionally oily, it's likely that the seals are worn out and should be replaced.

3. ***Front suspension sticks or won't fully compress***—Misalignment of the forks when the wheel is installed can cause this. Loosen the axle nut and the pinch bolt on the nut end of the axle **(Figure 24)**. Lock the front wheel with the brake and compress the front suspension several times to align the fork legs. Then, tighten the pinch bolt and then the axle nut.

The trouble may also be caused by a bent or dented fork slider **(Figure 25)**. The distortion required to lock up a fork tube is so slight that it is often impossible to visually detect. If this type of damage is suspected, remove the fork leg and remove the spring from it. Attempt to operate the fork leg. If it still binds, replace the slider; it's not practical to repair it.

4. ***Rear suspension does not damp***—This is usually caused by damping oil leaking past

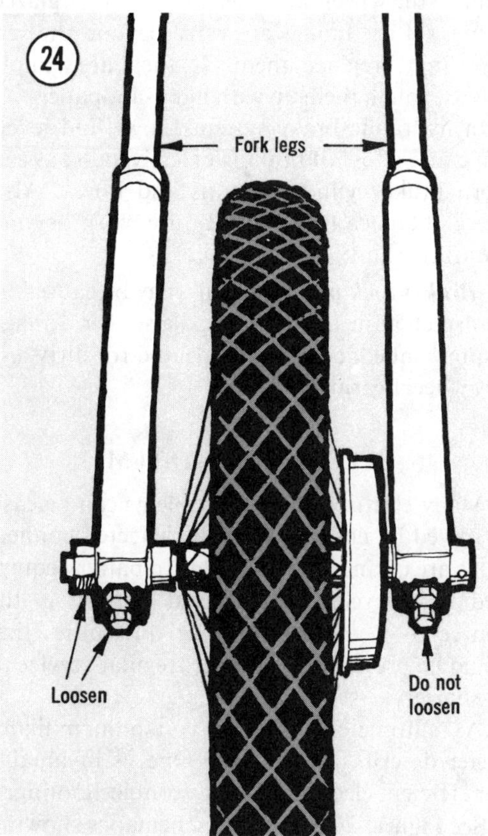

worn seals. Rebuildable shocks should be refitted with complete service kits and fresh oil. Non-rebuildable units should be replaced.

5. ***Rear suspension sticks***—This is commonly caused by a bent shock absorber piston rod (**Figure 26**). Replace the shock; the rod can't be satisfactorily straightened.

6. ***Steering is tight or "notchy"***—Steering head bearings may be dry, dirty, or worn. Adjustment of the steering head bearing pre-load may be too tight.

7. ***Steering is sloppy***—Steering head adjustment may be too loose. Also check the swing arm pivot; looseness or extreme wear at this point translate to the steering.

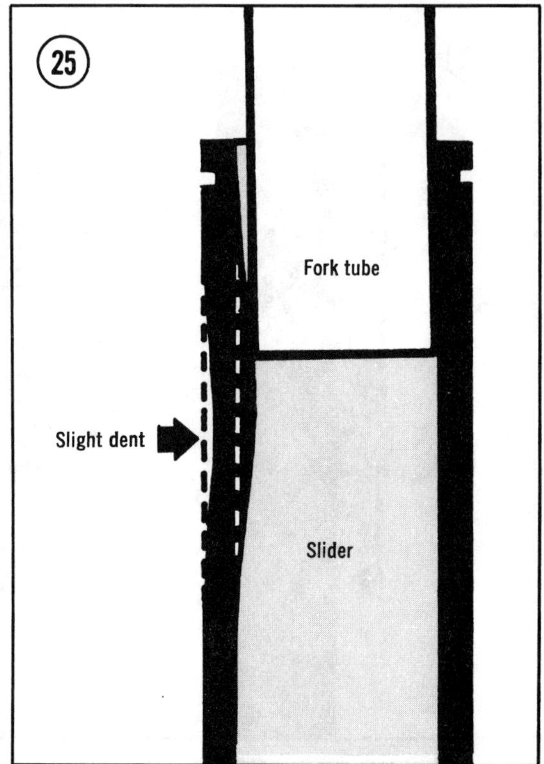

BRAKES

Brake problems arise from wear, lack of maintenance, and from sustained or repeated exposure to dirt and water.

1. ***Brakes are ineffective***—Ineffective brakes are most likely caused by incorrect adjustment. If adjustment will not correct the problem, remove the wheels and check for worn or glazed linings. If the linings are worn beyond the service limit, replace them. If they are simply glazed, rough them up with light sandpaper.

In hydraulic brake systems, low fluid levels can cause a loss of braking effectiveness, as can worn brake cylinder pistons and bores. Also check the pads to see if they are worn beyond the service limit.

2. ***Brakes lock or drag***—This may be caused by incorrect adjustment. Check also for foreign matter embedded in the lining and for dirty and dry wheel bearings.

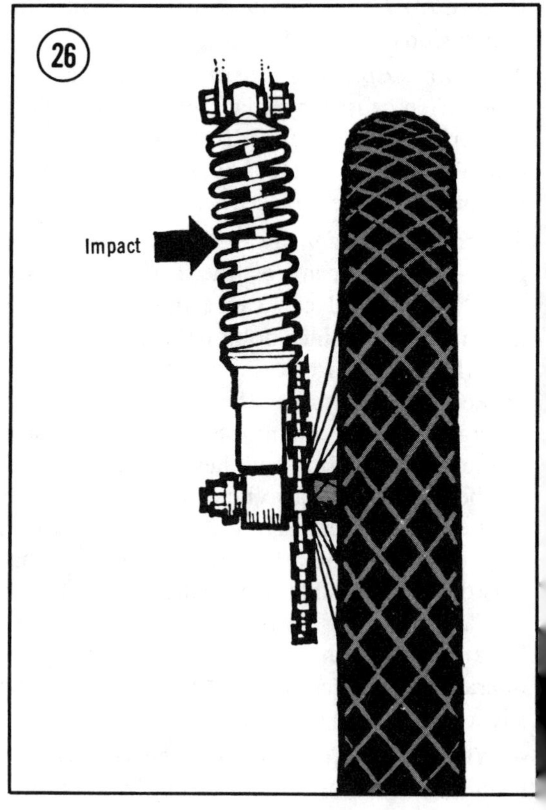

ELECTRICAL SYSTEM

Many electrical system problems can be easily solved by ensuring that the affected connections are clean, dry, and tight. In battery equipped motorcycles, a neglected battery is the source of a great number of difficulties that could be prevented by simple, regular service to the battery.

A multimeter, like the volt/ohm/milliammeter described in Chapter One, is invaluable for efficient electrical system troubleshooting.

See **Figures 27 and 28** for schematics showing

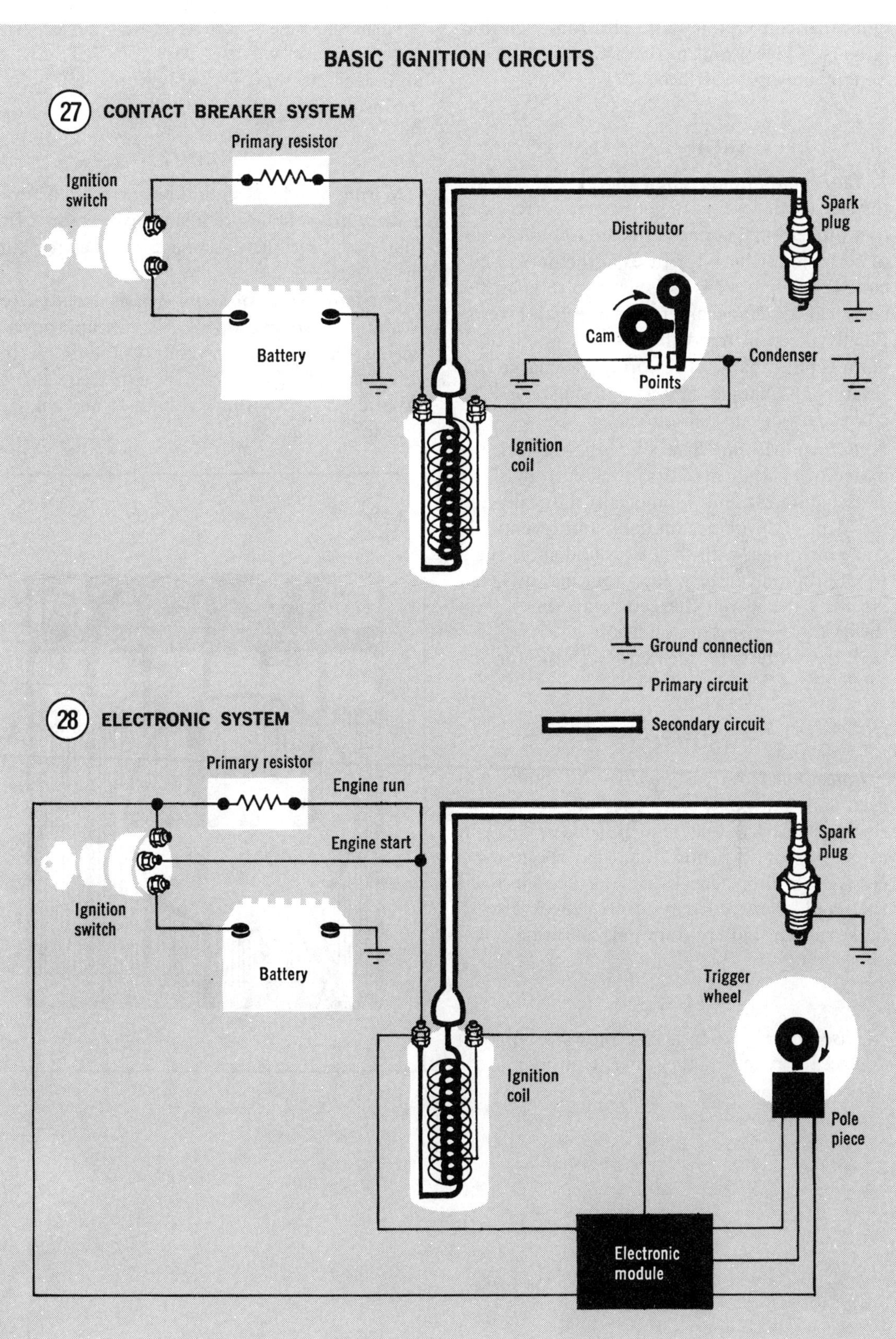
BASIC IGNITION CIRCUITS
27 CONTACT BREAKER SYSTEM
Primary resistor
Ignition switch
Spark plug
Distributor
Cam
Battery
Condenser
Points
Ignition coil
Ground connection
Primary circuit
Secondary circuit
28 ELECTRONIC SYSTEM
Primary resistor
Engine run
Engine start
Spark plug
Ignition switch
Battery
Trigger wheel
Ignition coil
Pole piece
Electronic module

simplified conventional and electronic ignition systems. Typical and most common electrical troubles are also described.

CHARGING SYSTEM

1. ***Battery will not accept a charge***—Make sure the electrolyte level in the battery is correct and that the terminal connections are tight and free of corrosion. Check for fuses in the battery circuit. If the battery is satisfactory, refer to the electrical system chapter for alternator tests. Finally, keep in mind that even a good alternator is not capable of restoring the charge to a severely discharged battery; it must first be charged by an external source.

2. ***Battery will not hold a charge***—Check the battery for sulfate deposits in the bottom of the case (**Figure 29**). Sulfation occurs naturally and the deposits will accumulate and eventually come in contact with the plates and short them out. Sulfation can be greatly retarded by keeping the battery well charged at all times. Test the battery to assess its condition.

If the battery is satisfactory, look for excessive draw, such as a short.

LIGHTING

Bulbs burn out frequently—All bulbs will eventually burn out, but if the bulb in one particular light burns out frequently check the light assembly for looseness that may permit excessive vibration; check for loose connections that could cause current surges; check also to make sure the bulb is of the correct rating.

FUSES

Fuse blows—When a fuse blows, don't just replace it; try to find the cause. Consider a fuse a warning device as well as a safety device. And never replace a fuse with one of greater amperage rating. It probably won't melt before the insulation on the wiring does.

WIRING

Wiring problems should be corrected as soon as they arise — before a short can cause a fire that may seriously damage or destroy the motorcycle.

A circuit tester of some type is essential for locating shorts and opens. Use the appropriate wiring diagram at the end of the book for reference. If a wire must be replaced make a notation on the wiring diagram of any changes in color coding.

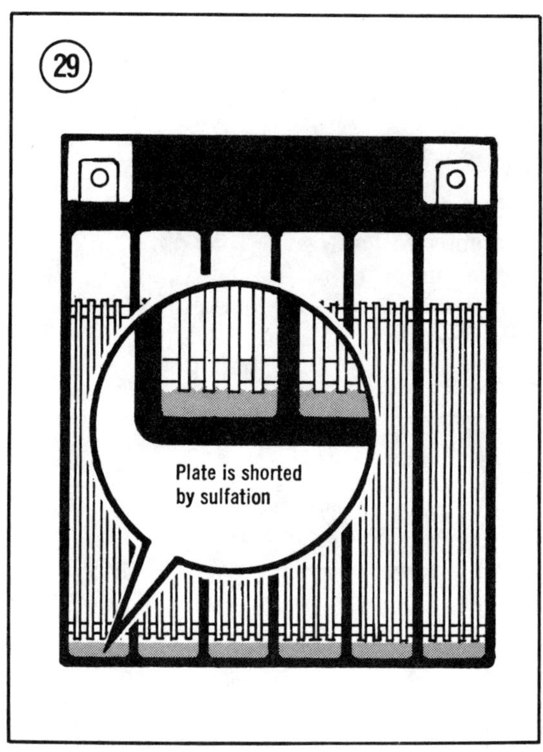

CHAPTER THREE

PERIODIC MAINTENANCE, AND TUNE-UP

Regular preventive maintenance is the best guarantee of a trouble-free motorcycle. An afternoon spent cleaning and adjusting the bike can prevent costly mechanical problems in the future and unexpected, inconvenient breakdowns on the road.

This chapter covers all maintenance procedures, including engine tune-up, required for the Honda Four. Any owner with average mechanical ability can perform the procedures with ordinary tools by following the step-by-step instructions.

TOOLS

The basic tools suggested in Chapter One are essential for most work. In addition, equipment required for a thorough tune-up includes a static timing light, strobe light, dwell tachometer, carburetor float gauge, sets of flat and round feeler gauges measured in millimeters and inches, and a vacuum gauge set to balance the carburetors.

The only expensive item is the vacuum gauge set — about $30-75 — but a less expensive alternative is discussed later in this chapter. See *Carburetion, Manometer Construction*.

DAILY CHECKS

Before starting the engine for the first time each day, check the following items. After a few days these checks will become second nature and can be performed in the time required for the engine to warm up.

1. Visually check tire pressure.
2. Check brake fluid level and brake operation.
3. Check brake lights and horn.
4. Check headlight, taillight, and turn indicators.
5. Check fuel level.

PERIODIC CHECKS

The following checks should be made weekly or at every fuel stop.

Front Brake

1. Have an assistant apply the front brake.
2. Shine a light between the caliper and the disc and inspect the brake pads (**Figure 1**).
3. If either pad has worn enough so that its red line is touching the disc, replace both pads as a set (**Figure 2**). See Chapter Eleven for more detail.

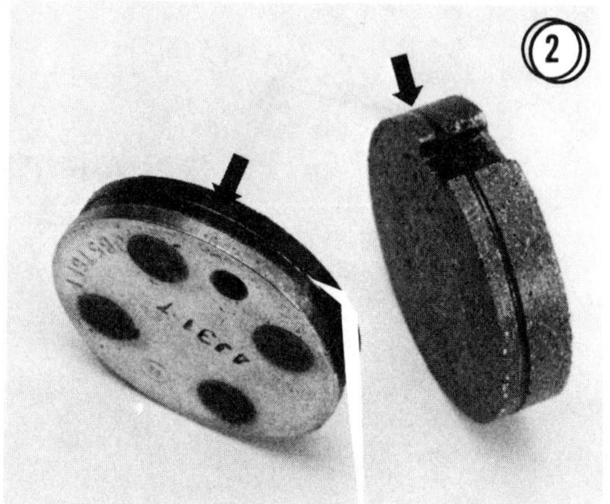

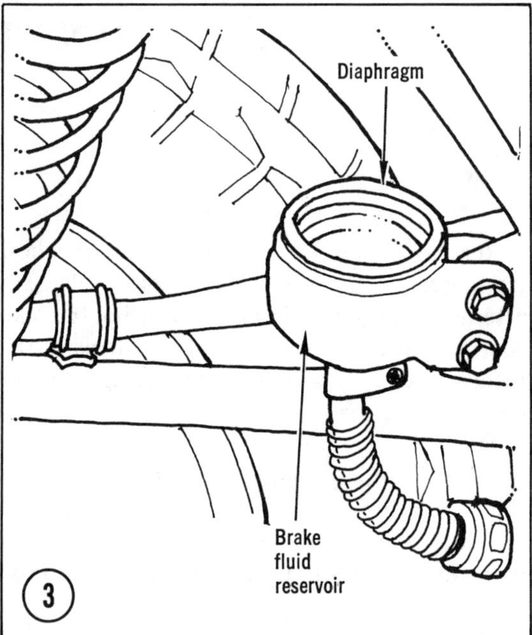

4. Check the fluid level. If the reservoir is less than ½ full, add enough fluid to bring the level up to the line on the side of the reservoir. Use DOT 3 brake fluid.

Rear Brake (Disc)

1. Remove the cap from the brake fluid reservoir on the side of the frame and check the fluid level. See **Figure 3**. Add enough DOT 3 brake fluid to bring the level to the FULL mark.
2. Press on the rear brake lever. It should not feel spongy or reach the limits of its travel.
3. Place the transmission in NEUTRAL and apply the rear brake. Try to move the motorcycle back and forth. This will assure that the brake pads are clamping the disc.
4. If the brake feels spongy or there is too much lever travel, bleed the system as described in *Brake Hydraulic System Bleeding,* Chapter Eleven.

Rear Brake Pedal

1. Check the position of the rear brake pedal at rest. The top of the pedal should be slightly below the top of the front footpeg.
2. Push the pedal down by hand. It should move approximately ¾-1¼ in. (20-30mm). See **Figure 4**. The brake cam lever should then form an angle of 80-90° with the brake rod (**Figure 5**).
3. If brake pedal travel exceeds 1½ in. (40mm), adjust the linkage. See *Rear Brake Linkage Adjustment (Drum Brakes),* this chapter.

Tire Pressure

1. For normal solo riding, inflate the front tire to 26 psi. Inflate the rear tire to 28 psi.

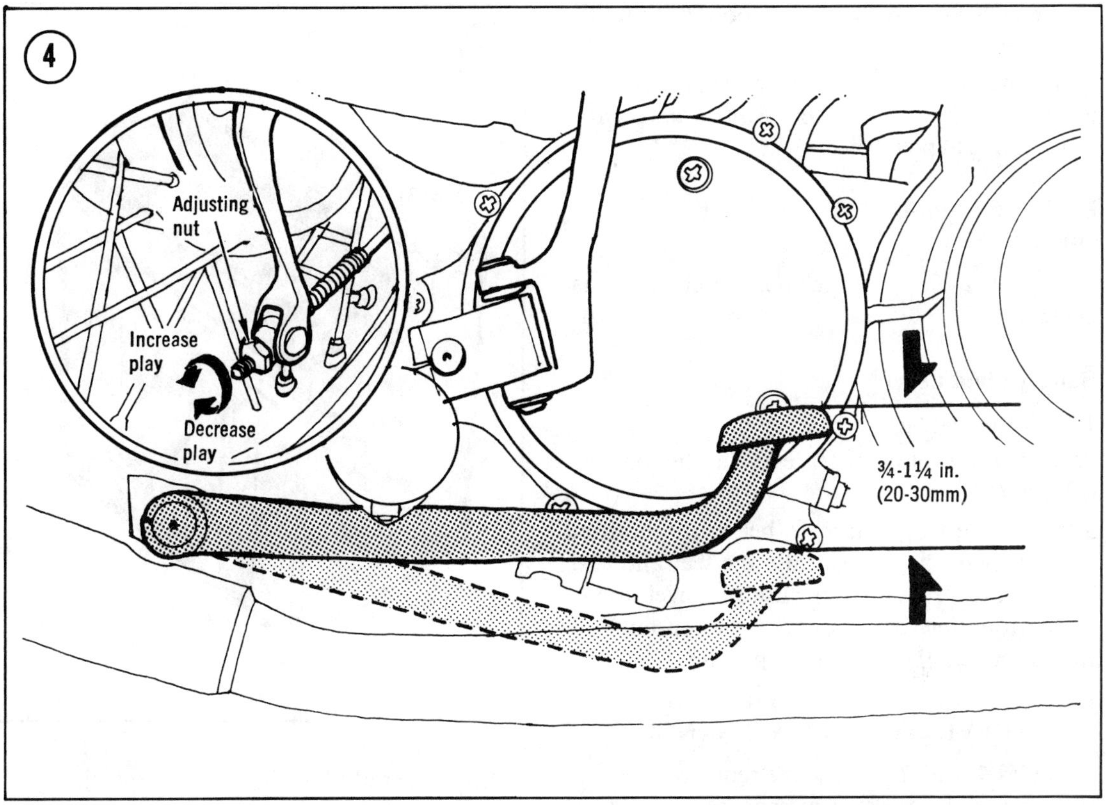

4

Adjusting nut

Increase play

Decrease play

¾-1¼ in. (20-30mm)

2. For normal double riding (with passenger), inflate front tire to 26 psi and rear tire to 30 psi.

3. For sustained high-speed riding, increase both tire pressures to 2 psi over normal.

4. Remove any stones or debris from the tire tread. Check each tire for cracks or cuts, and replace the tire if you find any. For replacement procedure, see Chapter Ten, *Tire Changing and Repair*.

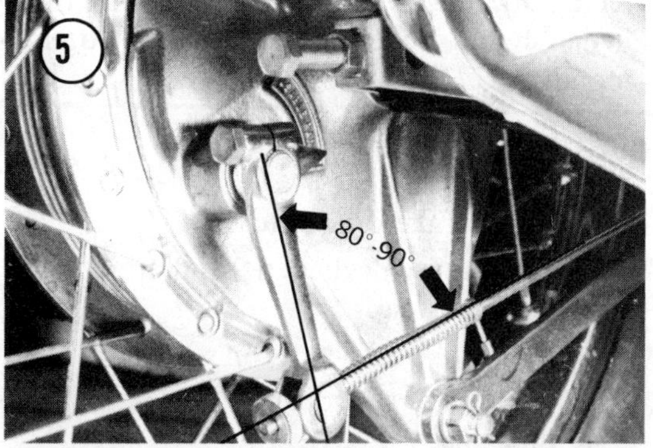

Tire Wear

1. With a depth gauge or a machinist's scale, measure the depth of the tread on each tire **(Figure 6)**.

2. Replace the front tire when its tread is less than 0.04 in. (1.0mm) deep. Replace the rear tire when its tread is less than 0.08 in. (2.0mm) deep.

Wheel Spoke Tension

1. Tap each spoke with a wrench. The higher the pitch of sound it makes, the tighter the spoke. The lower the sound frequency, the

looser the spoke. A "ping" is good; a "klunk" indicates a loose spoke.

2. If one or more spokes are loose, tighten them. See the *Spokes* and *Rim Truing* procedures in Chapter Ten.

Engine and Automatic Transmission Oil Level

See *Periodic Lubrication,* later in this chapter.

Battery Fluid Level

1. Lift the seat.

2. Check the electrolyte level in the battery **(Figure 7)**.

3. If the electrolyte level is below the bottom line in any of the 6 cells, raise the seat and add enough distilled water to raise the level above the bottom line (but not above the top line) on the battery case. Do not use tap water.

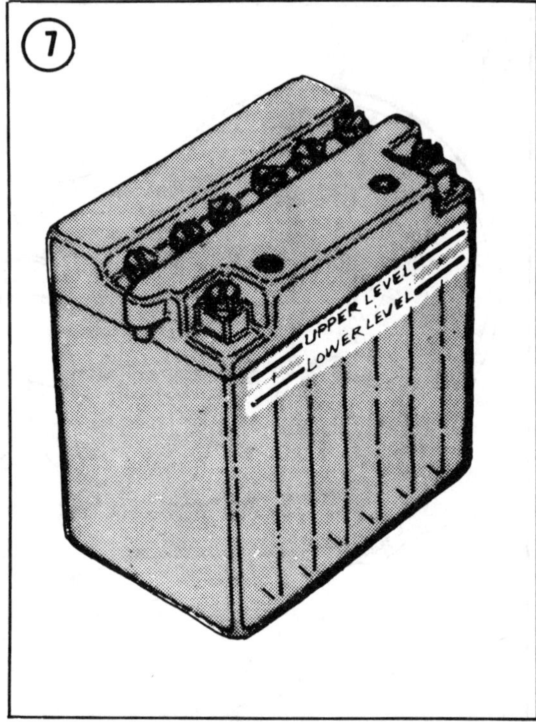

PREVENTIVE MAINTENANCE

Tables 1 and 2 summarize required preventive maintenance. Perform each item at the interval specified. In addition, the following items should be carefully inspected after 24 months or 12,000 miles (20,000km).

- a. Disc brake hydraulic hose(s)
- b. Brake cable
- c. Front brake light switch
- d. Brake master cylinder(s) and primary secondary caps
- e. Disc brake caliper piston seal
- f. Carburetor rubber dust caps
- g. Fuel lines

Tightness of Nuts and Bolts

Every 3,000 miles (5,000km):

1. Check for looseness of the following items:

- a. Engine mount bolts
- b. Handlebar clamp bolts
- c. Top triple clamp bolts
- d. Bottom triple clamp bolts
- e. Front axle clamp nuts
- f. Shock absorber mounting nuts
- g. Swing arm pivot nut
- h. Rear brake backing plate torque link
- i. Rear axle nut

2. Check the engine cover screws for tightness.

3. Check the remaining nuts and bolts on the motorcycle for tightness.

Rear Brake Linkage Adjustment (Drum Brakes)

1. When at rest, the top of the brake pedal should be positioned about 1/16 in. (1.6mm) lower than the bottom of the right front footpeg. If it is not, loosen the locknut on the brake pedal stop bolt **(Figure 8)**.

2. To lower the pedal, back out the stop bolt. To raise the pedal, screw in the stop bolt.

3. When the pedal is positioned correctly while at rest, tighten the stop bolt locknut.

4. Push down the rear brake pedal by hand. The brake cam lever and the brake rod should form an angle of 80-90°.

Parking Brake Adjustment

1. Check cable free play. There should be no more than 0.08 in. (2.0mm) between the knob and its stop.

Table 1 LUBRICATION AND PREVENTIVE MAINTENANCE—1976 AND EARLIER

Every 1,000 miles (1,600 km)
- Inspect, clean, and gap spark plugs
- Inspect, lubricate, and adjust drive chain
- Inspect, adjust, and lubricate controls and linkage

Every 2,000 miles (3,200 km) or 2 months
- Change engine oil (change filter every 4,000 miles)

Every 3,000 miles (5,000 km) or 6 months
- Check contact breaker condition and gap — lubricate
- Check timing
- Check valve clearance
- Check clutch free play
- Check all fasteners for tightness
- Clean and inspect battery
- Clean fuel filter, fuel lines and tank
- Clean air cleaner (more frequent for dusty conditions
- Check, adjust, and synchronize carburetors
- Check fork pinch bolts
- Check and lubricate swing arm pivot
- Inspect wheels and spokes*
- Inspect brake linings and pads for wear
- Check brake fluid level — replace annually
- Adjust rear brake pedal
- Lubricate rear brake cam
- Inspect frame and handlebar mount
- Check steering play*
- Check and clean exhaust system
- Check sidestand pad — lubricate pivot
- Inspect drive sprockets
- Check operation of lights, switches and horn
- Check instrument operation

Every 6,000 miles (10,000 km) or 12 months
- Change oil filter screen
- Inspect ignition wiring
- Lubricate cables
- Lubricate steering head bearings*
- Change fork oil
- Inspect and lubricate wheel bearings and axles
- Inspect hydraulic brake lines and connections
- Adjust parking brake (A models)

*Refer to a dealer unless you have experience with wheels and steering

Table 2 LUBRICATION AND PREVENTIVE MAINTENANCE—1977 AND LATER

Every 600 miles (1,000 km)
- Inspect drive chain condition and adjustment

Every 1,800 miles (3,000 km)
- Change engine oil

Every 3,600 miles (6,000 km)
- Replace oil filter
- Drain crankcase breather*
- Clean air cleaner (more frequent for dusty conditions)
- Check fuel lines
- Check spark plug gap and condition
- Check valve clearance
- Check contact breaker condition and gap — lubricate
- Check timing
- Adjust cam chain tension
- Check throttle operation and free play
- Check idle speed (curb and high-speed)
- Synchronize carburetors
- Clean and inspect battery
- Check brake fluid (monthly is less than 3,600)— Replace annually
- Check brake shoes and pads for wear
- Inspect brake lines, rod, controls — lubricate
- Check brake light switch operation
- Check headlight aim
- Check clutch free play
- Check sidestand pad — lubricate pivot
- Inspect suspension — swing arm pivot, shock and fork damping — change fork oil annually
- Lubricate swing arm pivot
- Lubricate controls and cables
- Check all fasteners for tightness
- Check wheels and spoke tension**
- Check tire condition

Every 7,200 miles (12,000 km)
- Lubricate and adjust steering head bearings**
- Adjust parking brake (A models)

*Drain more frequently if motorcycle is ridden in rain or extensively at wide throttle openings.
**Refer to a dealer unless you have experience with wheels and steering.

3

2. Loosen the locknut to adjust.
3. Turn the adjusting nut to reduce or increase play as needed.
4. Tighten the locknut.
5. Remove brake pedal and dust cover.
6. Check inside housing for dust or lack of lubrication.
7. Check to make sure the ratchet lever pushes on the switch.
8. The parking brake should engage at each detent position as the pedal moves approximately ¾ in. (20mm). If the brake does not engage, remove the case ratchet and inspect the pawls.

Headlight Adjustment

Proper headlight adjustment is essential to safe night riding. If the lights are set too low, the road will be invisible. If set too high, they will blind oncoming cars. Adjustment is very simple and should be a part of routine maintenance. The procedure is as follows.

1. Place the machine approximately 15 feet from a white or light colored wall. Refer to **Figure 9**.
2. Make sure the bike and wall are on level, parallel ground and that the front wheel is pointing directly ahead.
3. Measurement should be made with one person on the seat and both wheels on the ground.
4. Draw a cross on the wall equal in height to the center of the headlight.
5. Put on the high beam. The cross should be centered in the concentrated beam of light.
6. If the light does not correspond to the mark, loosen the 2 bolts and adjust. Tighten bolts and recheck positioning.

PERIODIC LUBRICATION

The procedures that follow apply after initial break-in. Maintenance and lubrication intervals are summarized in **Tables 1 and 2**.

Crankcase Breather

CB750 models manufactured after December 31, 1977, are equipped with a crankcase breather. The breather should be drained every 3,600 miles in dry weather and when the engine

8

is operated mostly at moderate throttle settings. If the motorcycle is used often in heavy rain or at sustained wide throttle openings, the breather should be drained more often. To clean the breather, remove the plug **(Figure 10)** and allow the breather tube to drain. Then reinstall the plug.

Rear Chain

At the intervals shown in **Tables 1 and 2**, lightly oil the drive chain with SAE 30 motor oil, or a good quality commercial chain lube. Make certain the oil penetrates between the plates and the rollers.

Wipe off excess oil so that it will not attract dirt. With a rider on the motorcycle, check the adjustment of the chain. It should move up and down no more than ¾ in. midway between the sprockets on the bottom run. If adjustment is required, refer to *Drive Chain, Adjustment* at the end of this chapter.

Engine Oil Change Frequency

For 1977 and earlier models, the oil change interval is 2,000 miles (3,000km) or 2 months.

9

HEADLIGHT ADJUSTMENT

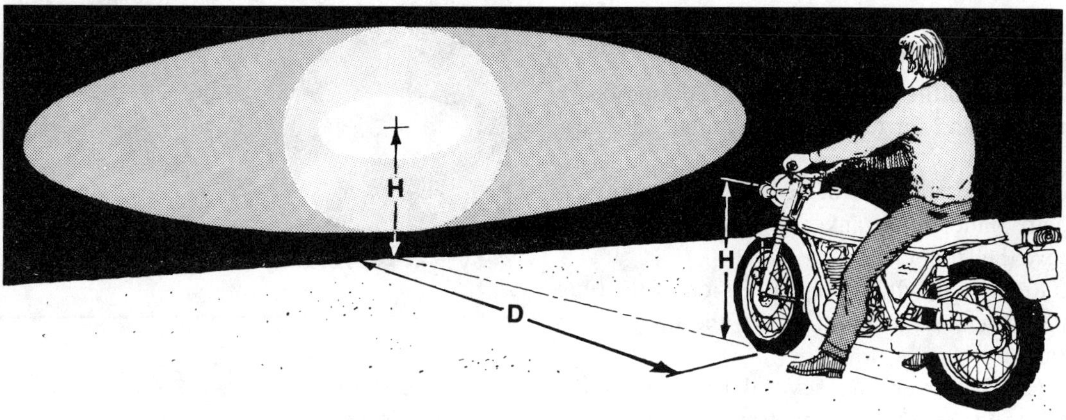

H

H

D

H = Height from center of headlight to floor
D = Distance from headlight to wall

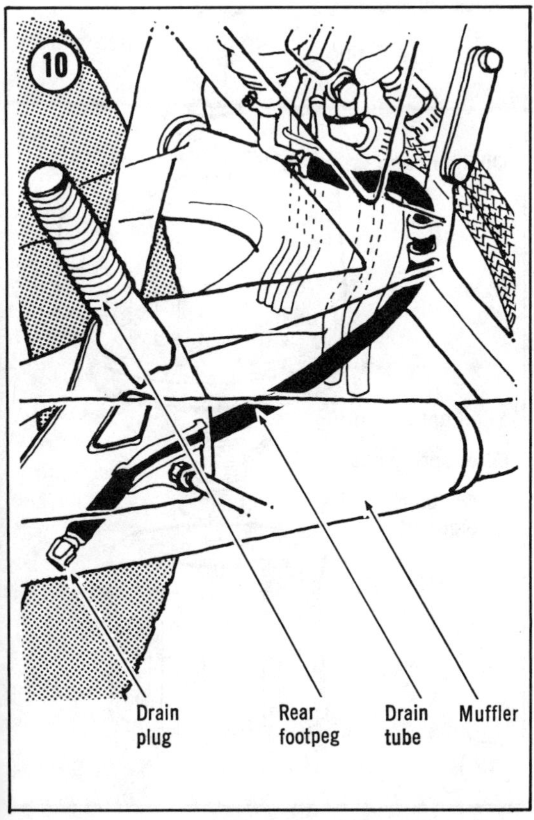

For 1978 models, the recommended interval is 1,800 miles (2,700 km) or 2 months. The time interval is as important as accumulated mileage; acids formed by gasoline vapor blown by the piston rings will contaminate the oil even if the engine is not run for several weeks.

Engine Oil Quality and Viscosity

Use only a detergent oil with an API classification of G. The classifications are stamped on the top of the container. Always use the same brand of oil when topping up.

SAE 10W-40 oil is recommended for normal operation in moderate climates. Contrary to some editions of the Honda 750 owner's manual, heavier weight oils should be used if the motorcycle is to be run hard in high temperatures. SAE 10W-50 is recommended.

The factory recommends the following alternate weight oils according to prevailing temperature:

59° F and above (15° C)	SAE 30 or 30W
32-59° F (0-15° C)	SAE 20 or 20W
32° F and below (0° C)	SAE 10W

CAUTION
Never use oil additives in a Honda engine. The clutch is lubricated by the same oil used in the crankcase. Do not use automatic transmission fluid (ATF) in the CB750A. Use only normally recommended motor oil or severe engine damage will result.

Draining Engine Oil

1. Warm up the engine. Warm oil drains faster than cold and carries more accumulated impurities with it.
2. Place a catch pan of at least one gallon capacity under the crankcase drain plug and remove the filler cap.
3. Remove the drain plug. Location of the plug is shown in **Figure 11**. Allow the dirty oil to drain.
4. Crank the engine several times with the kickstarter to force out oil trapped in the inner recesses.
5. Repeat Steps 2-4 for the oil tank drain plug.

CAUTION
Do not permit the engine to start; keep the ignition off.

NOTE: *Pour the used oil into plastic bottles, such as those used for laundry bleach. Cap them tightly and discard according to local regulations.*

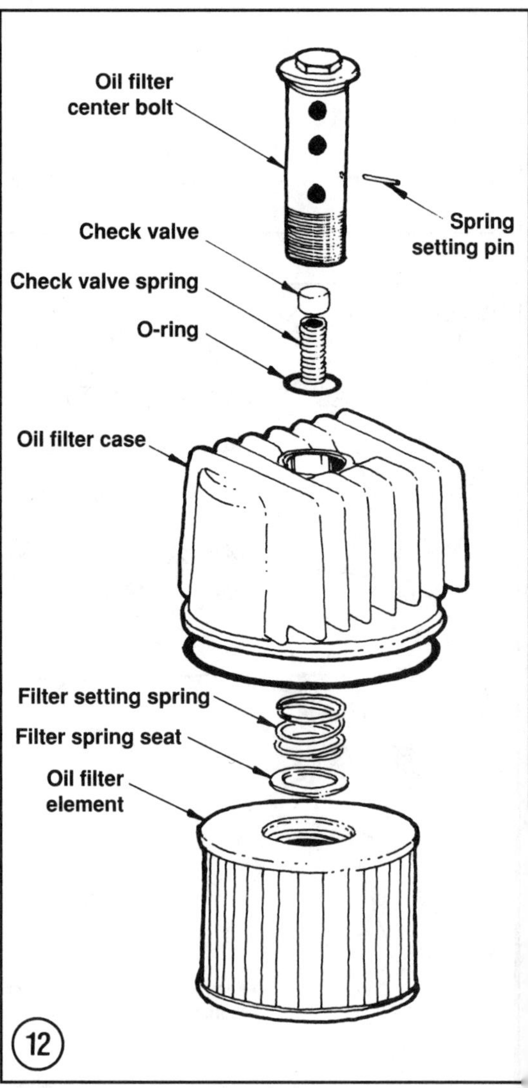

Changing Oil Filter

The Honda 750 has 2 different types of oil filter housings, depending on when the machine was manufactured.

Figure 12 is an exploded view of the later version.

Replace the oil filter element every other oil change.

1. Remove the center bolt from the housing and pull the assembly from the engine. Watch out for oil dripping from the filter.
2. Discard the old filter element according to local regulations and inspect the O-ring seal for damage. Clean the dirty oil and sludge from the inside of the housing with solvent and wipe or blow dry.
3. Install new filter element and new O-ring.
4. Install the assembly on the engine. Torque center bolt to 19-24 ft.-lb. (2.7-3.3 mkg).

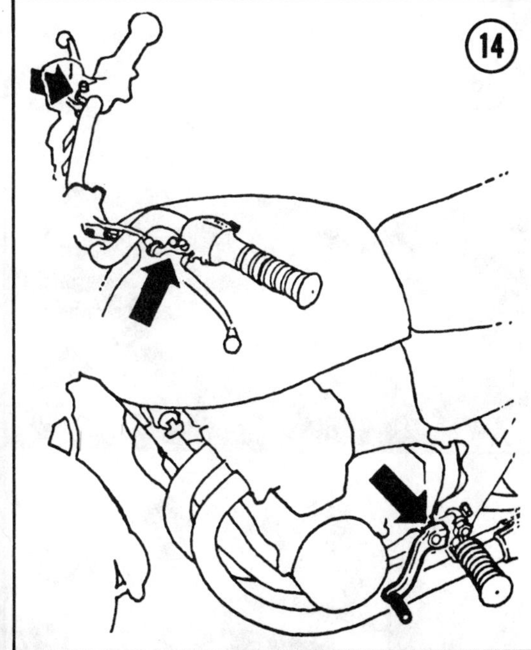

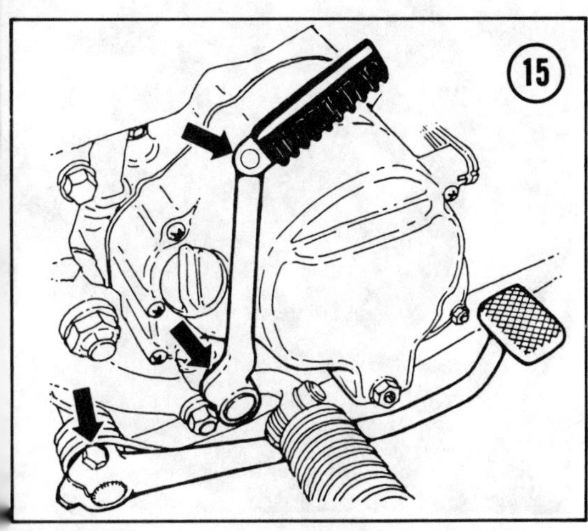

Filling Engine With Oil

1. Install the drain plugs in the crankcase and oil tank with their gaskets. Be careful not to overtighten or they will be difficult to remove the next time. Torque to 25-29 ft.-lb. (3.5-4.0 mkg).

2. Fill the oil tank with 3.7 quarts (U.S.), 6.2 pints (Imp), or 3.5 liters of recommended oil. Check the level with the dipstick.

3. Run the engine at 1,000-1,500 rpm for 2 minutes, then check for oil seepage around the drain plug and filter housing. Check the oil level and top up if necessary.

Contact Breaker Points

1. Remove the 2 screws that mount the breaker point cover (**Figure 13**). Remove the cover and its gasket.

2. Rub a small amount of high-temperature grease into the felt that bears against the breaker point cam.

CAUTION

If you use too much grease, the cam will sling it into the points and foul them.

3. Install gasket and cover.

Control Linkage

Every 1,000 miles (1,500km) or after washing the motorcycle, use a long-spout oil can to lubricate the points shown in **Figures 14 and 15**. Use SAE 30 motor oil.

Throttle Cable

Every 6,000 miles (10,000km) or when the cables begin to bind:

1. Loosen the nuts (at the carburetor pulley) and remove the 2 throttle cables from the pulley.

2. Remove the screws (at the handlebars) that assemble the twist grip housing. Remove the top half of the housing.

3. Remove the throttle cable(s) from the twist grip. Note which cable goes where on A, F, and K series models.

4. Examine the exposed parts of the inner cables. Pull each inner cable up and down in its housing to determine whether it is clean or gritty.

5. If the cables are clean, hold the top part of one cable vertical and spray it with Dri-Slide or one of the thin spray-on chain lubricants.

6. Hold the spray can close to the inner cable, near the top ferrule of the cable housing, so that lubricant will run down between the inner cable and its housing. Spray the cable until lubricant runs out of the bottom of the cable housing. Lubricate other cable in the same way.

7. If the cables are dirty, spray them instead with a lubricant/solvent, such as LPS-25, or WD-40. Continue spraying the upper portion of the inner cable until lubricant, running out the bottom of the cable housing, is clean.

8. Lubricate the twist grip assembly with grease.

9. Reassemble throttle linkage in reverse order of disassembly. Refer to *Throttle Cable Adjustment,* earlier in this chapter.

Clutch Cable

Every 3,000 miles (5,000km):

1. At the clutch lever mount, loosen the locknut and cable adjuster **(Figure 16)** to provide slack in the cable.

2. If there is enough slack in the cable, pull the cable housing (outer cable) free of the lever, and lift the inner cable out. Bend the inner cable around to match the slot in the lever, and pull the cable and its fitting out of the lever.

3. If there is not enough slack in the cable, loosen the locknut on the clutch adjusting screw. This will provide enough slack in the clutch cable so that it can be freed from the handlebar lever.

4. At the top of the clutch cable, examine the exposed portion of the inner cable. If it is clean, hold the cable vertical and spray it with Dri-Slide or one of the thin spray-on chain lubricants. Hold the spray can close to the inner cable, near the top ferrule of the cable housing, so that the lubricant will run down between the inner cable and its housing. Spray the cable until it is lubricated along its entire length.

5. If the exposed portion of the inner cable is dirty, or the cable feels gritty while moving it up and down in its housing, spray it instead with a lubricant/solvent, such as LPS-25 or WD-40.

6. Attach the cable to the clutch lever, and then fit it to the lever mount. To adjust the clutch adjustment screw and/or the cable linkage, refer to *Clutch, Free Play Adjustment,* later in this chapter.

Disc Brake Fluid Change

Every 12,000 miles (20,000km) or whenever the fluid becomes dirty or watery:

1. Remove rubber cap from caliper bleeder valve. See **Figure 17**.

2. Attach one end of a piece of clear plastic tubing to the bleeder valve. Stick the other end into an empty can.

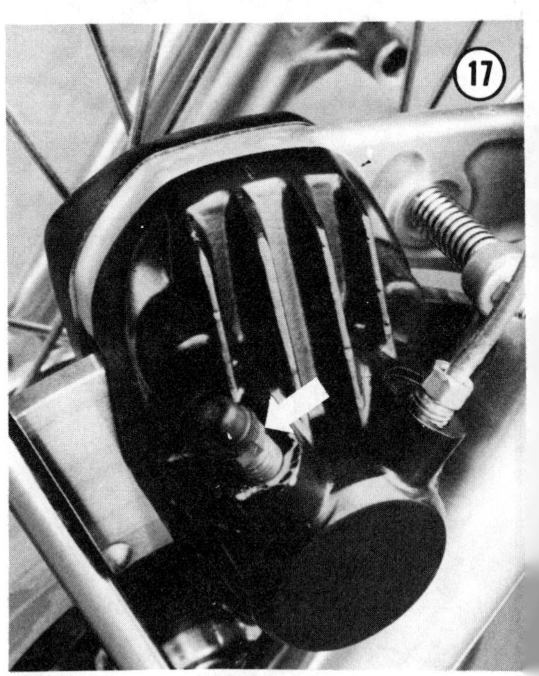

3. Unscrew the bleeder valve body enough to open the valve fully.

4. Squeeze and release the front brake lever until all of the fluid has been drained out of the reservoir, the line, and the caliper.

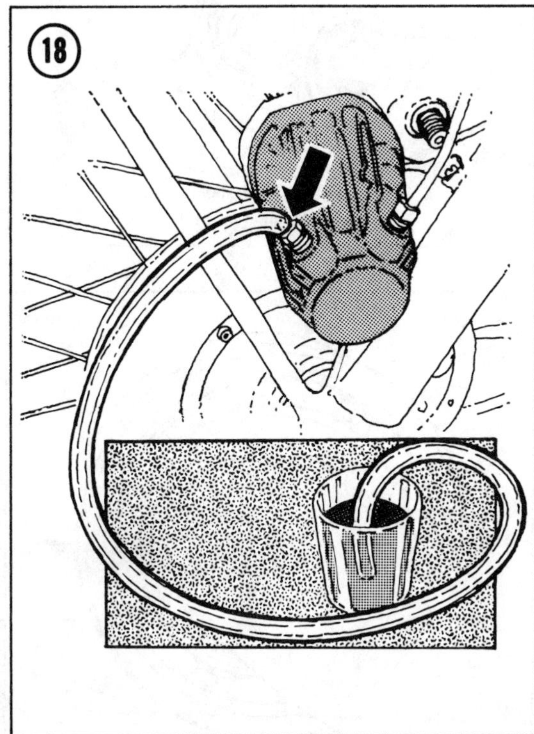
18

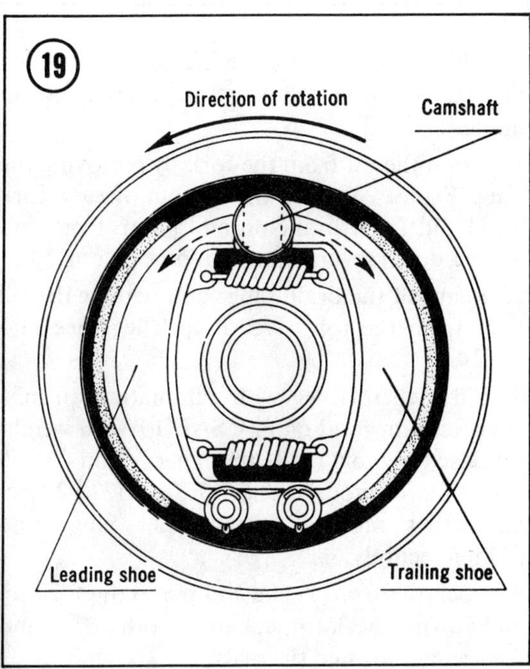

19

5. Screw in the bleeder valve to close the valve. Discard the used fluid and stick the bottom end of the tubing into a clean jar.

6. Unscrew the cap from the handlebar fluid reservoir. Fill the reservoir with fresh fluid.

CAUTION
Use only DOT 3 brake fluid. Use fluid only from a recently opened can.

7. Open the bleeder valve. See **Figure 18**. Squeeze the brake lever and hold it down. Close the valve, and quickly release the lever. Continue this operation until brake fluid starts coming out of the bleeder valve. Add fluid as necessary to prevent reservoir from running dry.

8. Bleed air from the system. See *Brake Hydraulic System, Bleeding,* Chapter Eleven.

Rear Brake Cam (Drum)

Every 12,000 miles (20,000km), or whenever the rear wheel is removed:

1. Remove the rear wheel. Refer to *Rear Wheel Removal,* Chapter Ten.

2. Take out the brake backing plate.

3. Wipe away the old grease, being careful not to get any of it on the brake shoes.

4. Sparingly apply high-temperature grease to camming surfaces of the camshaft, camshaft grooves, brake shoe pivots, and ends of the springs **(Figure 19)**. Do not get any grease on the brake shoes.

5. Assemble the rear wheel and install it.

Wheel Bearings

Lubricate the front and rear wheel bearings every 12,000 miles (20,000km), as follows:

1. Remove the wheels from the motorcycle and remove the bearings **(Figures 20 and 21)**. For front and rear wheel removal and disassembly procedures, see Chapter Ten, *Rear Wheel Removal/Disassembly*.

2. Clean old grease out of the hub.

3. Wash each wheel bearing in kerosene and dry it.

CAUTION
Do not spin the wheel bearing during the cleaning process.

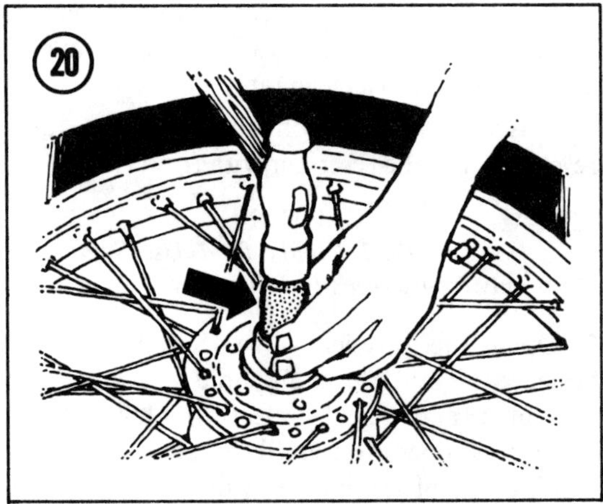

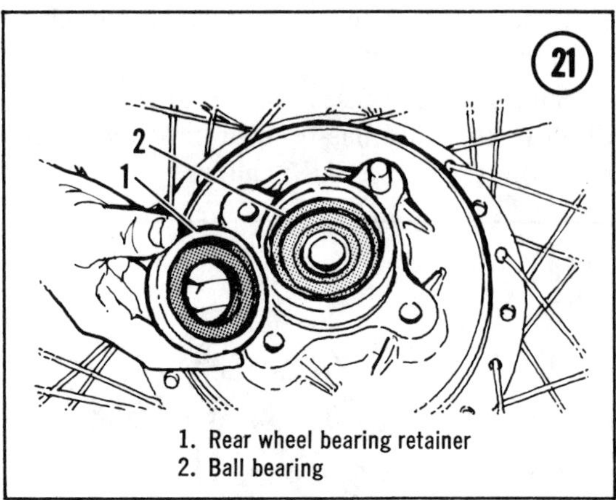

1. Rear wheel bearing retainer
2. Ball bearing

4. Oil each bearing, and spin it slowly. See **Figure 22**. If it will not spin smoothly, is noisy, or has rough spots, replace it with a new one. Safe steering requires that the wheel bearings be in good condition.

5. Pack the bearings with good quality bearing grease.

6. Grease the front hub speedometer gearbox.

7. Assemble and install the wheel.

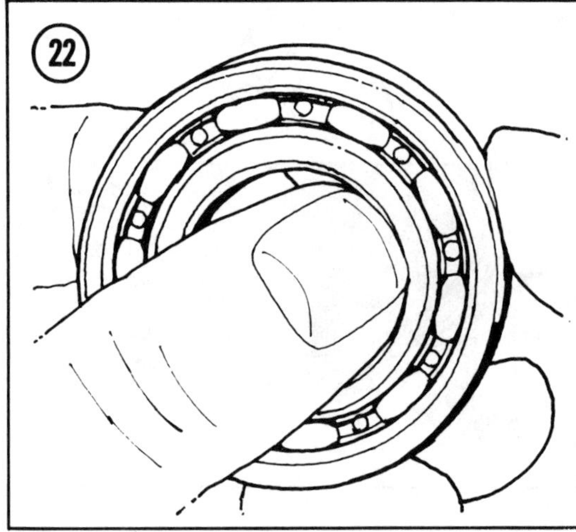

Swing Arm

Every 3,000 miles (5,000km):

1. Use a gun to force grease into the fitting on the swing arm, until the grease runs out both ends (fittings can be installed by a dealer if your model is not already so equipped).

2. Clean off excess grease.

3. If grease will not run out of the ends of the swing arm, unscrew the grease fitting from the swing arm. Clean it, and make certain that the ball check valve is free. Install fitting.

4. Apply the grease gun again. If grease does not run out both ends of the swing arm, remove the swing arm (see *Swing Arm*, Chapter Nine). Clean out the old grease, install the swing arm, and lubricate it.

Front Fork Oil

There is no simple method for checking fork oil level. It is a reasonable assumption that if there is no evidence of leakage and the forks are damping properly, the oil level is correct.

Oil in the front forks should be changed every 6,000 miles (10,000km) to maintain good handling, and prolong the life of the damping mechanism. The following steps apply to all models:

1. Drain the oil from the fork by removing the plug **(Figure 23)** from the bottom of each fork leg. Hold front brake on and pump front end up and down several times to force oil out.

2. Reinstall the drain plugs and remove the fill plug from the top of each fork leg. See **Figure 24.**

3. Fill each fork leg with automatic transmission fluid or good quality SAE 10W-30 weight oil. Use 6-6.5 oz. (180-200cc) per leg on CB750 K3 and later models, and 7-7.3 oz. (220-230cc) on earlier models. Install filler plugs and tighten securely.

4. Lock the front brake and pump the fork up and down. Check for lack of smooth action and for seepage around the seals.

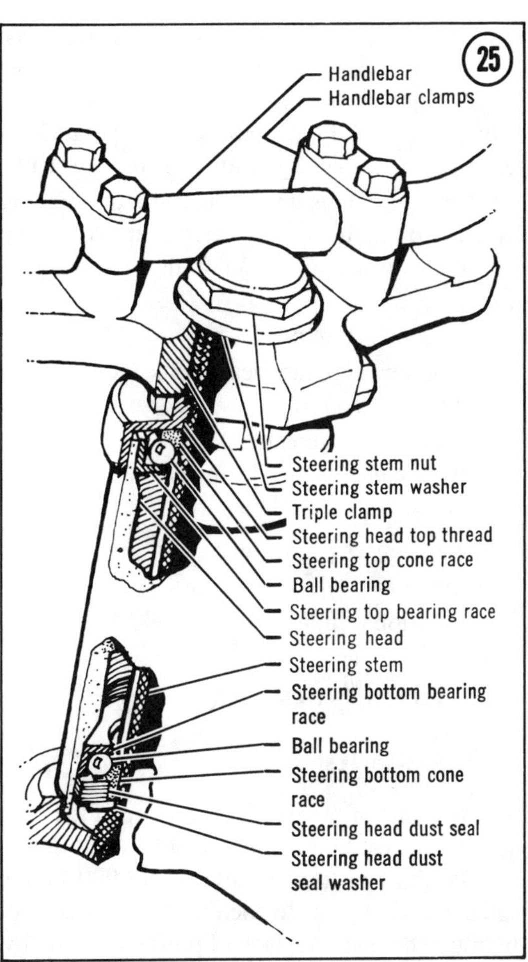

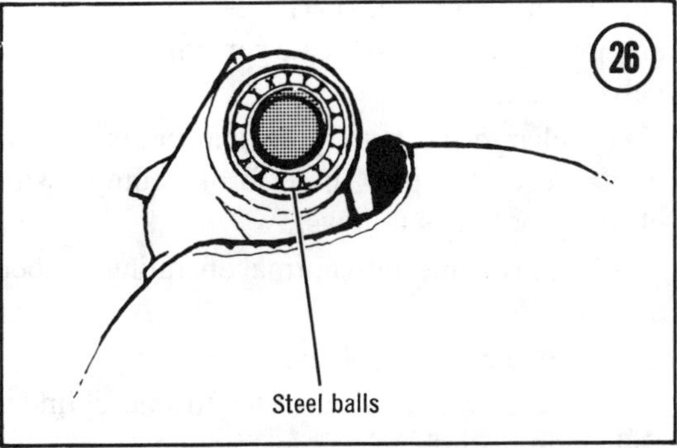

Steering Stem Bearing

Every 12,000 miles (20,000km):

1. Remove the steering stem (**Figure 25**). See Chapter Eight, *Steering Assembly*.
2. Clean the upper race, lower race, and balls of each bearing in kerosene.
3. Inspect the balls and races of each bearing for wear or damage. If any component shows wear or damage, replace the entire bearing with new parts.
4. Coat all 4 races with chilled grease, and position the balls on their races (**Figure 26**).
5. Install the steering stem.

ENGINE TUNE-UP

For 1977 and earlier models, a complete tune-up is recommended every 3,000 miles

(5,000km) or 6 months under normal conditions. For 1978 models, the interval is 3,600 miles (6,000km) or 6 months. More frequent tune-ups may be required if the motorcycle is operated extensively in stop-and-go traffic or for short trips.

Different systems interact in a smooth running engine and cannot be considered apart. A tune-up should always be performed in the following order:

a. Compression test
b. Tighten cylinder head bolts (see Chapter Four, *Camshaft*)
c. Cam chain adjustment
d. Valve clearance adjustment
e. Spark plugs
f. Condenser (capacitor)
g. Breaker points
h. Ignition timing
i. Air cleaner
j. Carburetion (if needed)

Compression Test

This is one of the simplest, yet one of the most significant test to determine engine condition. It should be performed every 12,000 miles (20,000km) or prior to each tune-up if indicated by rough engine idle, lack of power, or blow-by

A compression tester measures pressure buildup in each cylinder. The results, when properly interpreted, can indicate general cylinder and valve condition.

Full charge the battery so that cranking rpm will exceed 250 rpm. To perform a compression check, proceed as follows:

1. Run the engine until normal operating temperature is reached.
2. Remove all spark plugs.
3. Connect compression tester to one cylinder, following manufacturer's instructions.
4. Open choke and throttle fully.
5. Use a remote starter switch or have an assistant crank the engine until the reading on the compression tester stabilizes. This is usually about 8 revolutions.
6. Remove the tester and record the reading. Reset tester.
7. Repeat above steps for each cylinder.

If compression reading does not differ between cylinders by more than 10 psi, the rings and valves are in good condition.

If a low reading (10% or more) is measured on one cylinder, it indicates valve or ring trouble. To determine which, pour about a teaspoon of engine oil through the spark plug hole onto the top of the piston. Turn the engine over once to distribute the excess oil, then take another compression test and record the reading. If compression increases significantly, the valves are good but the rings are defective in that cylinder. If compression does not increase, the valves require servicing. A valve could be hanging open but not be burned, or a piece of carbon could be on a valve seat or valve face.

Low compression in 2 adjacent cylinders may indicate that the head gasket has blown between the cylinders and that gases are leaking from one cylinder to the other. Torque the cylinder head bolts and take another set of readings. If the condition persists, replace the head gasket.

Valve Clearance Adjustment

Incorrect valve clearance between tappets and valve stems hampers performance and may damage the valves if the condition is prolonged. Adjust clearances every 3,000 miles (5,000km) with the engine cold.

1. Turn the fuel valve off and disconnect both fuel lines.
2. Raise seat and remove fuel tank. See Chapter Six, *Fuel Tank and Fuel Valve*.
3. Remove the breaker point cover.
4. Refer to the cylinder head cover illustration in **Figure 27** and remove the 8 caps that cover the tappet access holes. There are 4 holes in back (intake) and 4 holes in front (exhaust).

NOTE: *Cylinders are numbered 1-4, starting from the rider's left.*

5. Slowly rotate the crankshaft clockwise with the kickstart pedal until the "T 1-4" mark, seen through the peephole in the breaker base plate, is even with the outer index mark as shown in **Figure 28**.
6. At this point, either No. 1 or No. 4 cylinder will be at the top dead center (TDC) point of its

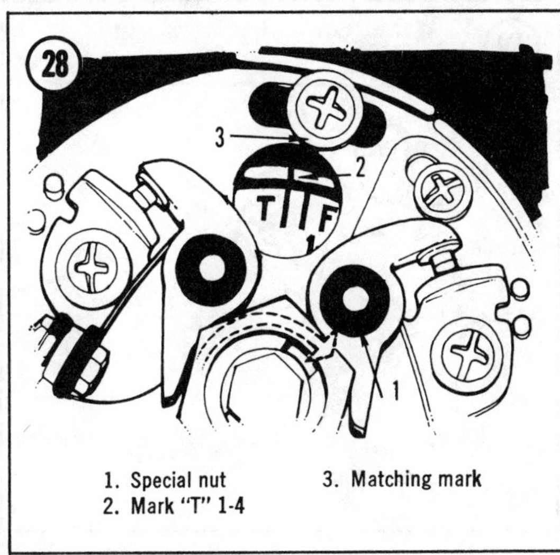

1. Special nut
2. Mark "T" 1-4
3. Matching mark

compression stroke. Find out which one it is by feeling the rocker arms of both cylinders through the adjustment holes. A cylinder at TDC will have both its rocker arms loose, indicating that both intake and exhaust valves are closed.

7. Check valve clearances as shown in **Figure 29** by sliding the proper sized feeler gauge between the adjusting screw tip and the top of the valve stem. The feeler blade should slide through with a slight amount of drag.

Standard valve clearances are:

Intake (rear)	0.002 in. (0.05mm)
Exhaust (front)	0.003 in. (0.08mm)

8. To adjust, loosen the locknut on the tappet adjusting screw **(Figure 30)**.
9. Turn the adjusting screw clockwise to reduce clearance and counterclockwise to increase it.
10. When clearance is correct, tighten the locknut while holding the adjusting screw in position. Check clearance again to make sure tightening did not upset the setting.
11. These adjustments should be performed for both intake and exhaust valves of the cylinder that is at TDC.
12. Rotate the crankshaft 360° until "T 1-4" mark once again is lined up with the index mark.
13. The other cylinder, either No. 1 or No. 4, is now at TDC. Check and adjust if necessary according to Steps 7 through 11.

14. Set up the valves for No. 2 and No. 3 cylinders by rotating the crankshaft until the "T 2-3" mark on the timing ring is aligned with the index line (**Figure 31**).

15. Determine which cylinder is at TDC and then check and adjust clearance.

16. Rotate the crankshaft another 360° until the "T 2-3" mark once again is lined up properly and adjust the valves for the final cylinder.

17. Replace the tappet hole caps with their gaskets. Torque to between 7.2-10 ft.-lb. (1-1.4 mkg) or until snug.

> NOTE: *If cam chain tension is to be adjusted (next procedure), do not install the caps for No. 1 cylinder or the breaker point cover.*

Cam Chain Adjustment

The cam chain tensioner bears against the chain to absorb shock while a chain guide damps vibration. See **Figure 32**. A loose cam chain is noisy and can change valve timing. The tension is easy to set.

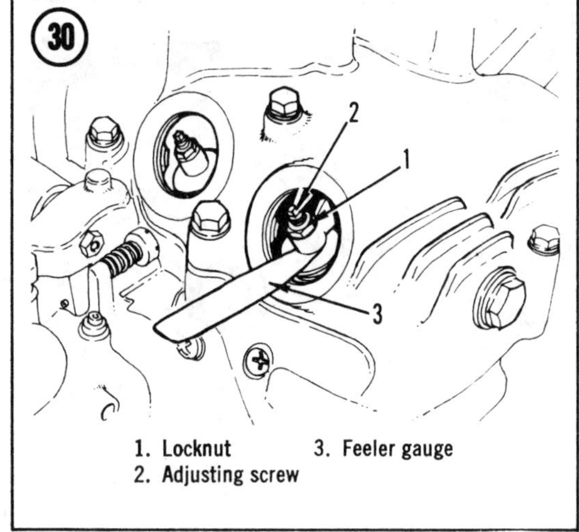

1. Locknut
2. Adjusting screw
3. Feeler gauge

1. Rotate crankshaft clockwise until it is 15° after top dead center (ATDC) for the No. 1 cylinder. See **Figure 33**. This position puts the chain slack at the rear of the engine and duplicates running conditions.

> NOTE: *When the No. 1 piston is at* TDC, *both valves will be closed and the rocker*

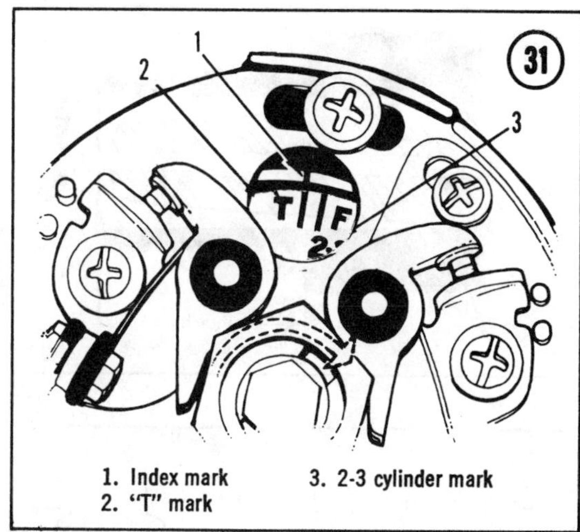

1. Index mark
2. "T" mark
3. 2-3 cylinder mark

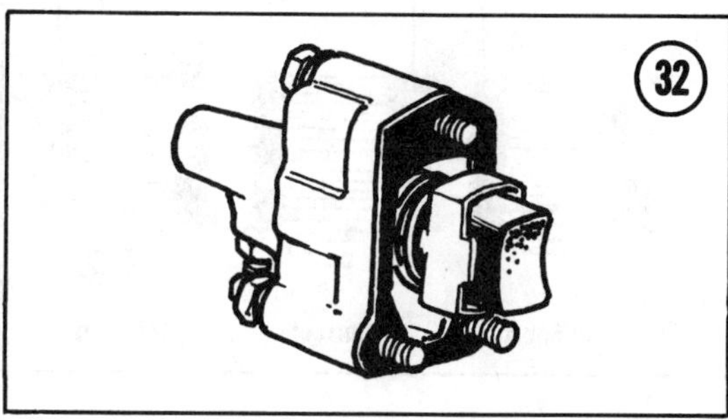

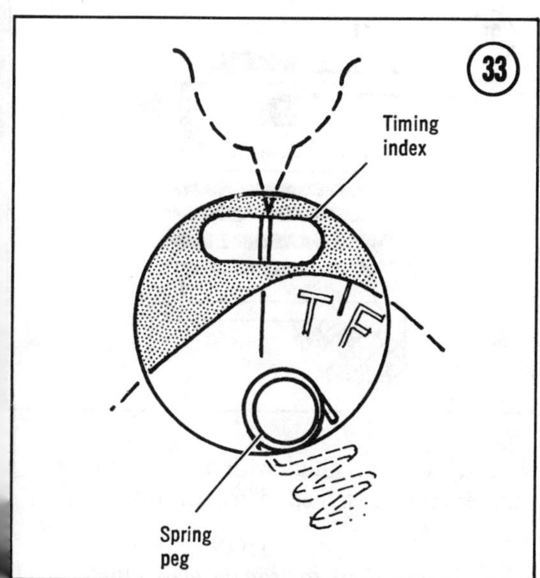

arms will be loose. Remove tappet adjusting caps, if necessary, to check.

The drawing shows the timing setting for 15° after top dead center.

2. Loosen the locknut (refer to **Figure 34**).

3. Loosen the adjusting bolt. This releases the bar and allows the spring to automatically exert the correct amount of tension on the chain.

4. Tighten the adjusting bolt.

5. Tighten the locknut.

6. Install the cap over the tappet adjusting hole of the No. 1 cylinder. Use a new O-ring if the old one is worn or damaged.

Spark Plugs

Spark plugs are available in various heat ranges, hotter or colder than plugs originally installed at the factory.

Select plugs of a heat range designed for the loads and temperature conditions under which the bike will run. Use of incorrect heat ranges can cause seized pistons, scored cylinder walls, or damaged piston crowns.

In general, use a lower numbered plug for low speeds, loads, and temperatures. Use a higher numbered plug for high speeds, engine loads, and temperatures.

NOTE: *Use the highest numbered plug that will not foul.*

In areas where seasonal temperature variations are great, the factory recommends a "2-plug system" — a high numbered plug for hard summer riding and a lower numbered plug for slower winter operation.

The reach (length) of a plug is also important. A longer than normal plug could interfere with the valves and piston causing permanent and severe damage. Refer to **Figures 35 and 36**.

NOTE: *The standard spark plugs are Champion A8Y-MC, NGK, D8ES, Bosch X260T2, and Autolite HG1.*

Testing Plugs

A quick and simple test can be made to determine if the plug is correct for your type of riding. Accelerate hard through the gears and maintain a high, steady speed. Shut the throttle off, and kill the engine at the same time, allowing the bike to slow, out of gear. Do not allow the engine to slow the bike. Remove the plugs and check the condition of the electrode areas. A spark plug of the correct heat range, with the engine in a proper state of tune, will appear light tan. See **Figure 37**.

If the insulator is white or burned, the plugs are too hot and should be replaced with colder ones. Also check the settings of the carburetors for they may be too lean.

A too-cold plug will have sooty deposits ranging in color from dark brown to black. Replace with hotter plugs and check for too-rich carburetion or evidence of oil blow-by at the piston rings.

If any one plug is found unsatisfactory, discard the set.

Removal/Installation

Remove and clean the spark plugs at least once every 1,000 miles (1,500km) of riding. Electrode gap should be measured with a round feeler gauge and set at 0.024-0.028 in. (6-7mm) as shown in **Figure 38**.

Often heat and corrosion can cause the plug to bind in the head making removal difficult. Do not use force; the head is easily damaged.

Here is the proper way to replace a plug:

1. Blow out any debris which has collected in the spark plug wells. It could fall into the holes.
2. Gently remove the spark plug leads by pulling up and out on the cap. Do not jerk the wires or pull on the wire itself.
3. Apply penetrating oil to the base of the plug and allow it to work into the threads.

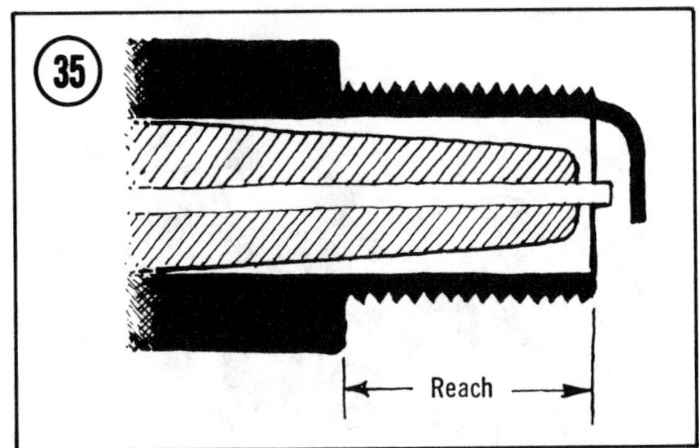

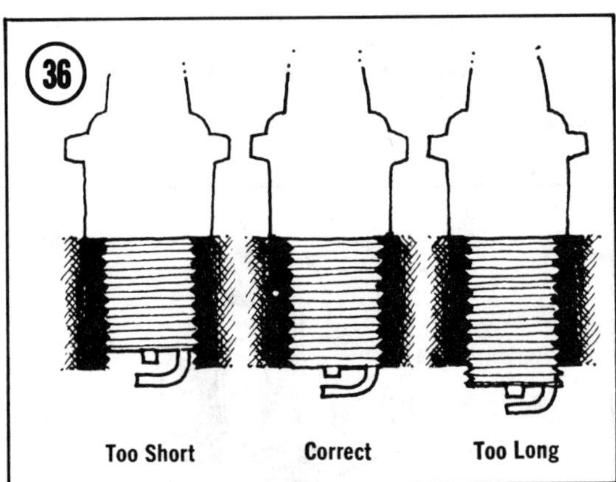

4. Back out the plugs with a socket that has a rubber insert designed to grip the insulator.

CAUTION
Be careful not to drop the plugs into the cooling fins where they could become lodged.

5. Clean the seating area after removal and apply graphite to the thread to simplify future removal.

SPARK PLUG CONDITION

(37)

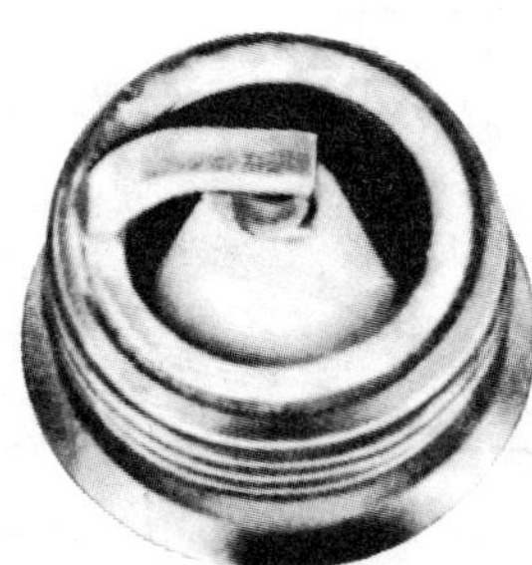

NORMAL

- Identified by light tan or gray deposits on the firing tip.
- Can be cleaned.

GAP BRIDGED

- Identified by deposit buildup closing gap between electrodes.
- Caused by oil or carbon fouling. If deposits are not excessive, the plug can be cleaned.

OIL FOULED

- Identified by wet black deposits on the insulator shell bore and electrodes.
- Caused by excessive oil entering combustion chamber through worn rings and pistons, excessive clearance between valve guides and stems, or worn or loose bearings. Can be cleaned. If engine is not repaired, use a hotter plug.

CARBON FOULED

- Identified by black, dry fluffy carbon deposits on insulator tips, exposed shell surfaces and electrodes.
- Caused by too cold a plug, weak ignition, dirty air cleaner, too rich a fuel mixture, or excessive idling. Can be cleaned.

LEAD FOULED

- Identified by dark gray, black, yellow, or tan deposits or a fused glazed coating on the insulator tip.
- Caused by highly leaded gasoline. Can be cleaned.

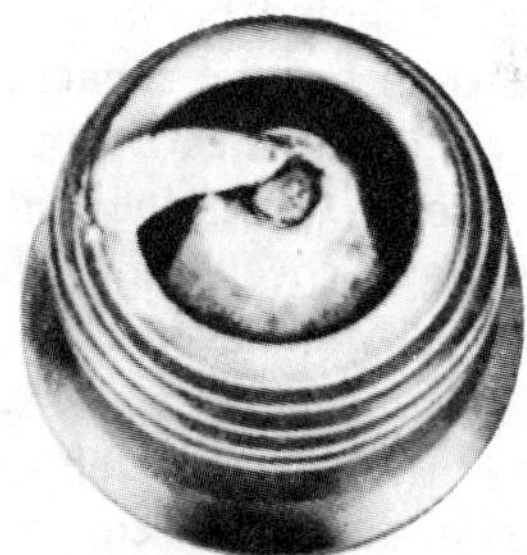

WORN

- Identified by severely eroded or worn electrodes.
- Caused by normal wear. Should be replaced.

FUSED SPOT DEPOSIT

- Identified by melted or spotty deposits resembling bubbles or blisters.
- Caused by sudden acceleration. Can be cleaned.

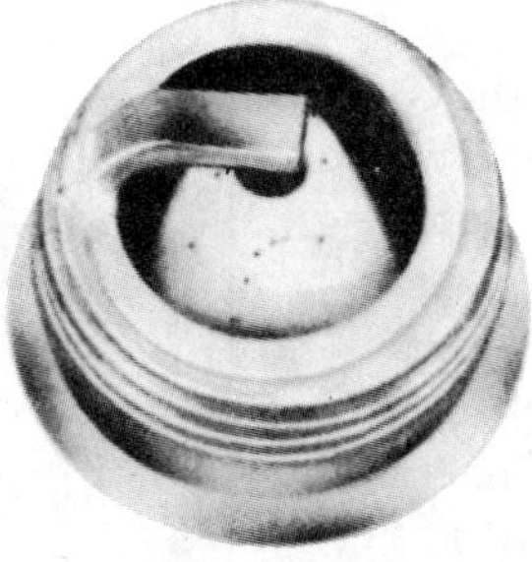

OVERHEATING

- Identified by a white or light gray insulator with small black or gray brown spots and with bluish-burnt appearance of electrodes.
- Caused by engine overheating, wrong type of fuel, loose spark plugs, too hot a plug, or incorrect ignition timing. Replace the plug.

PREIGNITION

- Identified by melted electrodes and possibly blistered insulator. Metallic deposits on insulator indicate engine damage.
- Caused by wrong type of fuel, incorrect ignition timing or advance, too hot a plug, burned valves, or engine overheating. Replace the plug.

3

6. Clean the tips of the plugs with a sandblasting machine (some gas stations have them) or with a wire brush and solvent.

7. Always use a new gasket if old plugs are to be reused after cleaning.

8. Run the plug in finger-tight and tighten ¼ turn more with a wrench. Further tightening will only flatten the gasket and cause binding.

> NOTE: *A short piece of fuel line can be used to install the plug initially in areas where space is a problem.*

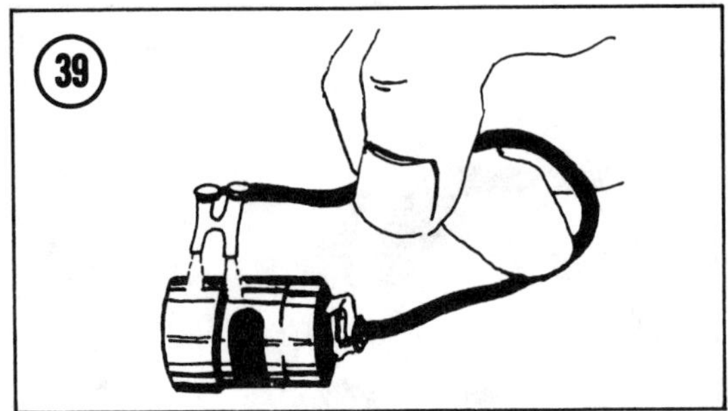

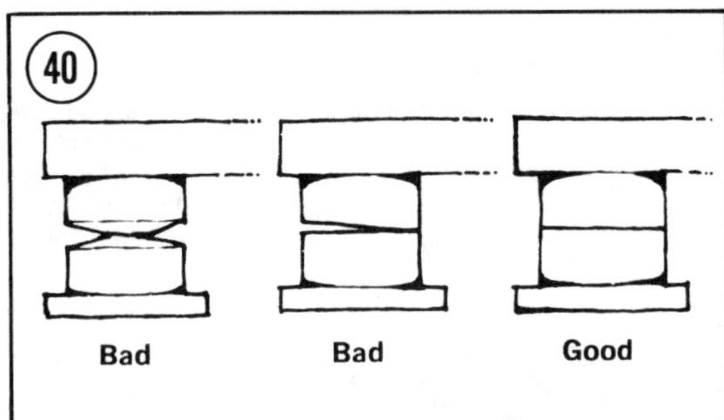

Condenser (Capacitor)

The condenser (capacitor) is a sealed unit and requires no maintenance. Be sure the connections are clean and tight.

The only proper test is to measure the resistance of the insulation with an ohmmeter. The value should be 5,000 ohms. A make-do test is to charge the capacitor by hooking the leads, or case and lead, to a 12V battery. After a few seconds, touch the leads together, or lead to case, and check for a spark, as shown in **Figure 39**. A damaged capacitor will not store electricity or spark.

Most mechanics prefer to discard the condensers and replace them with new ones during engine tune-up.

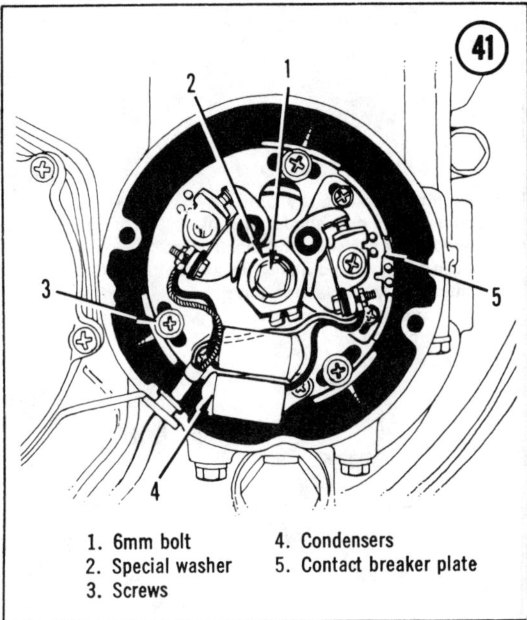

1. 6mm bolt
2. Special washer
3. Screws
4. Condensers
5. Contact breaker plate

Breaker Points

Inspection

1. Remove the breaker point cover. If the cover does not come off easily, try tapping it loose with a rubber or rawhide mallet.

CAUTION
Do not use a metal hammer.

2. Pry open the points gently with a finger and check the 2 sets for alignment and wear. **Figure 40** shows what to look for. Replace the points if they are severely pitted or worn.

Cleaning

1. Gray discoloration of the contacts is normal. Dress the surfaces with a point file. Never use sandpaper or emery cloth for this purpose.

2. Blow away the residue and then clean the contacts with chemical point cleaner or a piece of unwaxed stiff paper such as a business card. Make certain the contacts are absolutely clean. Even fingerprint oil can affect performance.

3. If the same points are to be used, skip the next section on removal and replacement procedure. If new points will be installed, replace the 2 condensers. These parts usually are sold in sets.

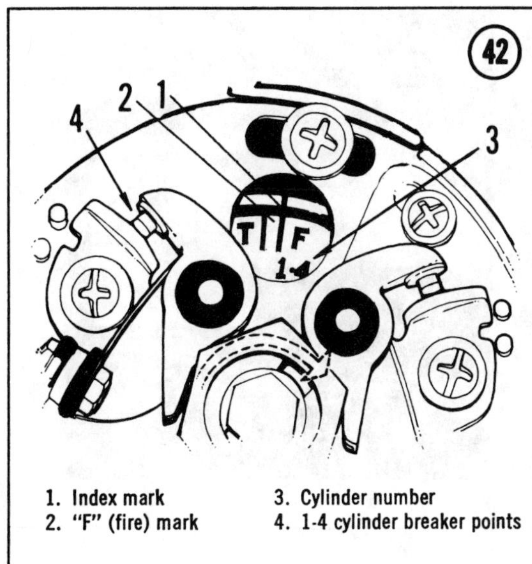

1. Index mark
2. "F" (fire) mark
3. Cylinder number
4. 1-4 cylinder breaker points

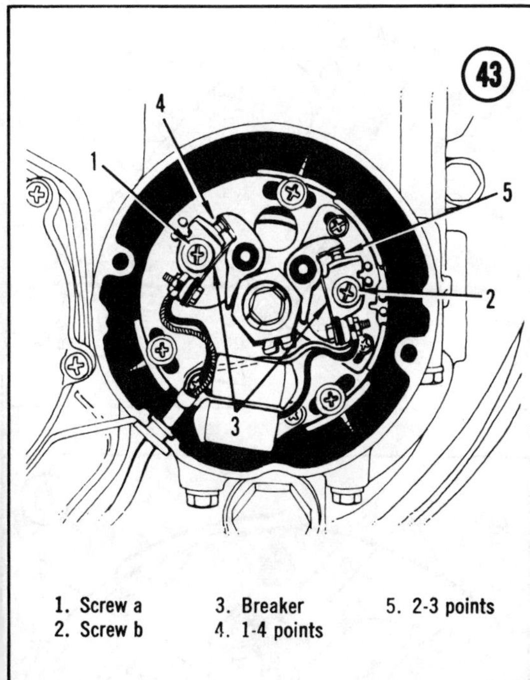

1. Screw a
2. Screw b
3. Breaker
4. 1-4 points
5. 2-3 points

Replacement

1. Disconnect the yellow and blue leads at the junction box located near the lower right side of the center of the frame. Remove the hex bolt and its washer. Refer to **Figure 41**. Loosen the 3 breaker plate holding screws and lift out unit.

2. Remove the points and condensers. Install new parts.

Adjusting Point Gap

There are 2 methods for measuring point gap; with a feeler gauge or a dwell meter. In either case, the points must be adjusted manually.

Point Gap Adjustment

1. Rotate the crankshaft (use a socket on the big retainer bolt in the center shaft) until points for No. 1 and No. 4 cylinders are fully open. See **Figure 42**.

2. Point gap should be 0.012-0.016 in. (0.3-0.4mm). Check with a wire feeler gauge.

3. To adjust, loosen the lockscrew (1, **Figure 43**). Set the tip of a screwdriver in the notch in the point arm and shift it by gently prying against the 2 leverage buttons set into the plate on which the points rest.

4. When the gap is correct, tighten the lockscrew. Check the gap a final time with the feeler gauge, which should slip between the contact points with a slight amount of drag.

NOTE: *Tightening the lockscrew may change the point gap. The points may have to be adjusted several times.*

5. To adjust the other set of points (for cylinders No. 2 and No. 3), rotate the crankshaft clockwise until points are fully open. Repeat Steps 3 and 4, this time loosening the opposite screw.

6. Finally, lubricate the cam with a thin coating of special cam grease. Do not apply an excessive amount or it will contaminate the contact surfaces and lead to premature failure.

NOTE: *Adjust ignition timing as described under* **Ignition Timing**, *later in this chapter.*

Dwell Measurement

Dwell is the number of degrees that the breaker point cam rotates while the points remain closed. The longer the dwell, the smaller the point gap. The shorter the dwell, the wider the gap.

Dwell should be between 92° and 98° if the points are clean and correctly adjusted. A dwell meter is an extremely accurate method of measuring point gap. Of course, the points must still be adjusted statically if the distance and dwell are incorrect.

Figure 44 shows one type of dwell meter suitable for motorcycle engines. Make sure the meter is calibrated for small gasoline engines of 2 cylinders (one point set controls 2 cylinders). On a 4-cylinder scale, the correct dwell would be 46-49°; and on an 8-cylinder scale, 23-24.5°.

1. Hook up the meter according to its instructions. One lead attaches to the points and the other grounds to the engine.

2. Start the engine and read the dwell angle on the meter.

3. If the points require adjustment, refer to *Point Gap Adjustment,* earlier in this chapter.

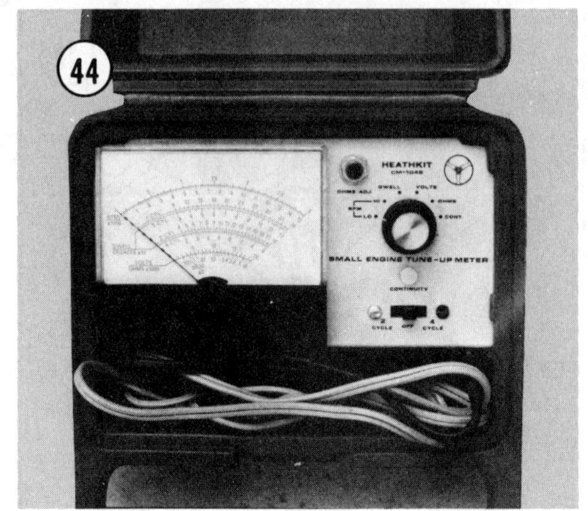

Ignition Timing

There are 2 methods used to adjust ignition timing — the static procedure and a more precise method using a stroboscopic (strobe) light.

Static Method

The static method requires something that can signal when an electronic circuit is opened or closed. This can be a buzz box (ignition on), and ohmmeter (ignition off), or a continuity light (ignition on). This later method, often called a timing light, is the least expensive. It is available for under $2 at parts stores.

A homemade timing light consists of a 12-volt light bulb, a socket to hold it, and 2 wires attached to the socket with alligator clips at the ends of each wire. See **Figure 45**.

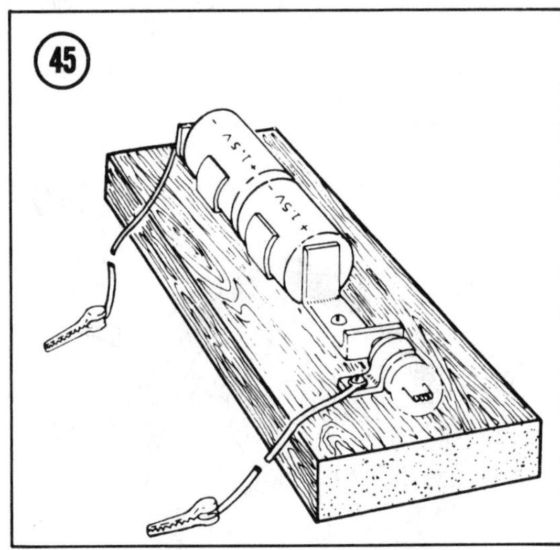

1. The cylinders controlled by each set of points are stamped next to the breaker set on the base plate. See **Figure 46**. Start the timing procedure with the set for No. 1 and No. 4 cylinders.

2. Hook up the timing light at the blue wire. Ground the other lead wire as shown in **Figure 47**.

3. View through the peephole in the base plate where the timing marks are visible. See **Figure 48**. Rotate the crankshaft with a wrench on the retaining bolt of the center shaft until the "1-4 F" mark is even with the index, or matching, mark on the outer ring. At this instant the points should begin to open and the timing light should come on. If it does not, ignition timing is off and should be adjusted.

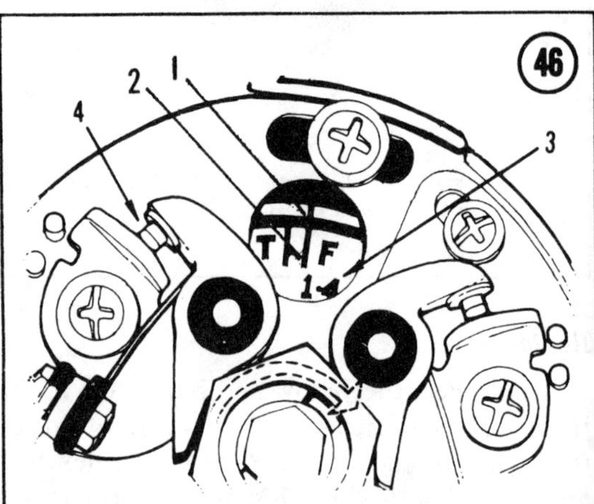

1. Index mark
2 "F" (fire) mark
3. Cylinder number
4. 1-4 cylinder breaker points

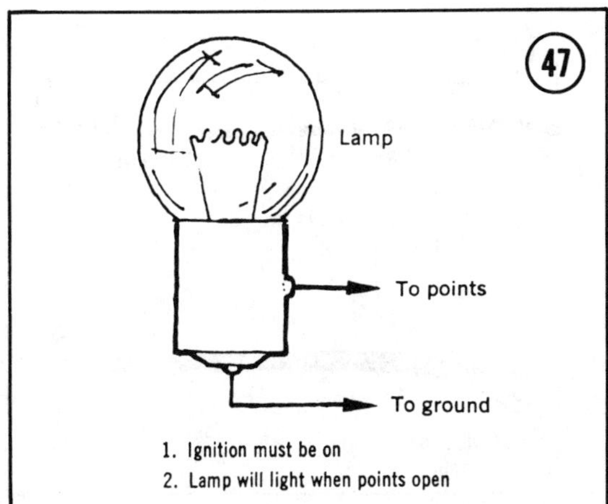

1. Ignition must be on
2. Lamp will light when points open

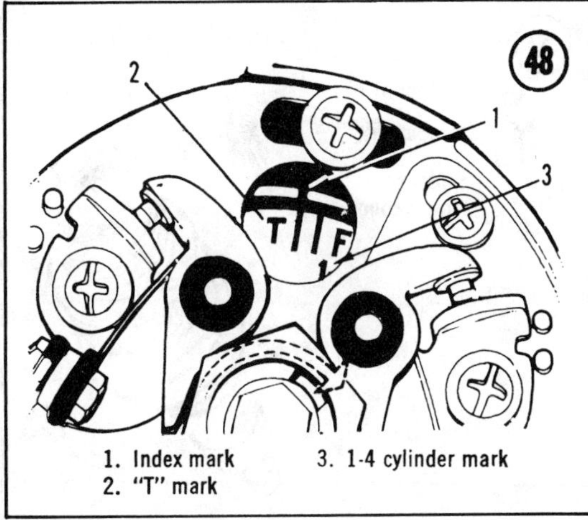

1. Index mark
2. "T" mark
3. 1-4 cylinder mark

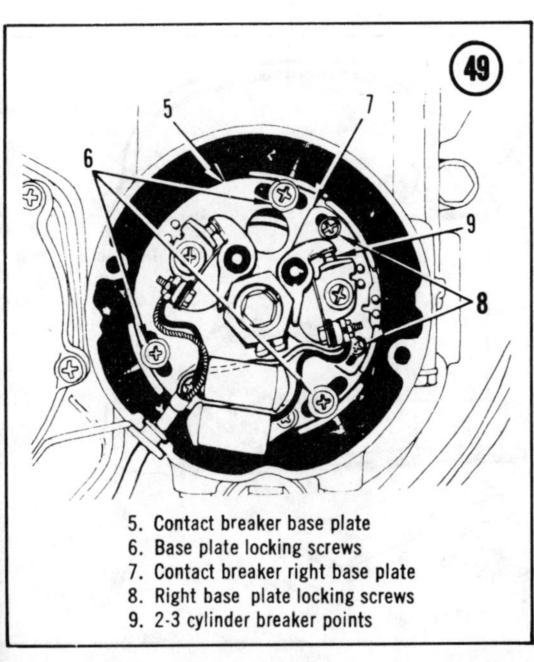

5. Contact breaker base plate
6. Base plate locking screws
7. Contact breaker right base plate
8. Right base plate locking screws
9. 2-3 cylinder breaker points

4. To adjust, refer to **Figure 49** and loosen the 3 base plate screws to retard or advance timing until the light flickers. Tighten the 3 screws, being careful not to change the adjustment. Check the point gap before proceeding to the next step to make sure it has not changed.

5. Connect the timing light to the other set of breaker points which control cylinders No. 2 and No. 3.

6. Rotate the crankshaft ½ revolution until the "2-3 F" is aligned with index mark inscribed on the outer ring.

7. If the light does not flicker at this point, adjust by loosening the 2 right base plate locking screws (8, **Figure 49**). Note that these are different from the screws used to make the earlier adjustment.

8. Disconnect the timing light and turn off the ignition. Replace point cover unless advanced timing is to be checked (below).

Strobe Light Method

A strobe light enables the timing to be checked under actual running conditions. See **Figure 50**. Such lights are commonly available, but beware of inexpensive ones because they usually produce a weak light or are not durable.

A homemade adapter will simplify this task and eliminate the risk of possible personal injury. **Figures 51 through 53** show construction details.

WARNING

Do not allow the exposed end of the old plug to get near the frame, exhaust headers, or other metal. Do not touch the exposed end with your bare fingers or you will receive a severe shock.

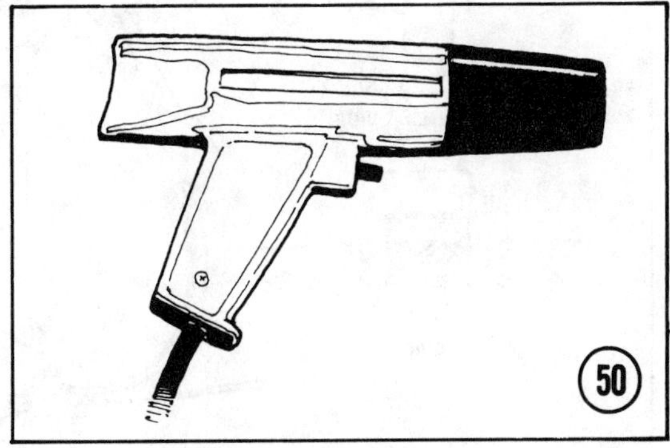

1. Connect the light according to the manufacturer's instructions. The light's spark plug lead should be connected to the plug either in cylinder No. 1 or No. 4.

2. Start the engine and set it at idling speed — between 850 and 950 rpm.

3. Aim the flashing light at the peephole in the breaker base plate. The "1-4 F" mark should appear to line up with the outer index mark when illuminated by the light.

4. If the marks do not line up, adjust the timing according to Step 5, *Static Timing Method,* preceding.

5. Increase engine speed to 2,500 rpm to check the timing advance mechanism.

6. Point the light at the peephole. Spark advance is correct if the index mark appears between the 2 lines located 23.5-26.5°, or in advance, of the "F" mark. See **Figure 54**.

7. Shut off the engine and connect the plug lead to either the No. 2 or No. 3 cylinder spark plug.

8. Repeat the operations for checking the timing at idle and at 2,500 rpm and adjust if necessary.

Air Cleaner Service

A clogged air cleaner can decrease the efficiency and life of the engine. It should be

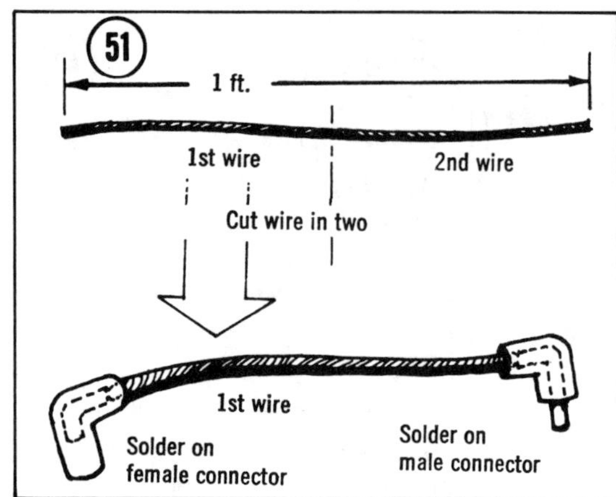

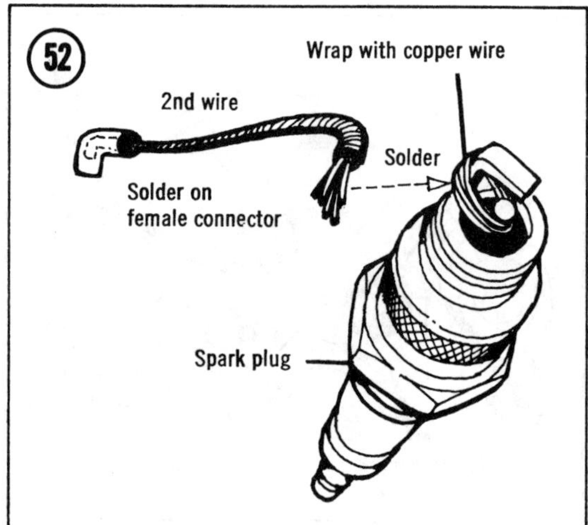

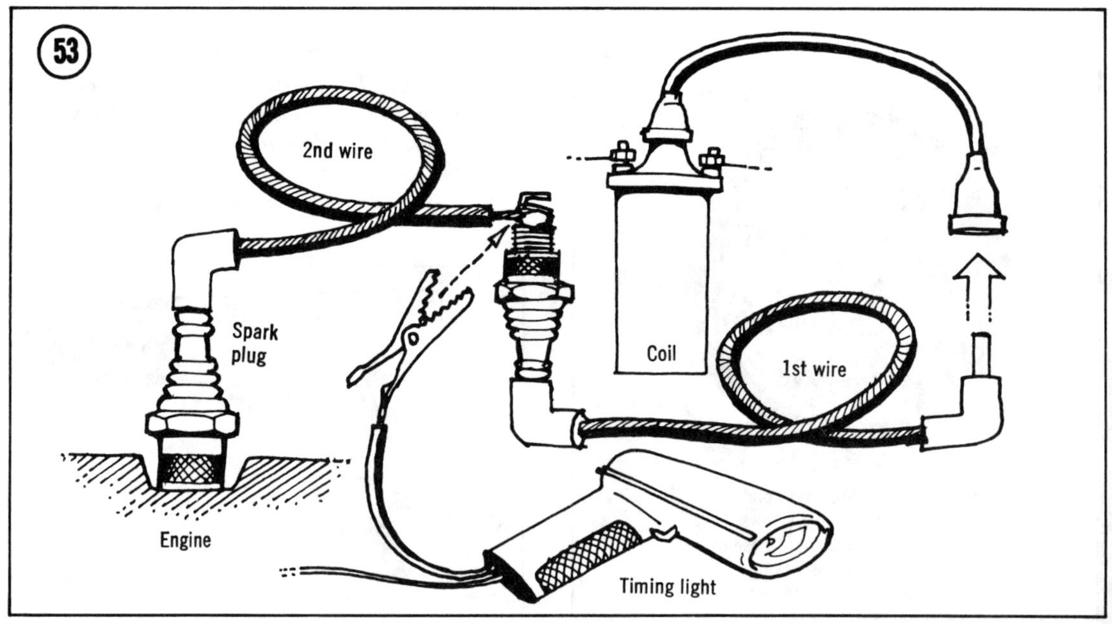

checked at each oil change, or more often if the motorcycle is operated under dusty conditions. Refer to **Figure 55**.

1. Loosen the 2 wing nuts on the underside of the cover and remove the lower half. Refer to **Figure 56**.
2. Remove the filter element. Replace it with a new one if the filter is clogged with dirt, oil soaked, or if the bonding material is cracked.
3. Light dust can be shaken off the element by tapping it while using a soft brush on the outside. A better method, if compressed air is available, is to force air through the element from the inside.

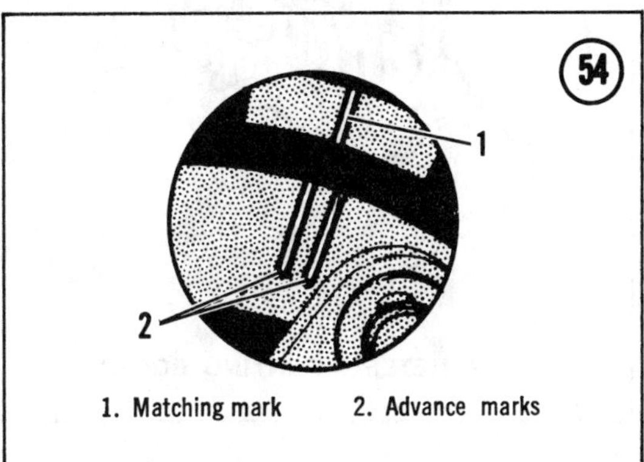

1. Matching mark 2. Advance marks

4. Replace the lower housing and the filter element. If the carburetors are to be adjusted, remove the upper case by loosening the 4 clamps on the air hoses and removing the mounting bolts. See **Figure 56**.

Carburetion

Unless the carburetors have been disassembled, they normally should not require adjustment. They should be worked on only as a last resort when all other possible causes of problems, such as rough idling or misfiring, have been checked out.

Two different carburetor throttle linkages are used on the Honda 750. Early versions use a single throttle cable from the twist grip to the carburetor linkage, with a spring employed to close the throttle. Starting in late 1970, this was modified to a 2-cable arrangement designed to give a more positive "push-pull" action to opening and closing the throttle. The CB750 has the single cable. The CB750 K1's and later have 2 cables. The adjustment and synchronization operations for each model are outlined separately in this section.

A special set of gauges is required for this procedure. Honda sells a set of 4 vacuum

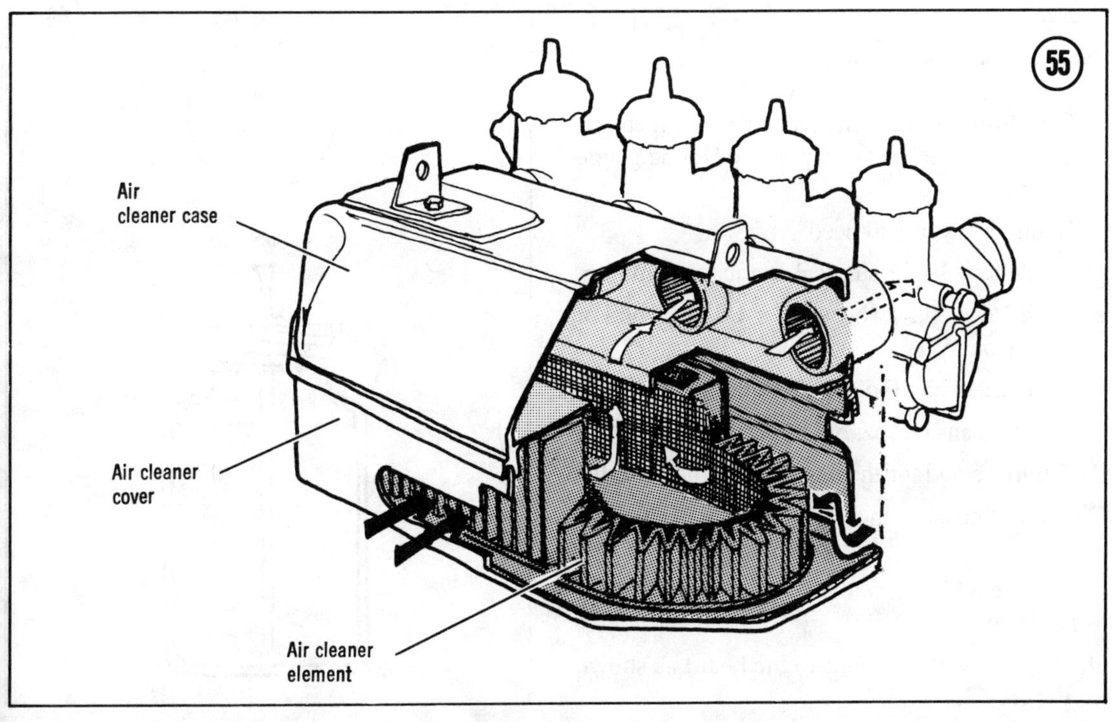

gauges with tubes and adapters to connect them to the carburetors. This unit enables synchronization to be performed quickly and easily.

Other gauges are available from aftermarket suppliers and results are just as accurate if they are used carefully. An alternative is to make your own manometer as described under *Manometer Construction*, following.

In the sequence of *Adjustment Operations* described in this section, the factory gauges are used, but any manometer may be substituted.

Manometer Construction

This do-it-yourself manometer is inexpensive and works as well as the expensive Honda gauge set.

To build it, you will need:

a. 40 ft. of 3/4-in. surgical or aquarium tubing

b. A 3/4-in. thick sheet of 2 x 4 ft. plywood or masonite

c. 4 large baby food jars with lids

d. 4 tin cans (12 oz. or larger)

1. Build a stand for the board to keep it upright.

2. Attach the jars 6 inches from the bottom of the board.

3. Cut the tubing into four 4-ft. sections and four 6-ft. sections.

4. Affix the 4-ft. sections to the board as shown in **Figure 57**.

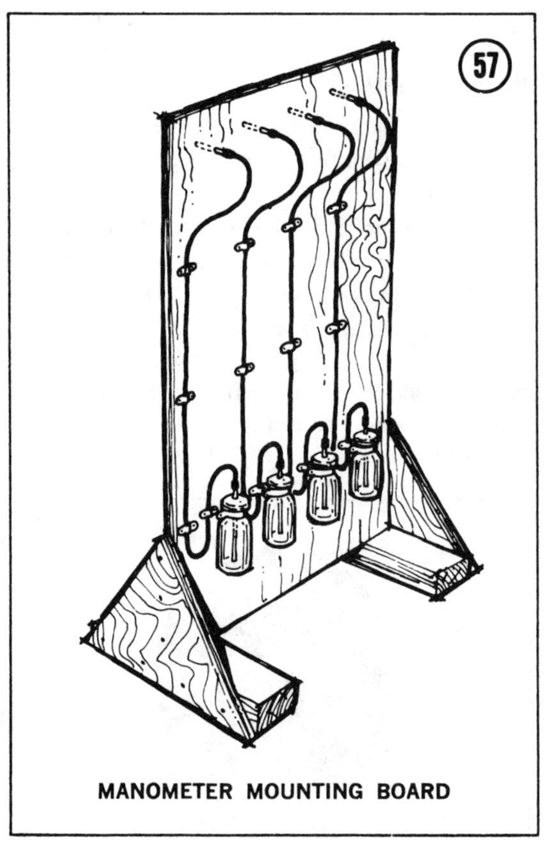

MANOMETER MOUNTING BOARD

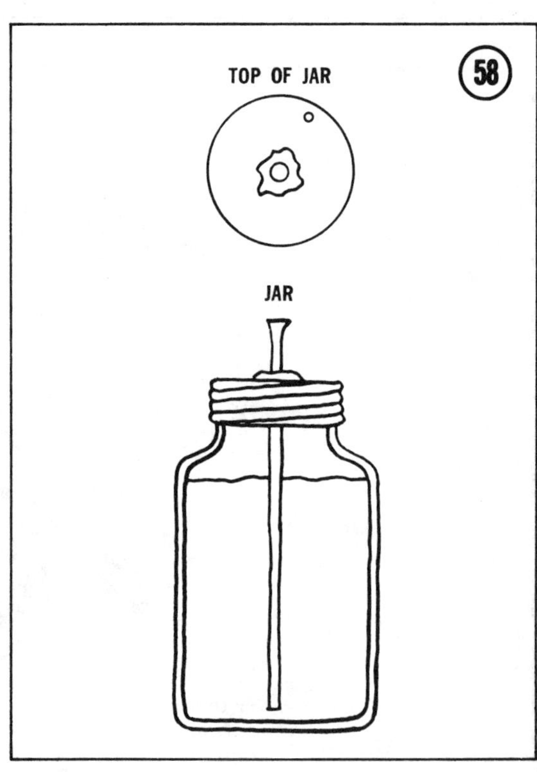

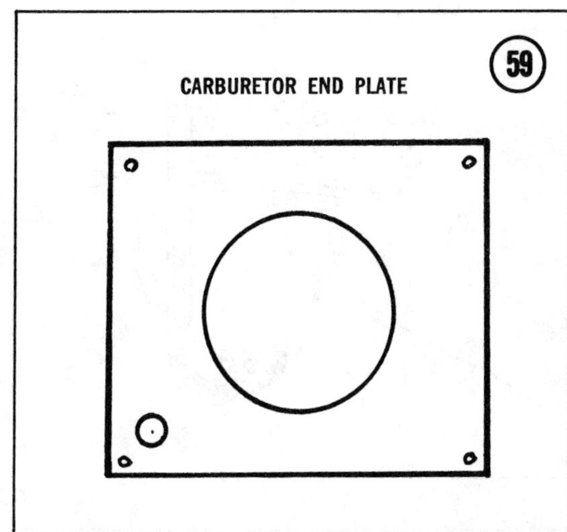

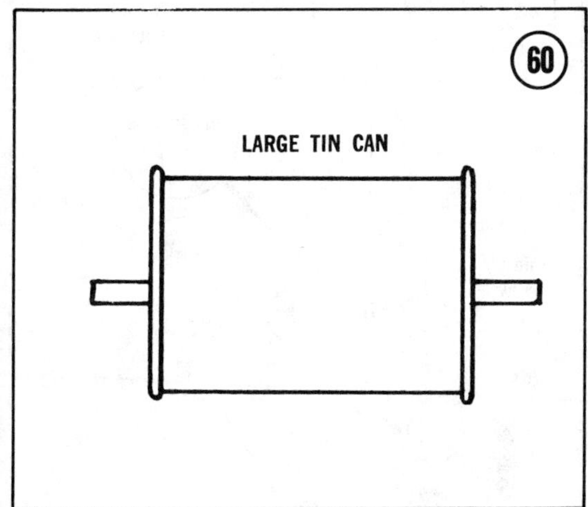

5. Scrape the paint off the center section of the top surface of the 4 jar lids.

6. Drill one ¼-in. and one ⅛-in. hole in each lid. The ¼-in. hole should be in the center of the lid. The smaller hole is a vent and can be anywhere. See **Figure 58**.

7. Solder a piece of tubing to the jar lids so the bottom edge nearly touches the jar and the top section protrudes at least ½ in. as shown in **Figure 58**.

8. Push the clean plastic tubing onto the brass tubing.

9. Drill four ¼-in. holes in the top of the plywood directly above each jar and insert four 2-in. lengths of brass tubing.

10. Connect the 4-ft. lengths of tubing to the four 2-in. tubes.

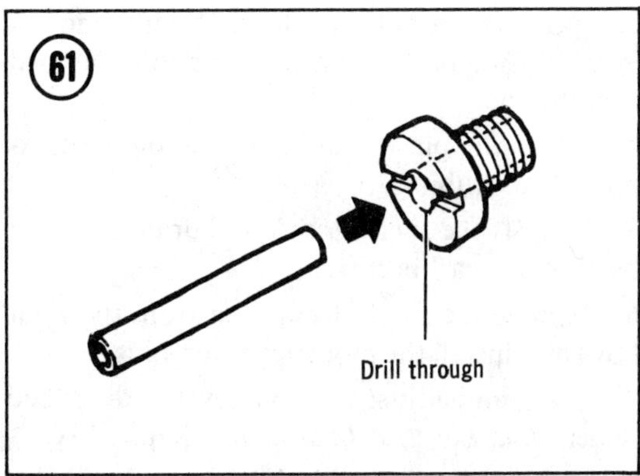

11. Fill the jars ¾ full of water. Tint with food coloring. Suck all air out of the U-shaped pieces of tubing.

12. Fabricate 4 plates of aluminum or steel to be ½-in. larger in diameter than the carburetor throat. Drill a hole ⅔ the size of the carburetor intake in the center of each plate and a ¼-in. hole just to the side. See **Figure 59**.

13. Epoxy a short piece of brass tubing in the ¼-in. plate hole for each unit.

14. Glue pieces of gasket material around each orifice plate to ensure a good seal against the carburetor.

15. Connect each orifice plate to one of the 6-ft. sections of tubing and connect the other end to the brass tubing at the top of the manometer board.

Using a Manometer

Place orifice plates over carburetor throats. Make sure that plates seal well against throats. Adjust synchronization as described later in this chapter.

If the water levels fluctuate too widely, make stabilizers out of tin cans as shown in **Figure 60**. This set-up can be used with any multi-cylinder motorcycle or car. The orifice size is unimportant as long as it and the small tube hole are less than the carburetor intake.

Float Level Check

1. Purchase a single carburetor drain plug screw from a dealer.

2. Drill the end of the screw to snugly accept a piece of brass tubing approximately one inch (25mm) long. See **Figure 61**.

3. Epoxy the tubing in place, leaving enough exposed for a piece of clear tubing to be slipped over the end.

4. Clamp the plastic tubing to the piece of exposed brass tubing.

5. Shut off the fuel petcock and drain the float bowl of one carburetor.

6. Remove the stock drain plug from the float bowl and install the modified drain plug.

7. Check and adjust the float level as described under *Float Level, Adjustment,* Chapter Six.

8. Install the bowl and hold the plastic tube as shown in **Figure 62**.

9. Turn on the fuel petcock and wait for the fuel to reach its level in the exposed tube. Record this level by scoring a mark on the float bowl. This mark can be used for adjusting the other 3 carburetors and all of them at any time in the future.

10. Make any necessary adjustments and reinstall all of the float bowls.

Adjustment (prior to K Series)

The major parts of the carburetor involved in the adjustment process are shown in **Figure 63**.

1. Remove the fuel tank, making sure to disconnect the fuel lines at the valve assembly underneath. Remove the air cleaner.

2. Check each of the 4 throttle stop screws **(Figure 64)** to make sure the "T" mark is aligned with the index mark on the carburetor body. If not, adjust to the setting shown in **Figure 65**. Check all 4 carburetors.

3. Loosen the locknut and turn the throttle cable adjusting nut so that free play in the cable is between 0.04-0.05 in. (1-2mm). Refer to **Figure 66**. Tighten the locknut. Play should be even on all 4 carburetors. See **Figure 67**.

4. Turn each of the idle air screws **(Figure 68)** in until they seat gently. Back each out counterclockwise one full turn.

5. Install air cleaner and fuel tank.

6. Start the engine and let it warm up to operating temperature.

7. Stop engine and remove plugs from the vacuum gauge attachment holes **(Figure 69)**.

8. Connect the vacuum gauges as shown in **Figure 70**. Long adapters are for the inside car-

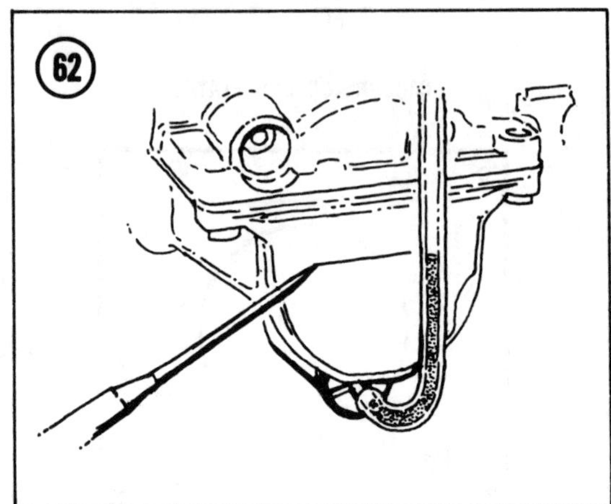

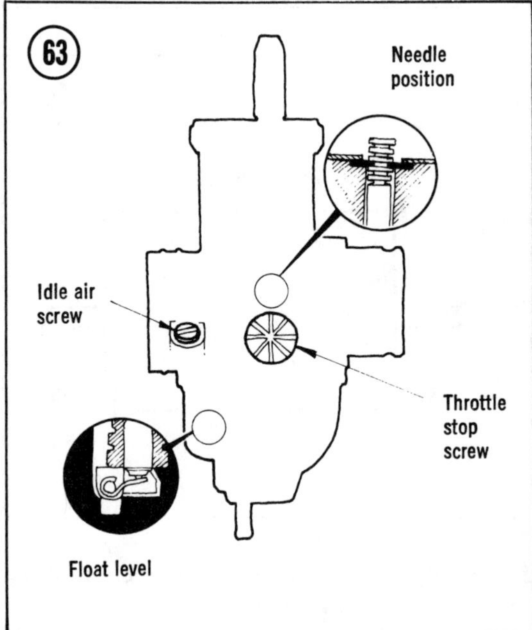

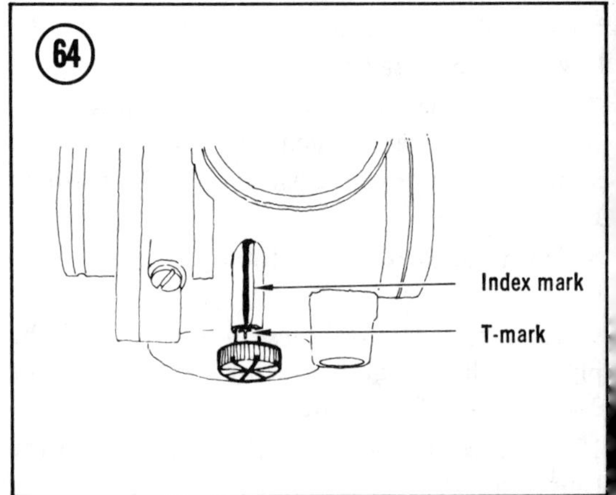

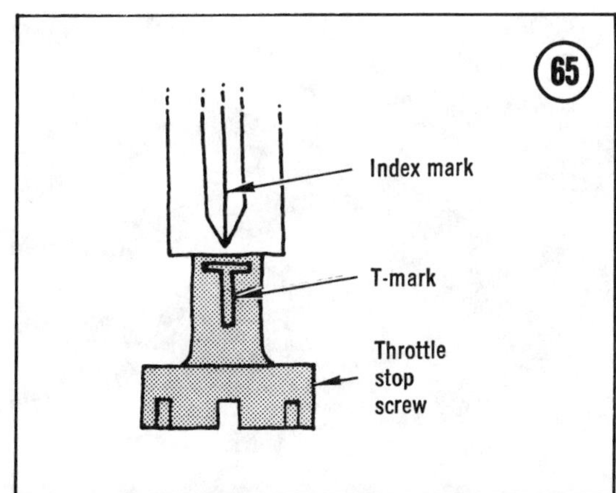

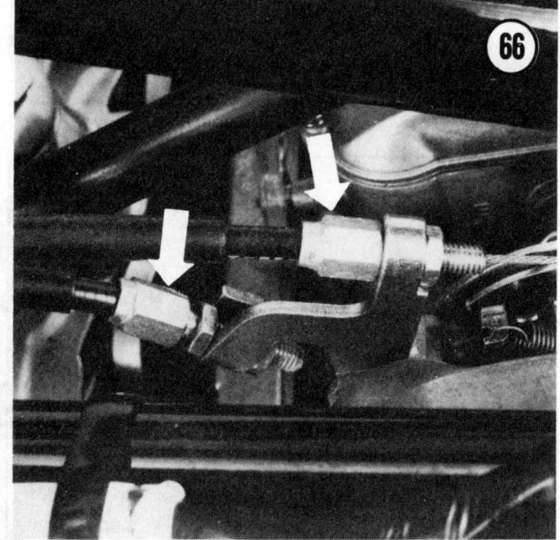

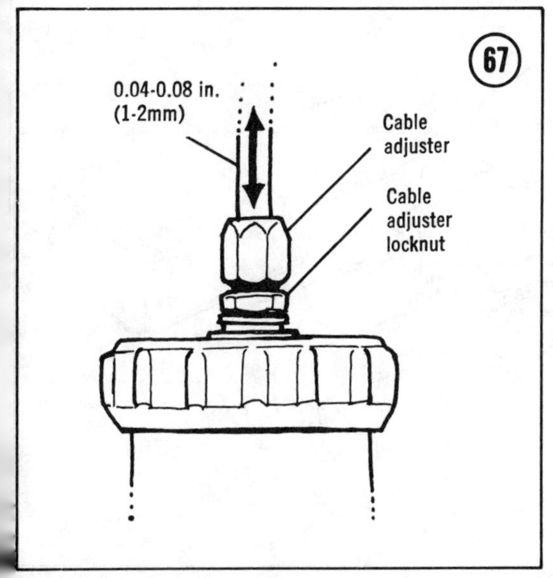

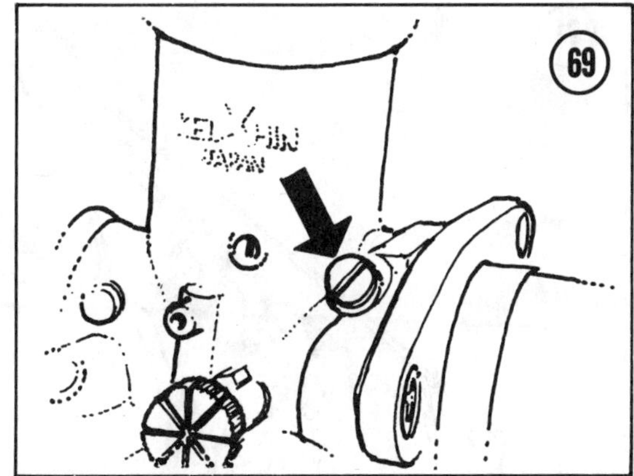

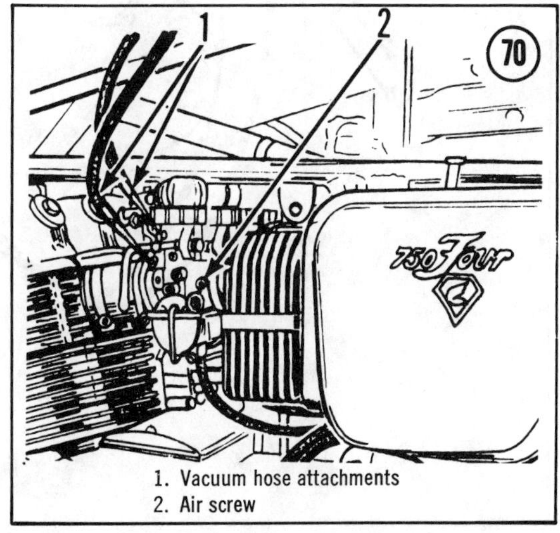

1. Vacuum hose attachments
2. Air screw

buretors and short ones are for the outboard carburetors. Rig the gauges over the handlebars. See **Figure 71**.

9. Start the engine and let it idle. Adjust idle speed to between 850 and 900 rpm by loosening the locknut and turning the adjuster screw at the throttle grip **(Figure 72)**.

10. Steady the gauge needles by adjusting the damping valves in the hoses (**Figure 73**). The needles will flutter slightly but should not move beyond one graduation mark.

11. Vacuum readings are not as important as an equal balance between carburetors. Generally, 8 inches of vacuum is average for machines with less than 30,000 miles (50,000 km).

12. If vacuum readings vary between carburetors, adjust them as outlined in the follow-

71

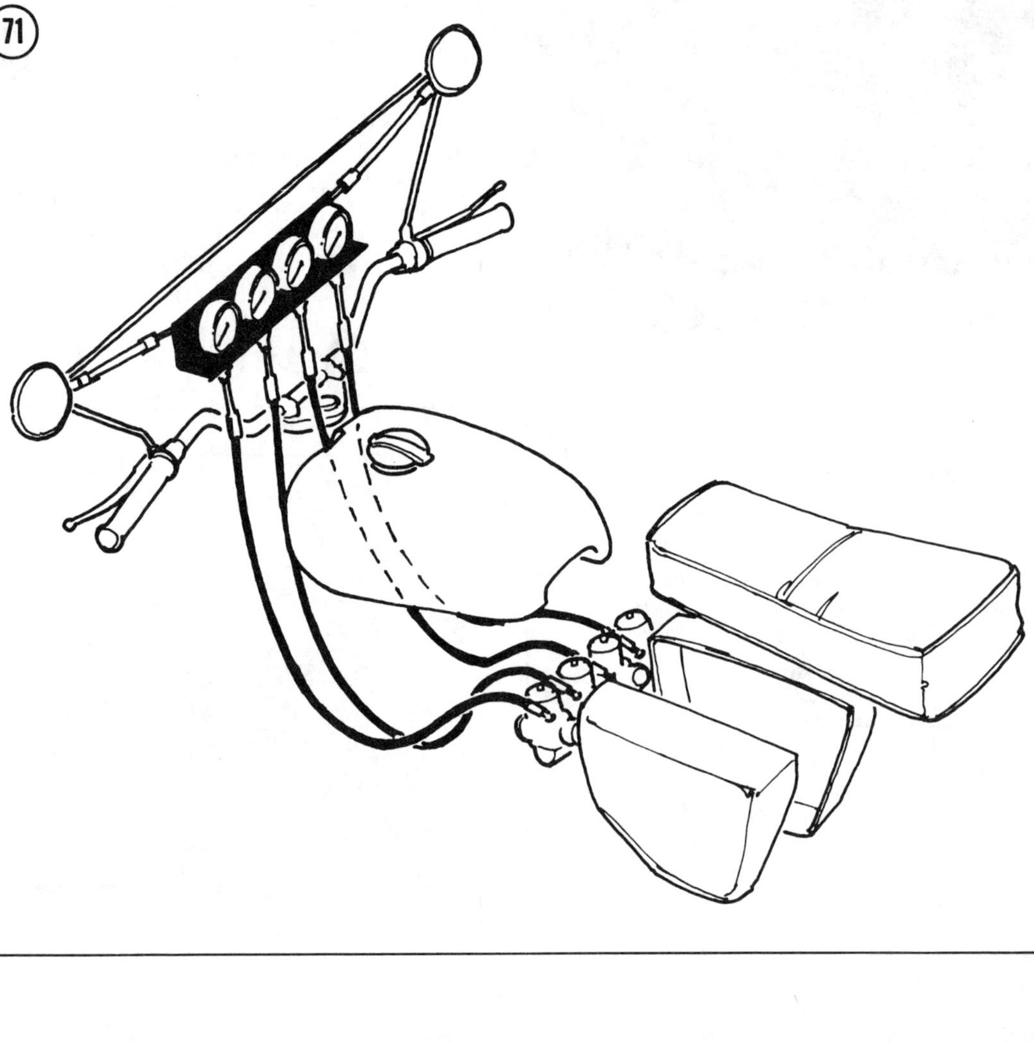

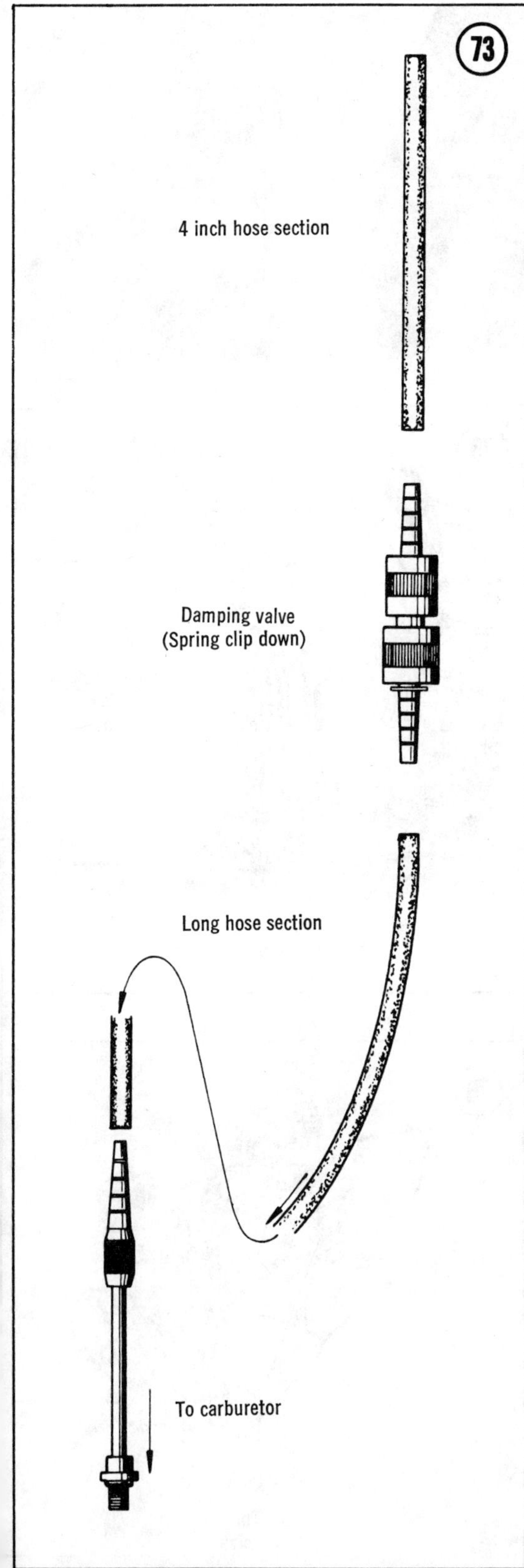

ing steps, using the one with the lowest vacuum as a reference.

13. Raise the dust boot from the top of the carburetor.

14. Loosen the locknut at the base.

15. Rotate the adjuster clockwise to increase the vacuum, or counterclockwise to decrease the vacuum.

> NOTE: *Check the balance with the throttle grip opened about ¼ turn. Note if the vacuum drop of one carburetor is not equal to the others when the throttle is opened. If the drop is faster, turn the adjuster clockwise. Turn it in the opposite direction if the drop is slower.*

16. After carburetors are synchronized, tighten the locknuts and install the dust covers.

17. Slack off the main throttle cable by backing off the adjustment screw near the grip. See **Figure 72**.

18. Turn the idle speed screws slowly clockwise until the idle speed is between 850 and 900 rpm with the vacuum balanced.

19. Adjust the throttle cable at the grip. Refer to **Figure 72**. For the most positive engine response, free play in the grip should be between 10° and 15° of total rotation.

20. To adjust, loosen the locknut to free the adjuster screw. Turn the screw until desired free play is achieved.

> NOTE: *A similar locknut and adjusting screw setup is used to adjust the damping action of the grip. See **Figure 72**.*

21. Stop engine and remove gauge set from the carburetors.

Adjustment (1977 and Earlier K and F Series)

Major carburetor parts involved in the adjustment process are shown in **Figure 74**.

1. Warm up the engine to operating temperature. Make sure the chokes are open.

2. Turn the 4 idle air screws (**Figure 75**) in until they gently seat; then back each out one full turn.

3. Refer to **Figure 76** and set engine idle speed to 900 rpm by adjusting the throttle stop screw.

Turn it clockwise to increase idle speed or counterclockwise to reduce it.

4. Stop the engine. Open the seat and prop up fuel tank to provide access to the carburetors.

CAUTION

Be careful not to stretch the fuel lines.

5. Remove the rubber dust covers from the throttle rod adjusters on top of the 4 carburetors.

6. Remove the plugs from the vacuum gauge attachment holes in the carburetors **(Figure 74)** and hook up the gauge hoses—the long hoses to the inside carburetors, and the short ones to the outside carburetors. Start the engine.

7. Stabilize the gauges by adjusting the damping valves on the hoses until the needles flutter only slightly and do not move more than one graduation mark. See **Figure 77**.

8. Equalize the vacuum readings between the 4 gauges either to around 8 in. or until all are equal to the lowest initial reading.

9. To raise or lower vacuum of an individual carburetor, refer to **Figure 78** and adjust the throttle rod by loosening the locknut and turning the adjusting nut. Turn nut clockwise to reduce vacuum. Turn nut counterclockwise to increase vacuum.

CAUTION

*When performing synchronization, leave the throttle rods extended at least one thread above the locknut, as in **Figure 79**.*

10. When carburetors are balanced, tighten the locknut.

CAUTION

Hold adjusting bolt with a wrench when tightening locknut. If the adjustment nut is left loose, torque can transfer through to the throttle rod and twist or break it. Locknut torque should be 0.8-1.4 ft.-lb. (12-20 mkg).

11. Rev the engine several times and check vacuum readings again. Readjust if the carburetors are not balanced.

12. Refer to **Figure 80** and oil and grease the throttle linkage. Apply grease to the throttle rods with the throttle grip opened all the way.

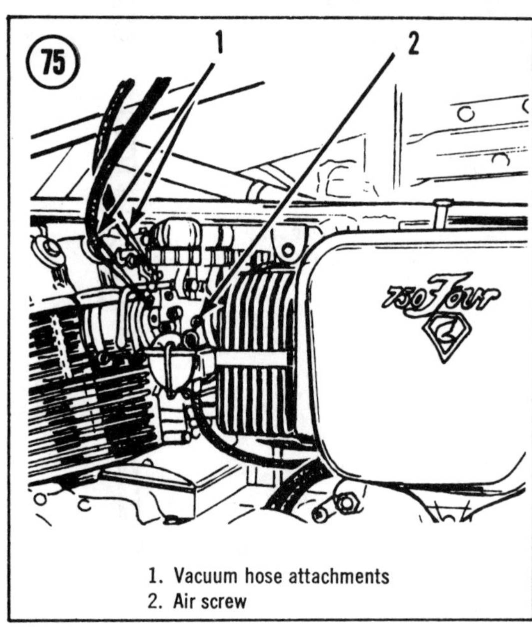

1. Vacuum hose attachments
2. Air screw

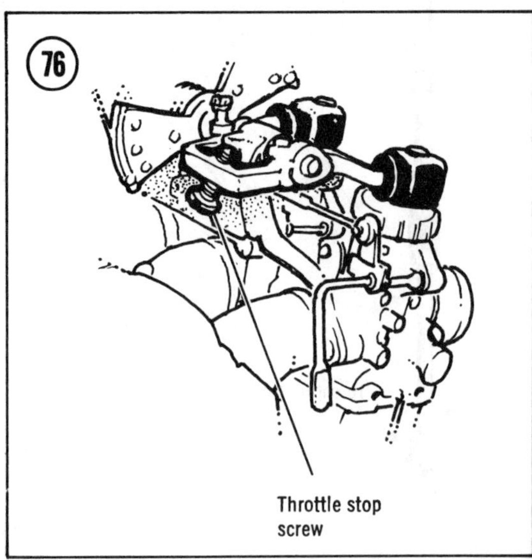

Throttle stop screw

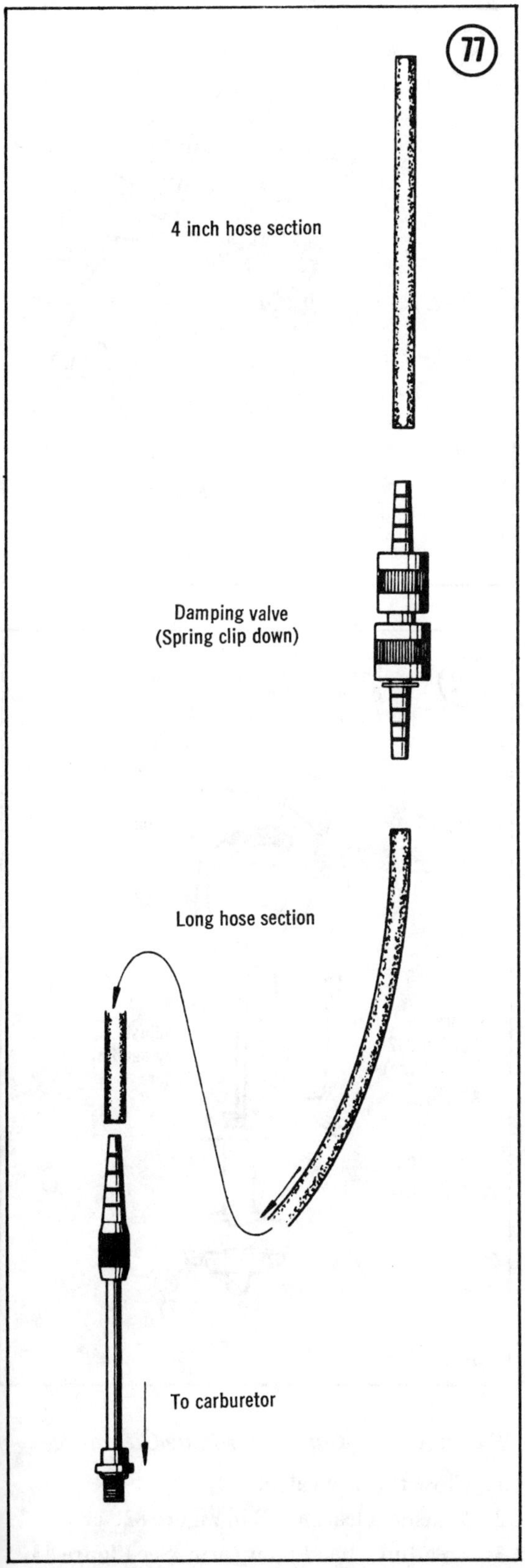

77
4 inch hose section
Damping valve
(Spring clip down)
Long hose section
To carburetor

Throttle rod
Locknut
Throttle rod adjuster nut
Lever arm
Dust cover
Carburetor top
78

79
Rod height
too low
Rod height
correct
Locknut
Throttle
rod

Lubricate with motor oil
80
Apply a thin coating
of light grease

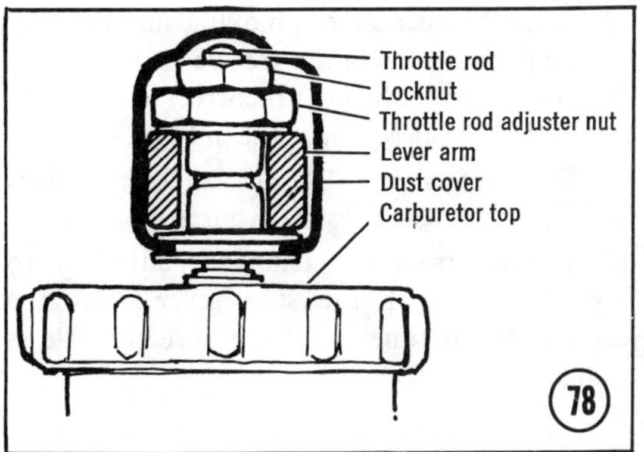

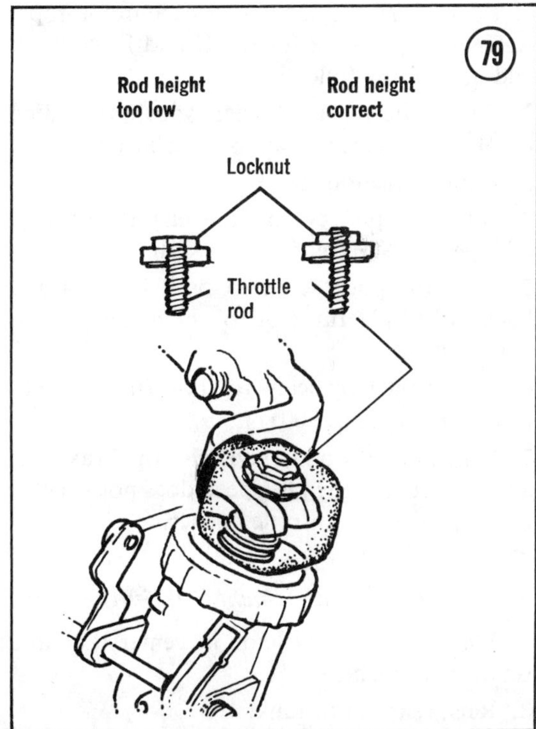

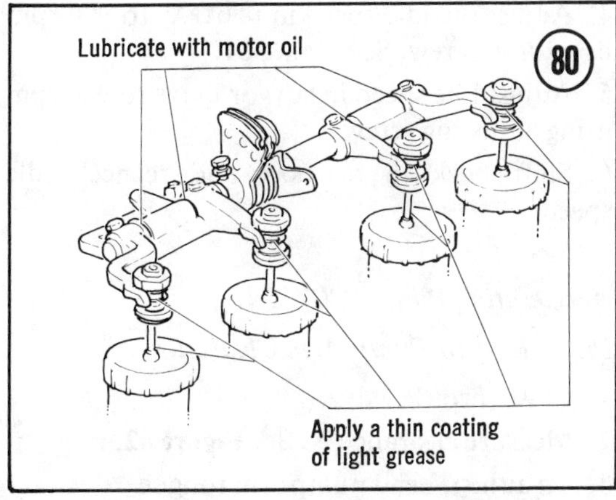

13. Reinstall dust covers, making sure the bottom rims are seated in the groove at the base of the throttle rod adjuster. Incorrect seating can interfere with operation of the linkage.

14. Stop the engine. Remove vacuum gauges and replace plug screws in carburetor orifices.

15. If idle speed has changed, adjust it to 850-900 rpm with the stop screw. Rev the engine several times to make sure the idle is stable.

Adjustment (CB750A)

1. Remove No. 1, 3, and 4 carburetor tops. Refer to adjustment for the K and F series, in addition the the following.

2. Turn adjuster until each vacuum reading becomes the same as for No. 2 carburetor.

3. Connect tachometer.

4. Adjust stop screw to allow engine to run at idle speed of 900 rpm in NEUTRAL and DRIVE.

5. Turn the pilot screw in until it stops and back off ¾-1¾ turns or to obtain the highest engine speed.

6. Adjust the stop screw to allow the engine to run at idle speed of 900 rpm.

7. Shift into LOW and DRIVE with the brakes on and be sure that the idle speed does not vary. If it does, adjust the throttle opener.

Throttle Opener Adjustment (CB750A)

1. Place the motorcycle on its centerstand and set the parking brake.

2. Raise rear of fuel tank.

3. Connect tachometer.

4. Adjust the idle speed in NEUTRAL to 900 rpm using stop screw. See **Figure 81**.

5. Adjust idle speed in LOW or DRIVE to 900 rpm using adjusting screw.

6. Shift back to NEUTRAL and recheck idle speed.

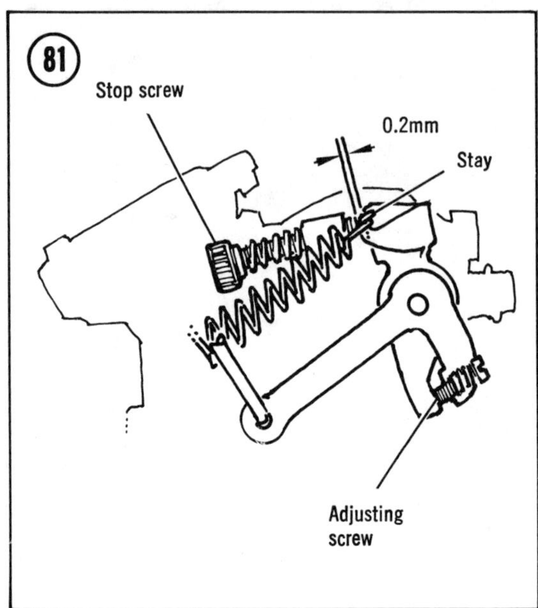

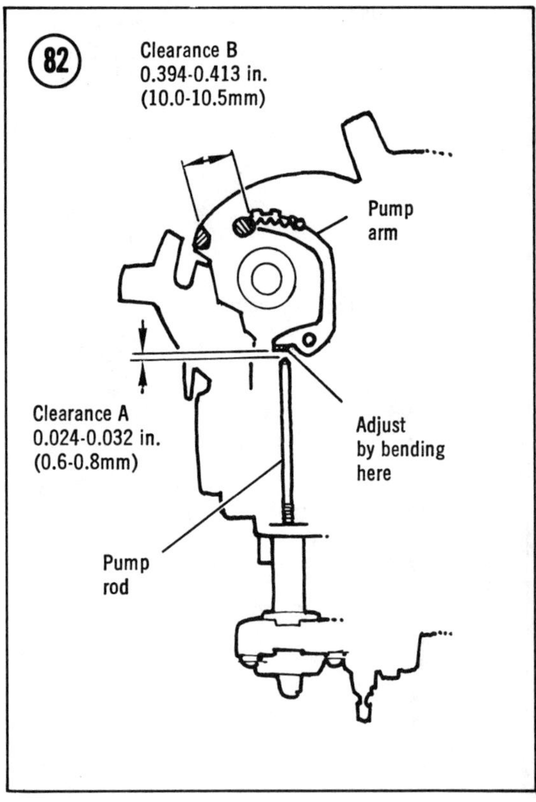

Accelerating Pump (CB750A)

Pump Rod-to-Pump Arm Clearance

1. Close throttle valve.

2. Measure clearance A. See **Figure 82**.

3. To adjust, bend pump arm tongue.

Pump Arm-to-Carburetor Plate Clearance

1. Close throttle valve.

2. Measure clearance B in **Figure 82**.

3. To adjust, bend pump arm. See **Figure 83**.

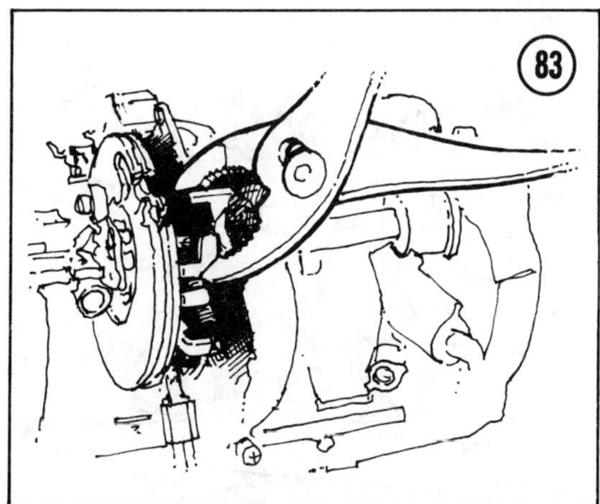

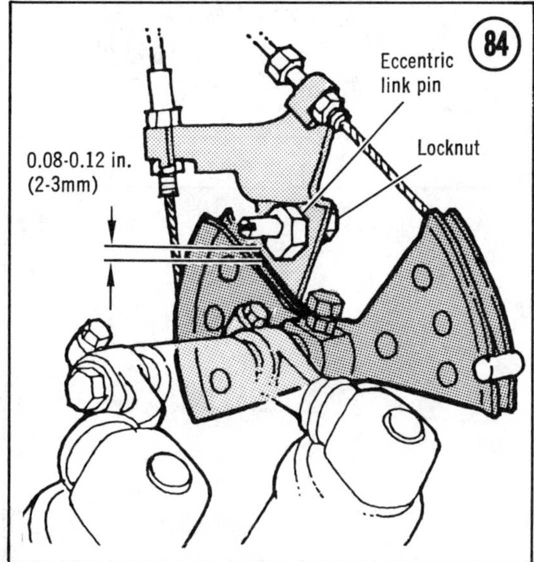

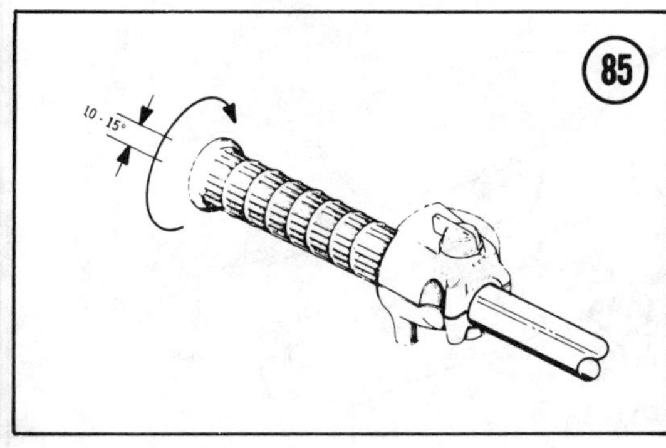

Throttle Cable Adjustment

The last procedure in adjusting the carburetors is to set the throttle cable. There are 3 points in the linkage that must be adjusted.

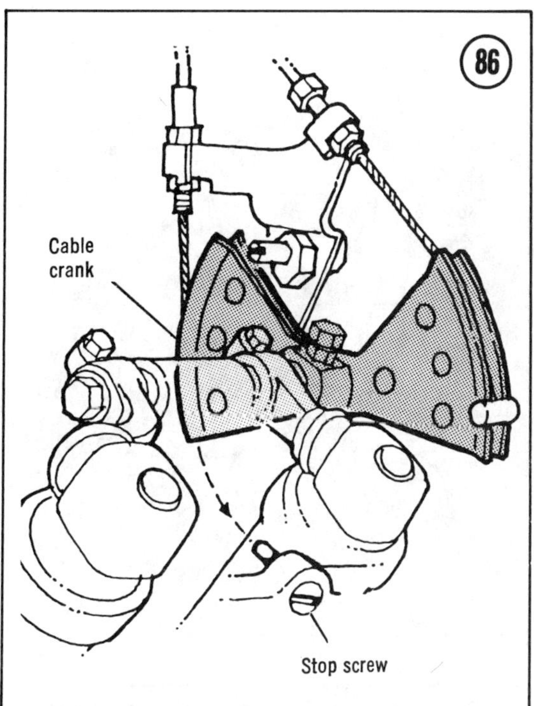

1. **Figures 84 and 85** show the linkage for preventing overtravel when the throttle grip is snapped to the closed position.
2. Adjust by loosening the locknut and turning the eccentric link pin until clearance between the throttle lever and pin is from 0.081 in. to 0.12 in. (2-3mm).
3. The stop screw limits opening travel and excessive pressure on the throttle valve. Refer to **Figure 86**. The air cleaner must be removed to gain access.
4. There are 2 methods of adjustment; both are with the throttle grip held open all the way.
    a. Turn the stop screw so that the gap between the top and the screw is 1.28-1.29 in. (32.5-33mm).
    b. Back out the stop screw, and turn it in so it just touches the throttle lever. Then turn it in an additional ¾-1 turn.
5. Final adjustment is made as shown in **Figure 87**. The throttle cable should have about 0.12 in. (3mm) of free play when measured as rotation of the throttle grip.
6. Loosen the locknut at the carburetor end of the cable, and turn the adjusting nut to provide 0.12-0.16 in. (3-4mm) play at the grip flange.

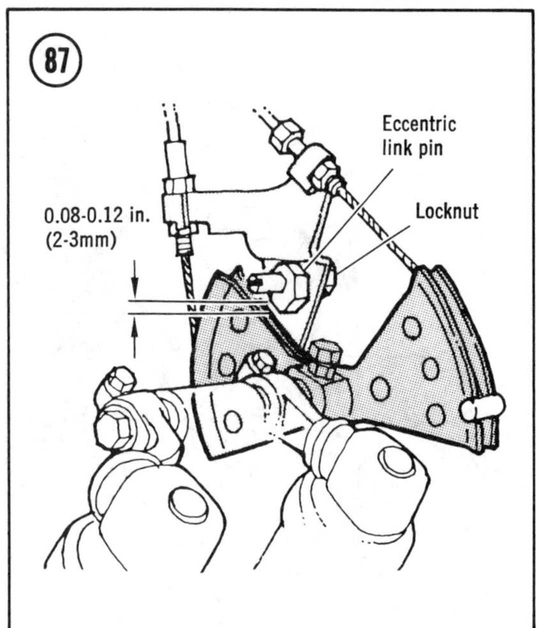
87
Eccentric
link pin
Locknut
0.08-0.12 in.
(2-3mm)

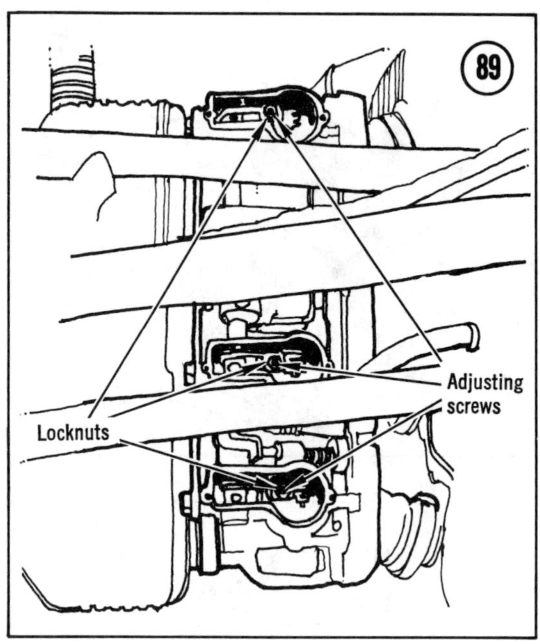
89
Adjusting
screws
Locknuts

88

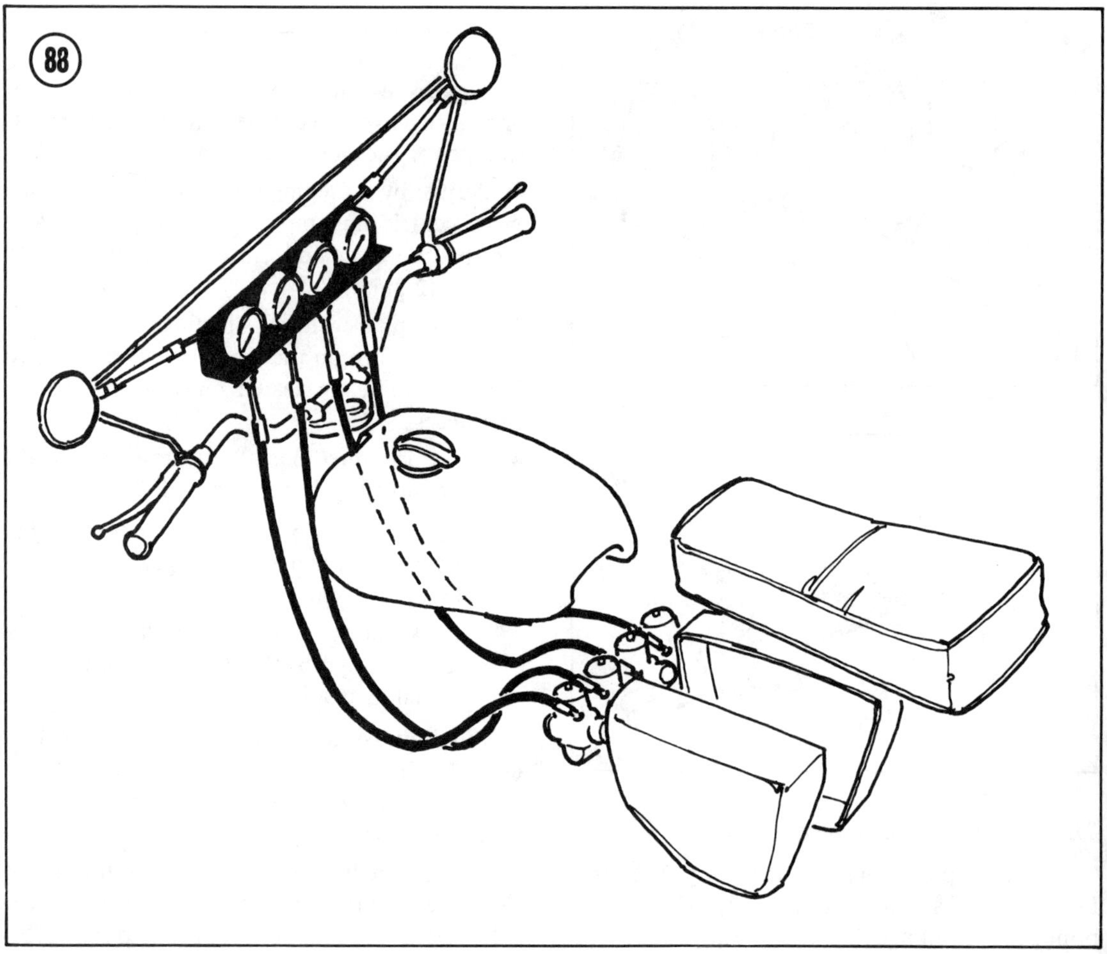

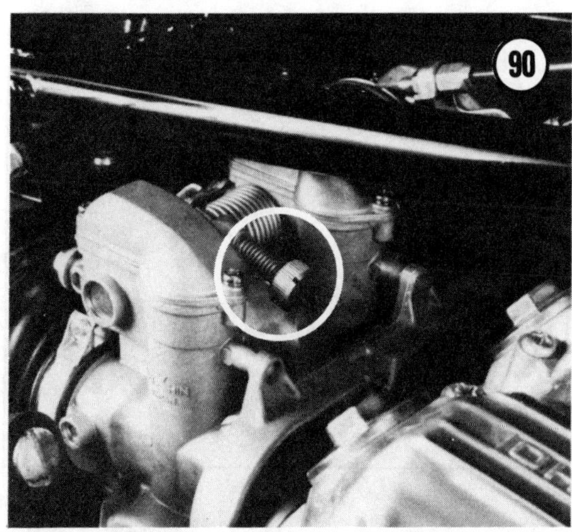

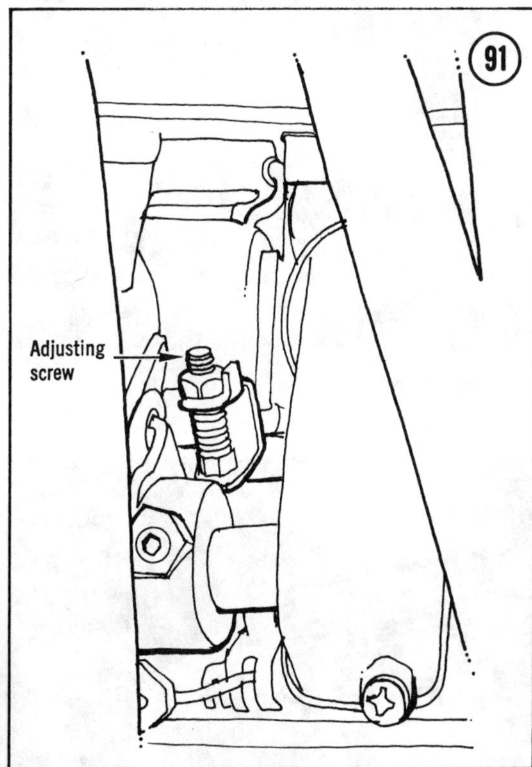

Neutral Return Rod (CB750A)

1. Place motorcycle on the centerstand.
2. Retract the side stand.
3. Shift transmission into DRIVE.
4. Loosen the locknut on the end of the NEUTRAL return rod.
5. Turn the tie rod in until it stops and turn it back one full turn.
6. Tighten the locknut.
7. Set the side stand and be sure that the shift pedal is in the NEUTRAL position. There should be no clearance between the side stand and its stop.
8. Retract the side stand and be sure that the transmission can be shifted into DRIVE and LOW.

3

Adjustment (CB750 K8 and CB750 F3)

1. Adjust the throttle opener cable so there is about ⅛-¼ in. (3-6mm) of free rotation of the hand grip.
2. Start the engine and allow it to warm up to normal operating temperature. Then shut it off. Shut off the fuel valve, disconnect the line, and remove the fuel tank. Locate the tank higher than its normal position and connect it to the carburetors with a longer length of hose.
3. Remove the plugs from the vacuum ports in the carburetors, install the adapters, and connect the vacuum gauge set (**Figure 88**). Start the engine and adjust the idle, if necessary, to 900-1,100 rpm. Check the vacuum gauges. If the readings are within a range of 1.6 in. (40mm) Hg difference, the synchronization is correct. If the difference is greater, remove the tops from carburetors 1, 3, and 4; carburetor No. 2 is the base and cannot be adjusted. Loosen the locknuts on the throttle lifters and turn the adjusting screws until all the readings are within a range of 1.6 in. (40mm) Hg. Then tighten the locknuts. See **Figure 89**. Reinstall the carburetor tops. Disconnect the vacuum lines, remove the adapters, and install the plugs.
4. Recheck the idle speed. If it is not 900-1,100 rpm, adjust it by turning the throttle stop screw **(Figure 90).** *Do not turn the air screws;* they are preset at the factory.
5. Allow the engine to cool. Then, pull the choke all the way out and start the engine. Check the fast idle speed. It should be 2,000-3,500 rpm. Shut off the engine. If adjustment is required, pull the choke all the way out and screw in the adjuster **(Figure 91)** until it contacts the cam. Then, push the choke in and turn the adjuster in 2 additional turns. Reinstall the fuel tank.

CLUTCH

If the clutch slips when it is engaged, or if the motorcycle creeps forward with the clutch disengaged, the free play is probably out of adjustment.

Free Play Adjustment

1. Measure free play at the tip of the lever. See **Figure 92**. It should measure between 0.4-0.8 in. (10-20mm).

2. Major adjustment, if needed, should be made at the lower end of the clutch cable and fine adjustment at the grip end. See **Figure 93**.

3. Screw in the clutch cable adjusting bolt at the grip lever until it stops against the bracket.

4. Turn the adjusting bolt at the clutch housing to slack off the cable. Refer to **Figure 93**.

5. Remove the clutch cover, loosen the locknut, and turn the lifter adjusting screw clockwise until a slight resistance is felt. Refer to **Figure 94**. Turn the screw ¼ turn back (counterclockwise).

6. Tighten the locknut and replace the cover.

7. Final adjustment is made with the adjusting bolt at the clutch grip lever. In Step 3, this was screwed up to the bracket.

8. Back off the adjusting bolt until standard free play of 0.4-1.0 in. (10-25mm) is achieved.

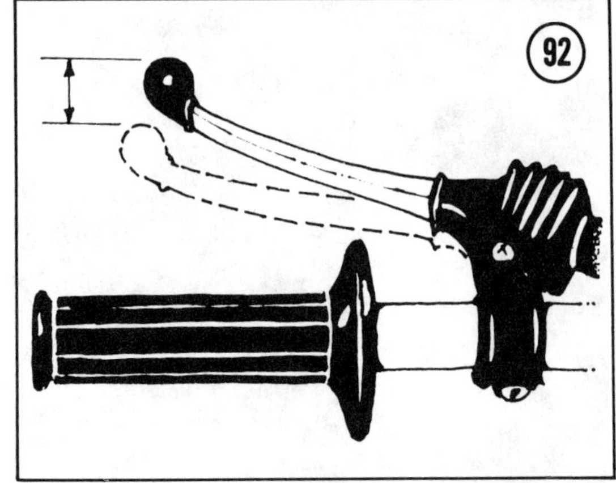

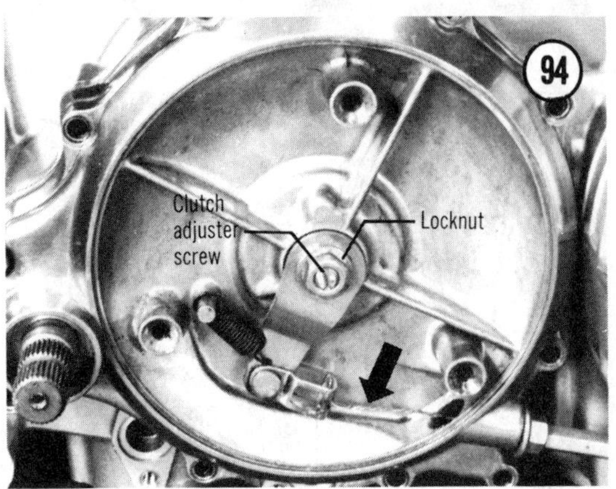

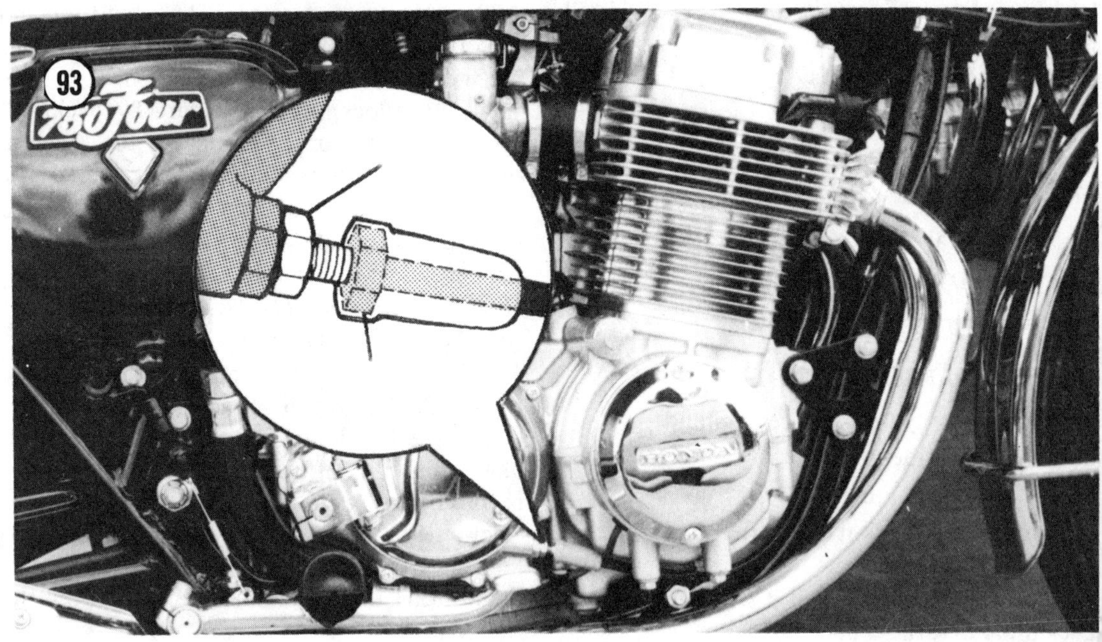

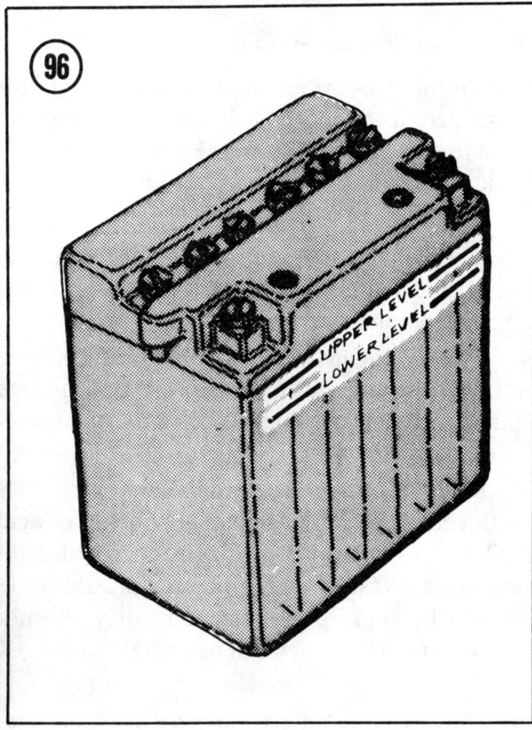

BATTERY CHECK

The battery is the heart of the electrical system. Its condition should be checked regularly.

Battery charging procedures are covered in the electrical system chapter.

1. Remove the left side cover. See **Figure 95**.
2. Check the electrolyte level. **Figure 96** shows the maximum and minimum marks. If necessary, top up with distilled water only. Be careful not to overfill.

CAUTION

Painted surfaces will be damaged if corrosive battery electrolyte is spilled on them. Flush away all spills with water, and neutralize with baking soda if necessary.

3. Inspect the terminals for corrosion. Flush off any oxidation with a solution of baking soda and water. Coat the terminals lightly with Vaseline or a silicone grease to retard new corrosion.

DRIVE CHAIN

Cleaning and Initial Lubrication

Follow the recommended service intervals listed in **Tables 1 and 2**. More frequent attention is required when the machine has been ridden over dusty or muddy terrain.

Failure to clean the chain regularly will result in faster chain wear.

1. Remove the chain and clean with solvent and a stiff brush.

CAUTION

Always check both sprockets every time the chain is removed. If any wear is visible on the teeth, replace the sprocket. Never install a new chain over worn sprockets or a worn chain over new sprockets.

2. Rinse thoroughly in clean solvent and dry with a clean rag or compressed air.
3. Put the chain in a pail of melted grease or motor oil and then hang it to drain excess lubricant. As an alternate, use one of the chain lubes sold by most motorcycle dealers.

Inspection

1. After cleaning the chain, examine it carefully for wear or damage. If any signs are visible, replace the chain.

2. Lay the chain alongside a ruler (**Figure 97**) and compress the links together. Then stretch them apart. If more than 0.25 in. (0.6mm) of movement is possible, replace the chain.

3. Check the inner faces of the inner plates. They should be lightly polished on both sides. If they show considerable wear on both sides, the sprockets are not aligned. Adjust alignment as described in the following section.

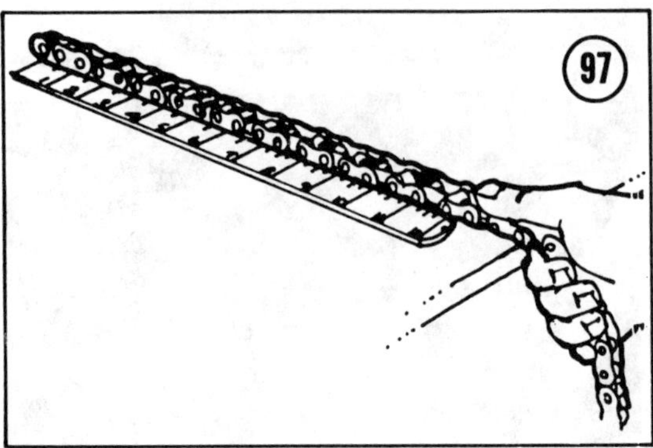

Adjustment

1. Loosen rear axle nut and brake anchor bolt.

2. Turn the chain adjuster nuts equally until the chain has 0.75 in. (20mm) slack on the bottom run with the rider on the machine. See **Figure 98**.

3. Make sure that the sprockets are aligned by sighting along the top run of the chain. A straight chain is readily visible from the rear sprocket.

4. Tighten the axle nut and recheck alignment and slack.

5. Tighten the brake anchor bolt.

STORAGE

Several months of inactivity can cause serious problems and a general deterioration of bike condition. This is especially important in areas of extreme cold weather.

Selecting a Storage Area

Most cyclists store their bikes in a home garage. Facilities suitable for long-term storage are readily available for rent or lease in most areas. In selecting a building, consider the following points:

1. The storage area must be dry, free from dampness and excessive humidity. Heating is not necessary, but the building should be well insulated to minimize extreme temperature variations.

2. Buildings with large window areas should be avoided, or such windows should be masked (a good security measure) if direct sunlight can fall on the bike.

3. Buildings in industrial areas, where factories emit corrosive fumes, are not desirable, nor are facilities near bodies of salt water.

4. The area should be selected to minimize the possibility of loss by fire, theft, or vandalism. It is strongly recommended that the area be fully insured, perhaps with a package covering fire, theft, vandalism, weather, and liability. The advice of your insurance agent should be solicited on these matters. The building should be fireproof and items such as the security of doors and windows, alarm facilities, and proximity of police should be considered.

Preparing Bike for Storage

Careful pre-storage preparation will minimize deterioration and will ease restoring the bike to service in the spring. The following procedure is recommended:

1. Wash the bike completely, making certain to remove any accumulation of road salt that may have collected during the first weeks of winter. Wax all painted and polished surfaces.

2. Run the engine for 20-30 minutes to stabilize oil temperature. Drain oil regardless of mileage since oil change and replace with normal quantity of fresh oil.

3. Remove battery and coat cable terminals with petroleum jelly. If there is evidence of acid spillage in the battery box, neutralize with baking soda, wash clean, and repaint. Batteries should be kept in an area where they will not freeze, and where they can be recharged every 2 weeks.

4. Drain all gasoline from the fuel tank, settling bowl, and carburetor float bowls. Leave fuel cock on RESERVE position.

5. Remove spark plugs and add a small quantity of oil to each cylinder. Turn the engine a few revolutions by hand. Install spark plugs.

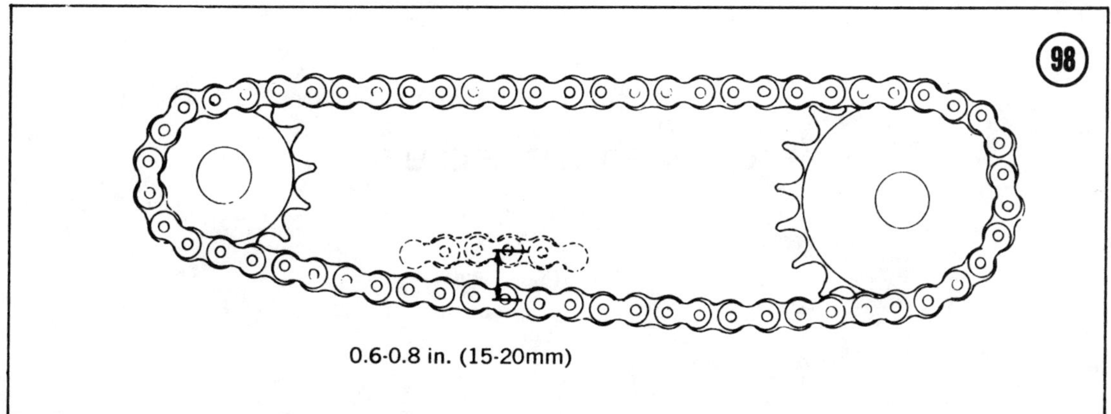

6. Insert a paper card, lightly saturated with silicone oil, between the points.

7. Check tire pressures. Move machine to storage area and store on centerstand. If preparation is performed in an area remote from the storage facility, the bike should be trucked, not ridden, into storage.

Inspection During Storage

Try to inspect bike weekly while in storage. Any deterioration should be corrected as soon as possible. For example, if corrosion of bright metal parts is observed, cover them with a light film of grease or silicone spray after a thorough polishing.

Restoring Bike to Service

A bike that has been properly prepared and stored in a suitable area requires only light maintenance to restore it to service. It is advisable, however, to perform a spring tune-up.

1. Before removing the bike from the storage area, reinflate tires to the correct pressures. Air loss during storage may have nearly flattened the tires, and moving the bike can cause damage to tires, tubes, and rims.

2. When the bike is brought to the work area, immediately install the battery (fully charged) and fill the fuel tank. (The fuel cock should be on the RESERVE position; do not move it yet.)

3. Check the fuel system for leaks. Remove carburetor float bowl or open the float bowl drain cock, and allow several cups of fuel to pass through the system. Move the fuel cock slowly to the CLOSE position. Remove the settling bowl and empty any accumulated water.

4. Perform normal tune-up, described earlier, adjust valve clearance, apply oil to camshaft, and, when checking spark plugs, add a few drops of oil to the cylinder. Be especially certain to degrease ignition points if an oily card was used to inhibit oxidation during storage; use a non-petroleum solvent such as trichloroethylene.

5. Check safety items (lights, horn, etc.), as oxidation of switch contacts and/or sockets during storage may make one or more of these critical devices inoperative.

6. Test ride and clean the motorcycle.

CHAPTER FOUR

ENGINE

In most ways, the Honda 4-cylinder 750 engine is simple in construction and easy to maintain. Most operations will take no longer than for a single or twin cylinder bike. Mechanics charge for their time rather than for the type of job. You will save money by doing the work yourself and have the added satisfaction of knowing that work was done properly.

SERVICING ENGINE IN FRAME

Many components can be serviced while the engine is mounted in the frame:

a. Electrical systems
b. Oil pump and filter
c. Gearshift mechanism
d. Clutch
e. Carburetors

Other jobs require that the engine be removed. Follow the *Engine Removal and Engine Installation* procedures later in this chapter.

EXHAUST SYSTEM

Removal/Installation

1. Loosen bolts which hold the muffler(s) to the frame.

2. Loosen 8 nuts holding the exhaust collars in place.

3. Remove the 4 exhaust pipe collars. See **Figure 1**.

4. Loosen the muffler band bolts and exhaust pipes on the 4-into-1 system. See **Figure 2**. Standard models have 4 separate mufflers and pipes.

5. Remove the 2 separate exhaust pipes on a 4-into-1 system.

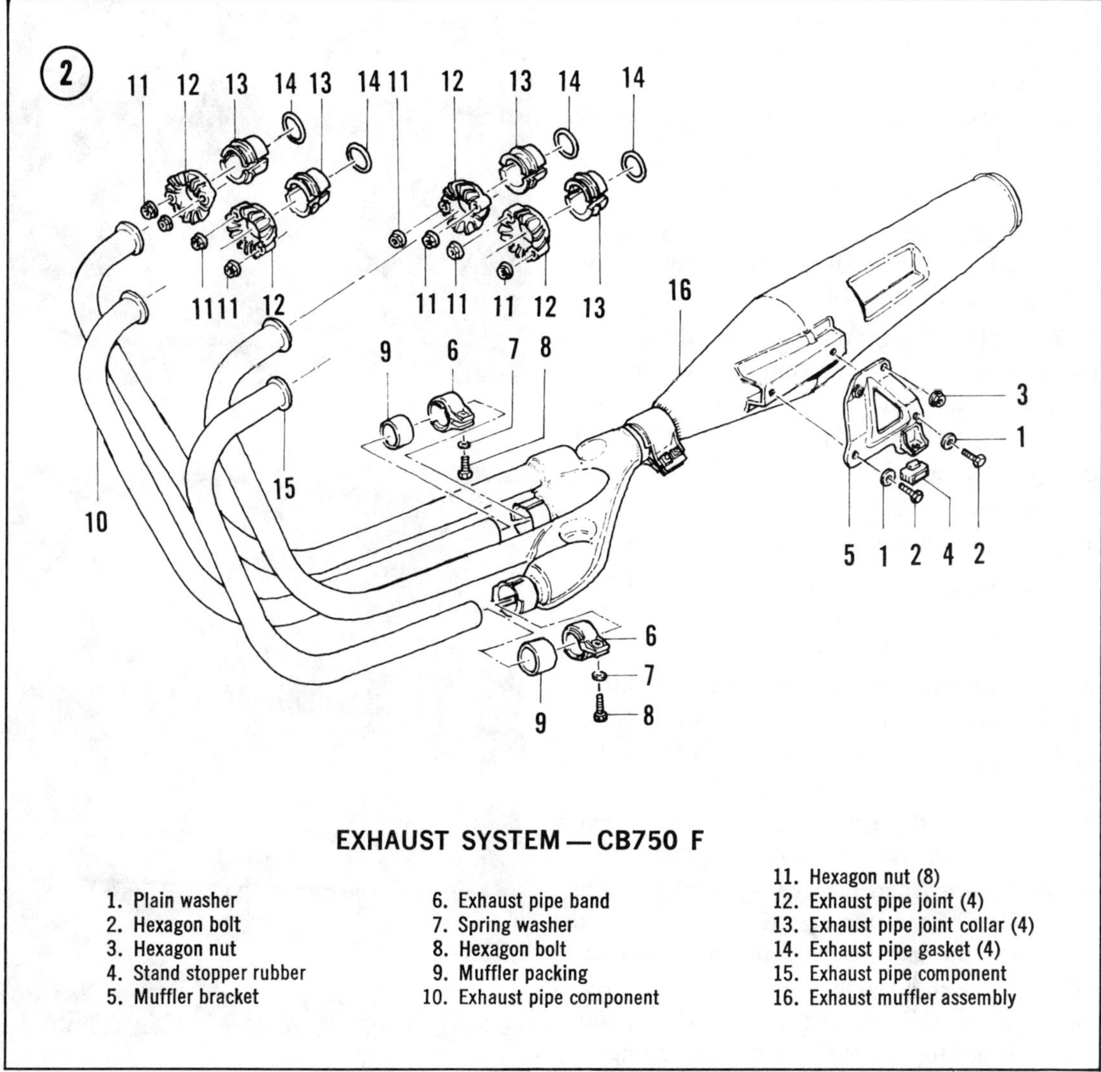

(2) EXHAUST SYSTEM — CB750 F

1. Plain washer
2. Hexagon bolt
3. Hexagon nut
4. Stand stopper rubber
5. Muffler bracket
6. Exhaust pipe band
7. Spring washer
8. Hexagon bolt
9. Muffler packing
10. Exhaust pipe component
11. Hexagon nut (8)
12. Exhaust pipe joint (4)
13. Exhaust pipe joint collar (4)
14. Exhaust pipe gasket (4)
15. Exhaust pipe component
16. Exhaust muffler assembly

6. Remove the mufflers and pipes.
7. Clean the pipes. Reverse procedure to install.

Cleaning

The exhaust system can be cleaned without removing the mufflers or tailpipes. Follow periodic intervals specified in Chapter Three, **Table 1**, or perform as necessary. The average 4-stroke exhaust system requires infrequent cleaning because there is not the oil-fouling or carbon buildup associated with a 2-stroke engine.

1. Remove the baffle setscrews at the end of the muffler(s).
2. Pull the baffle(s) out of the end of the muffler(s). It may be necessary to twist the baffle(s) slightly if buildup is severe.

CAUTION

Do not run the engine with the baffles removed. The engine has been designed to run properly at one fuel setting, which can be upset by any change in the exhaust or induction system. An unbaffled engine will run lean and hot, causing premature failure.

3. Remove heavy buildup from the baffles with a wire brush. Soak in solvent if necessary.
4. Clean the inside of the muffler(s) with a piece of old control cable frayed at one end and

chucked in a drill at the other. The flailing action will scrape away any carbon. Blow out any dust with compressed air.

5. Install the baffle(s) and replace the setscrew(s).

ENGINE REMOVAL

The engine, clutch, and transmission are a single unit attached to the frame by 4 mounting bolts. See **Figures 3 and 4**.

1. Turn off the fuel tank valve and disconnect the tubes running to the tank. Raise the seat and remove the fuel tank.
2. Drain oil from the crankcase and the oil tank, and remove the filter.
3. Remove the mufflers.
4. Disconnect the tachometer cable **(Figure 5)**.
5. Remove the throttle valves from the 4 carburetors, disconnect the carburetors from the inlet pipes, and remove them.
6. Remove the air cleaner case, kickstarter pedal, and clutch or torque converter cover.
7. Disconnect the clutch cable from the clutch lever (except CB750A). See **Figure 6**.
8. Disconnect the spring for the stop switch and remove the brake pedal and its step bar.
9. See **Figure 7** and remove the 2 oil hoses at the engine. Then remove the oil tank and disconnect the breather cap from the crankcase.
10. Remove the gearshift pedal and the drive chain cover. Disconnect the drive chain, and wire the ends together to keep it from coiling.
11. Disconnect the negative lead from the battery to prevent a short circuit, then disconnect the starter motor cable **(Figure 8)** at the magnetic switch. Also disconnect the alternator leads and the lead to the stop switch as shown. Disconnect the neutral switch wire.
12. **Figure 9** shows the location of the mounting bolts. Unscrew them, lift the rear of the engine, and remove it from the right side of the bike.

ENGINE INSTALLATION

1. Place engine in frame from the right side.
2. Install the mounting bolts. Note that the ground strap from the battery is connected to the frame at the upper rear bolt, shown in **Figure 10**. The mounting bolts also do double

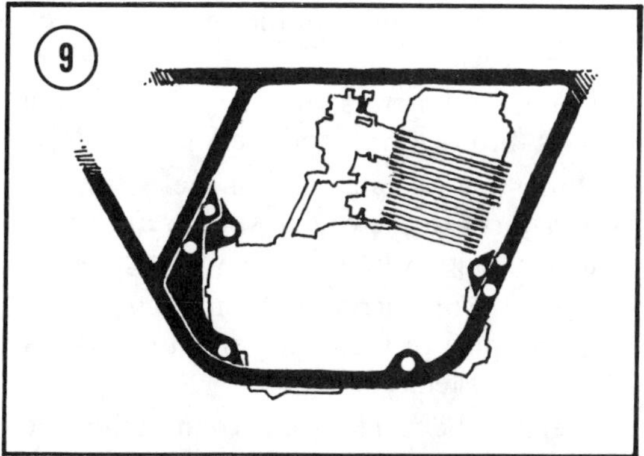

duty to connect the hanger plate and the stop switch stay.

3. Connect the electrical wiring and the tachometer cable.

4. Connect the drive chain and install its cover. Install the gearshift lever.

5. Refer to **Figure 11** and install the brake pedal and the spring for the stop switch.

6. Connect the clutch cable to the lever, install

the clutch pedal, and then the clutch cover (except CB750A).

7. Mount carburetors and air cleaner case. Connect throttle valves and spark plug leads.

8. Mount the oil tank, install the hoses, and connect them to the engine. Be careful not to mistake the supply hose for the scavenge hose.

9. Install the muffler(s). Refer to **Figure 12** for the positioning of the bands on all models except 4-in-1 systems.

10. Replace the fuel tank and connect the tubes to the fuel valve.

11. Refill with oil.

LUBRICATION SYSTEM

A dry sump lubrication system is used on the Honda 750. Oil from a reservoir tank is pressurized by a pump and forced through a filter to the engine components. A scavenge pump returns oil accumulated in the crankcase sump to the tank.

OIL FILTER

The full-flow, replaceable element filter cleanses the oil of impurities before it is routed to the engine.

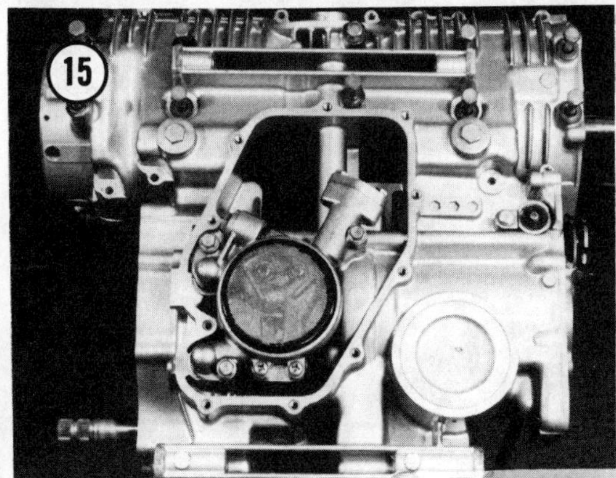

If the element becomes clogged, a bypass valve opens to allow a continued supply of oil to the engine.

OIL PUMP

Refer to **Figure 13** for construction of the oil pump. It is not necessary to remove the engine from the frame in order to remove and inspect the pump.

4

Disassembly

1. Remove the oil filter case by unscrewing the center bolt at the base of the cover.
2. Remove the oil pan from the base of the crankcase. See **Figure 14**.
3. Unscrew the 3 mounting bolts (**Figure 15**) and remove oil pump.
4. Take off oil pump left cover (**Figure 13**) and remove rotor from the delivery side.
5. Remove the dowel pin shown in **Figure 15**, and pull the shaft from the body. This will free the rotor so it can be removed from the scavenge side.
6. Remove the round mesh filter (**Figure 16**) and then the pump body by unscrewing the Phillips screws.
7. **Figure 17** shows the function of the stopper valve to cut off oil flow from the tank when the engine is stopped. To disassemble, remove the cap bolts (A, **Figure 18**). Remove the stopper cap, spring, and valve from the pump.

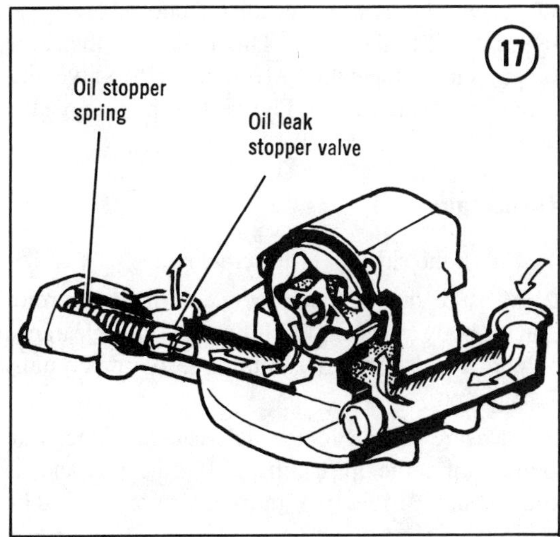

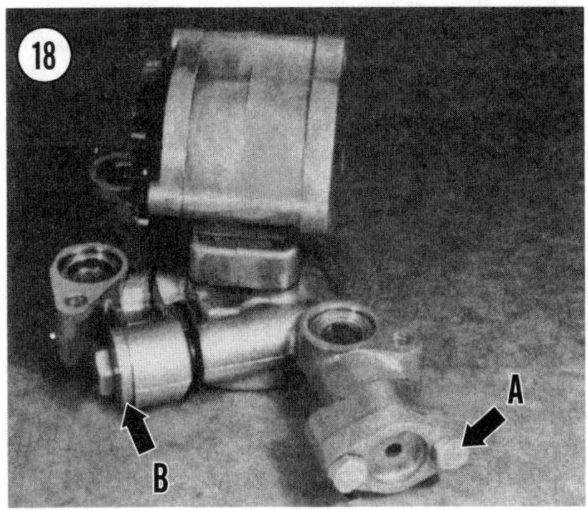

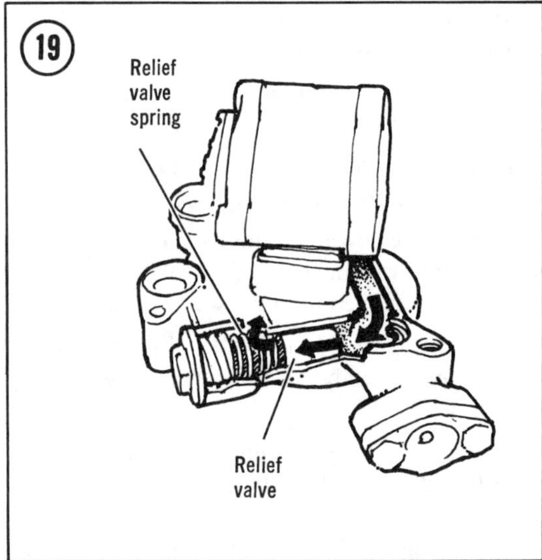

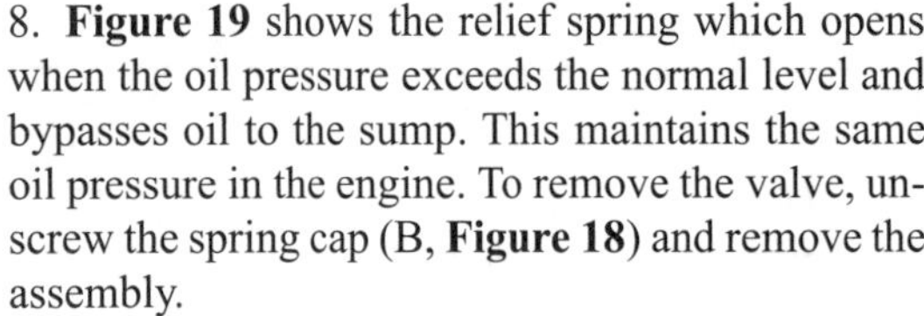

8. **Figure 19** shows the relief spring which opens when the oil pressure exceeds the normal level and bypasses oil to the sump. This maintains the same oil pressure in the engine. To remove the valve, unscrew the spring cap (B, **Figure 18**) and remove the assembly.

Inspection

1. Check the side cover for cracks.
2. Measure the clearance between the outer rotor and the body as shown in **Figure 20**. If the clearance is more than 0.014 in. (0.35mm), the worn part must be replaced.
3. Measure the clearance between the inner and outer rotor at the tip (**Figure 21**). If the clearance is more than 0.014 in. (0.35mm), the rotors should be replaced in a set.

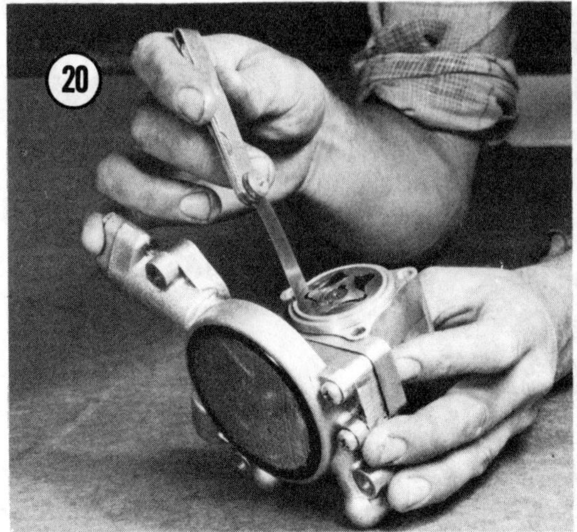

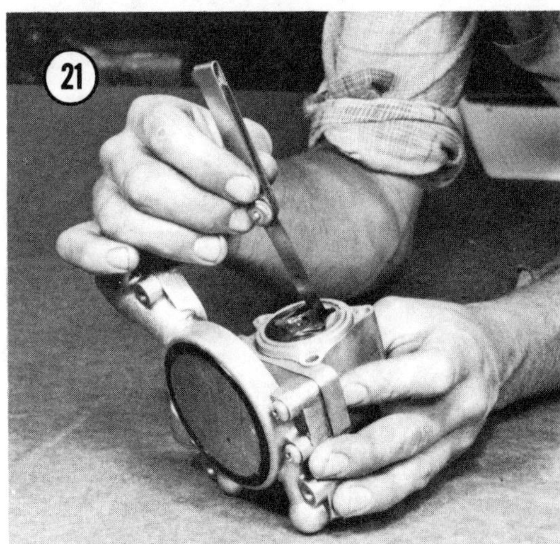

4. Use a dial gauge or micrometer to measure the inside diameter of the pump body, and the outside diameter of the oil leak-stopper valve (refer to **Figure 13**). If the difference between the 2 measurements is more than 0.007 in. (0.17mm), the worn part must be replaced.

5. Use a dial gauge or micrometer to measure the inside diameter of the body, and the outside diameter of the relief valve. If the difference is greater than 0.004 in. (0.1mm), the worn part should be replaced.

6. Measure the thickness of the rotor with a micrometer, and its depth using a depth micrometer. If clearance with body is more that 0.005 in (0.12mm), parts should be replaced.

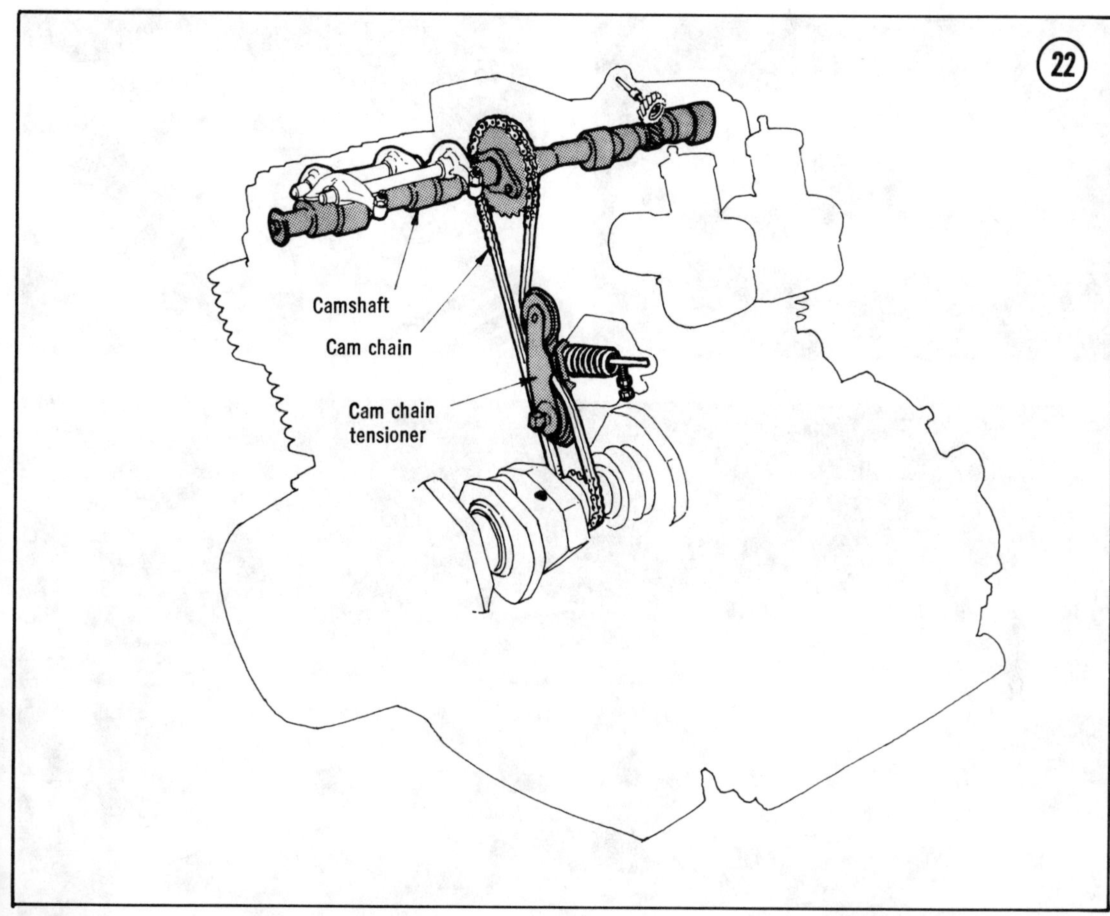

7. Before assembling the pump, clean the round strainer with solvent. If the seal is damaged, replace the part.

Assembly

1. Assemble the oil pump in reverse order of disassembly.
2. Assemble the relief valve and its spring, taking care to screw on the cap securely.
3. Assemble the stopper valve, its spring, the O-ring, and cap. Tighten the 2 bolts securely.
4. Mount inner and outer rotors (B) into the pump body, and insert the drive gear, making sure the dowel pin also is installed.
5. Mount inner and outer rotors (A).

TACH DRIVE CABLE

Oil Seal Repair

1. Remove the tach drive cable.
2. Screw a long, narrow wood screw into the hole alongside the tach drive shaft and seal. As the screw is turned, the seal will slowly come out. If care is taken, the only thing which will get damaged is the already bad seal.
3. Coat a new seal with Armor-All or silicone and place it on the tach drive shaft.
4. Seat the seal using a piece of tubing or a thin wall socket placed over the tach drive shaft.
5. Install the tach drive cable.

CAMSHAFT

The single overhead camshaft is driven by a chain off the timing sprocket at the crankshaft. **Figure 22** shows the drive system with the tensioner, guide roller, and chain guide.

Disassembly

1. Remove the breather cover by unscrewing the 3 Phillips screws (**Figure 23**).

2. Remove the cylinder head cover by unscrewing the Phillips screws shown in **Figure 24**.

3. Refer to **Figure 25** and rotate the crankshaft to align the timing marks on the cam end with the joint between the holder cap and head. The key groove should be at 12 o'clock.

4. Remove cam holder cap by loosening 2 bolts.

5. Refer to **Figure 26** and remove the cam chain tensioner from the engine.

6. Remove the 2 mounting bolts from the cam sprocket, and loosen the locknuts and the adjusting screws on the valve tappets.

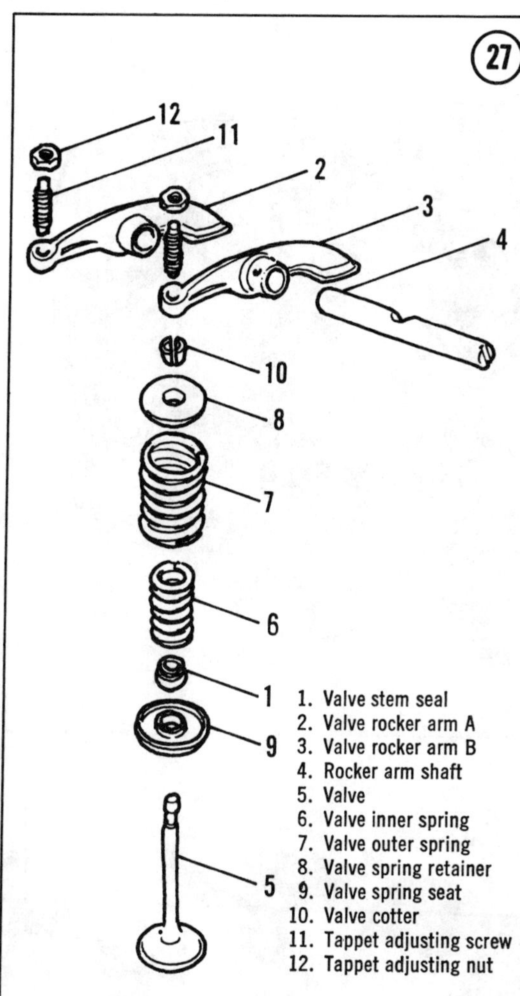

1. Valve stem seal
2. Valve rocker arm A
3. Valve rocker arm B
4. Rocker arm shaft
5. Valve
6. Valve inner spring
7. Valve outer spring
8. Valve spring retainer
9. Valve spring seat
10. Valve cotter
11. Tappet adjusting screw
12. Tappet adjusting nut

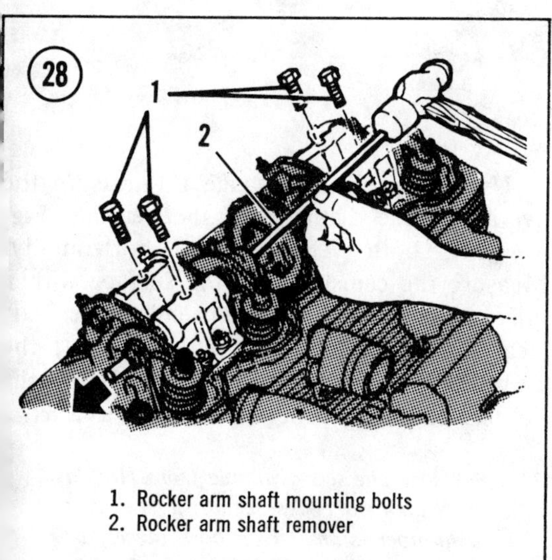

1. Rocker arm shaft mounting bolts
2. Rocker arm shaft remover

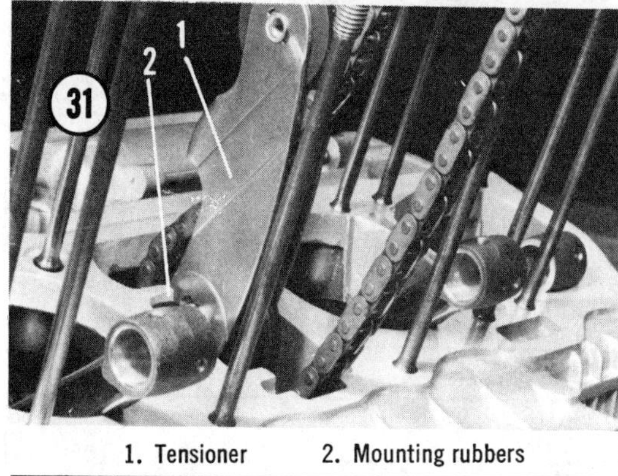

1. Tensioner 2. Mounting rubbers

7. Refer to **Figure 27** for construction of the rocker arm assembly. Unscrew the mounting bolts on the rocker arm shaft and remove the shaft as shown in **Figure 28**. **Figure 28** shows 2 bolts, the number of bolts varies from 2 to 4 with the different years.

NOTE: *Rocker arms No. 1 and No. 3, and No. 2 and No. 4 are identical. Tag them for identification when they are removed.*

8. Remove the cam chain from the sprocket (**Figure 29**) and pull out the cam from the holder on the left side.

9. Remove the holder from the head.

10. To remove the cylinder head, the 16 mounting nuts and the 6 mounting bolts, shown in **Figure 30** (next page), must be unscrewed.

11. Refer to **Figure 31**. Remove the 2 mounting rubbers, and then the chain tensioner assembly.

12. The guide roller can then be removed from the chain tensioner by pushing the roller pin. Refer to **Figure 32**.

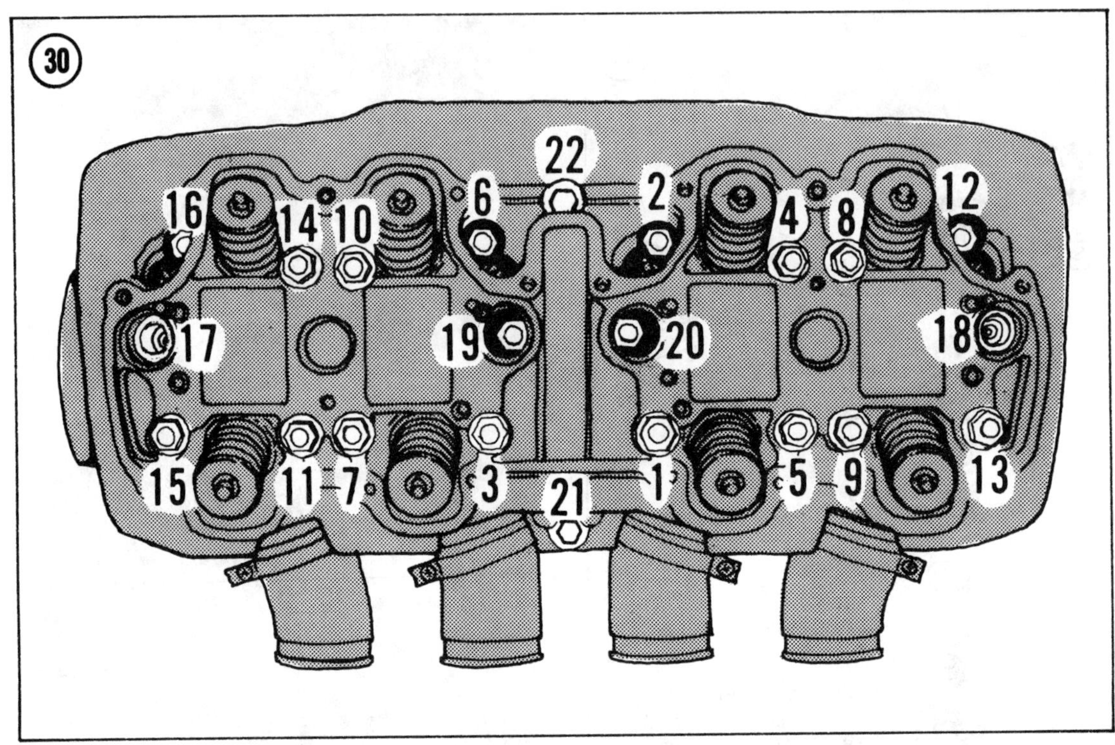

30

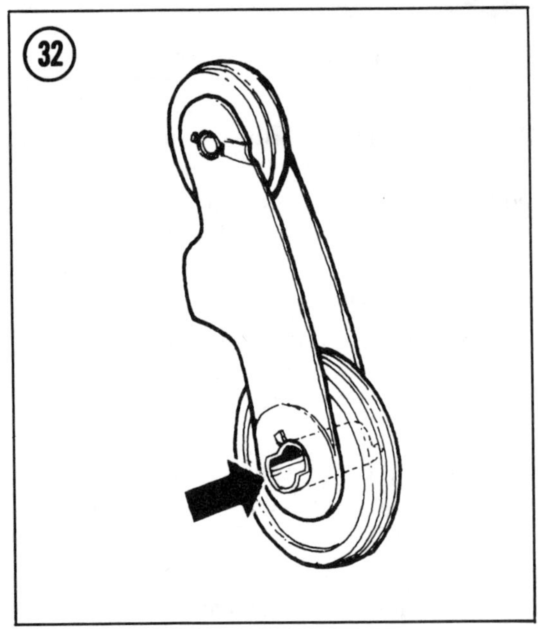

32

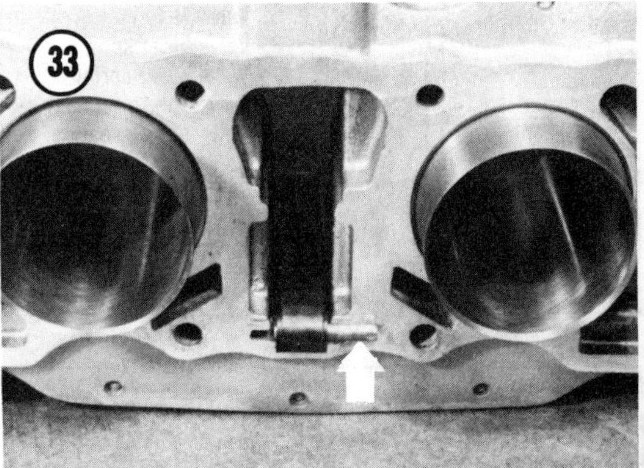

33

13. Remove the guide pin from the bottom of the block **(Figure 33)** and remove the guide.

Inspection and Measurement

1. Assemble the cam holder on the head, and torque down the cap to 6-8 ft.-lb. (80-110 mkg).

2. Use an inside dial gauge to measure the average inside diameter of the bearing **(Figure 34)**, both vertically and horizontally. Measure the camshaft bearing surface with a micrometer **(Figure 35)** and calculate the shaft clearance by subtracting the 2 values. If the clearance is more than 0.008 in. (0.21mm), the holder and the cap should be replaced as a set.

> NOTE: *The sets available from Honda have identical codes, usually a letter and a number, stamped on both pieces, as shown in **Figure 36**. There are 2 types*

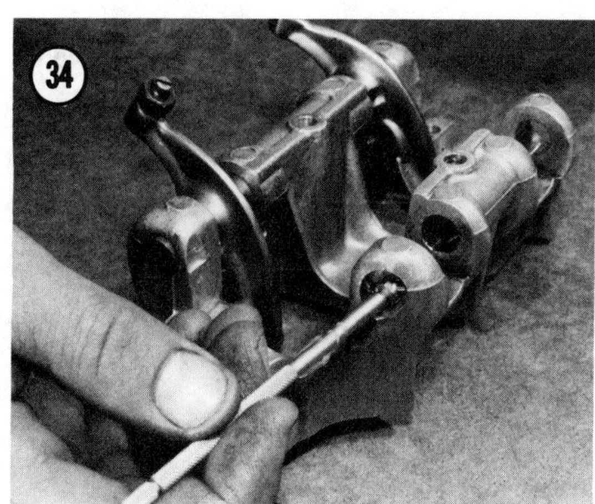

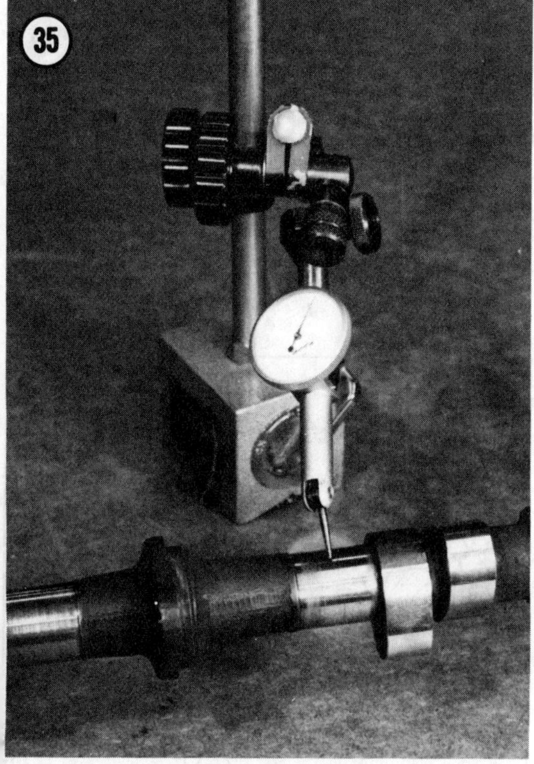

available, with the newer version for engine No. CB750E-1010338 and later numbers.

3A. *All models except CB750A*: Check cam lift by measuring the lobe with a micrometer, as shown in **Figure 37**. The camshaft should be replaced if the inlet cam height is less than 1.411 in. (35.86mm), or the exhaust cam height is less than 1.392 in. (35.36mm), or the base circle is less than 1.099 in. (27.93mm).

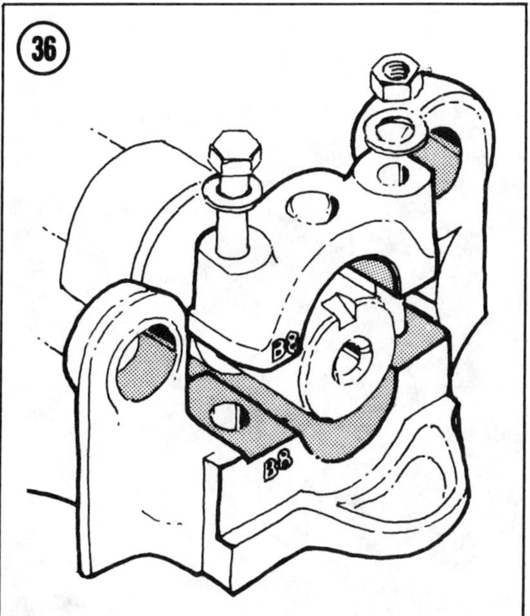

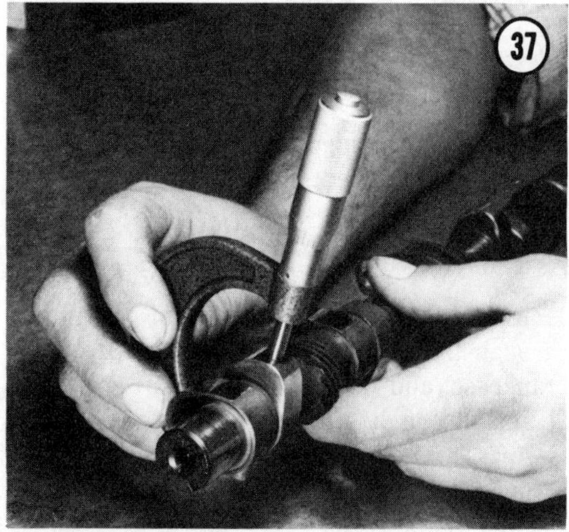

3B. *CB750A*: Check cam lift by measuring the lobe with a micrometer, as shown in **Figure 37**. The camshaft should be replaced if the inlet cam height is less than 1.387 in. (35.24mm), or the exhaust cam height is less than 1.371 in. (34.82mm), or the base circle is less than 0.862 in. (21.89mm).

4. Check for bend in the camshaft with a dial gauge as shown in **Figure 38**. If the runout is more than 0.005 in. (0.1mm), the camshaft should be replaced.

5. Check the camshaft and holder for cracks and scratches.

6. Check the chain guide roller (**Figure 39**) for wear. Replace if necessary.

Assembly

1. Refer to **Figure 40** and run the chain through the tensioner roller, mount it on the crankcase, and install the rubbers.
2. Install the head gasket, 2 dowel pins, 2 O-rings, and the cylinder head on the block (**Figure 41**). Be careful not to damage the pistons or the rings.
3. Torque down the head mounting nuts and bolts in the sequence shown in **Figure 42**. Tighten nuts to 13.7-15.2 ft.-lb. (1.9-2.1 mkg); tighten bolts to 6-9 ft.-lb. (0.8-1.2 mkg).
4. Time the valves by setting the No. 1 and No. 4 cylinders to top dead center (TDC) by aligning the "T 1-4" mark on the spark advance under the breaker points with the index mark, as shown in **Figure 43**.
5. Put the sprocket on the camshaft, and run the chain through the right side.
6. Put the camshaft in the holder and align the timing line on the shaft end (**Figure 44**), so it is parallel with the horizontal surface of the holder. The key groove should be at 12 o'clock.
7. Mount the sprocket and cam chain on the shaft with the 2 bolts as shown in **Figure 45**
8. Mount the rocker arms on the shaft and install the mounting bolts (**Figure 46**) making

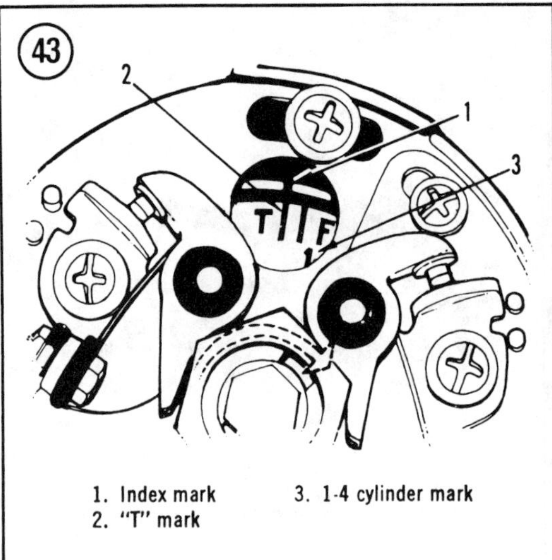

1. Index mark
2. "T" mark
3. 1-4 cylinder mark

41

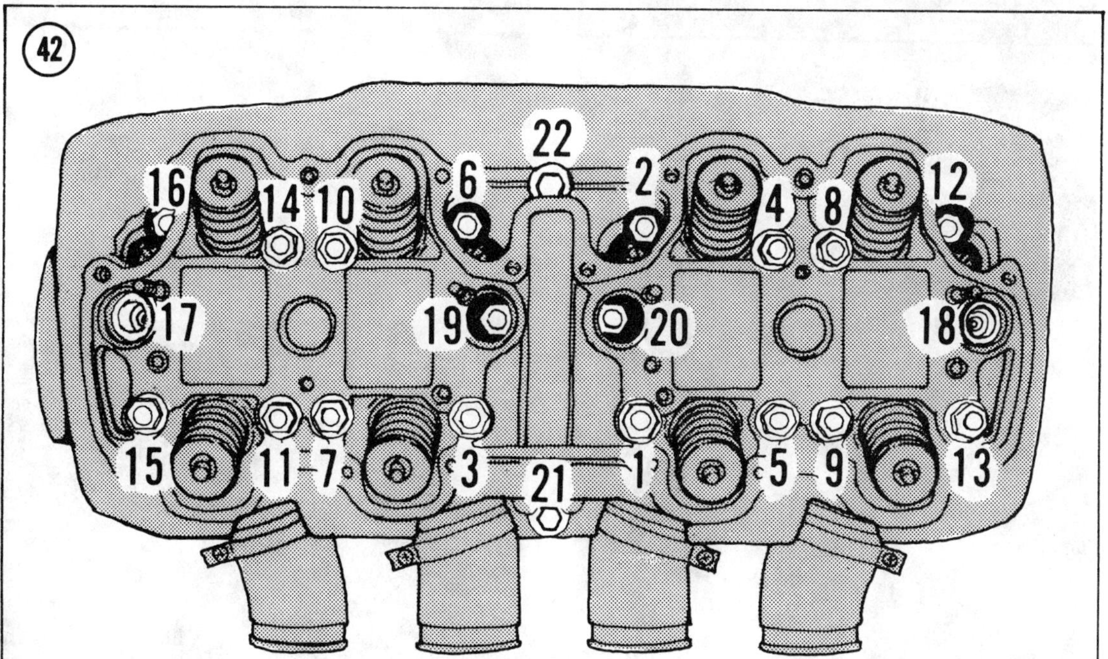

42

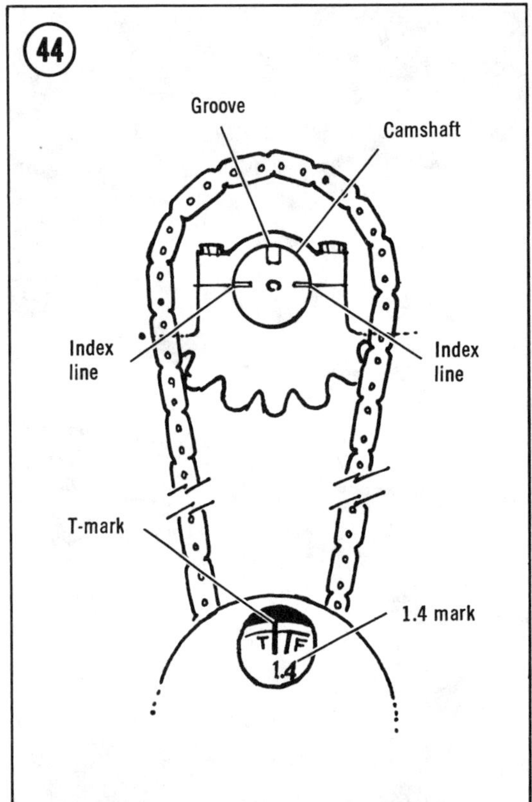
44
Groove
Camshaft
Index line
Index line
T-mark
1.4 mark
T
F
1.4

46

45

47

48

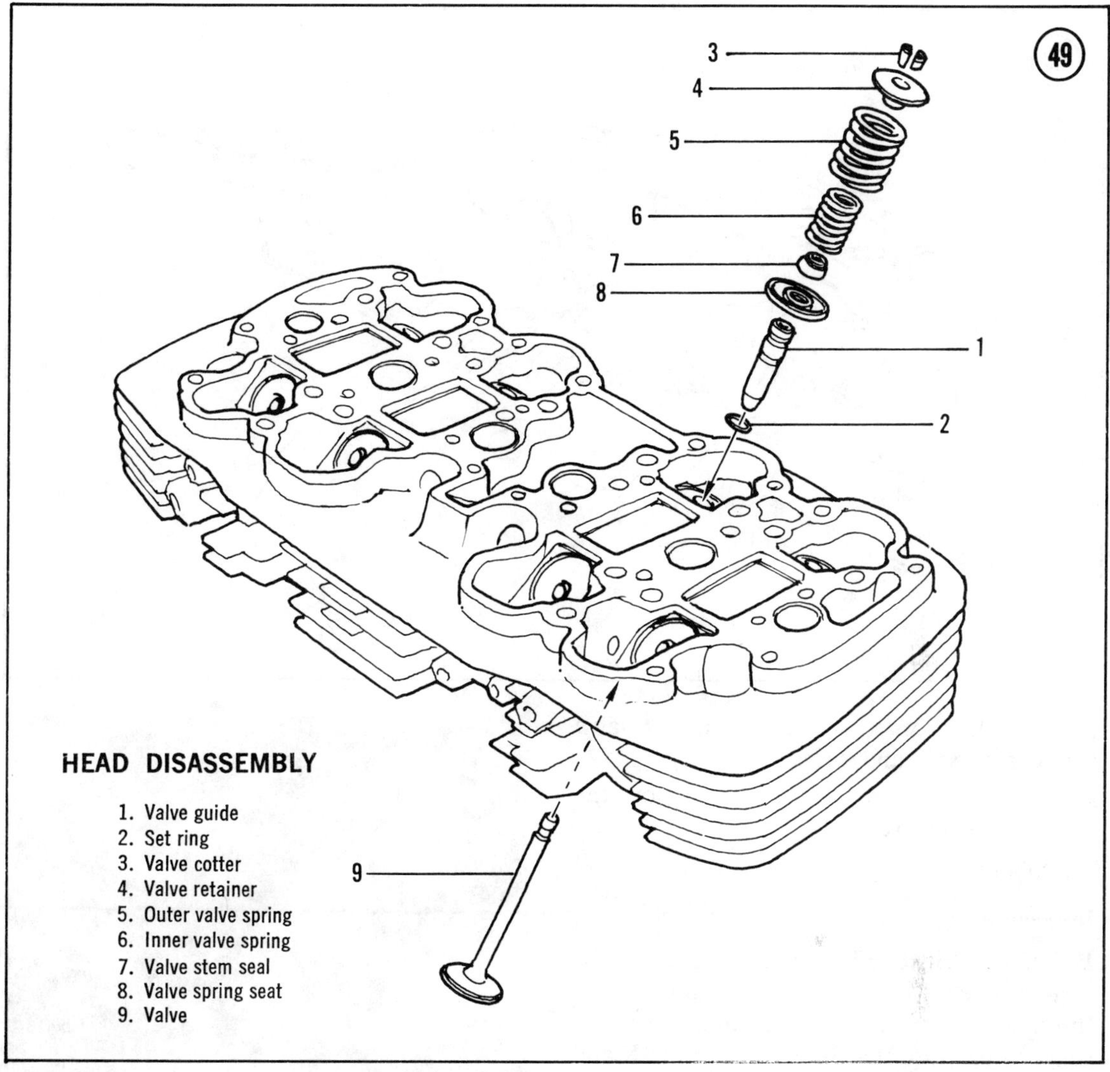

HEAD DISASSEMBLY

1. Valve guide
2. Set ring
3. Valve cotter
4. Valve retainer
5. Outer valve spring
6. Inner valve spring
7. Valve stem seal
8. Valve spring seat
9. Valve

sure that the No. 1 and No. 3 and the No. 2 and No. 4 rocker arms are put back in their original position. The number of bolts varies from 2 to 4 with the different years.

9. Install the camshaft holder and cap by torquing the bolts to 6.5-9.4 ft.-lb. (90-130 mkg). Note that sets are matched by identical codes stamped on the parts.

10. Install the push bar cam chain tensioner, and install housing on the engine (**Figure 47**). Loosen the adjusting bolt to allow the push bar to automatically tension the chain, and then tighten the bolt and the locknut.

11. Adjust the valve clearance as outlined in Chapter Three under *Valve Clearance Adjustment*. Refer to **Figure 48**, set gap with the valve closed by turning the adjusting screw. The clearance should be 0.002 in. (0.05mm) for the inlet valves and 0.003 in. (0.08mm) for the exhaust valves.

12. Install the cylinder head cover using the Phillips head screws, and mount the breather cover with its 3 screws.

CYLINDER HEAD

Disassembly

1. Remove the cylinder head from the blocks as outlined in the *Camshaft* section of this chapter.

2. Refer to **Figure 49** and disassemble the head using a valve remover. See **Figure 50**. Remove

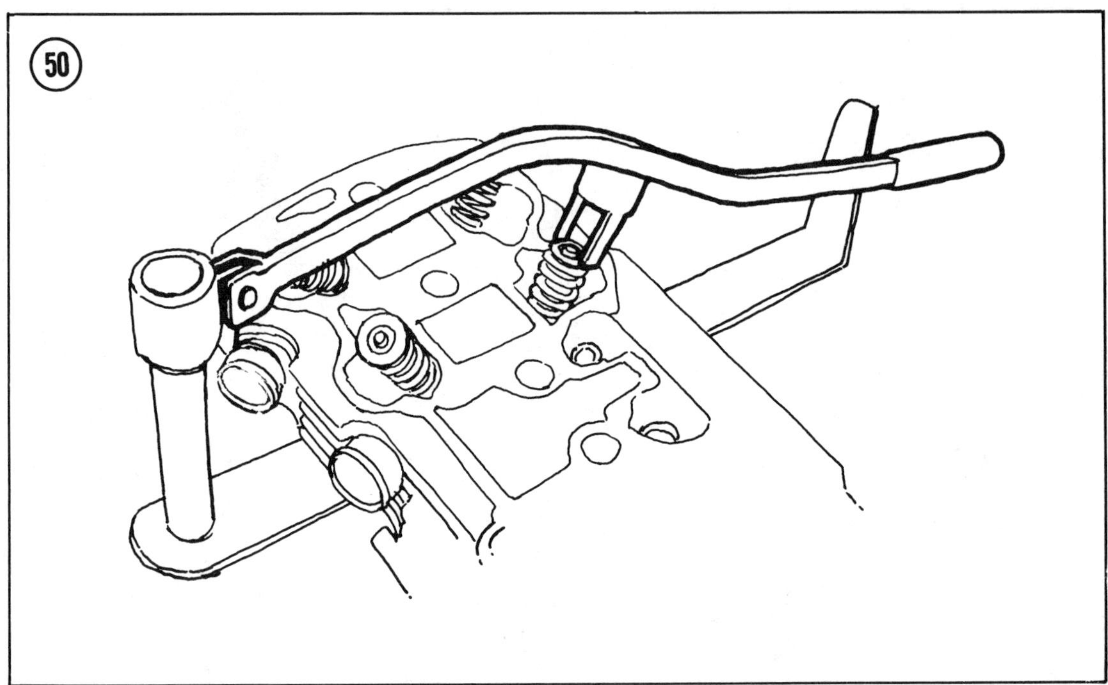

parts in this order: cotter, retainer, valve spring, stem seal, and spring seat.

3. Use valve guide removal tool to remove the valve guides (**Figure 51**).

Inspection

1. Refer to **Figure 52** for measurement of the clearance between the valve stem and its guide. Insert the valve into the guide and use a dial gauge to measure clearance for both the X and Y dimensions. If the clearance is more than 0.003 in. (0.08mm) for an intake valve or 0.004 in. (0.1mm) for an exhaust valve, the valve and its guide should be replaced as a set.

2. The new valve guide should be oversize. Drive the new guide into the head with a drift as shown in **Figure 53**. Ream out the oversize guide to the standard dimension with a reamer. The guide diameter should be 0.260-0.2603 in. (6.60-6.61mm).

3. Measure the vertical runout of the valve face with a dial gauge as shown in **Figure 54**. If the runout is more than 0.002 in. (0.05mm), replace the valve.

4. Measure the width of the contact area on the valve face. If it is more than 0.079 in. (2mm), replace the valve.

5. Check the edge of the valve for burned spots, and replace if necessary.

6. Check if the valve is seating in the head properly. If it is not seating completely, the

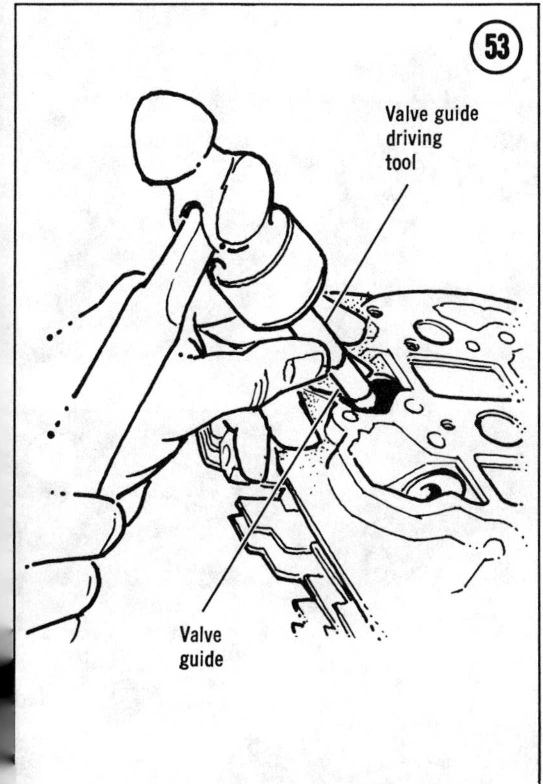

Table 1 VALVE SPRING SPECIFICATIONS

	Standard	Useable	Spring force
Inner spring	38.1mm (1.5 in)	37mm (1.457 in)	22.8kg-26mm to 25.8kg-26mm
Outer spring	41.2mm (1.622 in)	40mm (1.575 in.)	45.6kg-28mm to 51.6kg-28mm

seats must be reground. Refer this job to a machine shop.

7. Measure the free height of the valve springs with a vernier caliper (**Figure 55**), and measure the force it takes to compress the spring. Replace any which do not comform to the values in **Table 1**.

8. Measure the support area of the rocker arm shaft with a micrometer, and the bearing diameter with an inside micrometer, as shown in **Figure 56**. The clearance should not be greater than 0.005 in. (0.11mm). If it is, one or both of the parts must be replaced.

9. Insert the valves into the combustion chamber, and scrape or brush off the carbon, taking care not to scratch the metal.

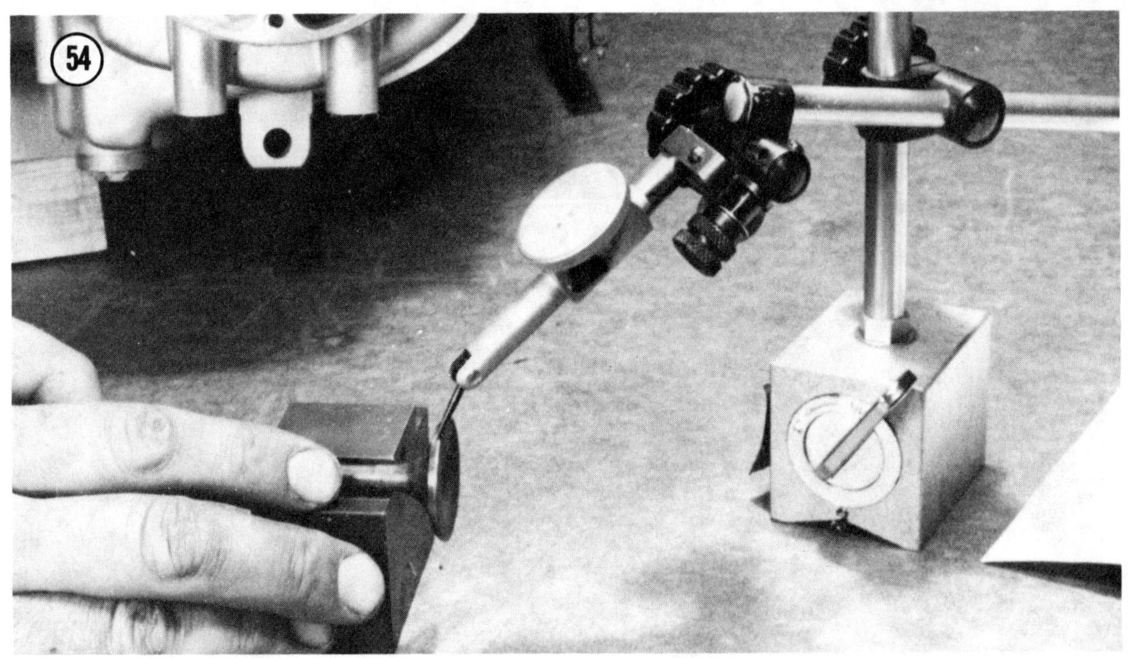

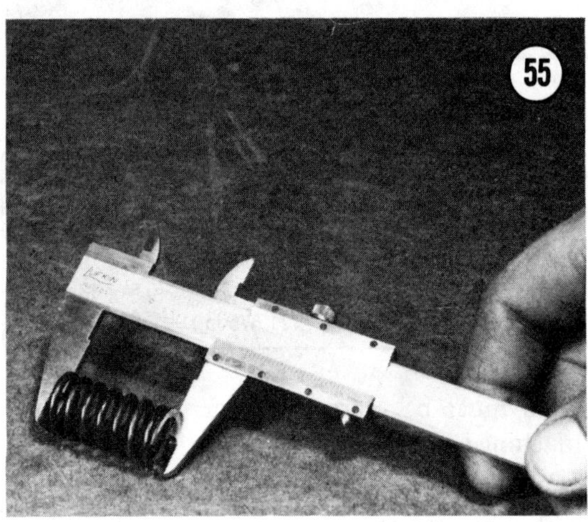

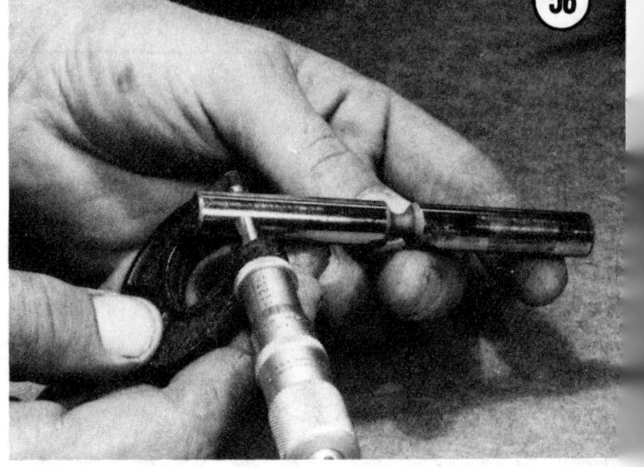

10. Check the trueness of the head by placing a straightedge across the surface **(Figure 57)** and checking the clearance with a feeler blade. If the clearance is greater than 0.010 in. (0.25mm), the head must be replaced or re-machined. The standard allowable warp is a maximum of 0.002 in. (0.05mm).

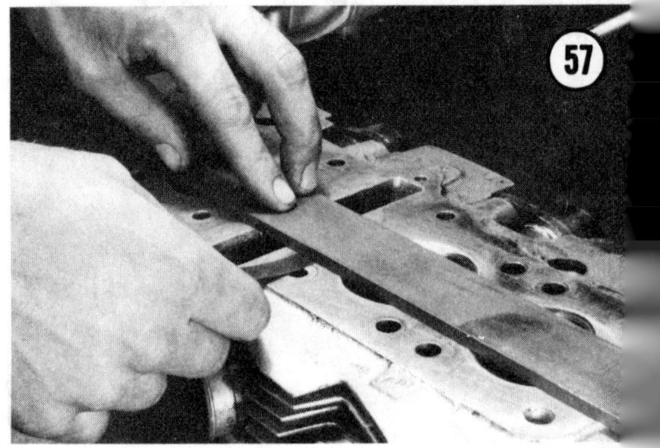

Assembly

1. Assemble the head in reverse order, referring back to **Figure 49** for the sequence of parts.

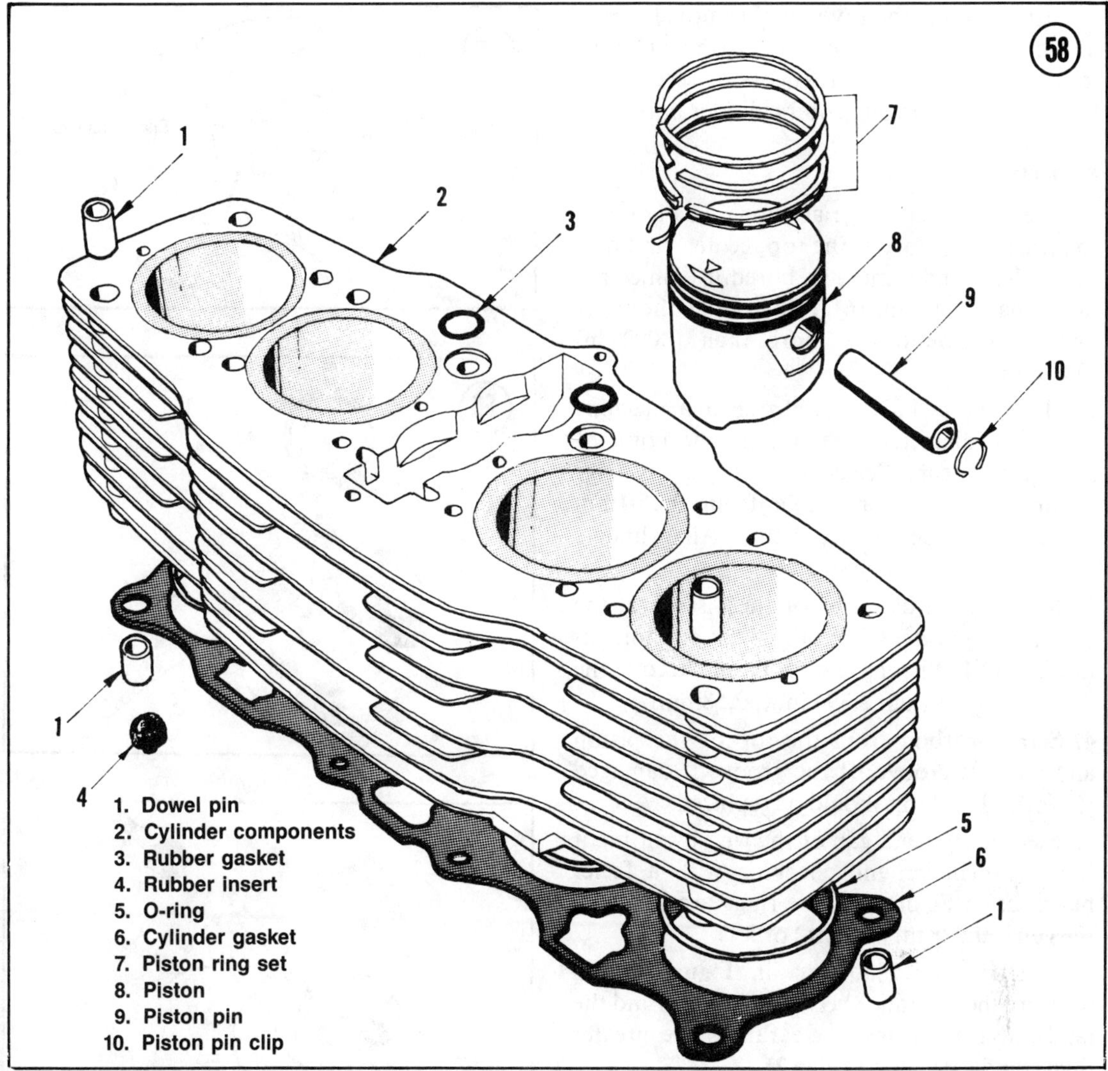

1. Dowel pin
2. Cylinder components
3. Rubber gasket
4. Rubber insert
5. O-ring
6. Cylinder gasket
7. Piston ring set
8. Piston
9. Piston pin
10. Piston pin clip

2. Set valve tappet clearance according to the *Valve Clearance Adjustment* procedure in Chapter Three. Briefly, the clearances between the tappets and the valve stem ends, with the valve closed, should be 0.002 in. (0.05mm) for inlet valves, and 0.003 in. (0.08mm) for the exhaust valves.

3. Install the cylinder head and breather covers.

PISTON AND CYLINDER

The pistons are made of light alloy aluminum. Their low weight increases high speed performance, while this metal dissipates heat rapidly. **Figure 58** shows block and pistons.

Disassembly/Assembly

1. Remove the cylinder head as desctibed in the *Camshaft* section of this chapter.
2. Pull the cylinder block up off the pistons. Don't lose the locating dowels.
3. Refer to **Figure 59**. Remove the clip, wrist pin and connecting rod from the piston. Be sure not to drop clip into the crankcase. Place a rag under the piston to catch it.
4. Remove the rings from the pistons.

5. Installation is the reverse of removal. Use a new cylinder base gasket and O-rings. Compress the rings with your fingers or screw-type hose clamps as pistons enter cylinder bores.

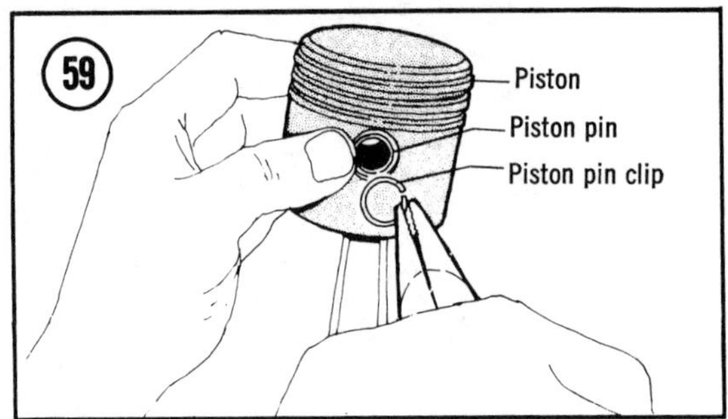

Inspection

1. Use a cylinder gauge as shown in **Figure 60** to measure the bore at the top, center, and bottom. The cylinder must be bored if diameter is more than 2.406 in. (61.1mm), or if the taper and out-of-round are more than 0.002 in. (0.05mm).
2. Have the cylinder bored out at a machine shop to a diameter greater than the point of maximum wear. Select the proper oversize pistons. They are available from 0.25-1mm oversize in 0.25mm increments. All cylinders must be bored to same size.
3. Measure the diameter of the pistons at the skirt and 90 degrees from the wrist pin hole, as in **Figure 61**. Pistons should be replaced if the diameter is less than 2.394 in. (60.58mm).
4. Scrape carbon from the top of the piston and the ring groove. If the groove is damaged or worn, the piston should be replaced.
5. Measure the end gap of the ring by fitting it into the cylinder and checking with a feeler blade, as in **Figure 62**. The rings are usable if the gap is 0.028 in. (0.7mm) or less.
6. Use a feeler blade, as in **Figure 63**, to measure the clearance between the rings and the lands. Replace rings if clearances are greater than standard values **(Table 2)**.
7. Use a dial gauge or an inside micrometer to measure the bore of the pin hole. Replace piston if reading is more than 0.594 in. (15.08mm).

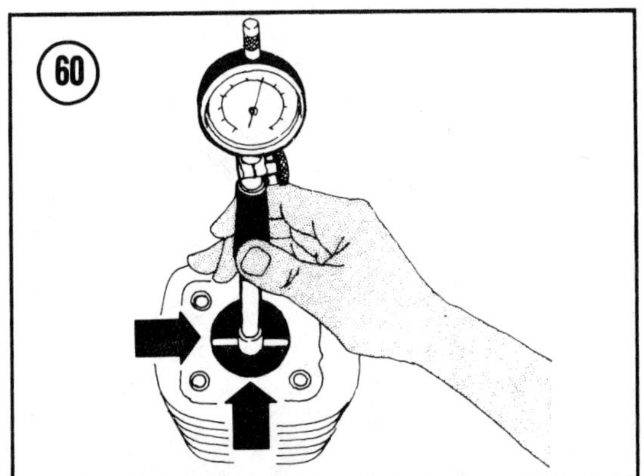

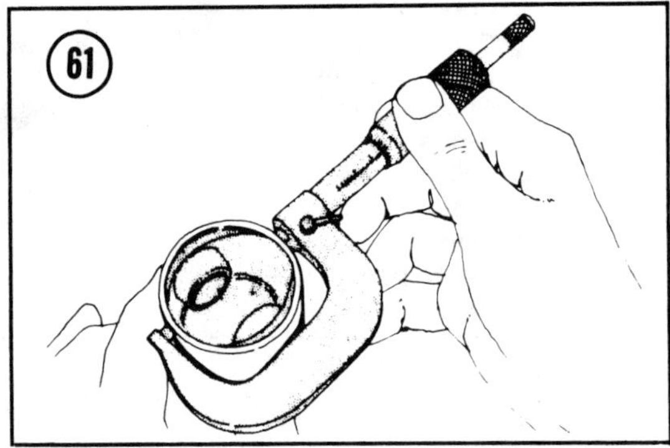

Assembly

1. Before putting new rings on a piston, roll the rings in the grooves as shown in **Figure 64** to make sure the clearances are correct.
2. Install the rings, making sure the manufacturer's mark is toward the top, and the gaps are spaced 120° apart.
3. Attach the piston to the connecting rod so that the arrow marks on the tops **(Figure 65)** are pointed forward toward the exhaust ports.
4. Use new pin clips when assembling.

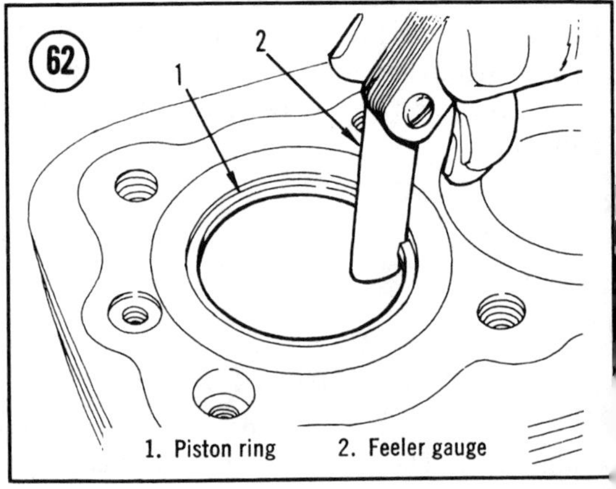

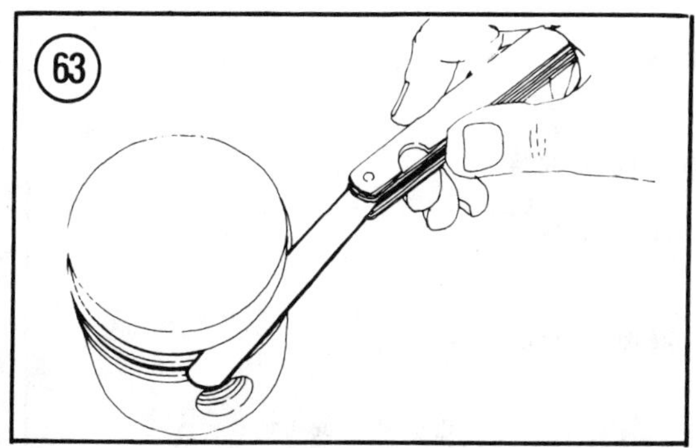

Table 2 PISTON RING CLEARANCES

Top ring	0.0071 in. (0.18mm)
Second ring	0.0065 in. (0.165mm)
Oil ring	0.0045 in. (0.114mm)

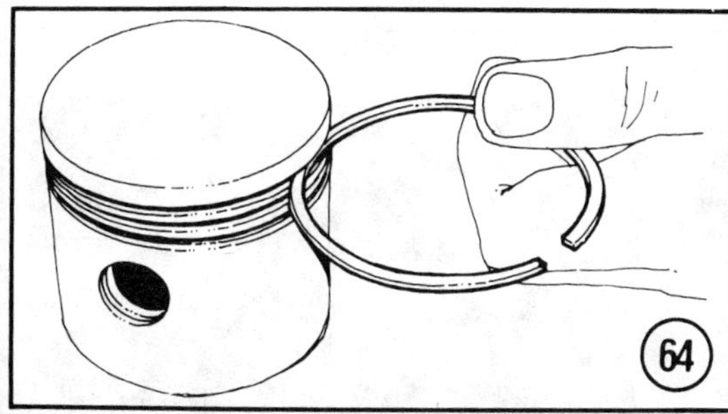

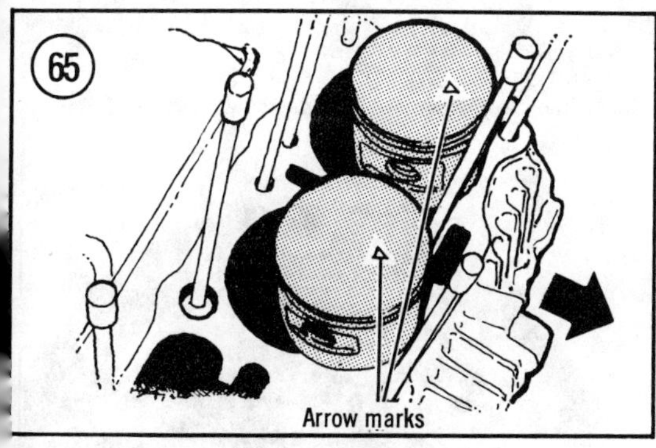

DRIVE SPROCKET

Removal/Installation

1. Remove the bolts securing the sprocket cover and remove the sprocket cover.

2A. On "F" models, perform the following:
  a. Straighten the tab on the lockwasher.
  b. Remove the bolt and lockwasher.
  c. Remove the drive sprocket and drive chain as an assembly.

2B. On all other models, perform the following:
  a. Remove the bolts securing the sprocket retainer plate.
  b. Rotate the sprocket retainer plate in either direction to clear the transmission shaft splines and slide the sprocket retaining plate from the transmission shaft.
  c. Remove the drive sprocket and drive chain as an assembly.

3. Install by reversing these removal steps noting the following.

4A. On "F" models, perform the following:
  a. Install a new lockwasher.
  b. Tighten the bolt securely and bend one side of the lockwasher up aginst one flat of the bolt.

4B. On all other models tighten the bolts securely.

CRANKSHAFT AND CONNECTING RODS

The forged crankshaft is supported by 5 main bearings. **Figure 66** shows crank and rod components.

These procedures apply to all models except the CB750A. Refer to Chapter Five under *Automatic Transmission* for procedures leading up to this point.

Disassembly

1. Remove the cylinder head, pistons, and cam chain tensioner according to the steps in the *Camshaft* section.

2. Remove the alternator cover, unscrew the alternator mounting bolt, and remove the rotor with a special puller as shown in **Figure 67**.

3. Remove the reduction and clutch gears. Refer to **Figure 68**.

4. Refer to **Figure 69** to remove the gearshift arm, drum stopper, and the positive stopper.

5. Remove the point cover and unscrew the hex nut **(Figure 70)** and remove it with the advance shaft washer. Unscrew the mounting screws and remove the breaker point unit.

6. Remove spark advancer and advance shaft.

7. Remove clutch as outlined in Chapter Five under *Clutch*.

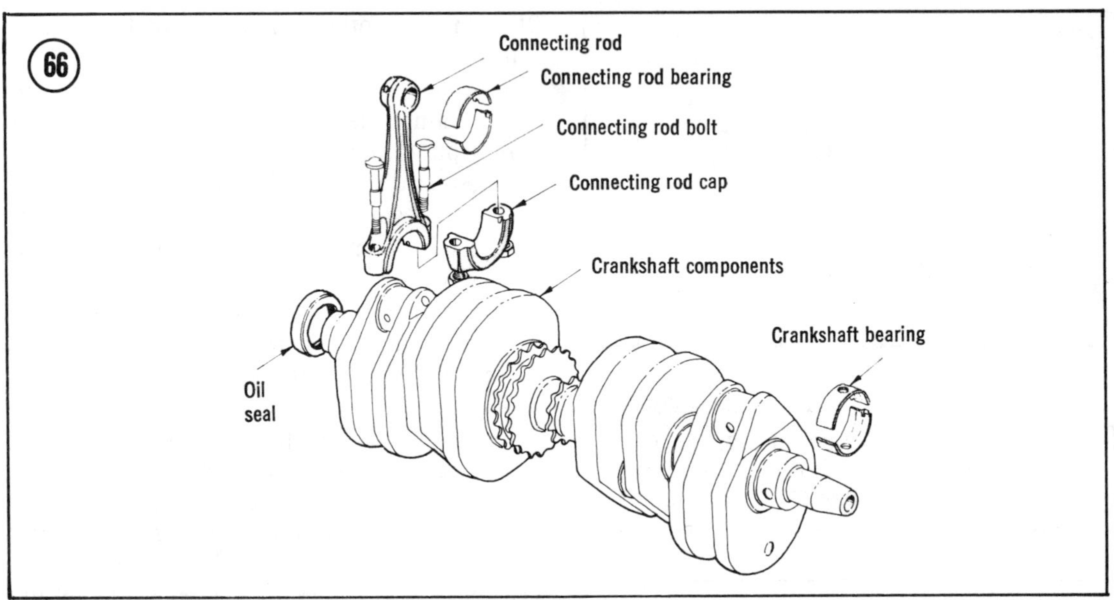
66
Connecting rod
Connecting rod bearing
Connecting rod bolt
Connecting rod cap
Crankshaft components
Crankshaft bearing
Oil
seal

67

69

68

70

8. Remove countershaft bearing holder, shown in **Figure 71**.

9. Remove the lower crankcase by loosening the upper mounting bolts, shown in **Figure 72**, and then removing the lower mounting bolts circled in **Figure 73**.

10. Lift up the transmission main shaft (**Figure 74**) and remove primary sprocket and chain.

11. Lift the crankshaft from the upper crankcase (**Figure 75**).

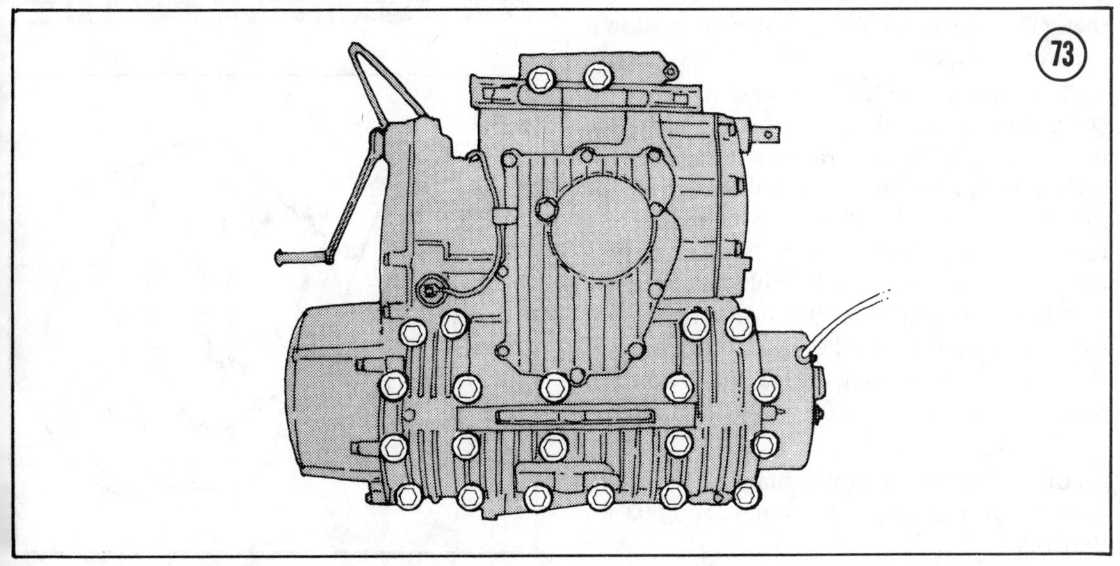

12. Remove the connecting rods (**Figure 76**) by unscrewing the cap bolts and removing the caps.

Inspection

1. Measure for bends in the crank with a dial gauge as shown in **Figure 77**. Runout should be 0.002 in. (0.05mm) or less. If it is greater than that value, the crank must be straightened in a press by an expert.

2. To measure wear in the crankshaft journals, cut a piece of Plastigage to the length of the bearing parallel to the crank. Keep it clear of the oil hole. Assemble the crankshaft into the lower case with the Plastigage in place, and torque down the mounting bolts. Do not turn the crankshaft. Now disassemble and read the Plastigage according to the instructions that came with it. Replace the bearings as a set if clearance is more than 0.0032 in. (0.08mm). Standard clearance is 0.0008-0.0018 in. (0.02-0.046mm).

3. Check each journal for damage or wear. The limit of taper or out-of-roundness is 0.002 in. (0.05mm).

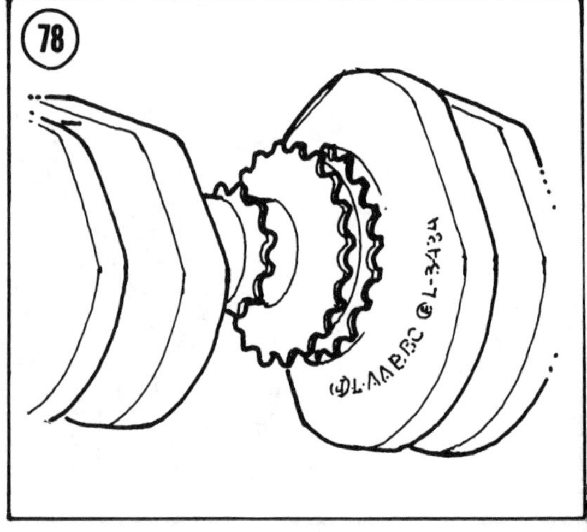

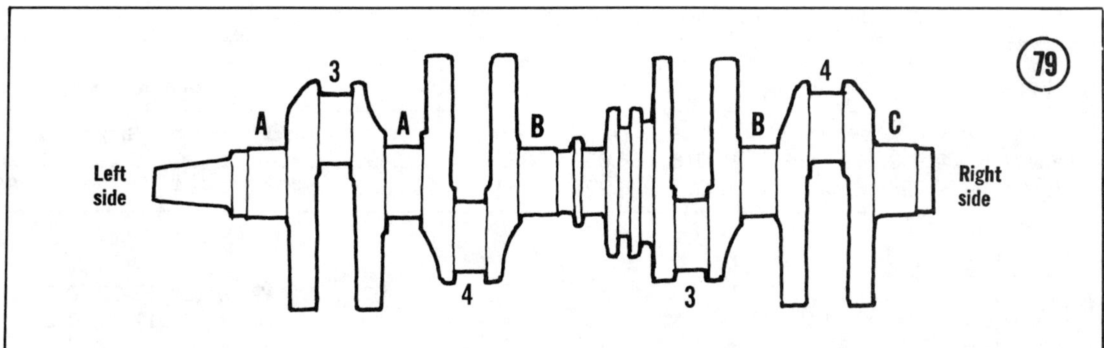

Table 3 CRANK PIN BEARING INSERTS

Code	Connecting Rod			Crank Pin			Bearing Insert			
	1	2	3	3	4	5	Black	Brown	Green	Yellow
Dimension (mm)	39.000-39.008	39.008-39.016	39.016-39.024	36.000-35.995	35.995-35.990	35.990-35.985	1.502-1.498	1.498-1.494	1.494-1.490	1.490-1.486
Clearance (mm)										
0.020-0.041		1			3		Yellow (13218-300-013)			
0.022-0.043		1			5		Green (13217-300-013)			
0.025-0.046		1			4		Yellow			
0.020-0.041		2			3		Green			
0.022-0.043		2			5		Brown (13216-300-013)			
0.025-0.046		2			4		Green			
0.020-0.041		3			3		Brown			
0.022-0.043		3			5		Black (13215-300-013)			
0.025-0.046		3			4		Brown			

4. The size of the bearings originally fitted to the crankshaft are identified by matching the code letters stamped on the side of the crankshaft weight adjacent to the drive sprocket, as in **Figure 78**. This system, effective from engine No. CB750E-1015587, supersedes the earlier code which used Japanese characters. The letters refer to the journals starting from left end of the crank. See **Figure 79**. Refer to **Table 3** for the corresponding sizes and color codes. The numbers refer to the crankpins, discussed later.

5. When inserting a new bearing, be careful not to damage the thin shell. When it is mounted into the crankcase, the top should extend above the flange 0.0027-0.0039 in. (0.068-0.098mm).

6. The connecting rod bearings are measured by first taking a micrometer reading of the crankpin diameter. Next, put the bearing into the connecting rod and torque the cap to 14.5 ft.-lb. (2 mkg). Measure the inside diameter of the bearing. An alternate method is using the press gauge following the same steps as in the crankshaft journal measurement section. The average clearance should be 0.0008-0.0018 in. (0.02-0.046mm). If the clearance is greater than 0.0032 in. (0.08mm), replace bearings as a set.

7. Refer to **Table 4** and **Figure 79** for the number code, to determine the original size of the bearings.

Assembly

1. Put the cam and primary chains on the crankshaft, and assemble it in the upper crankcase.

2. Put the primary chain on the sprocket (**Figure 80**) and install the sprocket on the main shaft.

3. Refer to **Figure 81** and install the 2 dowel pins, the oil pass collar, and the O-ring on the upper crankcase. Coat the mating surface with Permatex. Set the lower crankcase on top and install the mounting bolts.

Table 4 CRANKSHAFT JOURNAL BEARING INSERTS

Code	Crankcase			Crankshaft Journal			Bearing Insert			
	A	B	C	A	B	C	Black	Brown	Green	Yellow
Dimension (mm)	39.000-39.008	39.008-39.016	39.016-39.024	36.000-35.995	35.995-35.990	35.990-35.985	1.502-1.498	1.498-1.494	1.494-1.490	1.490-1.486
Clearance (mm)										
0.020-0.041	A			A			Yellow (13318-300-013)			
0.022-0.043	A			C			Green (13317-300-013)			
0.025-0.046	A			B			Yellow			
0.020-0.041	B			A			Green			
0.022-0.043	B			C			Brown (13316-300-013)			
0.025-0.046	B			B			Green			
0.020-0.041	C			A			Brown			
0.022-0.043	C			C			Black (13315-300-013)			
0.025-0.046	C			B			Brown			

1. Oil pass collar and O-ring 2. Dowel pins

4. Torque in sequence shown in **Figure 82** to 16.6-18.1 ft.-lb. (2.3-2.5 mkg).

5. Tighten the bolts in the upper crankcase.

6. Refer back to **Figure 69** and install the countershaft bearing, gearshift positive stopper, drum stopper, and shift arm.

7. Install the clutch as described in Chapter Five under *Clutch*.

8. Refer to **Figure 83**. Mount the spark advance shaft and advancer, making sure that the pin on the back side fits into the crankshaft pin hole.

9. Install the breaker point assembly with the washer and nut.

10. Install the starting motor reduction and clutch gears.

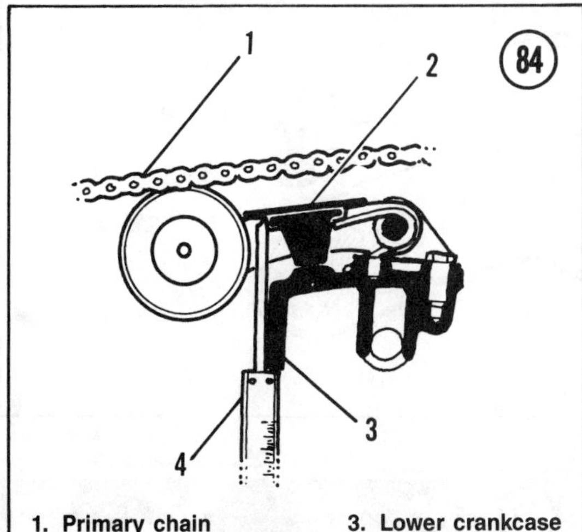

1. Primary chain
2. Primary chain tensioner
3. Lower crankcase
4. Vernier caliper

1. Primary sprocket 2. Main shaft

11. Install the generator, then torque mounting bolt to 73 ft.-lb. (10 mkg).

12. Install the pistons and cylinder head according to the previous sections on the camshaft, pistons, and rods.

PRIMARY DRIVE (All Models Except CB750A)

Power is transmitted from the crankshaft through 2 chains to the primary sprocket, and then through the clutch to the transmission. Refer to *Automatic Transmission* in Chapter Five for CB750A.

NOTE: *The stretch of the primary drive chain can be checked without disassembling the engine.*

Inspection

1. Drain the oil from the crankcase, and drop the pan by removing the mounting bolts.
2. Refer to **Figure 84**. Use a vernier caliper to measure the distance between the primary tensioner bracket and the pan mounting flange. Replace the chain if the distance between them is greater than 2.8 in. (70mm).
3. Inspect the rubber roller for wear or deterioration, and replace if necessary.

Disassembly/Assembly

1. Remove the cylinder head, pistons, and crankcase, referring to the appropriate sections of this chapter.
2. Remove the primary sprocket **(Figure 85)** by lifting the transmission main shaft. Then remove the chain from the sprocket.
3. Raise the crankshaft and remove the chain.
4. Refer to **Figure 86**. Remove the primary chain and tensioner from the lower crankcase. See **Figure 87**.
5. Reverse the procedure to assemble the crankcase, pistons, and cylinder head.

KICKSTARTER

Disassembly

1. Remove the cylinder head, cam chain tensioner, and crankcase cover in accordance with sections of this chapter.

86

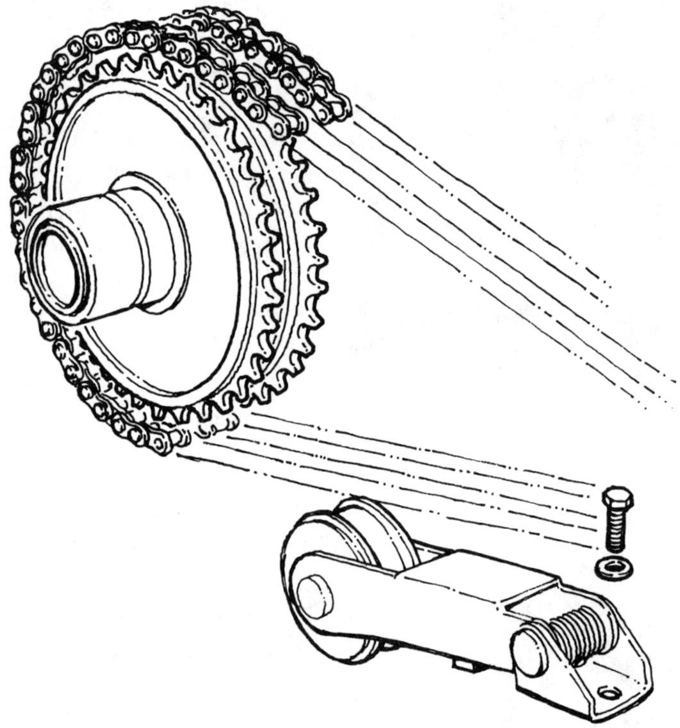

2. Refer to **Figure 88** to remove the stopper pin and the shaft.

3. Remove the gear assembly **(Figure 89)** and the return spring.

4. Remove the ratchet spring from the kickstarter flange, and then the starter pawl.

Inspection

1. Operate the kickstarter gear to make sure it turns smoothly in one direction and locks in the reverse direction.

2. Use an inside dial gauge to check the bore of the kick gear and a micrometer to check the starter shaft **(Figure 90)**. Replace the parts if the gear bore is more than 0.7904 in. (20.075mm), or the shaft diameter is less than 0.7847 in. (19.930mm).

Assembly

1. Assemble the kickstarter gear, starter flange, and return spring in the lower crankcase

87

(Figure 91). Make sure the return spring is hooked to the case. Use a screwdriver to force down the flange, and hook it onto the pin.

2. Install spindle **(Figure 92)** and stopper pin.

3. Assemble crankcase, pistons, and cylinder head as described earlier in this chapter.

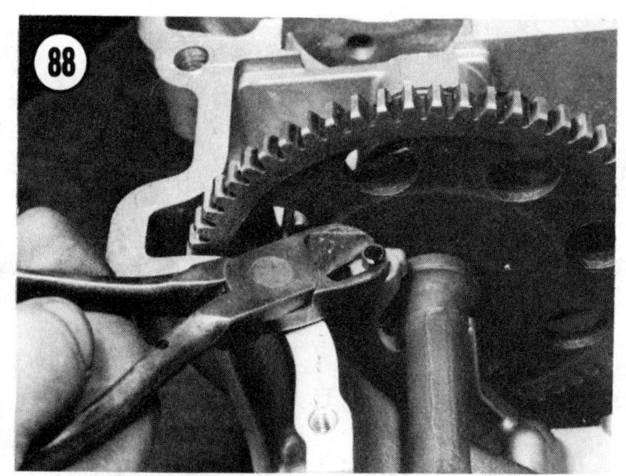

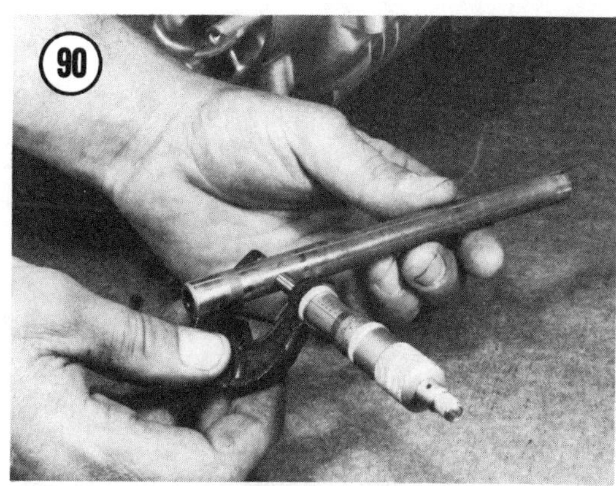

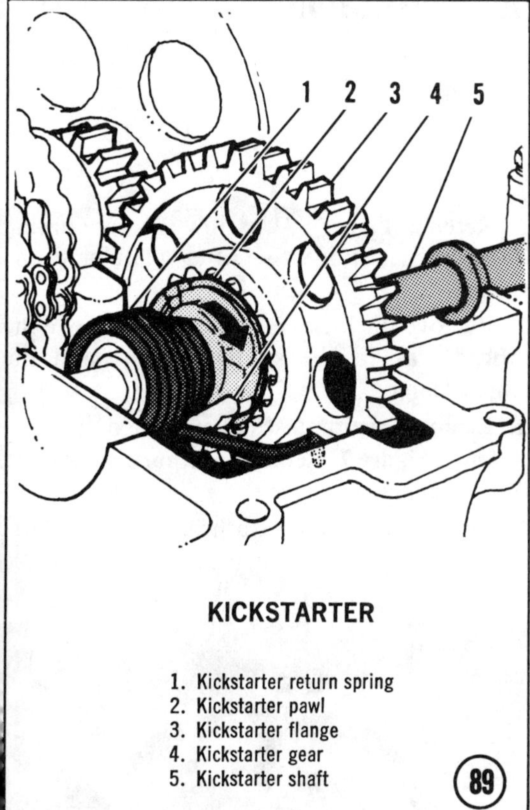

KICKSTARTER

1. Kickstarter return spring
2. Kickstarter pawl
3. Kickstarter flange
4. Kickstarter gear
5. Kickstarter shaft

CHAPTER FIVE

CLUTCH AND TRANSMISSION

CLUTCH
(All Except CB750A)

The Honda 750 has a multiple disc, wet type clutch with 7 fiber covered discs, 6 steel clutch plates, and 4 clutch springs. **Figure 1** is an exploded view of the clutch assembly. **Figure 2** is a cutaway diagram of the clutch mechanism.

Disassembly

1. Remove the clutch cover and disconnect the cable from the lever (**Figure 3**). Remove the mounting screw and clutch case. See **Figure 4**.

2. Refer to **Figure 5**. Unscrew the 4 mounting bolts, then remove the lifter plate and the spring.
3. Remove the locknut (**Figure 6**). Remove the tabbed washer, the spring washer, and the clutch center.
4. Remove friction disc (B) and the outer ring. Refer to **Figure 7**. Remove friction disc (A) and the clutch plates.
5. Remove the clutch washer, pressure plate, and the outer clutch from the main shaft.

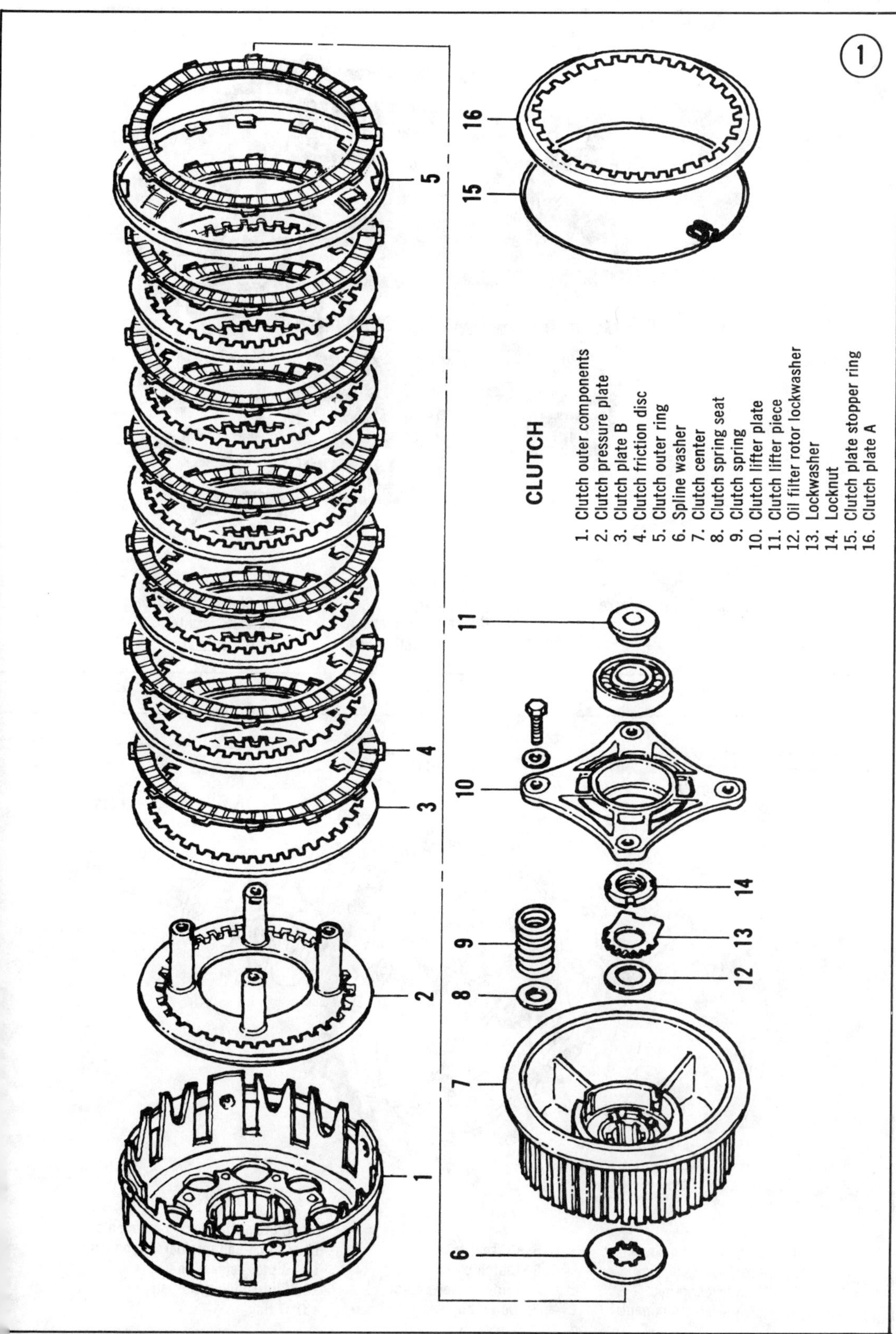
1
CLUTCH
1. Clutch outer components
2. Clutch pressure plate
3. Clutch plate B
4. Clutch friction disc
5. Clutch outer ring
6. Spline washer
7. Clutch center
8. Clutch spring seat
9. Clutch spring
10. Clutch lifter plate
11. Clutch lifter piece
12. Oil filter rotor lockwasher
13. Lockwasher
14. Locknut
15. Clutch plate stopper ring
16. Clutch plate A
5

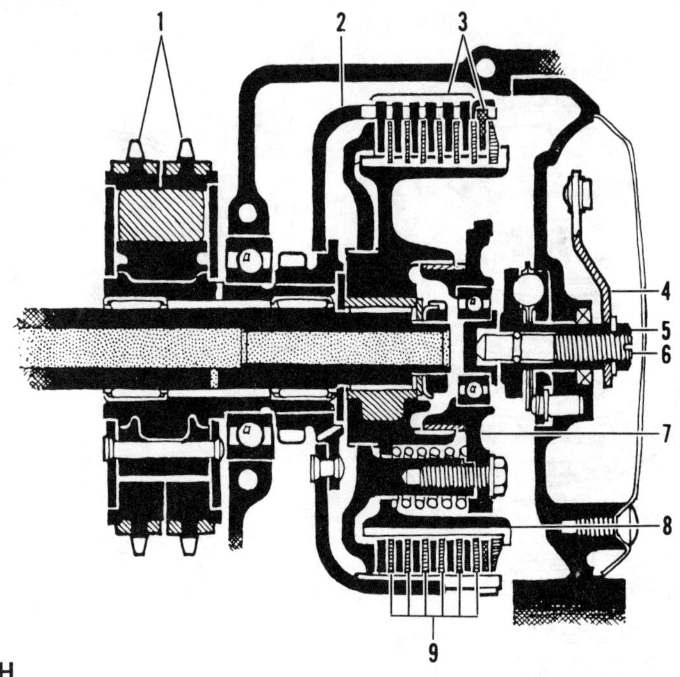

CLUTCH

1. Primary driven sprocket
2. Clutch outer
3. Friction disc
4. Clutch lever
5. Clutch release lever
6. Clutch adjusting bolt
7. Clutch lifter plate
8. Clutch center
9. Clutch plate

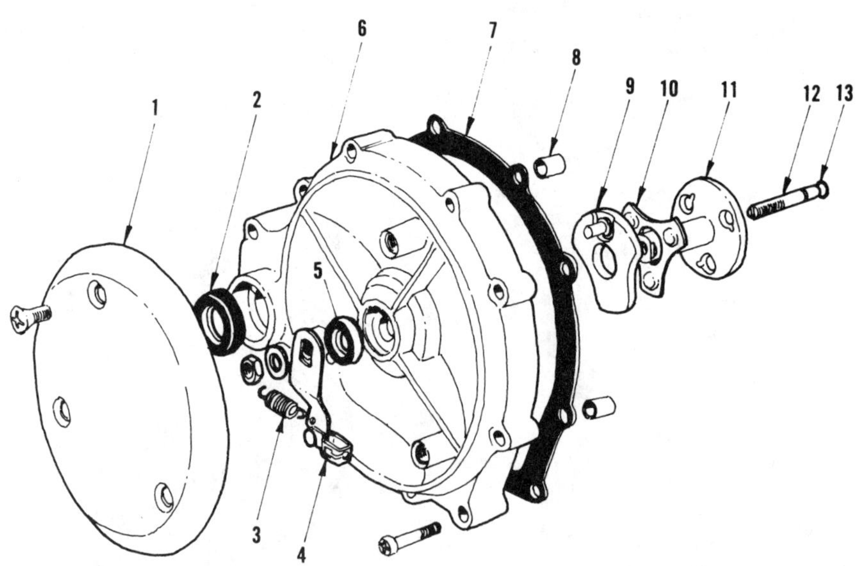

1. Clutch adjusting cover
2. Oil seal
3. Clutch lever spring
4. Clutch lever components
5. Oil seal
6. Clutch cover
7. Clutch cover gasket
8. Dowel pin
9. Clutch lifter cam components
10. Clutch ball retainer components
11. Clutch release shaft
12. Clutch adjusting bolt
13. O-ring

Inspection

1. Use a vernier caliper as shown in **Figure 8** to check the thickness of the friction disc. If the thickness is less than 0.122 in. (3.10mm) the disc should be replaced. Check the trueness of the clutch plate, and replace the disc if the plate is warped more than 0.012 in. (0.3mm).

2. Measure the uncompressed length of clutch springs with a vernier caliper **(Figure 9)**. Replace if length is less than 1.2 in. (30.5mm). All 4 springs should be the same length.

Assembly

1. Put the outer clutch and the spline washer on the main shaft. Then assemble the pressure plate.

2. Install the 6 friction discs (A), the clutch plates, and the clutch center into the outer clutch. Next, install the outer ring, making sure

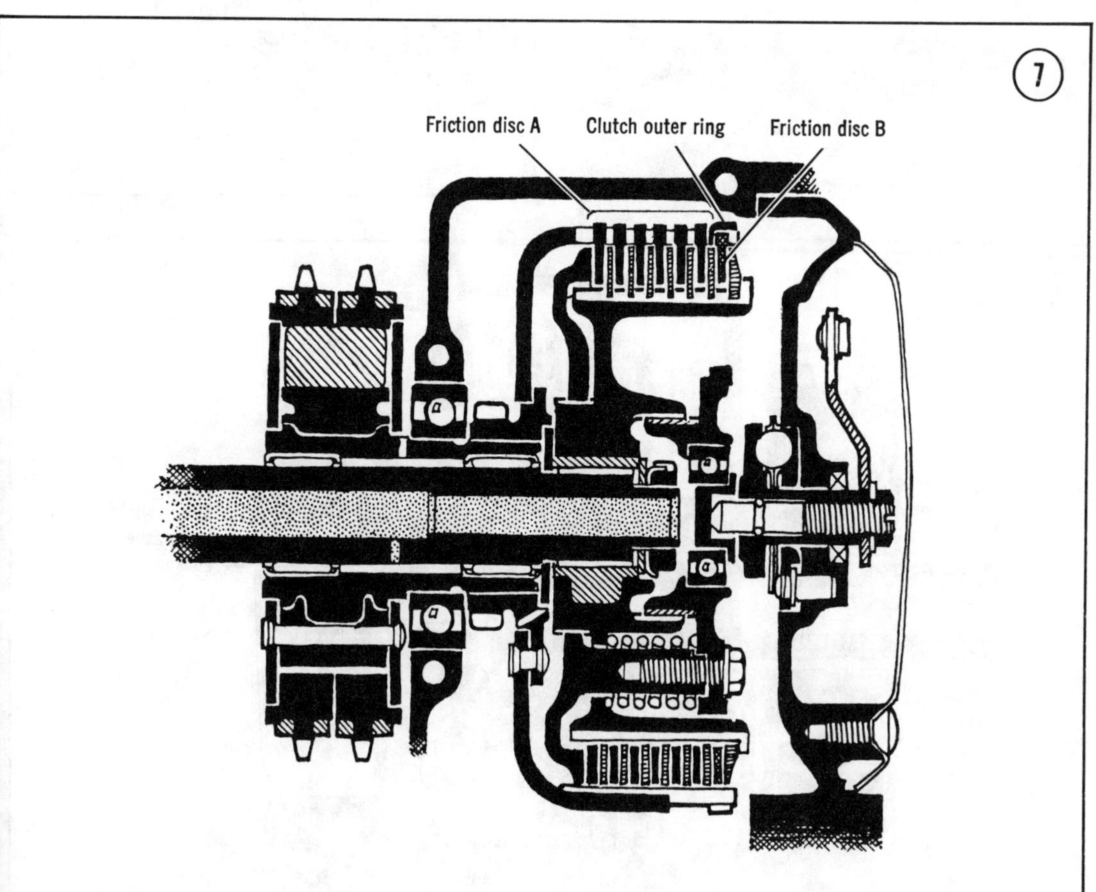

7

Friction disc A
Clutch outer ring
Friction disc B

the tabs are lodged in the friction disc grooves. See **Figure 7**.

3. Install friction disc (B). Refer to **Figure 7**.

4. Assemble the clutch center in the following order, referring to **Figure 10**: spring washer with its tab facing front, lockwasher, and locknut. Torque with the special tool to 32.5-36.2 ft.-lb. (4.5-5 mkg).

5. Assemble the springs, lifter, and bolts. Tighten the bolts progressively, one turn at a time, in a counterclockwise pattern (**Figure 11**), to 6-7 ft.-lb. (8-10 N•m).

6. Refer to the *Clutch* section in Chapter Three for adjustment.

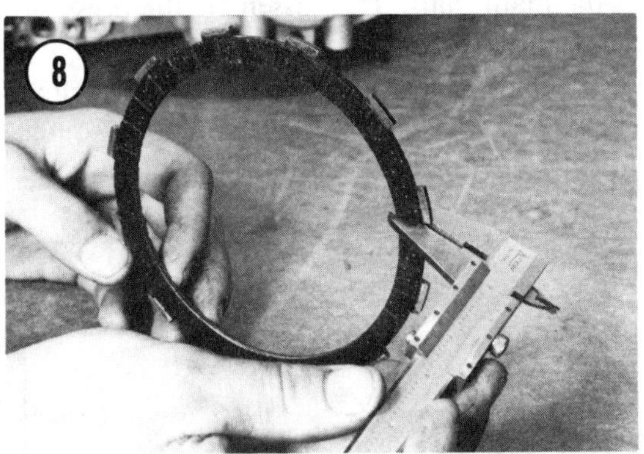

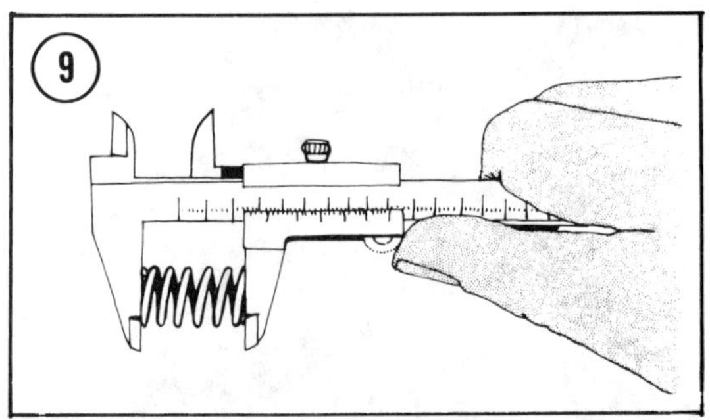

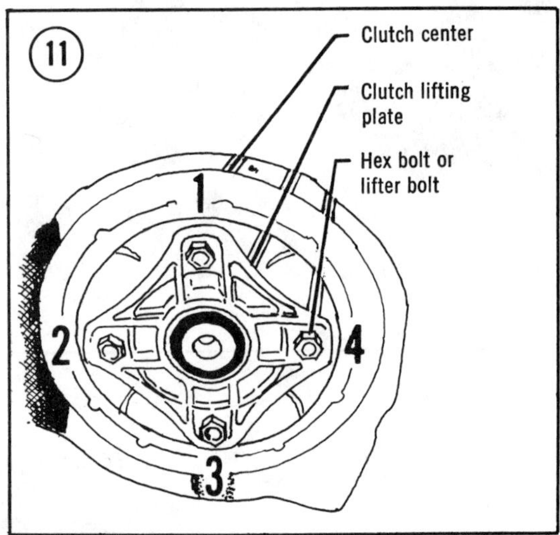

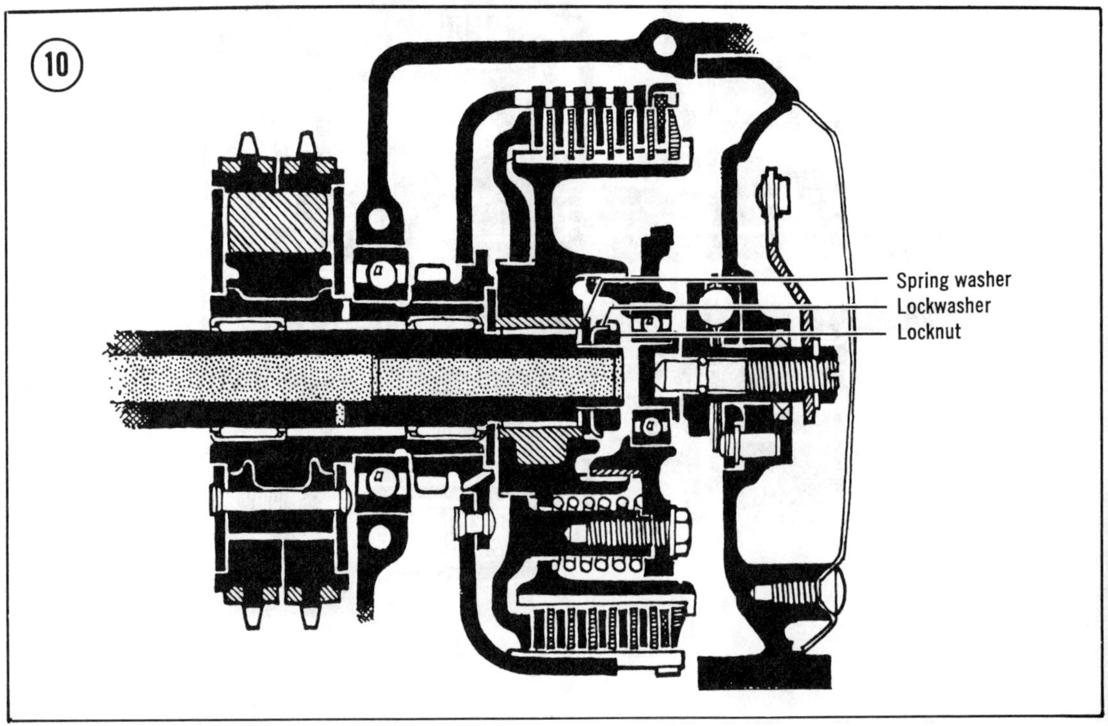

5-SPEED MANUAL TRANSMISSION

The Honda 750 has a constant mesh, 5-speed transmission.

The shift mechanism **(Figure 12)** incorporates 3 forks. When the shift pedal is depressed, the shift spindle rotates, causing the shift arm to turn the drum. The shift forks are moved sideways by the action of the groove cut in the body of the drum.

Disassembly

1. Refer to Chapter Four and remove the following: alternator cover, stator and field, clutch cover, point cover, point plate, gear selector arm, selector positive stopper, drum stopper, selector side plate, and countershaft bearing holder. Unscrew the crankcase bolts (top and bottom), tap along the mating line of the case halves with a soft mallet and separate the cases. Note that it's not necessary to disassemble the upper end.

2. Raise transmission main shaft **(Figure 13)** and remove the primary sprocket and the main shaft gear assembly from the upper crankcase.

3. Remove the oil guide shaft and the final shaft from the upper crankcase, shown in **Figure 14**.

5

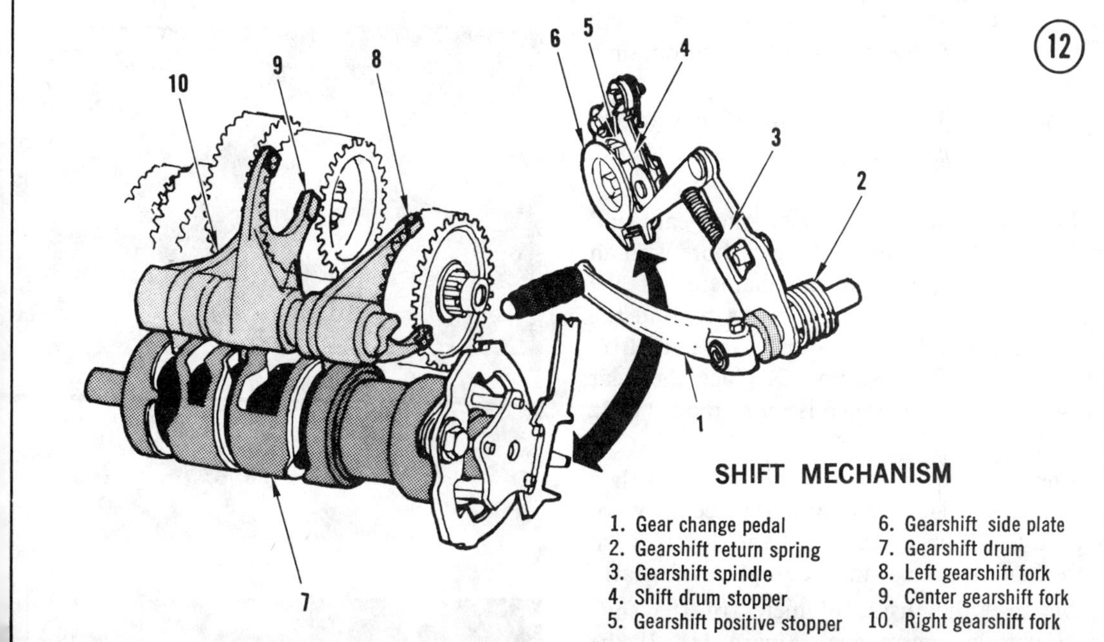

SHIFT MECHANISM

1. Gear change pedal
2. Gearshift return spring
3. Gearshift spindle
4. Shift drum stopper
5. Gearshift positive stopper
6. Gearshift side plate
7. Gearshift drum
8. Left gearshift fork
9. Center gearshift fork
10. Right gearshift fork

4. Pull out the shaft for shift forks **(Figure 15)** and then remove the forks.
5. Remove the neutral stopper bolt and the stopper. Remove the shift drum.
6. Remove top gear **(Figure 16)** from the countershaft and then remove the gear assembly.
7. Use a universal bearing puller to remove the right countershaft bearing from the lower crankcase, shown in **Figure 17**.
8. Refer to **Figure 18** and remove the gears from their shafts.

Inspection

1. Measure gear backlash with a small dial gauge. Place the pointer against the teeth **(Figure 19)**, lock the mating gear, and obtain a reading.
2. Inspect the dogs on the gears. If they are excessively worn or damaged, replace the respective gears.
3. Measure clearance between the gears and their shafts by measuring the gear bore with an inside micrometer, and the diameter of the shaft with a micrometer. Subtract to find the clearance. Standard clearances are 0.0016-0.0032 in. (0.04-0.082mm). Replace the gear and shaft if the clearance is more than 0.0072 in. (0.182mm).
4. Check the tines on the shift forks with a micrometer **(Figure 20)** and replace if worn beyond 0.240 in. (6.1mm). If the dog is worn more than the same standard, replace the gear.
5. Measure the inside diameter of the shift forks with a micrometer **(Figure 21)**. If the

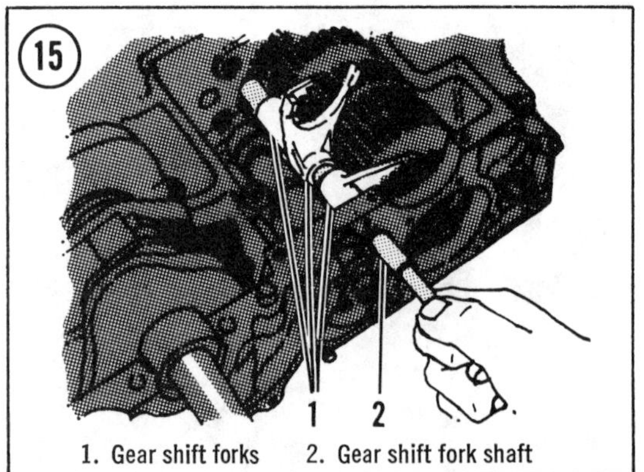

1. Gear shift forks 2. Gear shift fork shaft

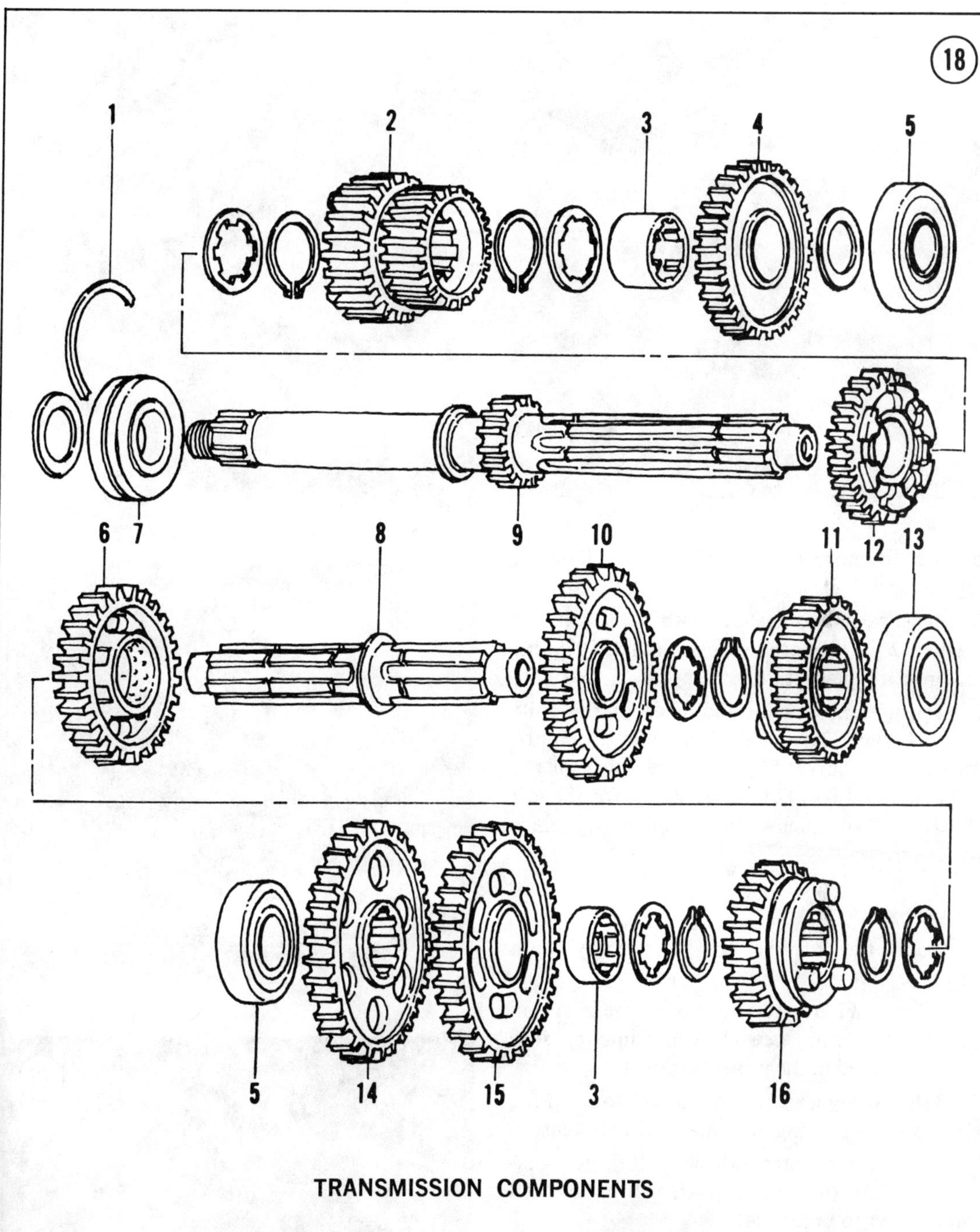

TRANSMISSION COMPONENTS

1. Ball bearing set ring A
2. Main shaft 2nd and 3rd gear
3. Bushing
4. Main shaft top gear
5. Radial ball bearing
6. Countershaft 3rd gear
7. Special ball bearing
8. Transmission countershaft
9. Transmission main shaft
10. Countershaft 2nd gear
11. Countershaft top gear
12. Main shaft 4th gear
13. Ball bearing
14. Final drive gear
15. Countershaft low gear
16. Countershaft 4th gear

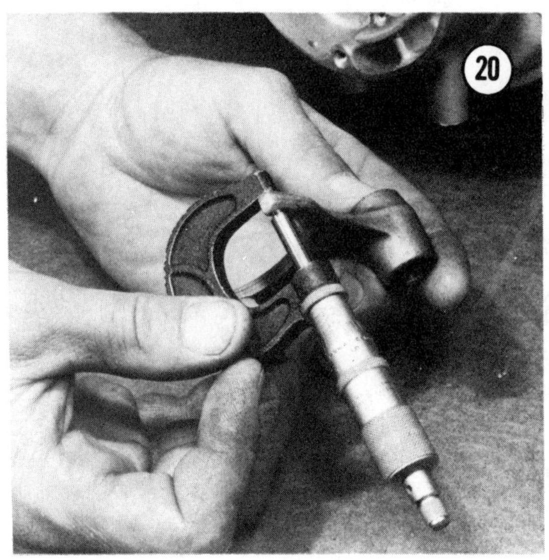

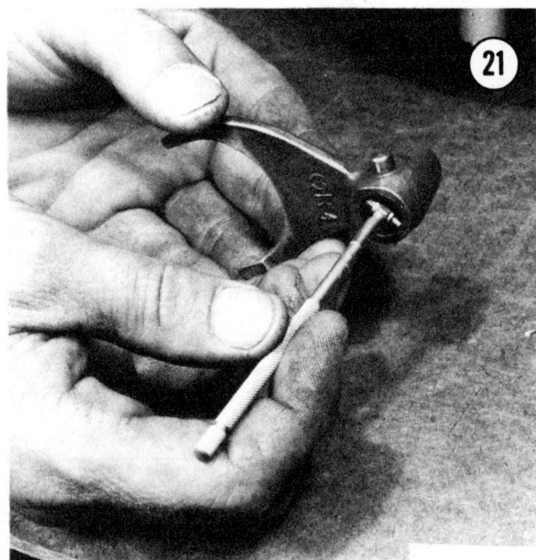

distance is more than 0.5134 in. (13.04mm), replace fork.

6. Measure the fork shaft with a micrometer (**Figure 21**). If worn to less than 0.5079 in. (12.9mm), replace it.

7. Measure the outside diameter of the shift drum (**Figure 22**) with a micrometer. Standard measurements are 0.5154 in. (11.95mm) for the right side and 1.4142 in. (35.92mm) for the left side. If it is worn below these standards, replace the drum.

Assembly

1. Mount the tensioner for the primary chain on the crankcase.

2. Refer to **Figure 18** and mount the gears on their shafts, using new clips and making sure they are seated in the proper grooves.

3. Refer to **Figure 23**. Use a driver to push the countershaft bearing into the lower crankcase.

4. Mount the countershaft with all its gears except for fifth (top) gear which will be inserted later. Refer to **Figure 24**.

5. Mount the shift drum and install the neutral stopper with its bolt. The depression on the drum is the neutral position.

6. Assemble the shift forks as in **Figure 25**. The letters, "R," "C," and "L," are stamped on the sides. Forks R and L are fitted into the fourth and fifth gears on the countershaft, while fork C is used with the main shaft's sec-

ond and third gears. The dog on the back of this fork fits into the groove on the shift drum.

7. Refer to **Figure 26** and install the final shaft assembly into the upper crankcase. Make sure to install the set ring. Install the final shaft oil guide.

8. Mount the primary sprocket on the main shaft assembly, and install the unit in the upper crankcase.

9. Install the 2 dowel pins, the oil collar, and the O-ring in the upper crankcase. Smear Permatex on the flange, and assemble lower crankcase.

> NOTE: *Make sure that the transmission is in* NEUTRAL, *with the center fork between second and third gears on the main shaft.*

10. Install the crankcase, cam chain tensioner, pistons, and cylinder head.

AUTOMATIC TRANSMISSION (CB750A)

The CB750A uses the 2-speed Hondamatic transmission. Service procedures are described below.

Torque Converter Removal/Installation

1. Remove foot pegs and brake pedal.
2. Remove the protector cover by unscrewing the single screw at the bottom of the cover. See **Figure 27**.
3. Remove the case cap. Be careful that the check valve and spring are not lost. Replace the gasket during installation.
4. Remove the torque converter case.
5. Use a universal puller to remove the torque converter assembly. A block of wood or a bearing driver can be used for installation. Do not try to disassemble and repair the unit yourself. This requires the tools and skill of an expert.
6. Installation is the reverse procedure of removal.

Oil Pump Removal/Installation

1. Remove the 3 screws attaching the left side case and remove case assembly. See **Figure 28**.
2. Remove oil pump assembly. See **Figure 29**.
3. Peel off the case gasket. Replace the old gasket with a new one during assembly.
4. Pull out the oil passage pipe.
5. Reverse the procedure to install.

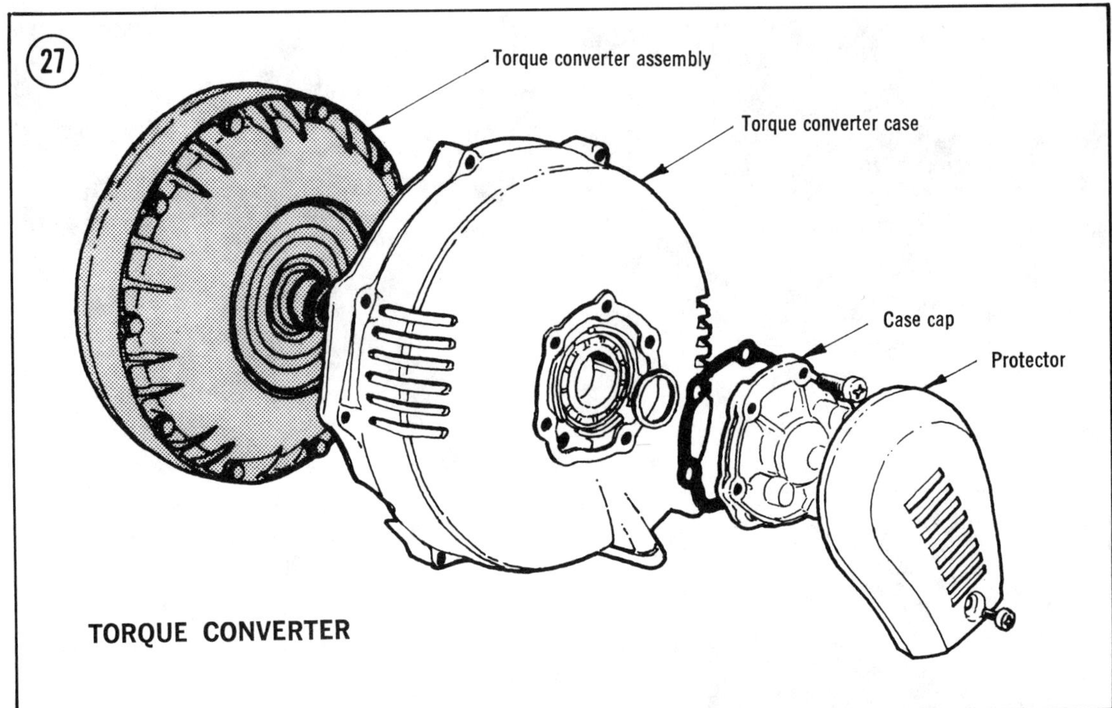

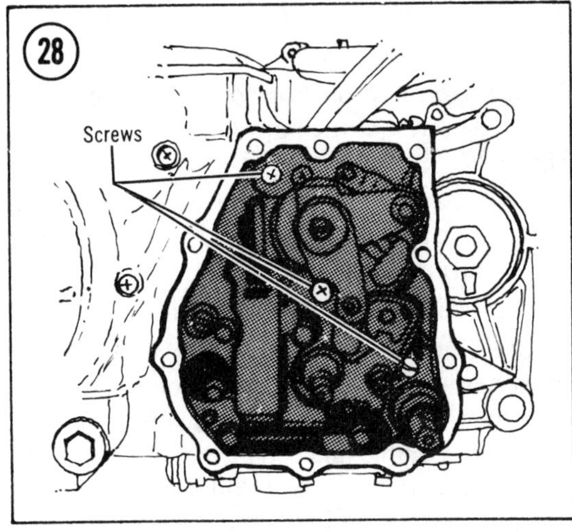

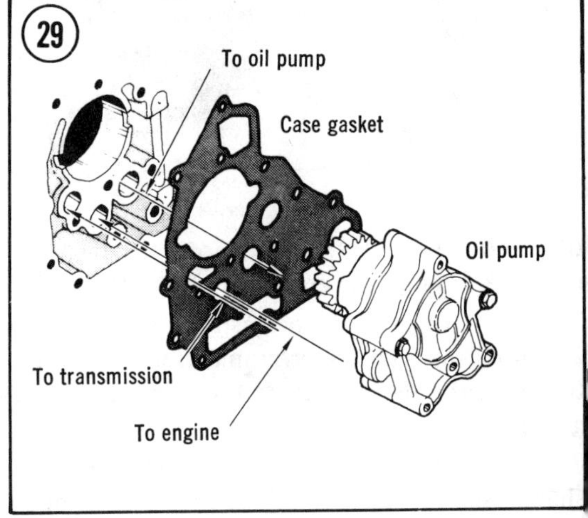

Oil Pump Disassembly/Assembly

1. Remove the 2 oil pump cover bolts. See **Figure 30**.
2. Remove the oil pump cover.
3. Slide the outer rotor off of the inner rotor and remove the pin from the inner rotor. Slide the inner rotor off of the oil pump shaft.
4. Remove oil pump body "B" and repeat Step 3.
5. Reverse the procedure to assemble.

Oil Pump Inspection

1. Measure oil pump body clearance to rotor Maximum allowable for either section is 0.013 in. (0.35mm).
2. Measure inner rotor tip to outer roto clearance at the tightest point. Maximum clear ance is 0.0079 in. (0.20mm).
3. Measure rotor surface to oil pump bod clearance. Maximum allowable is 0.0031 in (0.08mm) for either segment.

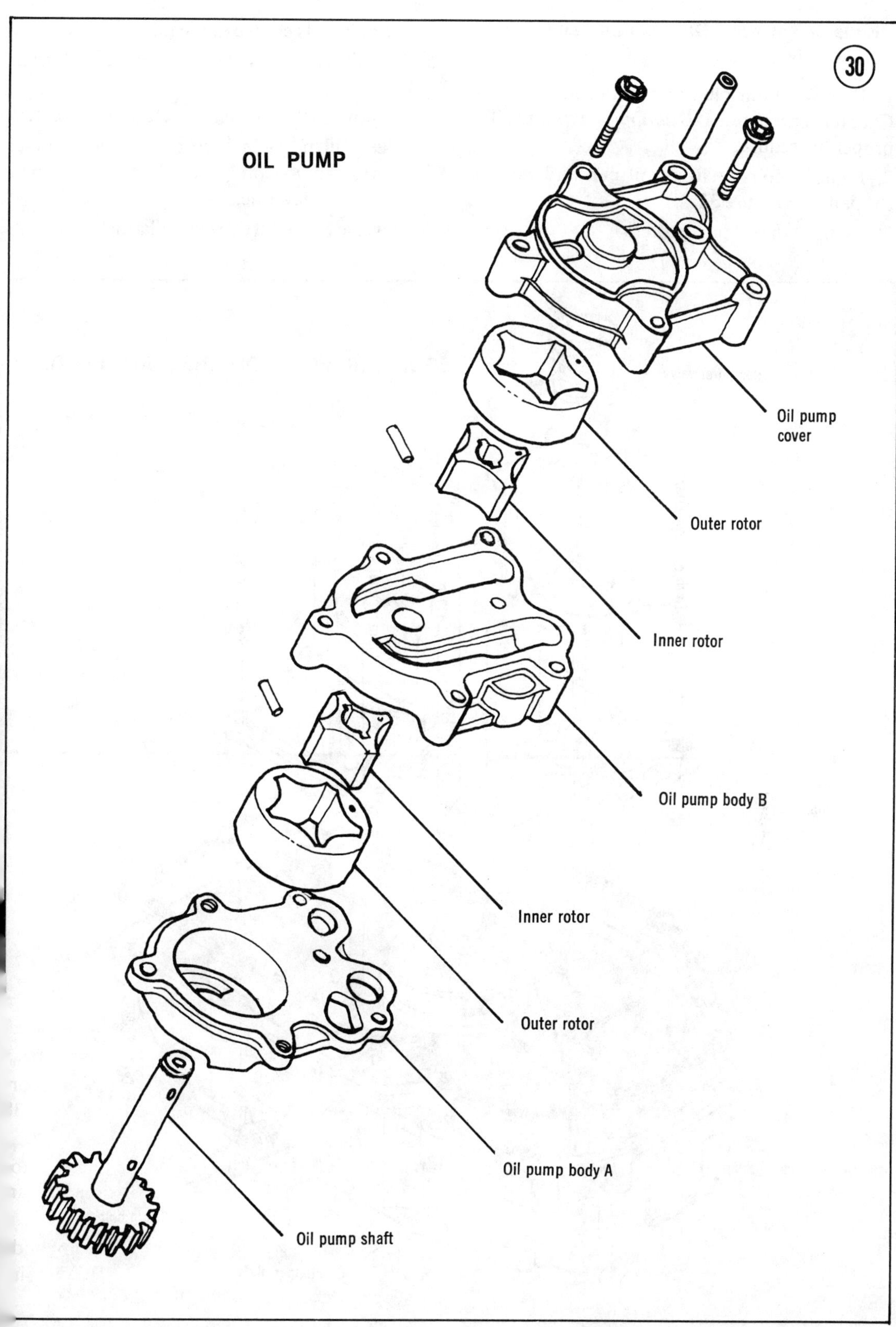
30
OIL PUMP
Oil pump cover
Outer rotor
Inner rotor
Oil pump body B
Inner rotor
Outer rotor
Oil pump body A
Oil pump shaft

5

Regulator Valve and Distribution Plate Removal/Installation

1. Remove drain plug and drain oil. Refer to Chapter Three under *Draining Engine Oil* for proper procedure.
2. Remove bolts securing oil pan and remove the pan. See **Figure 31**.
3. Remove the oil pan gasket.
4. Unbolt and remove the regulator valve.
5. Unbolt and remove the oil distribution plate.
6. Remove the oil screen and clean in solvent.
7. Clean all parts in kerosene or clean diesel fuel prior to assembly. Replace the oil pan gasket with a new one.
8. Reverse procedure for installation.

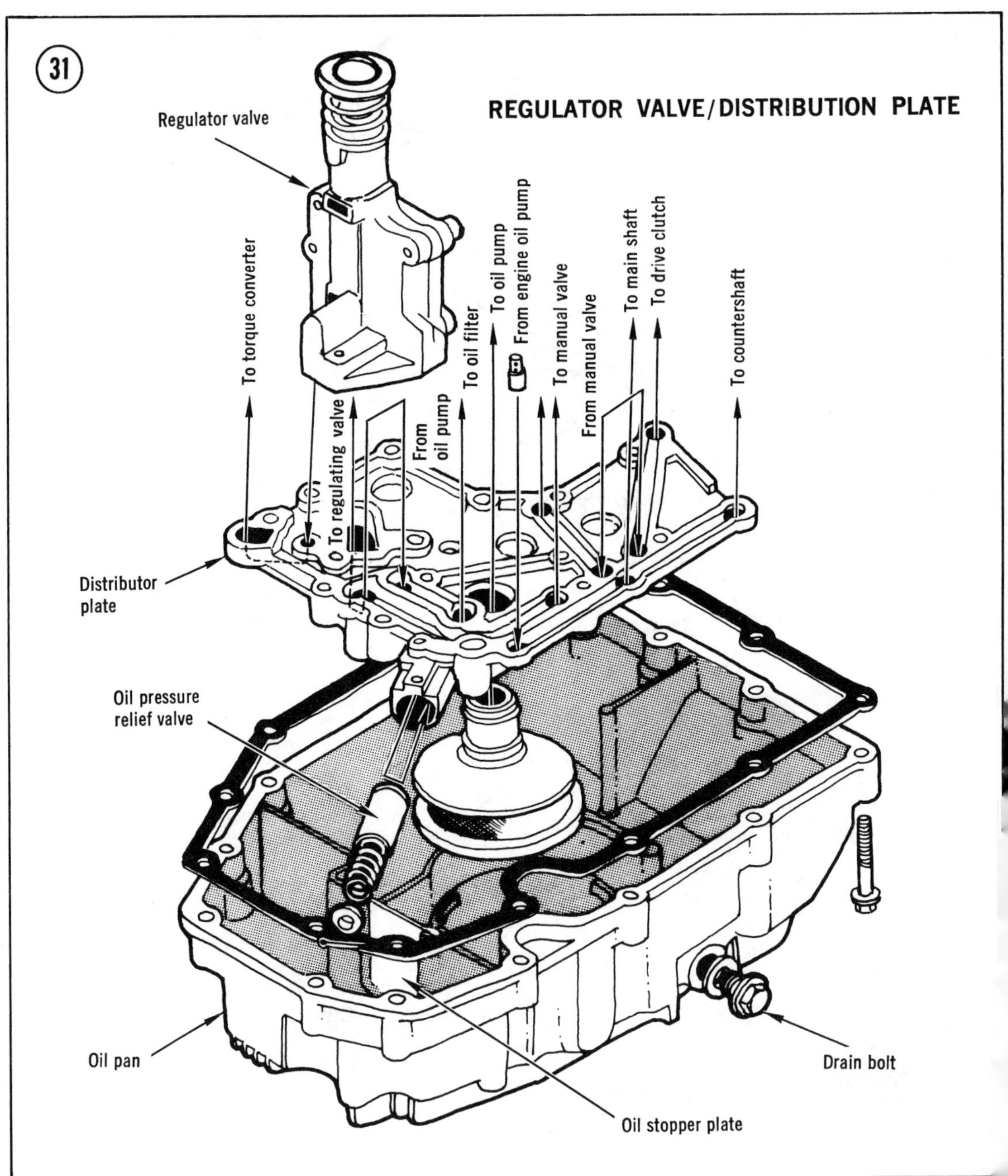

Shift Mechanism Disassembly/Assembly

1. Remove shift pedal, neutral return arm, and cover.
2. Remove gear shift inner actuator and outer housing as a unit. Refer to **Figure 32**.
3. Remove neutral spindle and spring.
4. Remove shift spindle and spring from case.
5. Remove neutral select arm and gearshift pivot shaft.
6. Unbolt and remove ratchet guide, shift stopper arm, and spring.
7. Remove gear indicator switch.
8. Unbolt and remove the manual valve.
9. Reverse procedure for assembly.

Transmission Removal/Installation

1. Remove the cylinder head, pistons, cam chain tensioner, and crankcase as described in Chapter Four.
2. Remove the torque converter, oil pump, shift mechanism, and regulator valve and distribution plate as described in this chapter.
3. Raise transmission main shaft and remove the primary sprocket and main shaft gear assembly from the crankcase.
4. Remove the stator and input shafts as complete assemblies.
5. Remove the countershaft and gears as a complete assembly.

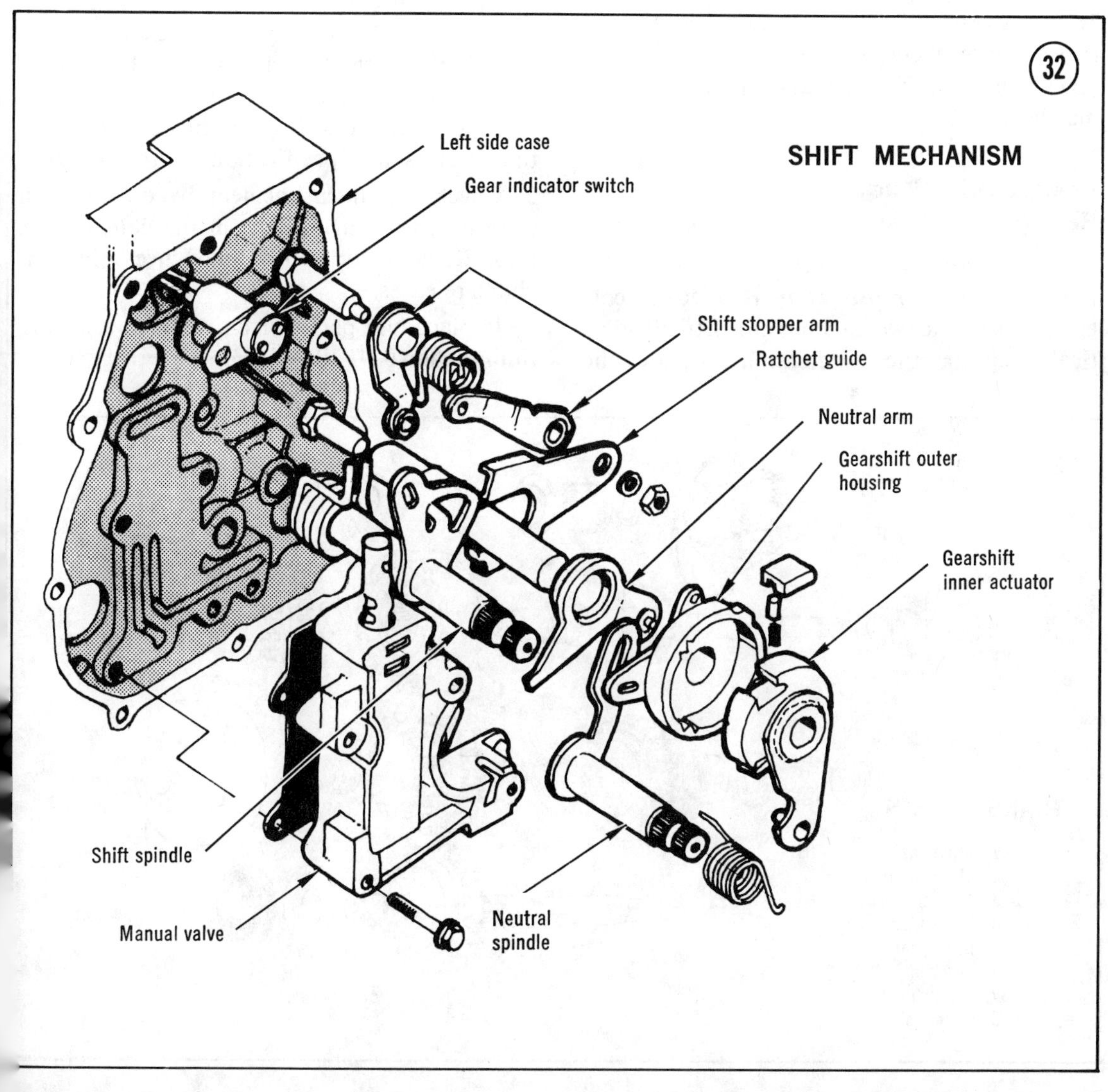

6. Refer to **Figure 33** and remove the gears and drive clutches from their respective shafts if necessary for repair or replacement.

7. Reverse procedure to install. Coat all moving parts with regular motor oil prior to assembly.

Transmission Inspection

1. Measure gear backlash with a small dial gauge. Place the pointer against the gear teeth and set the gauge on zero.

2. Lock the mating gear with each gear being tested, and rock back and forth. Add the 2 readings thus obtained or reset the gauge at one extreme and read at the opposite extreme. Maximum allowable backlash is 0.008 in. (0.2mm).

3. Inspect the dogs on each gear. Replace if they are excessively worn or damaged. Usually, you will have to replace gears in pairs with their match.

Low and Drive Clutch Removal/Installation

Refer to *Removal/Installation* procedure for the *Automatic Transmission (CB750A)*, covered earlier. The two clutches are virtually identical except that the LOW clutch has 4 plates and discs while the DRIVE clutch has 6 of each. See **Figure 34**.

Low and Drive Clutch Disassembly/Assembly

1. Use a pair of sockets, a bolt, and a nut to compress the return spring.

2. Remove the snap rings.

3. Remove the clutch piston, plates, and discs.

4. Replace the O-ring and oil seal rings during assembly.

5. Reverse the procedure for assembly.

Low and Drive Clutch Inspection

1. Replace any plates or discs which are worn, glazed, or warped.

2. Measure the clearance between the clutch end plate and the top clutch disc. If the clearance is more than 0.0317 in. (0.8mm), obtain a new clutch end plate of the thickness required to bring this into specification.

3. Check clutch engagement by directing air pressure to an oil passage in the clutch drum hub. Remove air source and check that the clutch releases.

4. Replace any plates or discs which are worn thinner than 0.075 in. (1.9mm).

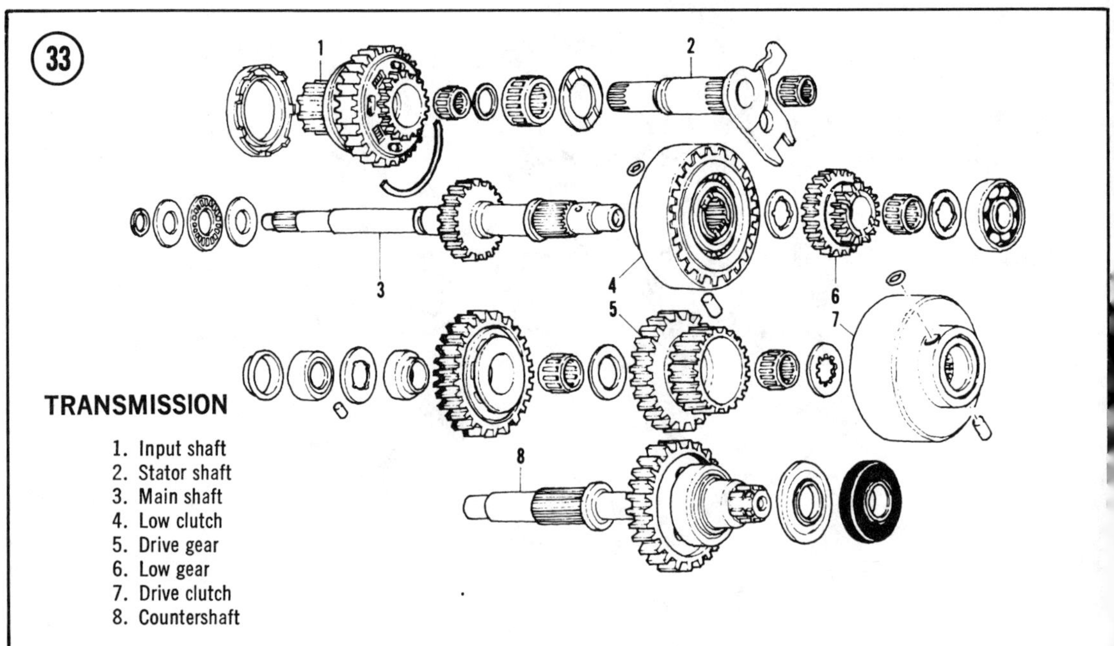

TRANSMISSION

1. Input shaft
2. Stator shaft
3. Main shaft
4. Low clutch
5. Drive gear
6. Low gear
7. Drive clutch
8. Countershaft

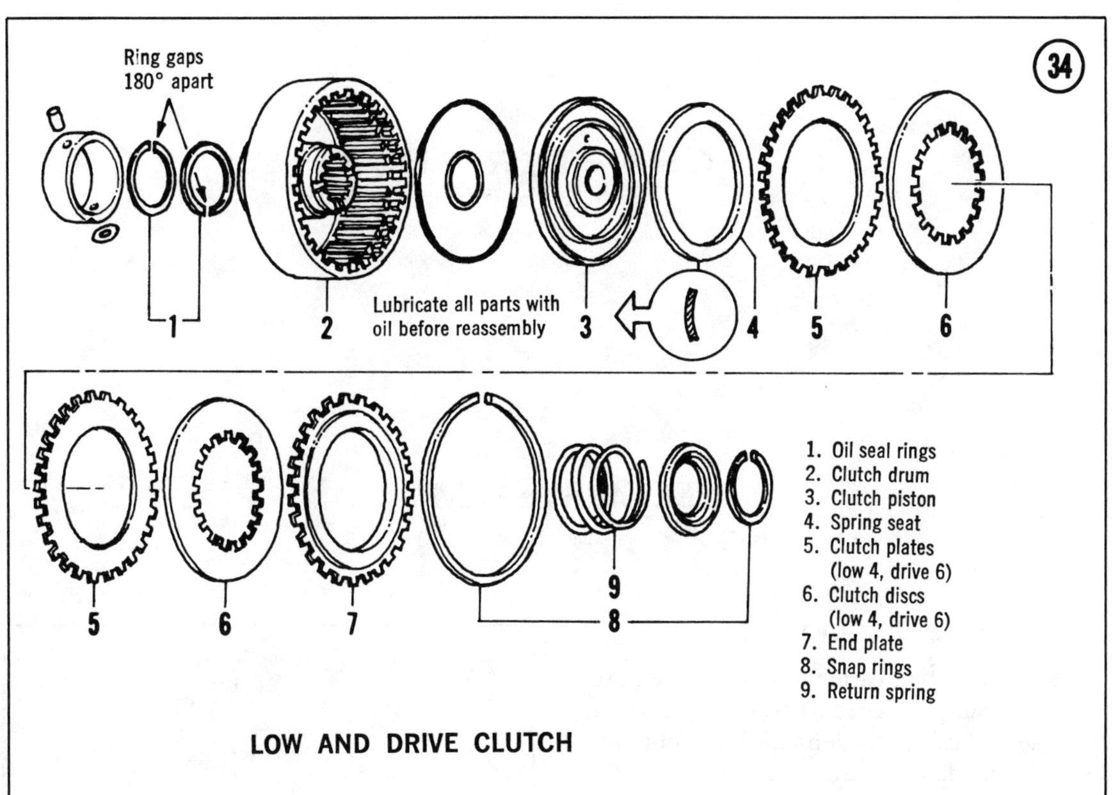

LOW AND DRIVE CLUTCH

CHAPTER SIX

FUEL SYSTEM

CARBURETORS

Several different carburetors have been used on the Honda 750. The earliest carburetors had a single pull cable. All subsequent carburetors, from K1 models on, use a 2-cable system that positively closes as well as opens the slides. The earliest version of this system employed a lifter assembly that was external to the carburetor. Carburetors for K7/8, A, and F models have an internal lifter and the system is equipped with an accelerator pump in the No. 2 carburetor that is actuated by a solenoid.

Routine adjustment procedures are covered in Chapter Three under *Carburetion*. This chapter covers disassembly and inspection.

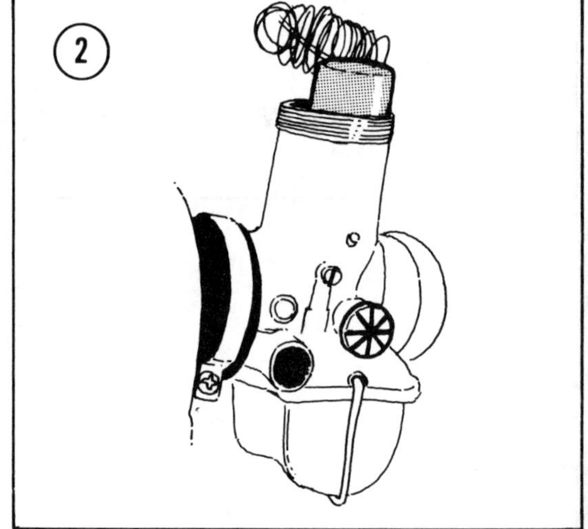

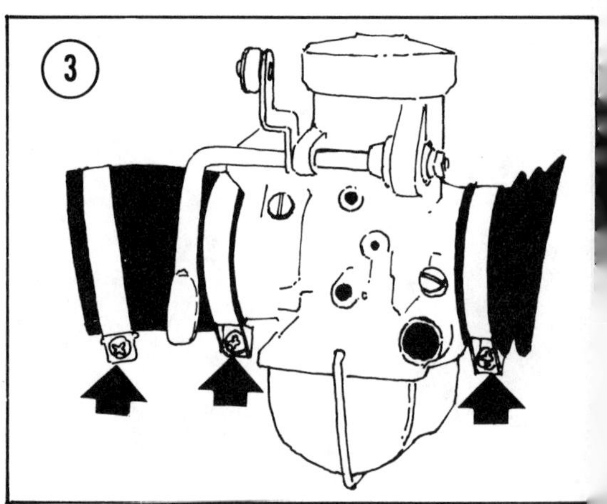

CB750 Removal/Disassembly

Figure 1 shows the major parts of the CB750 carburetor. Refer to it while performing the following operations:

1. Remove the fuel tank.
2. Remove the throttle valve (**Figure 2**) from each of the carburetors.
3. Remove the insulating and connecting bands (**Figure 3**) and then remove 4 carburetors as an assembly.
4. Refer to **Figure 4**. Remove the carburetors from the mounting plate by unscrewing the screws; 2 for each carburetor. Separate by disconnecting individual choke rods.

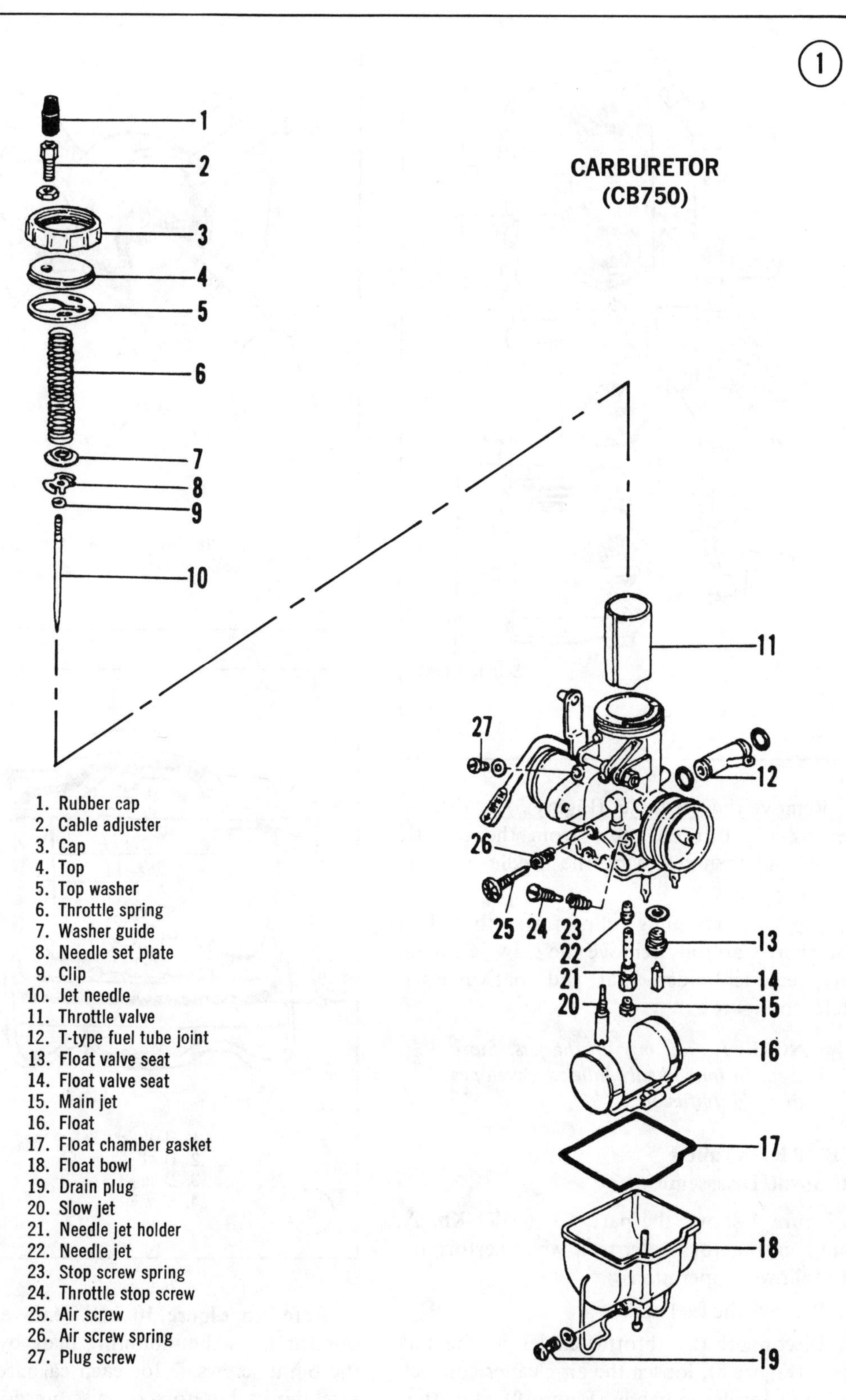
1
CARBURETOR
(CB750)
1
2
3
4
5
6
7
8
9
10
11
27
12
26
25 24 23
22
13
21
14
20
15
16
17
18
19
1. Rubber cap
2. Cable adjuster
3. Cap
4. Top
5. Top washer
6. Throttle spring
7. Washer guide
8. Needle set plate
9. Clip
10. Jet needle
11. Throttle valve
12. T-type fuel tube joint
13. Float valve seat
14. Float valve seat
15. Main jet
16. Float
17. Float chamber gasket
18. Float bowl
19. Drain plug
20. Slow jet
21. Needle jet holder
22. Needle jet
23. Stop screw spring
24. Throttle stop screw
25. Air screw
26. Air screw spring
27. Plug screw

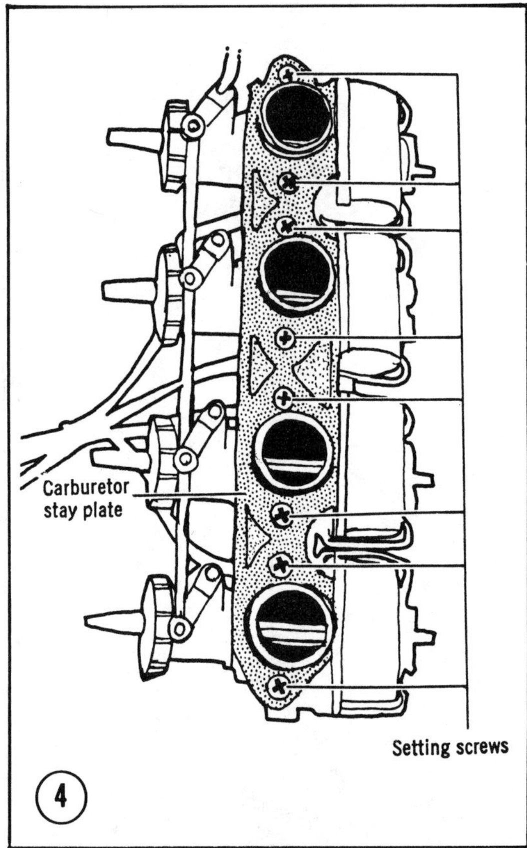

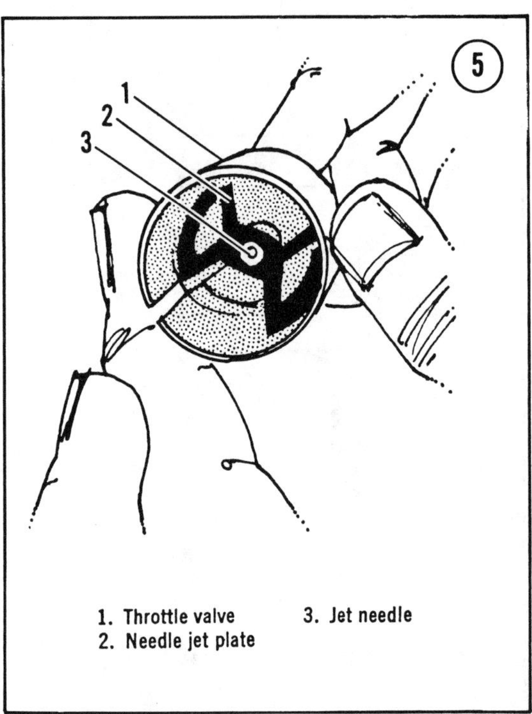

1. Throttle valve
2. Needle jet plate
3. Jet needle

5. Remove the needle jet (**Figure 5**) by disconnecting the throttle cable from the throttle valve, and then removing the needle jet plate from the valve.

6. Slip the retaining clip from the float chamber. Carefully remove the slow jet, main jet, needle jet holder, float, and float valve set. Refer to **Figure 6**.

> NOTE: *Do not mix up the jets. Store them in individually labeled envelopes to avoid confusion.*

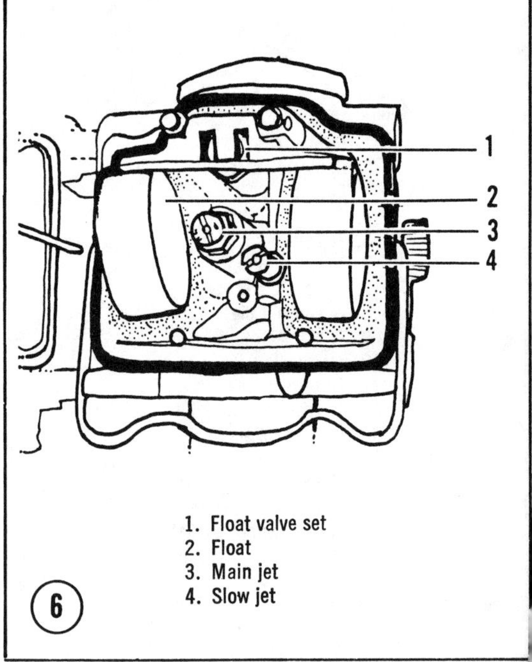

1. Float valve set
2. Float
3. Main jet
4. Slow jet

CB750 K1-K6 and F Removal/Disassembly

Figure 7 shows the parts of the K1-K6, A, and F carburetor. Refer to it while performing the following operations.

1. Remove the fuel tank.

2. Disconnect the throttle cables at the link lever (**Figure 8**), loosen the air cleaner connecting and insulator bands (**Figure 9**), and then remove the carburetors as an assembly.

3. Refer to **Figure 10** and remove each carburetor from the mounting plate by removing the 6mm screws, 2 for each carburetor. Separate the carburetors by disconnecting the individual choke rods.

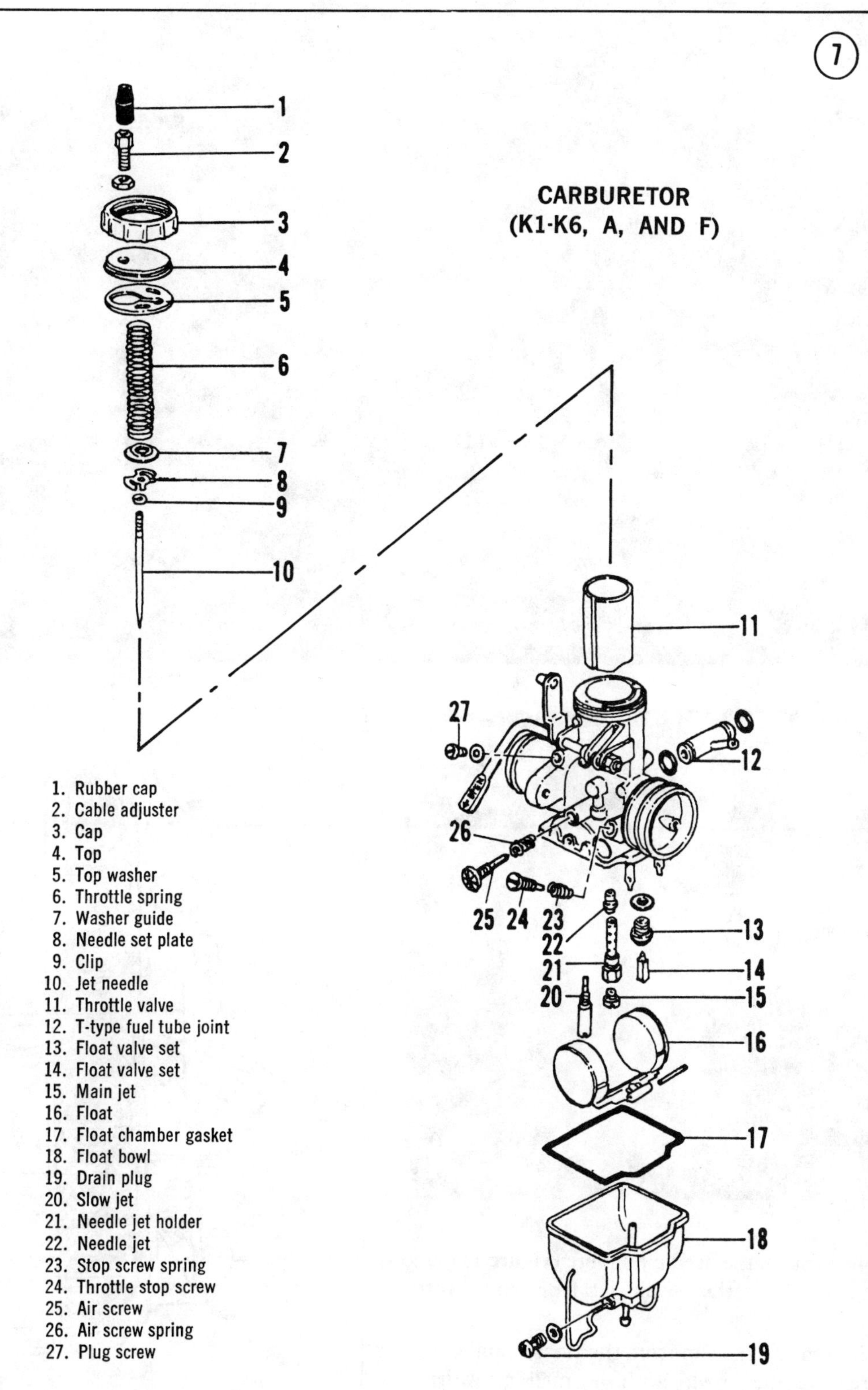
7
CARBURETOR
(K1-K6, A, AND F)
1
2
3
4
5
6
7
8
9
10
11
12
13
14
15
16
17
18
19
20
21
22
23
24
25
26
27
1. Rubber cap
2. Cable adjuster
3. Cap
4. Top
5. Top washer
6. Throttle spring
7. Washer guide
8. Needle set plate
9. Clip
10. Jet needle
11. Throttle valve
12. T-type fuel tube joint
13. Float valve set
14. Float valve set
15. Main jet
16. Float
17. Float chamber gasket
18. Float bowl
19. Drain plug
20. Slow jet
21. Needle jet holder
22. Needle jet
23. Stop screw spring
24. Throttle stop screw
25. Air screw
26. Air screw spring
27. Plug screw

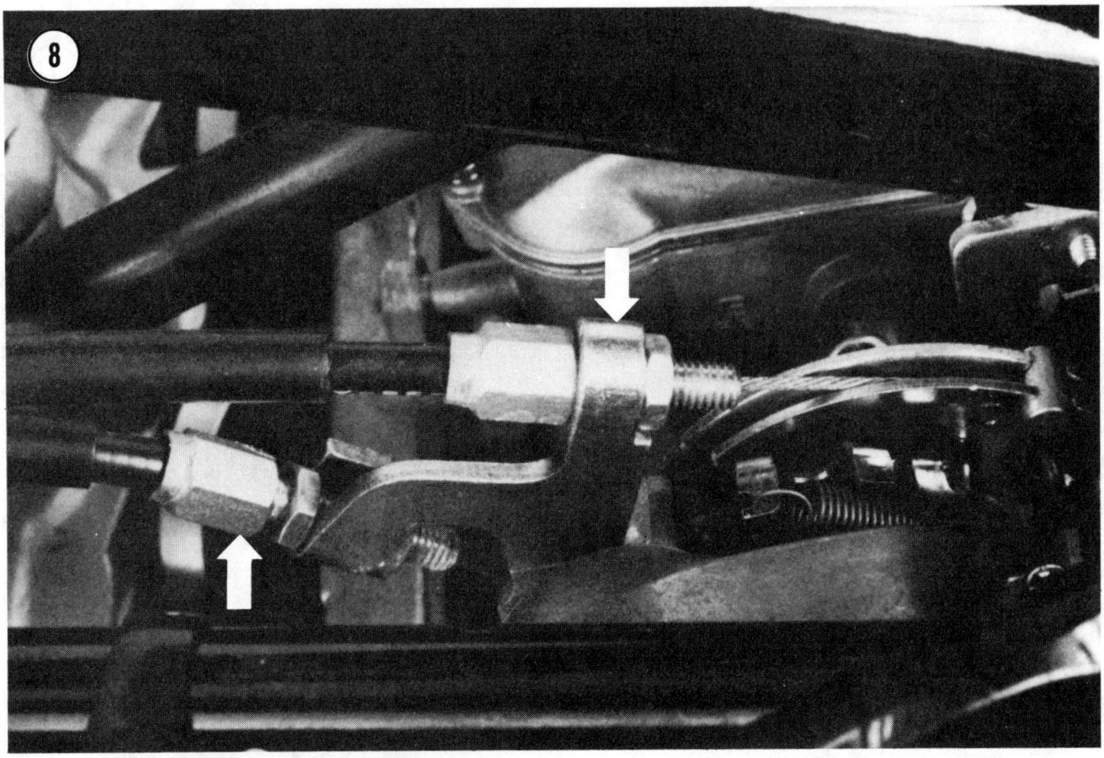

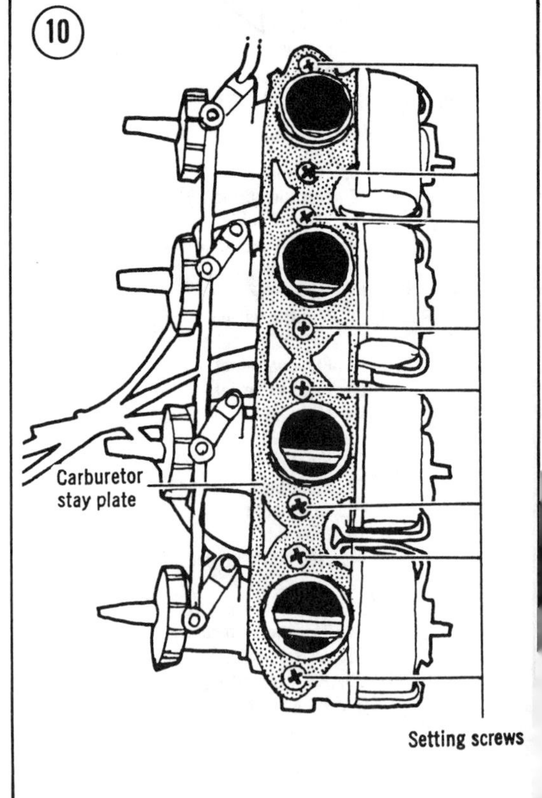

4. Remove the needle jet plate (**Figure 11**), and then remove the needle jet from the throttle valve.

5. Remove the clip from the float chamber and remove the bowl. With a small screwdriver (**Figure 12**), remove slow jet, main jet, needle jet holder, float, and float valve set.

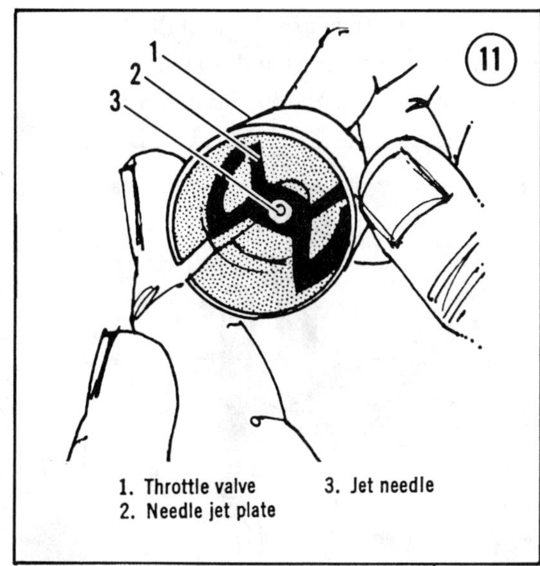

1. Throttle valve
2. Needle jet plate
3. Jet needle

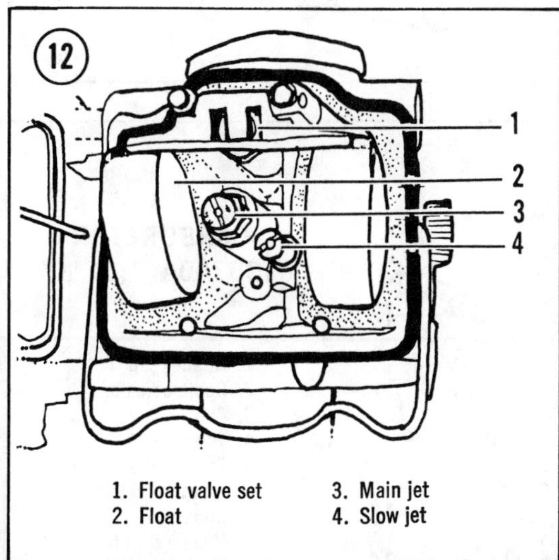

1. Float valve set
2. Float
3. Main jet
4. Slow jet

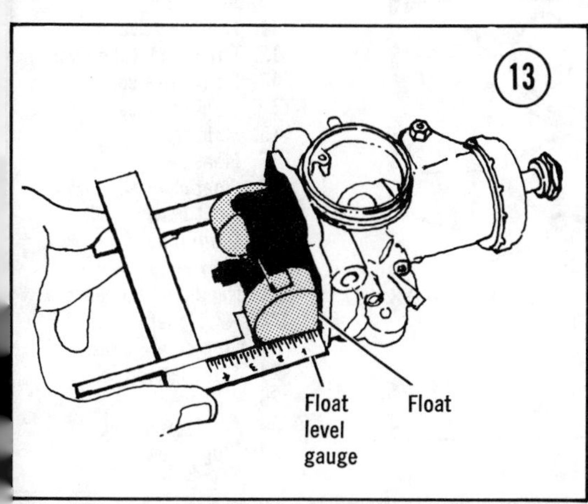

NOTE: *To avoid mixing up jets, store them in individually labeled envelopes.*

CB750, CB750 K1-K6 and F Inspection and Adjustment

1. Check the float level as described in this chapter under *Float Level*. The height of the float above the carburetor body should be 1.023 in. (26mm). Adjust by bending the float arm with a narrow screwdriver. See **Figure 13**.
2. Check the needle jet and its valve for wear. The needle moves constantly during operation, and if excessively worn it should be replaced.
3. Clean each jet by blowing out with compressed air. Never use a wire to poke dirt from the jets. A straw from a broom is permissible.
4. Clean metal parts, except carburetor body, in carburetor cleaner and blow dry with compressed air.

CAUTION

Non-metal parts may dissolve in carburetor cleaner. The plastic piston guide in the carburetor body will dissolve in these cleaners and is not available as a replacement part. If you accidentally destroy the guide, try running the engine without it before buying a new body.

CB750, CB750 K1-K6 and F Assembly/Installation

Assemble in reverse order of disassembly. Be careful not to overtighten jets.

CB750A and K Removal

1. Remove the fuel tank.
2. Disconnect throttle cables at link lever.
3. Loosen the air cleaner connecting and insulator bands and remove the carburetors as an assembly.
4. Unhook the throttle return spring from the throttle link lever. Be careful not to damage the hook.
5. Separate adjuster holders from the link arm.
6. Remove each of the carburetors from the mounting plate by removing the screws. Disconnect the connections for the accelerator pump on the No. 2 carburetor. Disconnect the interconnecting fuel lines from carburetor to carburetor.

6

CB750A and K Disassembly

Refer to **Figures 14 and 15** for the following procedure.

1. Remove the tops of each carburetor by unscrewing the 2 mounting screws.
2. Remove the valve plate by loosening the screw and turning the plate 90° in either direction so that the tab is aligned with the groove in the shaft.
3. Remove the needle from the throttle valve. Handle the needle carefully to avoid damage.
4. Remove the adjusting screw from the holder.
5. Remove float chamber by removing the 3 mounting screws.
6. Refer to **Figure 14** for the location of the components in the accelerator pump in the float chamber of the No. 2 carburetor. Remove the circlip to remove the pump rod arm and plunger.
7. Remove the float arm pin and float.
8. Remove the main jet and slow jet.
9. Remove the clip and the float valve seat.

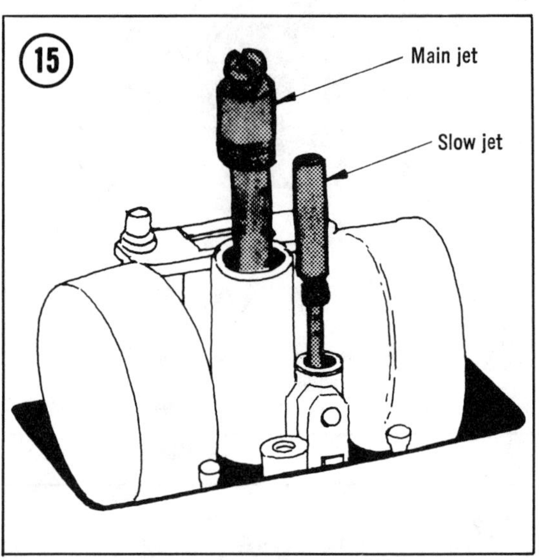

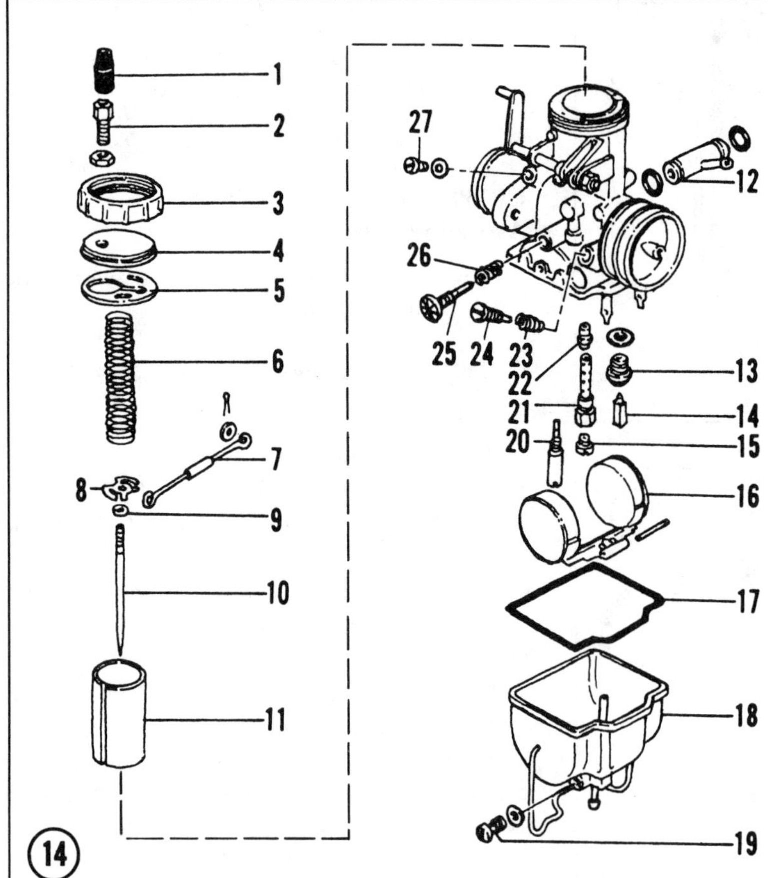

CARBURETOR (CB750A AND K)

1. Rubber cap
2. Cable adjuster
3. Cap
4. Top
5. Top washer
6. Throttle spring
7. Choke rod
8. Needle set plate
9. Clip
10. Jet needle
11. Throttle valve
12. T-type fuel tube joint
13. Float valve seat
14. Float valve seat
15. Main jet
16. Float
17. Float chamber gasket
18. Float bowl
19. Drain plug
20. Slow jet
21. Needle jet holder
22. Needle jet
23. Stop screw spring
24. Throttle stop screw
25. Air screw
26. Air screw spring
27. Plug screw

CB750A and K Assembly/Installation

Reverse procedure to assemble and install.

Inspection/Cleaning

1. Blow out the jets and passages with compressed air.
2. Clean all parts in carburetor cleaner and blow dry.

CAUTION
Non-metal parts may dissolve in carburetor cleaner. Clean all of these parts in clean kerosene or diesel fuel.

3. Check and adjust the float level as described in this chapter under *Float Level*.
4. Check the needle jet and its valve for wear and replace if necessary.

Float Level Adjustment (CB750, CB750 K1-K6, and A)

The procedures for cleaning carburetor float bowls and adjusting float levels, apply to all models.

Honda sells a special gauge to set the float level (tool No. 07144-99962).

1. Remove float bowls by slipping the snap ring toward the front of the engine.

NOTE: *Remove carefully. The bowls will contain gasoline. Be sure not to damage the floats or the float valves.*

2. Check float bowls for sediment, and wash out with kerosene.
3. Use the gauge to check the float setting. It should be 1.023 in. (26mm), measured from the base of the carburetor to the bottom edge of the float, for all models except the CB750A. Set the CB750A float at 0.571 in. (14.5mm).

NOTE: *The measurement should be taken when the float arm is just barely touching the valve, but not compressing the valve spring.*

4. Adjust the setting if necessary by carefully bending the float arm tab that contacts the valve. Use a narrow, flat-blade screwdriver. At the correct setting, the float should just barely touch the gauge.
5. Repeat the inspection and adjustment operations on all 4 carburetors.
6. Replace the bowls and gaskets, making sure the bowl lips are seated properly and that the clips are secure.

Accelerator Pump Removal/Installation (CB750A)

Half of this system is built into the float chamber and body of the No. 2 carburetor. Refer to procedures for the carburetor CB750A for the diaphragm, plunger, rod, and spring.

1. Remove fuel lines. Refer to **Figure 16**.

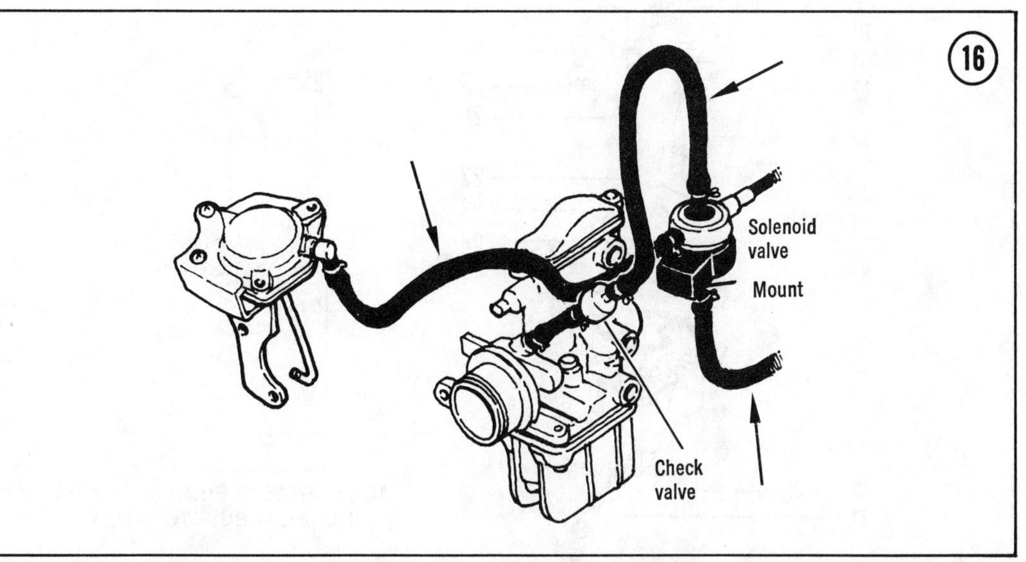

2. Remove the check valve
3. Remove the valve and mount.
4. Reverse the procedure for installation
5. Refer to Chapter Three under *Accelerating Pump* for Adjustments.

CB750 K7/8, F2/3
Removal/Disassembly

The carburetor is show in **Figure 17**. Refer to this illustration for the procedure that follows.

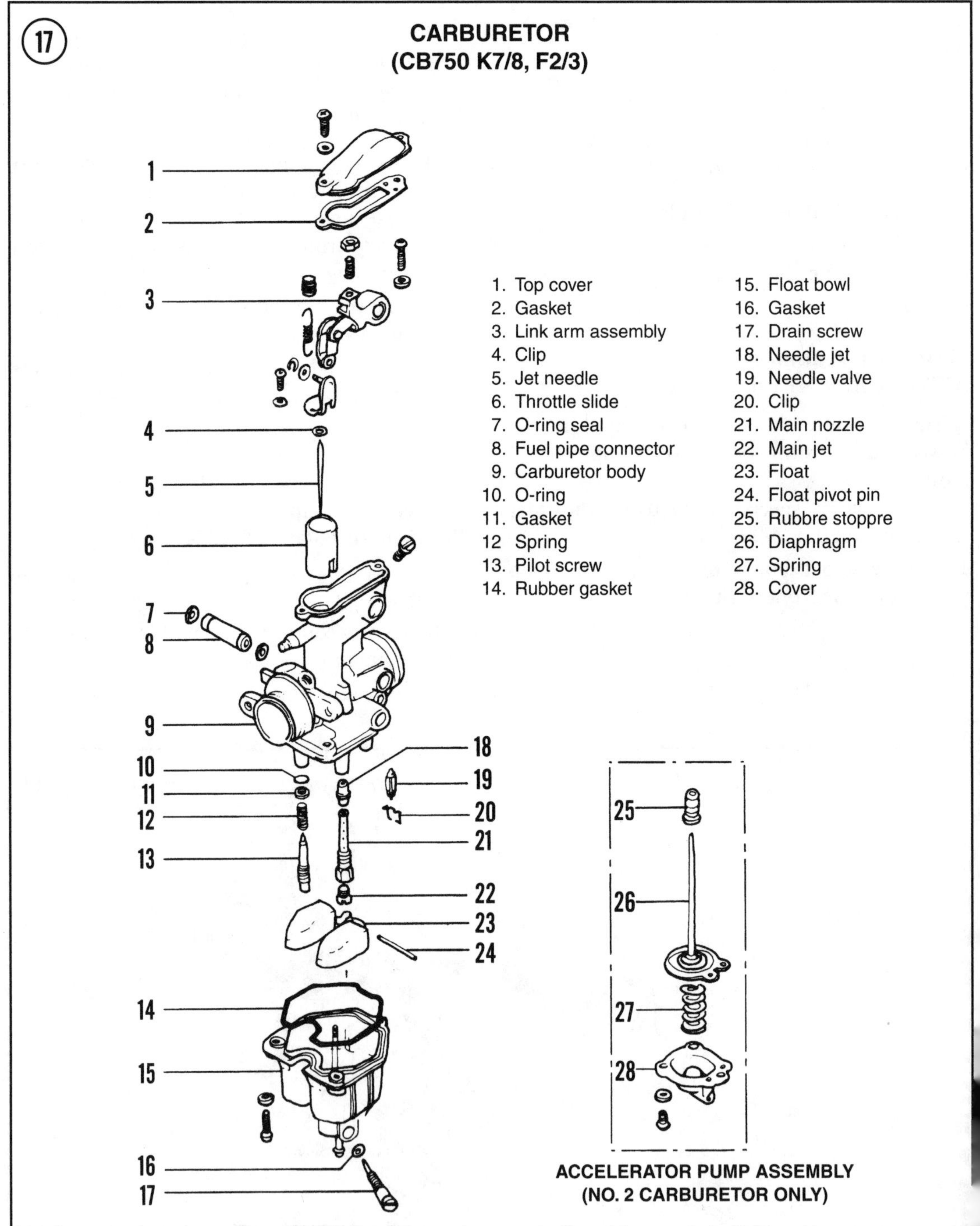

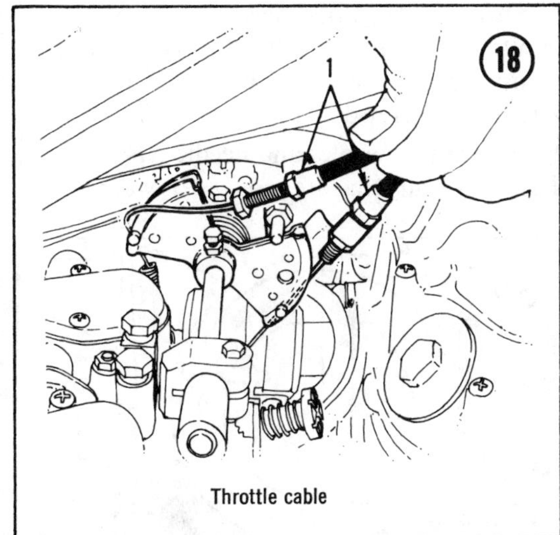

1. Remove the fuel tank.

2. Loosen the locknuts on the cable adjusters and disconnect the cables from the quadrant **(Figure 18)**. Disconnect the choke cable.

3. Remove the air cleaner — first the bottom half of the case, and then the upper **(Figure 19)**.

4. Loosen the carburetor clamping bands at the manifold **(Figure 20)** and remove the carburetors as an assembly.

5. Remove the rear stay from the carburetors. Unscrew the 8 screws that connect the carburetors to the mounting plate **(Figure 21)** and remove the carburetors.

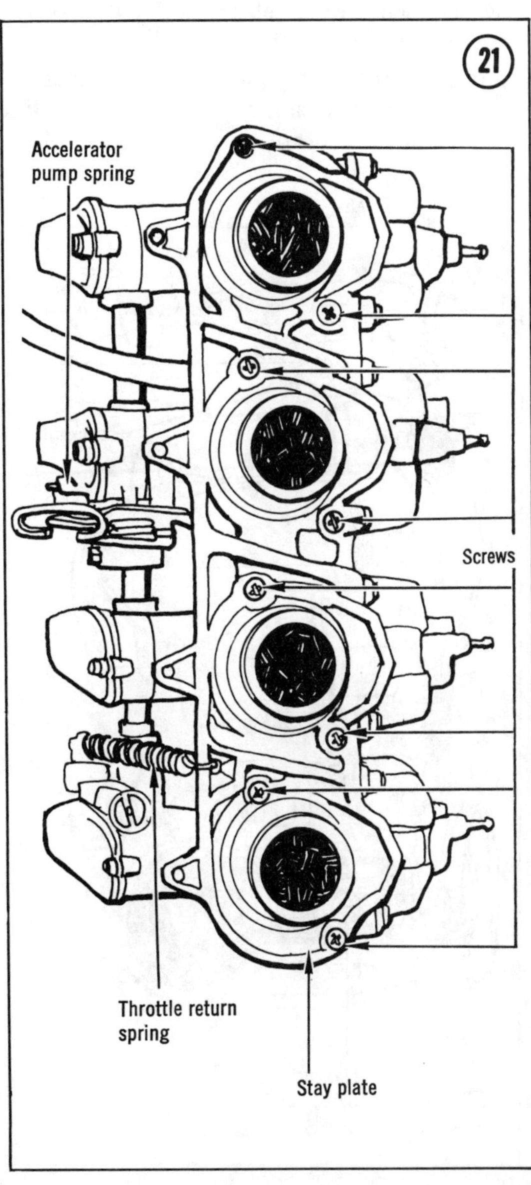

6

6. Remove the tops from the carburetors. Loosen the screw in the slide lifter **(Figure 22)**, and remove the throttle lever set screw after loosening the locknut.

7. Remove the choke plates **(Figure 23)** and separate the carburetors.

8. Remove the float bowls. Refer to **Figure 17** and disassemble the carburetors. Keep each carburetor and its parts separated from the others.

CB750 K7/8, F2/3
Inspection and Adjustment

1. Soak the metal parts in carburetor cleaner and dry them with compressed air. Do not use wire to clean the jets; they are easily damaged.

2. Inspect the slide for wear and scoring. Minor roughness can be removed with fine emery cloth but deep scores indicate replacement.

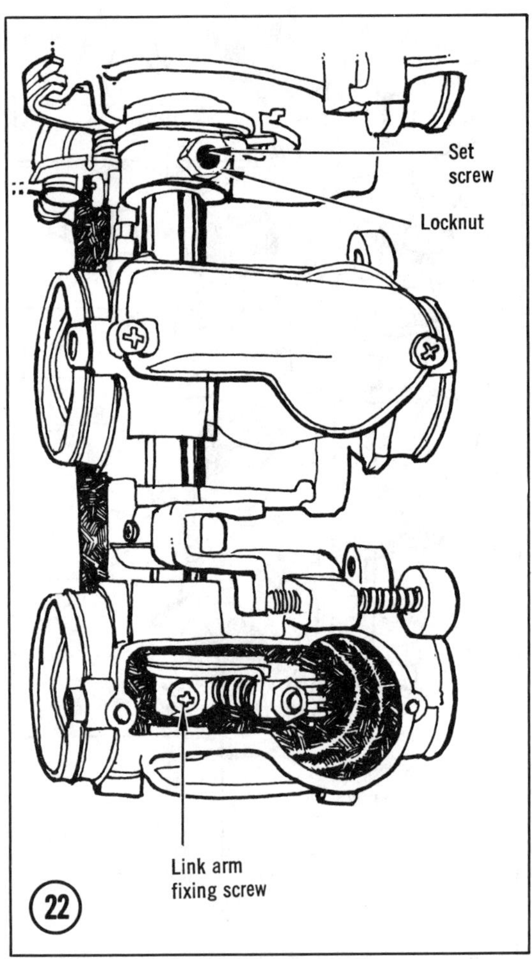

3. Measure the float height **(Figure 24)**. It should be between 0.55-0.59 in. (14-15mm). If adjustment is necessary, bend the float arm with a small screwdriver.

4. Inspect the needles and needle jets for wear and replace any that are grooved or worn.

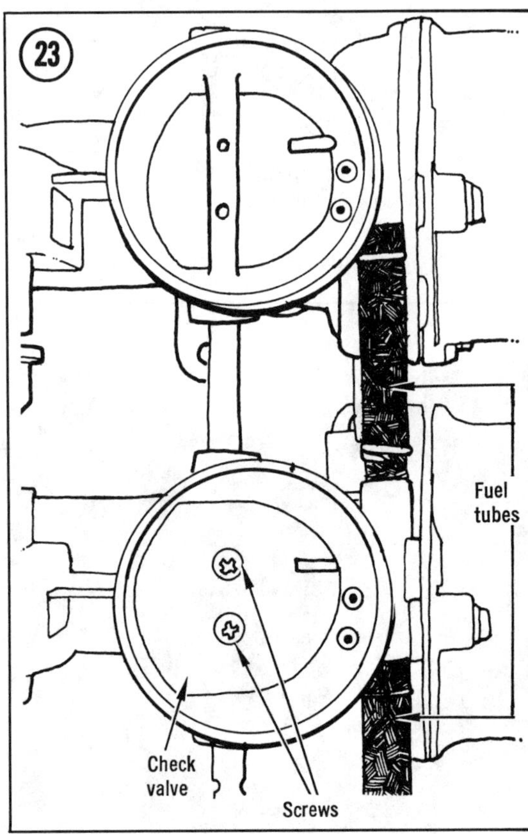

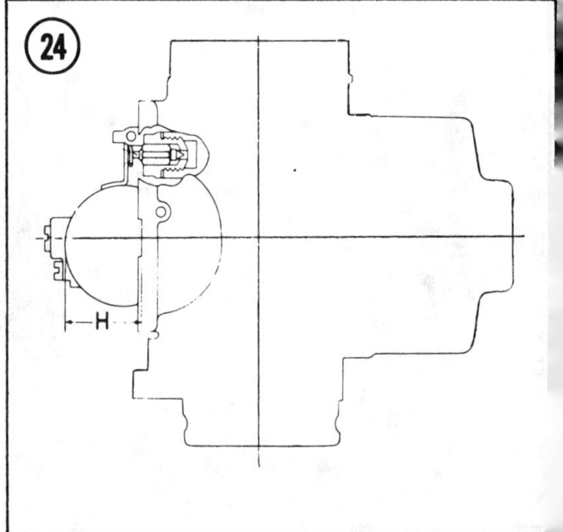

CB750 K7/8, F2/3 Assembly/Installation

Refer to **Figure 17** and assemble the carburetors by reversing the disassembly steps. Be careful not to overtighten the jets; they are easily damaged. When assembly and installation are complete, refer to Chapter Two, *Carburetion*, and adjust throttle free play, synchronize the carburetors, and adjust curb and high speed idle.

> NOTE: *If the pilot air screws were disturbed, the procedure that follows must be carried out to ensure compliance with emission control standards. Failure to do this could result in a citation.*

Idle Mixture Adjustment

1. Turn each pilot screw in clockwise until it just makes contact with the seat (**Figure 25**). Be careful not to overtighten them. On K models, back each screw out 1½ turns; on F models, back each screw out 1¾ turns. This is a preliminary setting.
2. Warm up the engine to operating temperature. Connect a shop type tachometer in accordance with the manufacturer's instructions; the motorcycle tachometer is not accurate enough for this procedure.

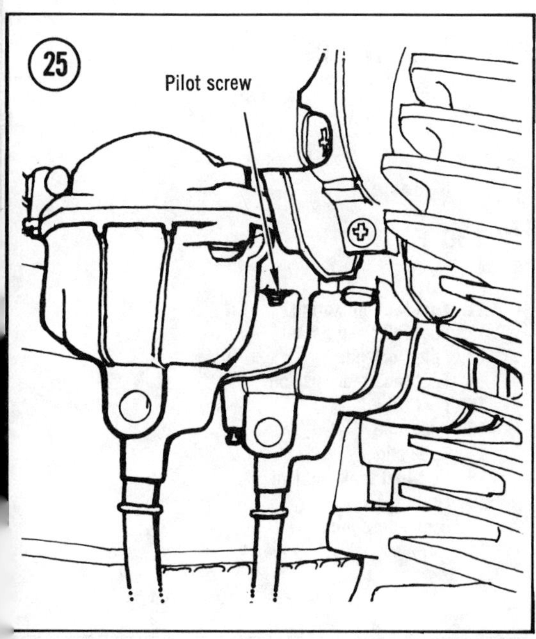

3. With the throttle stop screw, set the idle at 900-1,100 rpm.
4. Beginning with No. 2, the base carburetor, turn the pilot screw either in or out, while observing the tachometer, until the engine reaches the highest idle speed. Then, adjust the idle speed with the throttle stop screw until it is 900-1,100 rpm.
5. Turn the pilot screw in slowly until the engine speed has dropped 100 rpm. If the screw bottoms before the idle has dropped 100 rpm, open the screw 1¼ turns and readjust the idle with the throttle stop screw.
6. Adjust the pilot screw in the other carburetors in the manner just described. When adjustment is complete,refer to Chapter Three *Carburetion*, and adjust throttle free play, synchronize the carburetors, and adjust curb and high speed idle.

6

FUEL TANK AND FUEL VALVE

Figure 26 is a view of the fuel tank used on the 750 and 750 K1-K8 and A. **Figure 27** is an exploded view of the 750F fuel tank.

Removal

1. Shut the fuel valve and remove fuel tube from tank at the valve. See **Figure 28**, which is typical. Remove overflow tube, if so equipped.
2. Lift seat out of the way and pull fuel tank to the rear, raising it up and away.

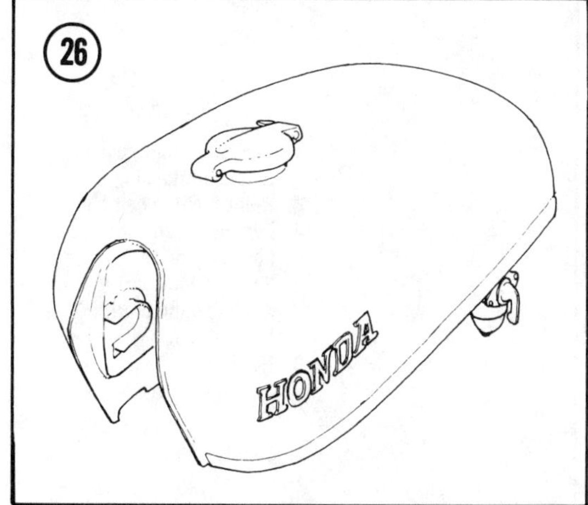

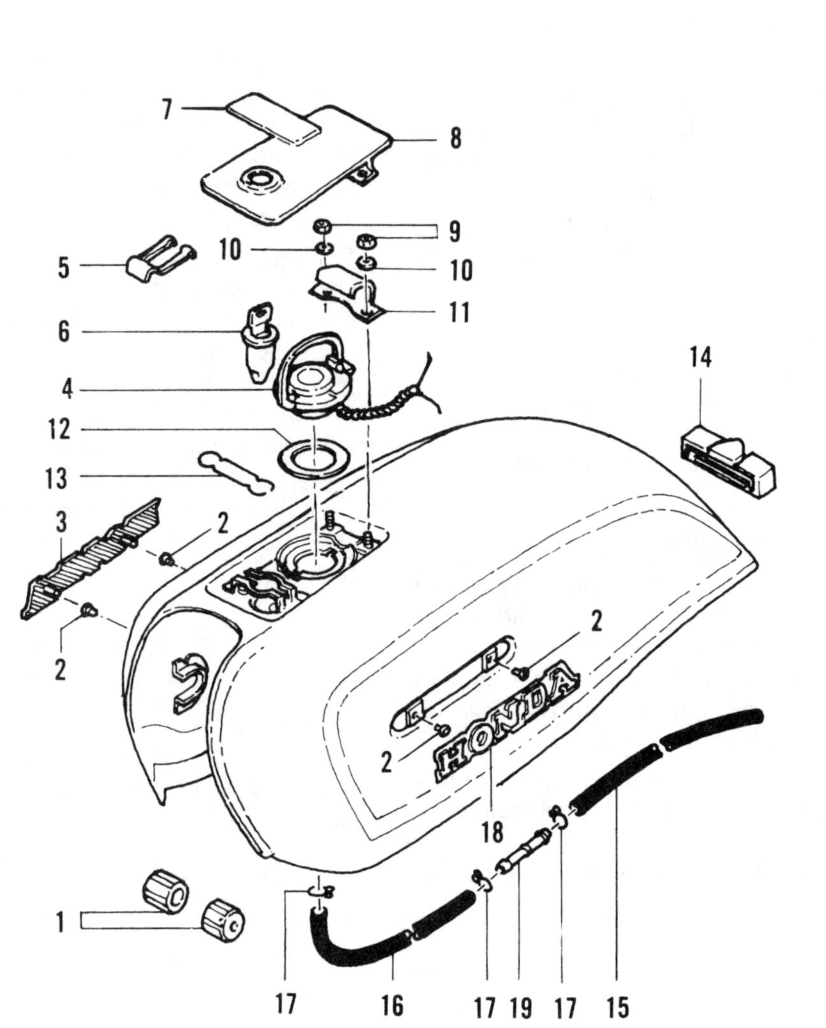

FUEL TANK — CB750 F

1. Fuel tank front cushion
2. Emblem attaching nut
3. Right fuel tank emblem
4. Fuel filler cap component
5. Lock set spring
6. Filler lid lock
7. Drive caution mark
8. Fuel tank lid
9. Hex nut
10. Spring washer
11. Fuel tank lid spring
12. Fuel filler cap gasket
13. Filler lock clip
14. Fuel tank rear cushion
15. Fuel tube
16. Fuel tube
17. Tube clip
18. Left fuel tank emblem
19. Drain tube connecting joint

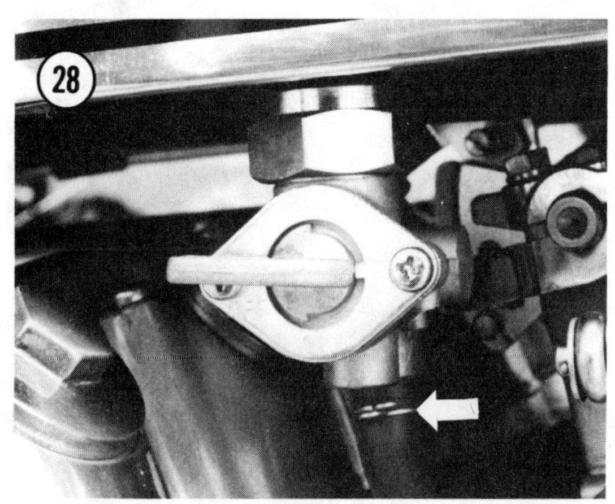

Inspection

1. Inspect the tank for leaks, and make sure the vent hole is not clogged.

2. Check the rubber mounts for deterioration, and replace if necessary.

3. Inspect the fuel line for leaks or cracks, and replace if required.

Installation

1. Assemble the fuel valve, if disassembled, and install it on the tank with the 2 mounting screws.

2. Install the front and rear rubber mounts on the frame. Fit the front mount by pushing the tank from the rear (**Figure 29**). Install the tank, being careful to route the wiring correctly.

3. Install the fuel line.

4. Turn the valve to open, and check for leaks.

CHAPTER SEVEN

ELECTRICAL SYSTEM

This chapter covers the ignition, battery, charging, starting, lighting, wiring, and instrument systems. Procedures for routine maintenance are given in Chapter Three under *Battery*. Wiring diagrams appear at the back of the book.

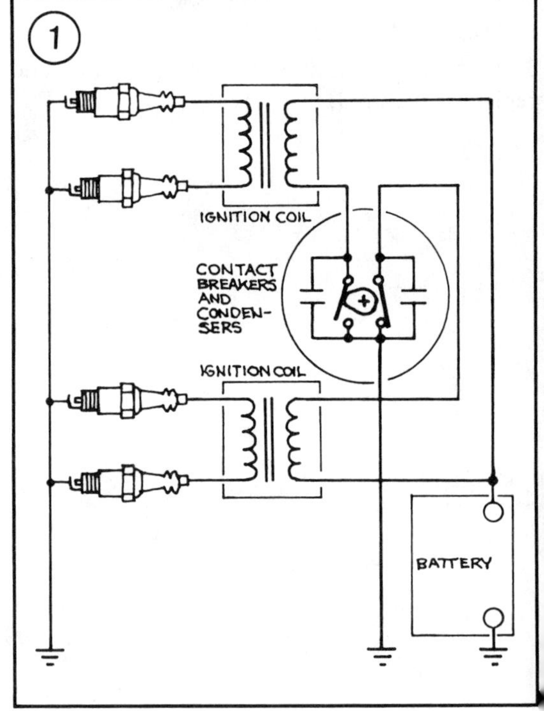

IGNITION

The Honda 750 ignition system consists of the battery, 2 coils, 2 sets of contact breaker points, and 4 spark plugs.

The schematic (**Figure 1**) traces the flow of current from the battery through the primary ignition windings to the breakers and then the plugs. One set of points supplies current to the No. 1 and No. 4 cylinders, and the other to cylinders No. 2 and No. 3.

This section gives instruction for removing and testing the coils, servicing point assemblies, and disassembly/assembly of the spark advance mechanism.

COIL

Removal

1. Remove the fuel tank.
2. Disconnect the 3 electrical leads, as shown in **Figure 2**. They are color-coded yellow, blue, and black/white.
3. Unscrew the 2 mounting bolts (**Figure 2**) and remove the coils from the frame.

Installation

1. Mount the coils with the 2 bolts.
2. Connect the yellow, blue and black/white lead to the wiring harness.

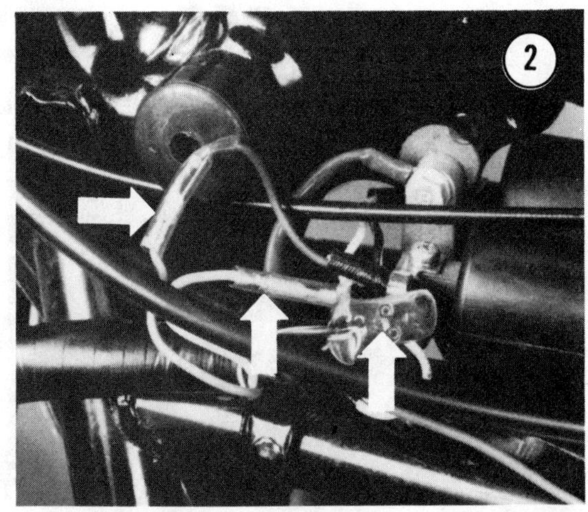

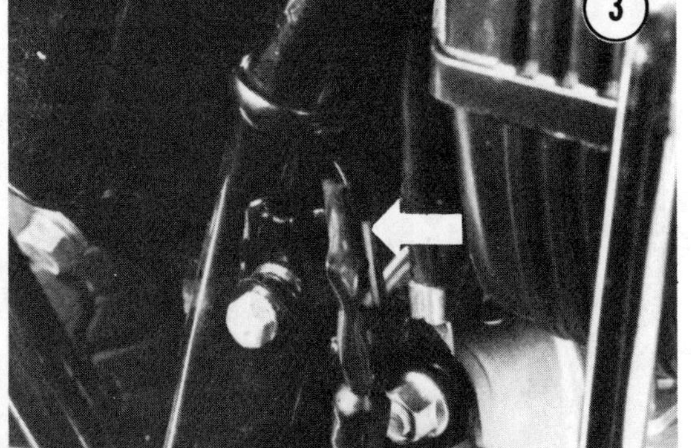

3. Install the fuel tank. Be careful not to crimp the electrical leads.

BREAKER POINTS

Servicing of the points and condensers is covered in Chapter Three under *Breaker Points and Condenser.* Only the removal of the assembly unit is outlined here.

1. Remove the point cover.
2. Disconnect the yellow and blue leads at the junction point in the center of the frame. See **Figure 3**.
3. Unscrew the nut and 3 base plate screws and remove the assembly. Refer to **Figure 4**.
4. Reverse procedure for installation.

> NOTE: *Do not install the breaker point assembly at the frame if the spark advance mechanism is to be serviced.*

SPARK ADVANCER

The spark advance mechanism is mounted on the crankshaft, inboard of the breaker point assembly. This device advances the point cam as the engine speed increases, to cause earlier ignition. Operation is by weights that move outward against spring tension as the rpm increases **(Figure 5)**.

Removal

1. Remove the breaker point assembly as outlined in the preceding sections.

2. Pull the advance mechanism from the advancer shaft (**Figure 6**).

Inspection

1. Check the advancer spring for loss of tension, and replace if necessary. See **Figure 7**.

2. Check the advancer shaft to make sure it is not bent or out-of-center. Turn the engine with the kickstarter while looking at the shaft. It should not wobble. A runout of 0.1mm or less is the permissible limit.

> NOTE: *The crankshaft hole for the advancer shaft is drilled slightly off-center. Thus, any advancer shaft, no matter how straight, will appear off-center at rest.*

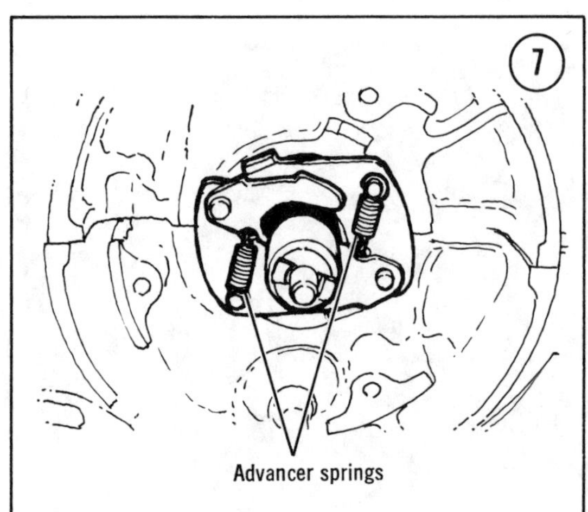

Installation

1. If necessary, install a new advancer shaft. The O-ring ridges are slightly oversize, and may have to be ground down to about 0.1mm to fit.

2. Install the advancer mechanism, making sure the pin is inserted into the hole at the end of the crankshaft.

3. Install the contact breaker assembly (**Figure 8**).

CHARGING SYSTEM

An alternator, voltage regulator, and rectifier comprise the charging system of a 750.

This system is notably different from those in other Honda motorcycles, and is similar to the type used in current model cars.

Testing Charging System

An ammeter is requires to perform the test. Refer to the schematic shown in **Figure 9** while following the operations.

1. Check that the battery voltage is normal. Measurement is described in the *Battery* section of this chapter.

2. Locate the positive battery terminal and disconnect the red/white rectifier lead, and the red power lead. Connect both of these to the positive terminal of the ammeter.

3. Connect the positive terminal of the battery to the minus terminal of the ammeter with a wire.

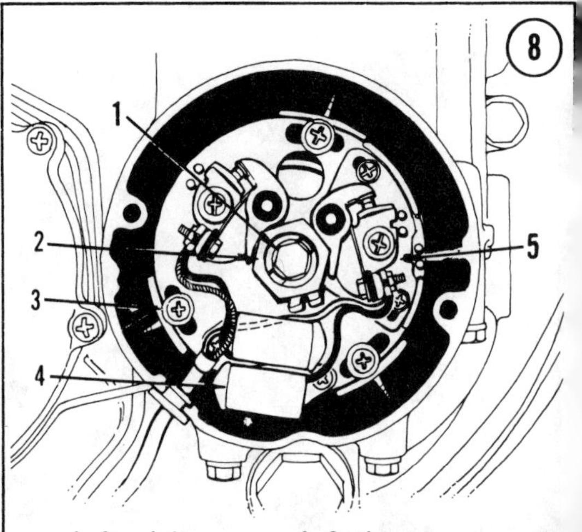

1. 6mm bolt
2. Special washer
3. Screws
4. Condensers
5. Contact breaker plate

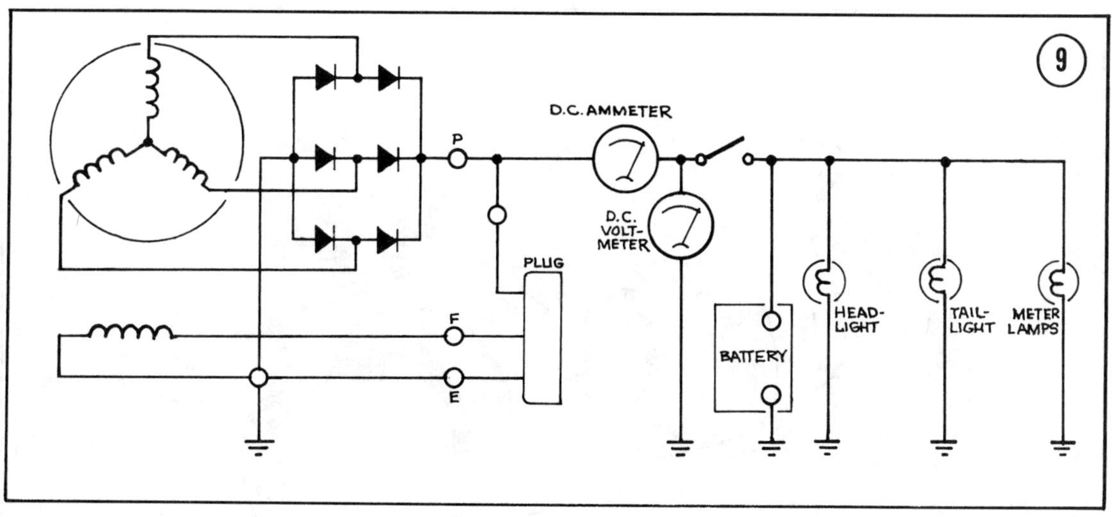

(9)

(10)

	Engine (rpm)							
Charging current (A)	1,000	2,000	3,000	4,000	5,000	6,000	7,000	8,000
Night riding	6.5	0	2.4	1.3	1.0	1.0	0.8	0.6
Day riding	2—3	1	1	1	1	1	1	1
Battery terminal voltage (V)	12	12.4	13.2	14.5	14.5	14.5	14.5	14.5

(11)

. Start the engine.

. Refer to **Figure 10**. Operate the engine at the arious speeds and check to see if the voltage measures up to the standard for night and day riding.

Night riding: Headlight high beam on.
Day riding: Turn signal and stoplights off.

ALTERNATOR

Figure 11 illustrates the components of the alternator: the field coil, stator coil, and the rotor. All parts are shown in **Figure 12**.

> NOTE: *The charge current reading on the ammeter may fluctuate, depending on the condition of the battery.*

Removal/Installation

1. Remove the alternator cover and pull out the rotor. A special rotor puller, shown in **Figure 13**, can be used for this operation.
2. Refer to **Figure 14**. Unscrew the 4 bolts and remove the stator coil from the cover.
3. Remove the field coil by unscrewing the 3 Phillips screws, shown in **Figure 15**.
4. Reverse procedure to install.

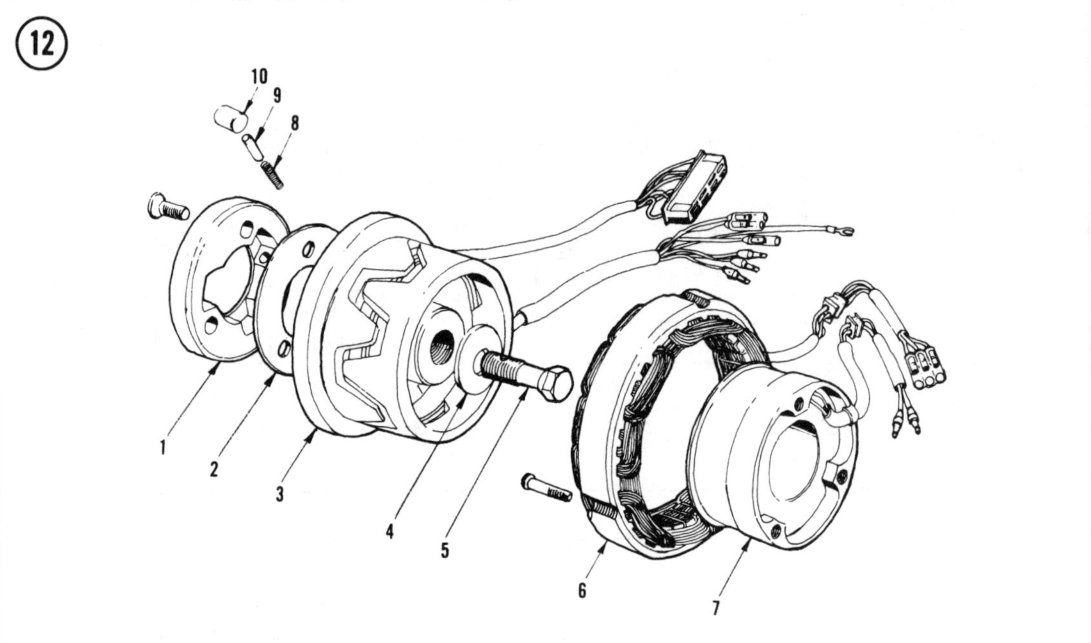

(12)

1. Starting clutch
2. Starting clutch side plate
3. Rotor components
4. Washer
5. Rotor set bolt
6. Stator components
7. Field coil components
8. Starting clutch roller spring
9. Starting clutch roller spring cap
10. Roller

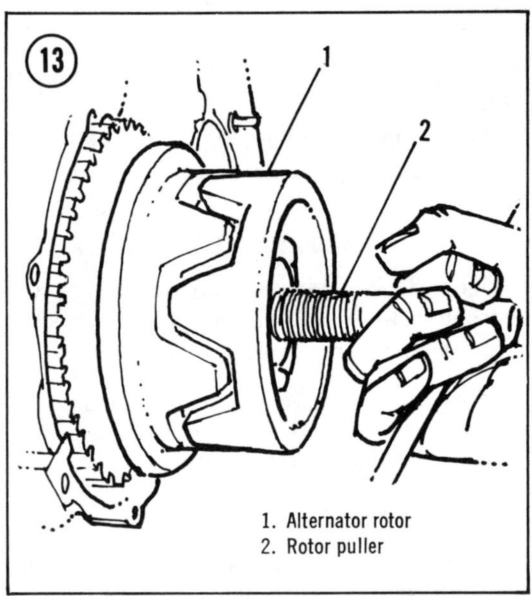

1. Alternator rotor
2. Rotor puller

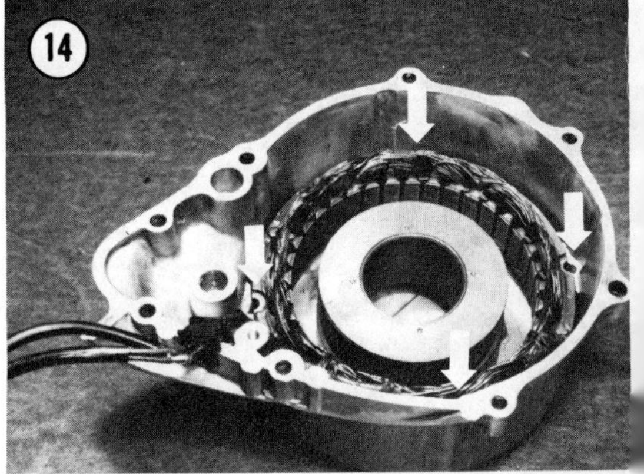

Testing Coil Continuity

A continuity tester is required to check continuity.

1. Hook the tester to the field coil according to the manufacturer's instructions. The rated re-

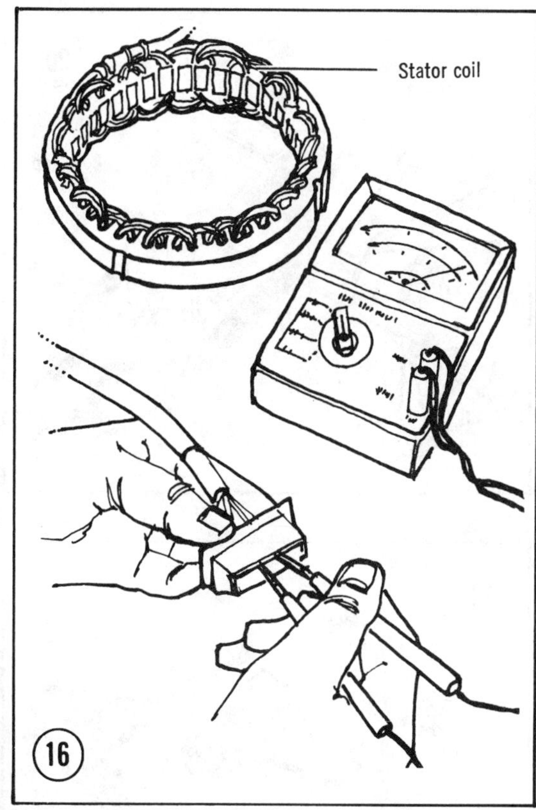

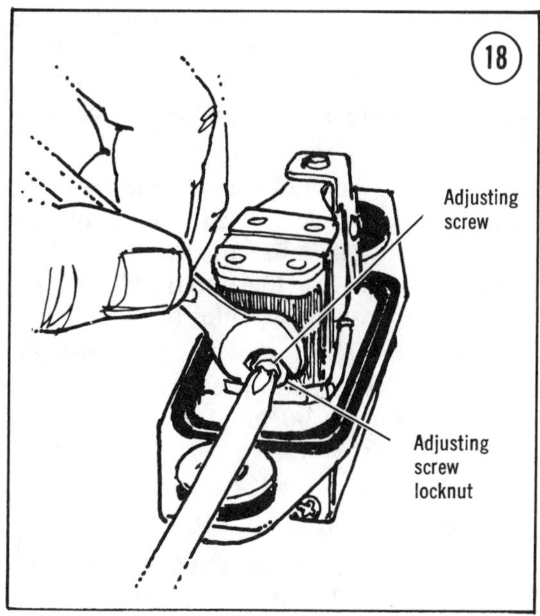

7

sistance is 7.2 ohms. Replace the coil if there is continuity between the lead wires and the coil (grounded coil), or if there is no continuity between the wires (open circuit).

2. Check continuity of stator coil (**Figure 16**). The rated resistance is 0.2 ohms.

REGULATOR

A dual contact voltage regulator is mounted inside the battery cover at the center of the frame.

Removal/Installation

1. Remove the battery cover and detach the regulator (**Figure 17**) by loosening the 2 set bolts.
2. Remove cover by loosening the 2 screws.
3. Reverse procedure for installation.

Inspection/Adjustment

The regulator must be adjusted if the charging system does not check out according to the test outlined earlier in this chapter.

1. **Figure 18** shows the location of the adjusting screw and its locknut.
2. The circuit is normal if a voltmeter shows an output from 14-15 volts at 5,000 rpm with no load. When the low speed contact circuit is

broken and changes to the high speed contact circuit, there should be 0.5 volt rise, as shown in **Figure 19**. If the increase is more than 0.5 volts, or if there is a drop, adjust the core gap (next step).

3. Refer to **Figure 20** for adjustment of the core gap. Clean the points with a point file, and check the gap with a feeler gauge. It should be from 0.025-0.04 in. (0.6-1mm). If different, reset the gap with the adjusting screw.

4. Check the point gap with a feeler blade as shown in **Figure 21**. The standard gap is 0.012-0.016 in. (0.3-0.4mm). Loosen the lock screw to adjust.

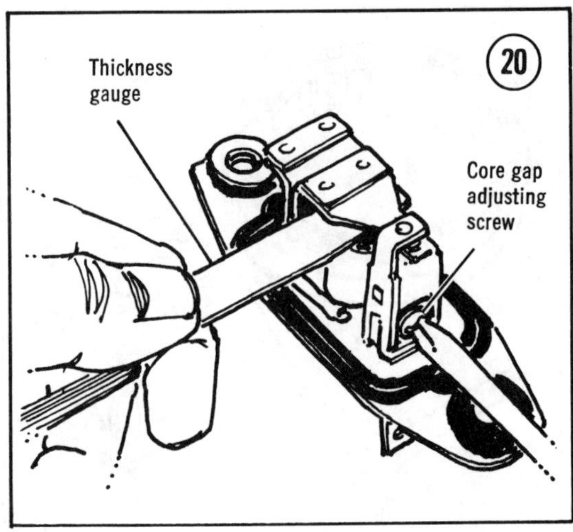

RECTIFIER

Six silicon diodes rectify alternator current to direct current. The assembly is attached away from the engine on the frame so it will remain cool. **Figure 22** shows its location in the charging schematic.

Remove the battery cover and unscrew the set nut **(Figure 23)** to detach the rectifier from the frame. Reverse procedure to install.

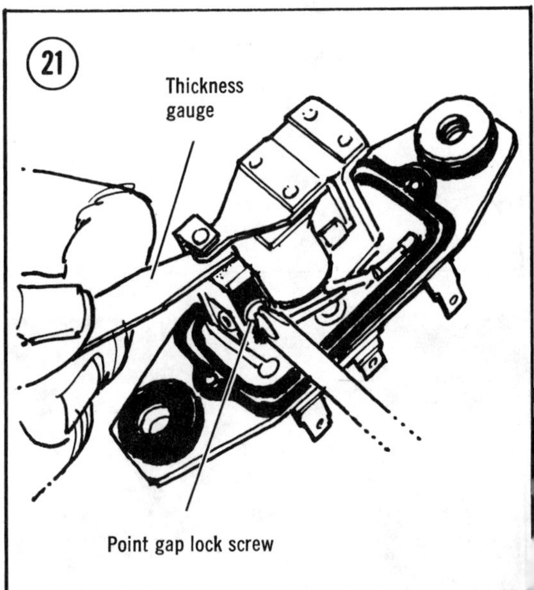

BATTERY

The Honda 750 12-volt, 14 ampere-hour battery is the heart of its electrical system.

Removal

1. Raise the seat and remove the strap from the battery.

2. First, disconnect the ground, or negative cable. Then remove the positive cable. Their locations are pointed out in **Figure 24**.

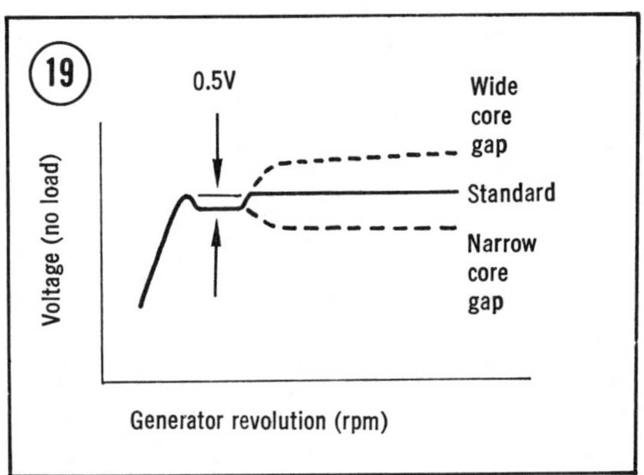

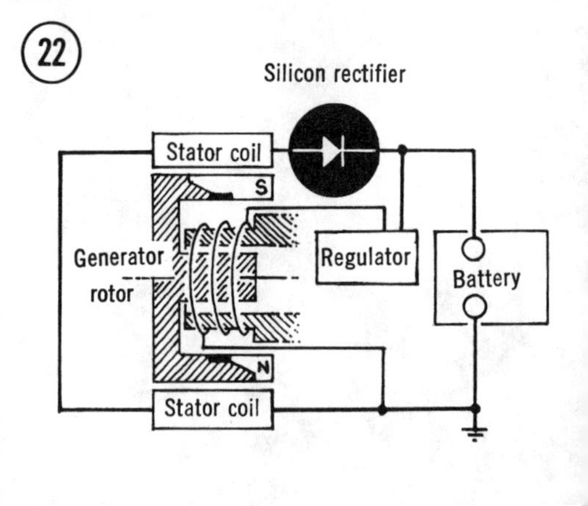

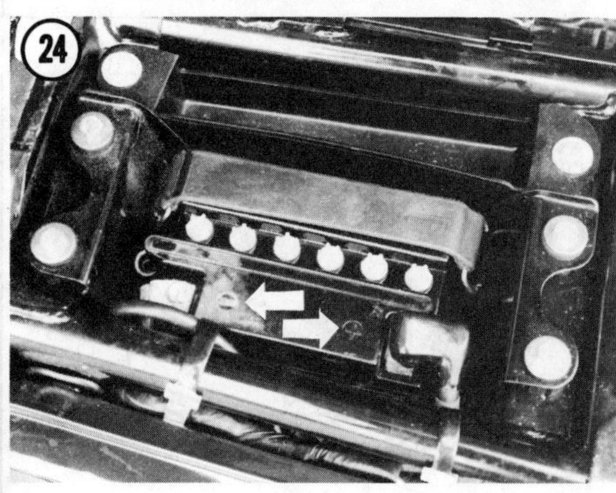

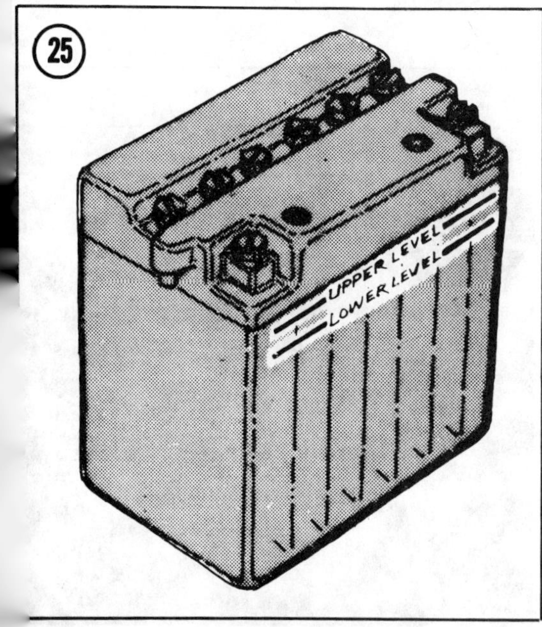

3. Lift the battery from the compartment. Be careful not to spill any of the corrosive acid electrolyte.

Inspection

1. Clean the terminals and clamps with a wire brush or a baking soda and water solution. Corrosion causes current leaks.

2. Check the electrolyte level. It should be between the upper and lower marks shown in **Figure 25**. Top up the low cells only with distilled water.

3. Measure the specific gravity of the electrolyte with a hydrometer, reading it as shown in **Figure 26**. Generally, the specific gravity should be between 1.26 and 1.28. If the value is less than 1.189 at 68°F (20°C), the battery is in poor condition and should be charged.

4. Specific gravity of the electrolyte varies with temperature, so it is necessary to apply a temperature correction to the reading obtained. For each 10° that the battery temperature exceeds 80°F, add 0.004 to the indicated specific gravity, and for every 10° that the battery is less than 80°F, deduct 0.004 from the indicated specific gravity.

Battery Charging

A "trickle" charger is recommended for restoring a low voltage battery. Most inexpensive automotive chargers have an output ranging from 2-6 amps.

So-called "quick" chargers should not be used on a fully discharged battery, and not used frequently to charge a low voltage battery because of the danger of overheating.

1. Connect the positive charger lead to the positive battery terminal, and the negative lead to the corresponding terminal. Remember, "positive to positive, negative to negative," or damage will result.

WARNING

During charging, highly explosive hydrogen gas is generated by and released from the battery. The battery should be charged only in a well-ventilated area, and open flames and lighted cigarettes should be kept away. Never check the charge of a battery by

7

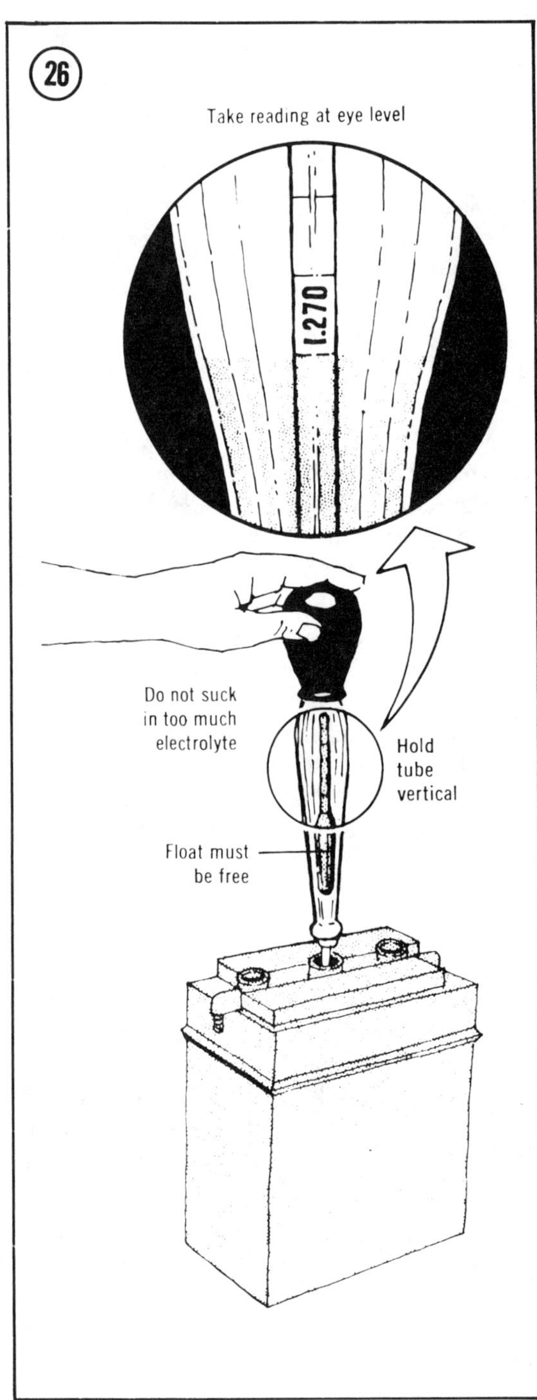

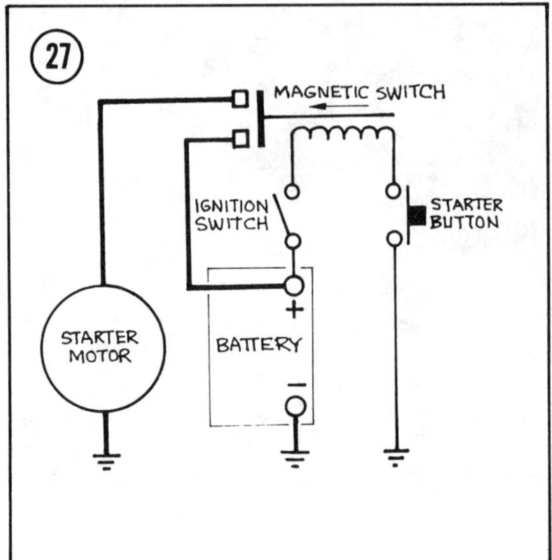

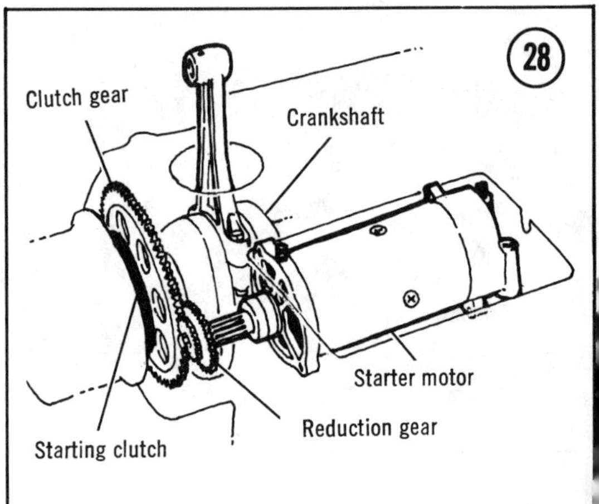

arcing across the terminals; the resulting spark can ignite the hydrogen gas.

2. Test with a hydrometer to see if the specific gravity is within standard range of 1.26-1.28. If the reading is standard over an hour's time, the battery is charged.

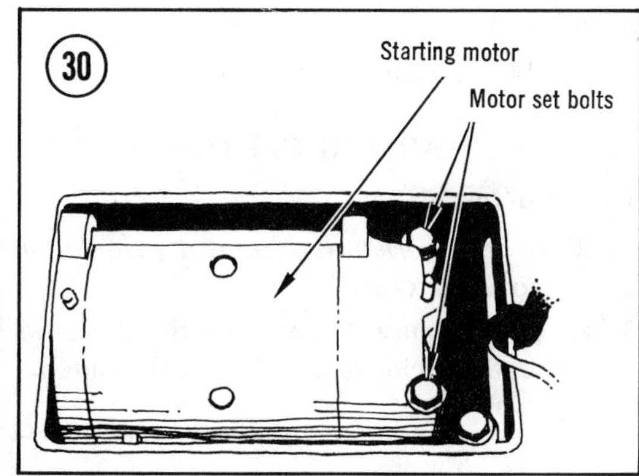

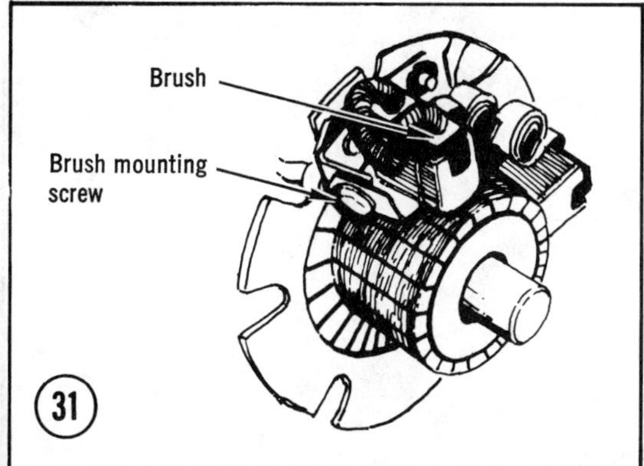

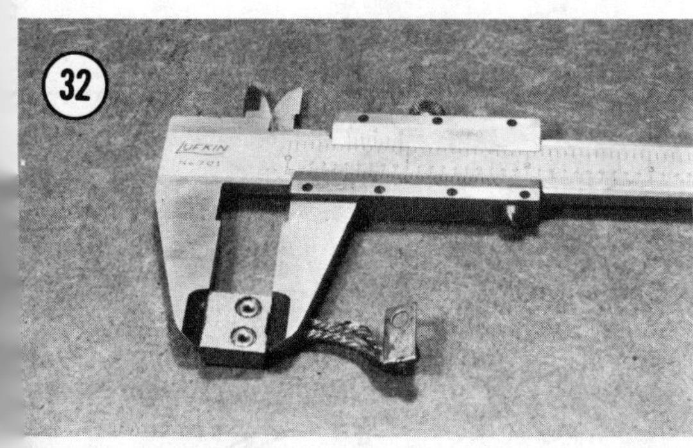

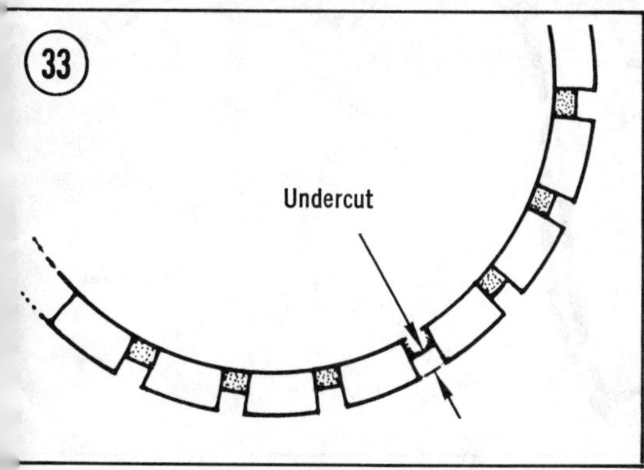

Installation

1. Make sure the battery terminals, cable clamps, and case are free of corrosion. Silicone spray can be applied to the terminals to retard decomposition of the lead.

2. Install the battery in reverse order of removal, being careful to route the vent tube so that it is not crimped. Connect the positive terminal first, then the negative one. Do not overtighten the clamps.

STARTING MOTOR

The layout of the electric starting system is shown in **Figures 27 and 28**. When the starter button is pressed, it engages the magnetic switch that closes the circuit. About 120 amperes flow from the battery to operate the starting motor.

The kickstarter is covered in Chapter Four of this manual. This chapter outlines the starter motor, its clutch, and the magnetic switch.

7

Removal

1. Take off the left side cover and disconnect the power cable **(Figure 29)** from the magnetic switch (solenoid).

2. Referring to **Figure 30**, remove the side cover and then detach the motor unit by unscrewing the set bolts. Remove the side cover from the motor.

3. Locate the brushes **(Figure 31)** and remove them from the holders by loosening the mounting screws.

Inspection

The overhaul of a starting motor is best left to an expert. This section shows how to determine if the unit is worn out.

1. Use vernier calipers **(Figure 32)** to measure the length of the brush. If it is worn beyond 0.217 in. (5.5mm), it should be replaced.

2. Refer to **Figure 33** and measure the amount of mica undercut (the depth of the grooves). If the cut is less than 0.012 in. (0.3mm), the commutator should be repaired.

3. Check electrical continuity between the armature and the shaft mounting. If there is a short, the armature should be replaced.

4. Measure the amount of current drawn by the motor with an ammeter, using the external shunt setting. Without a load, the starting motor should draw a maximum of 35 amperes.

Assembly

Refer to the exploded view of the starter (**Figure 34**) and assemble in the reverse order of disassembly.

Installation

Install by reversing *Removal* steps.

STARTING CLUTCH

Removal/Installation

1. Refer to *Alternator, Removal/Installation* and remove the rotor.

2. Refer to **Figure 12**, remove the 3 screws from the starter clutch, and remove the clutch.

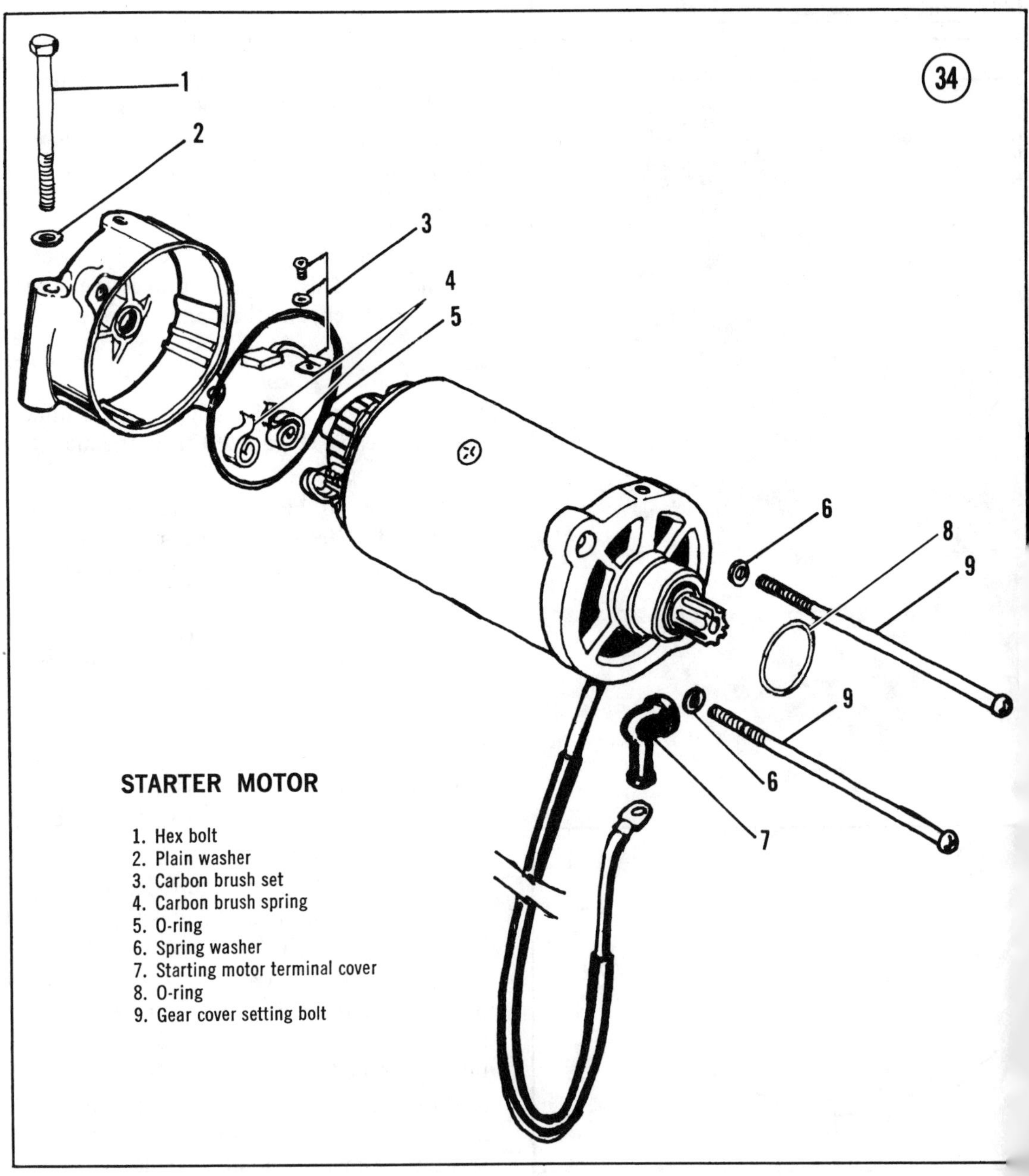

3. Reverse the above to install the clutch and alternator.

Inspection

Check the clutch roller to ensure it operates freely, and inspect the clutch for damage or wear.

MAGNETIC SWITCH

A solenoid switch is used to supply the heavy current for operating the starting motor. When the push button starting switch is pressed, the solenoid coil is energized and becomes an electromagnet that draws the iron core to it. The circuit is completed when the contacts meet. A return spring pulls the iron core back to break the circuit when the push switch is released.

1. Remove the left side cover and disconnect the lead from the starting motor (**Figure 35**). Remove the cover.
2. Depress the starter switch and listen for the click of the iron core contacting the coil.
3. Check the condition of the contact points and dress with a point file if they are pitted or burned.

STARTER MOTOR SAFETY UNIT

K3 and later models are equipped with a starter motor safety unit which prevents the starter from working when the transmission is in gear and the clutch is engaged. The unit permits operation of the starter when the transmission is in gear and the clutch is disengaged, or when the transmission is in neutral and the clutch is engaged or disengaged. The starter motor safety unit is shown in **Figure 36**. It appears schematically on the K3 and later wiring diagrams at the end of this chapter.

1. Depress the starter switch and listen for the click of the iron core contacting the coil.
2. Check the condition of the contact points and dress with a point file if they are pitted or burned.

INSTRUMENT GROUP

The speedometer and tachometer are driven by separate, flexible shafts. Repairs should only be attempted by an expert.

1. Remove the headlight unit according to the *Headlight* procedures, below.
2. Disconnect the speedometer and tachometer cables from the backs of the instruments.
3. Remove the bolts (**Figure 37**) and remove the instruments.

4. Unscrew the 2 cross screws and remove the underplate.
5. Remove the bulbs. See **Table 1**.
6. Reverse procedure to install.

HEADLIGHT — U.S., CANADA

1. Loosen the 3 mounting screws and remove the light unit from the case.
2. Disconnect the electrical leads (**Figure 38**).
3. Refer to **Figure 39**. Remove the 2 setscrews and the beam adjusting screw. Remove the light from the rim.
4. Remove the beam unit by loosening the 2 headlight screws. See **Table 1** for bulb type.
5. Reverse procedure to install.
6. Inspect the wiring for corrosion or fraying.

HEADLIGHT — U.K.

U.K. models use a prefocused headlamp bulb and a city (pilot) lamp. To replace either bulb:

1. Unscrew the 3 crosshead screws from the headlight rim and remove the rim from the housing.
2. Pull the city lamp out of the housing (**Figure 40**). Insert a new bulb and push it back into the housing.
3. Disconnect the spring that holds the headlamp socket in place (**Figure 41**). Remove the old bulb from the socket. Install a new bulb (**Table 1**), making sure the offset pins line up with their respective slots so that the prefocusing will not be disturbed. Note also that the socket can be installed only one way. Reconnect the spring.

Table 1 BULB TYPES

Bulb	U.S. & Canada	U.K.
Headlamp	12V 40/50W	12V 50/40W
Tail/stop	12V 8/27W (SAE 1157)	12V 7/23W
Directionals	12V 23W (SAE 1034/1073)	12V 24W
Instruments/ Indicators	12V 3.4W (SAE 57)	12V 3W
Parking light	12V 8W	—
Pilot (city)	—	12V 6W

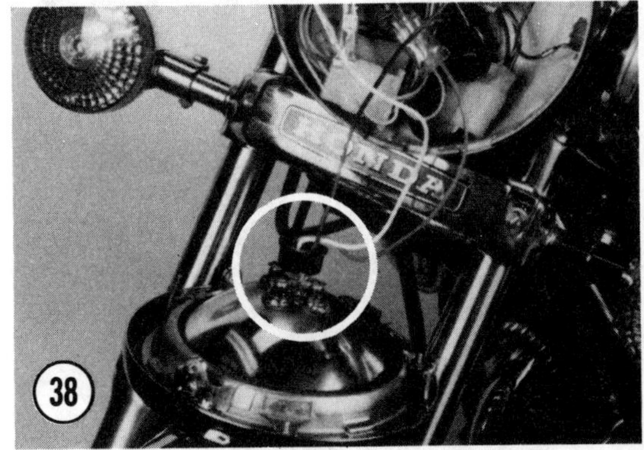

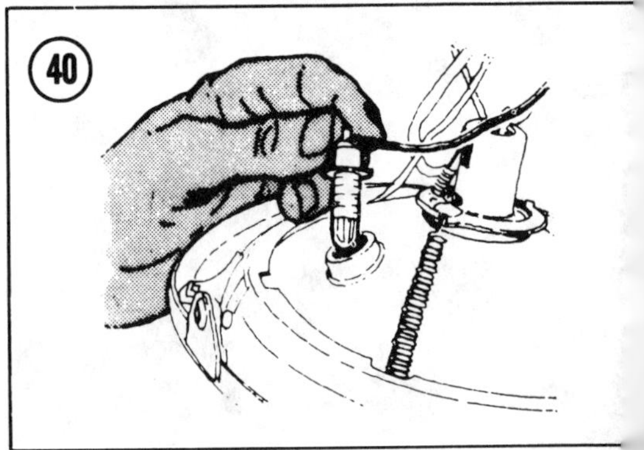

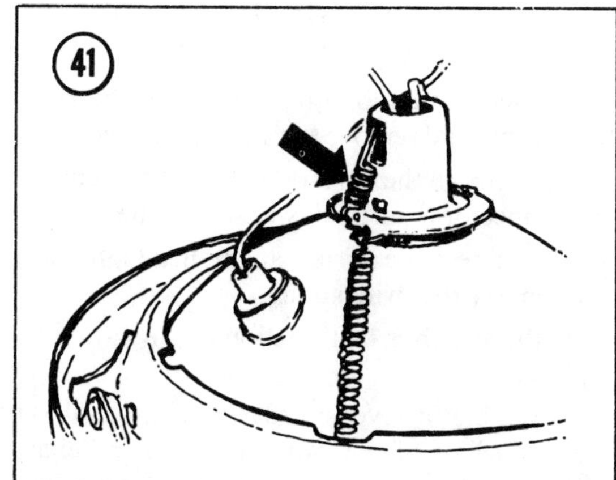

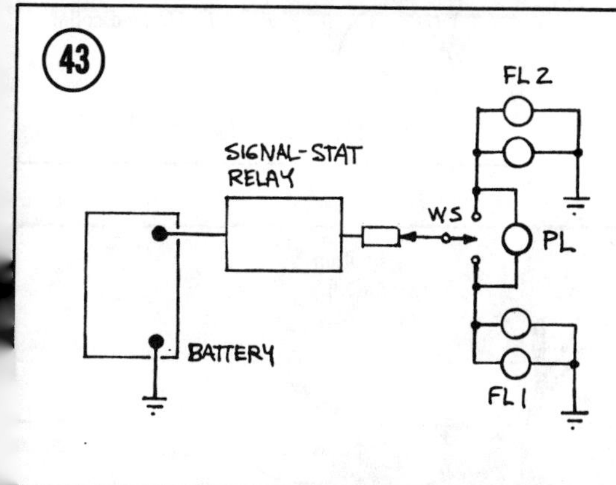

NOTE: ***Do not touch** the glass portion of the bulb with your fingers. Should you do so, wipe the bulb clean before installing it. Grease or oil from your fingers will shorten the life of the bulb.*

. Install the headlamp unit in the housing, install the rim, and screw in and tighten the 3 crosshead screws.

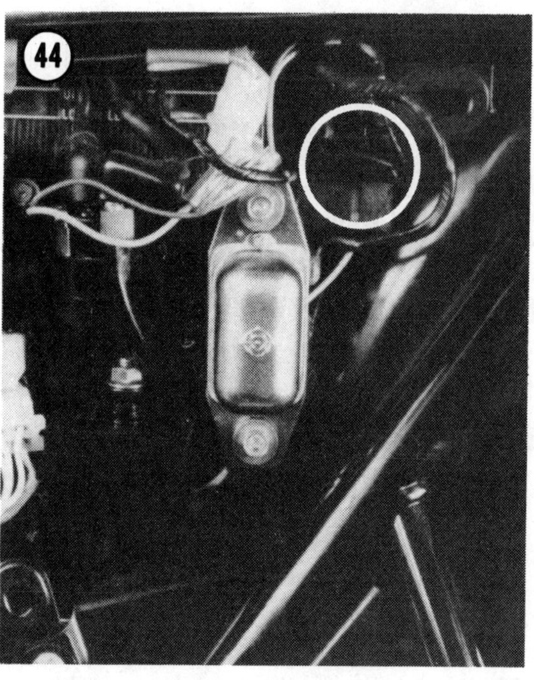

TAILLIGHT TURN INDICATOR AND STOPLIGHT

1. Disconnect the electrical leads **(Figure 42)** and remove bracket by loosening the 2 screws.
2. Remove lens and then the bulb. See **Table 1** for bulb type.
3. Reassemble in reverse order. Make sure not to overtighten the screws when installing the lens, or it may crack.

FLASHER RELAY

Figure 43 shows the wiring schematic of the flasher relay. The relay is located near the battery **(Figure 44)**.

1. Remove the battery cover.
2. Disconnect the electrical leads from the unit and remove.
3. Reverse the procedure to install.
4. If the flashing rate is abnormal, check the turn signal bulb rating. The rate is affected by the wrong wattage bulb.
5. Check the rate by connecting the relay unit to a 12-volt, 25-watt bulb, and grounding the circuit. The bulb should flash from 65-90 times per minute.

7

IGNITION SWITCH

This key switch controls all electrical circuits of the motorcycle. On the CB750 K7/8, F, and A, the switch also serves as a fork lock.

Removal/Installation CB750 and CB750 K1-K6

1. Remove the fuel tank.
2. Refer to **Figure 45** and unscrew the locknut.
3. Disconnect wires at the junction and remove the unit.
4. Reverse the procedure to install.

Removal/Installation CB750 K7/8, F, and A

1. Remove nuts from the meter mount bolts and remove bolts. See **Figure 46**.
2. Carefully lift the speedometer/tachometer/indicator assembly out of the way.
3. Carefully lift headlight bracket assembly out of rubber grommets in lower fork bridge and place assembly to one side, out of the way.
4. Unplug wiring harness connector from ignition switch assembly. See **Figure 47**.
5. Remove bolts attaching switch to fork top bridge and remove switch.
6. To install, reverse the procedure. Securely tighten all nuts and bolts.

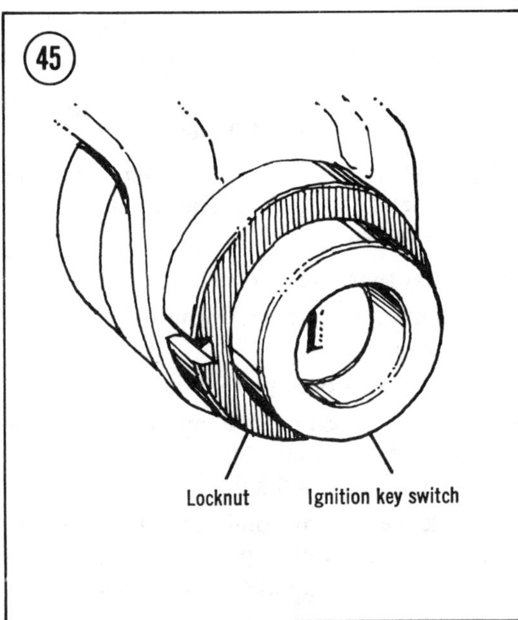

STARTER, LIGHTING, AND IGNITION SWITCH

1. Loosen the 2 mounting screws on the right handlebar, and remove the switch bracket.
2. Disconnect the throttle cable, then remove the connector from the lower side of the switch.
3. Disconnect the wiring at the headlight case and remove the switch unit.
4. If the switch is malfunctioning, it should be replaced as a unit.
5. Assemble in reverse order. When installing the lower half of the switch on the handlebar, make sure the pin is inserted into the stopper hole on the bar and is tightened with the upper half of the switch.

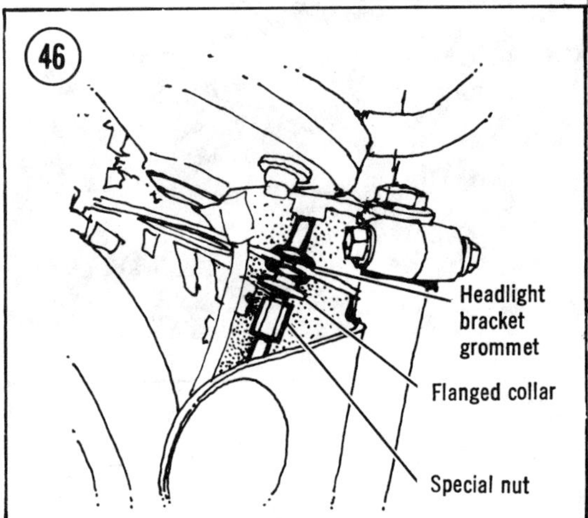

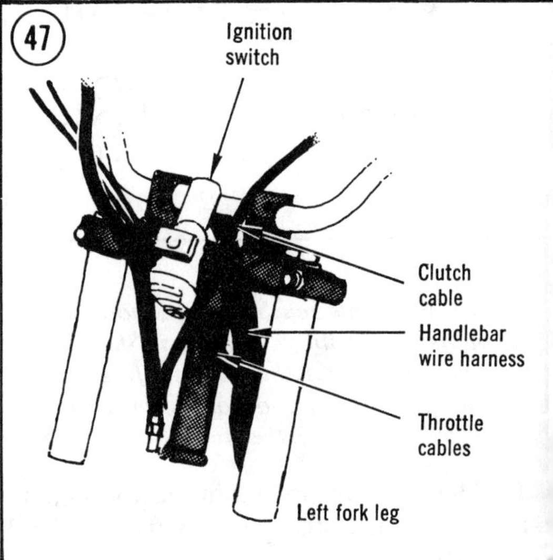

TURN SIGNAL AND HORN SWITCH

1. Remove the headlight and disconnect the wiring at the case.

2. Remove the 2 mounting screws and remove the upper and lower halves of the switch.

3. Replace the switch as a unit if it is malfunctioning.

4. Assemble in reverse order. Make sure the pin on the lower half of the switch is inserted into the stopper hole on the handlebar. Tighten the lower half together with the upper half.

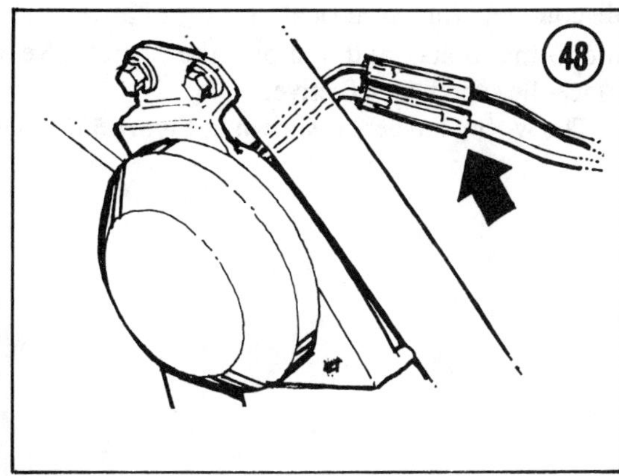

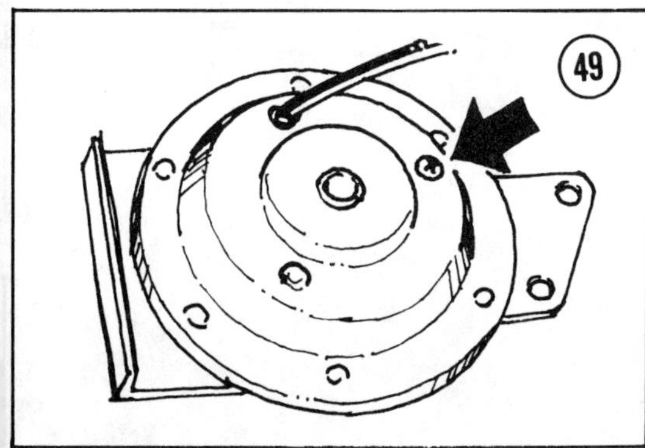

HORN

1. Disconnect the electrical leads at the connections **(Figure 48)**.

2. Unscrew the 2 mounting bolts and remove the horn unit.

3. The volume of the horn can be increased by turning adjusting screw **(Figure 49)** clockwise.

4. Reverse procedure to install.

FRONT STOPLIGHT SWITCH

The switch is activated by pressure in the brake hose and is located next to it.

1. Disconnect the electrical leads.

2. Loosen the mounting bolts and remove the switch from the joint.

3. Replace the switch as a unit if it is defective.

4. Reverse procedure to install.

REAR STOPLIGHT SWITCH

The rear stoplight switch is activated by the brake pedal **(Figure 50)**.

1. Disconnect the electrical leads, and remove the switch from the bracket. Reverse procedure to install.

2. Adjust the brake pedal, according to the instructions under Chapter Three, *Rear Brake Linkage Adjustment*.

3. The switch should function at the point where the rear brake just starts to take hold. Screw in the locknut to make the light turn on earlier, screw it out to make the light come on later.

OIL PRESSURE SWITCH

The switch is mounted on the upper crankcase behind the block. It functions when oil pressure is greater than 57-85 psi (4-6 kg/cm^2).

To replace, remove the switch from the crankcase **(Figure 51)** and disconnect the electrical lead. Replace the unit if defective.

NEUTRAL SWITCH

The neutral switch is mounted under the lower crankcase, as shown in **Figure 52**, and

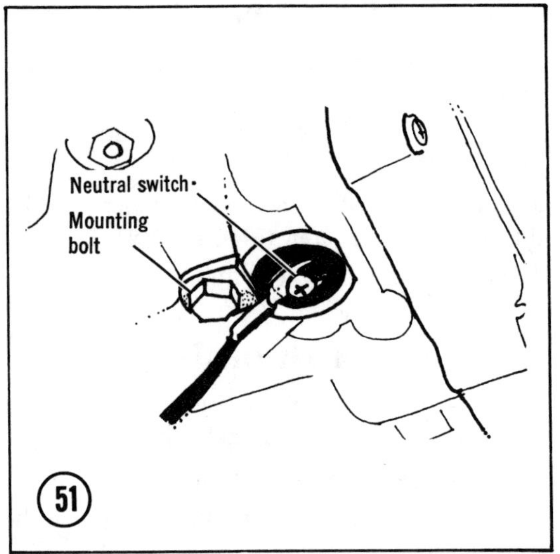

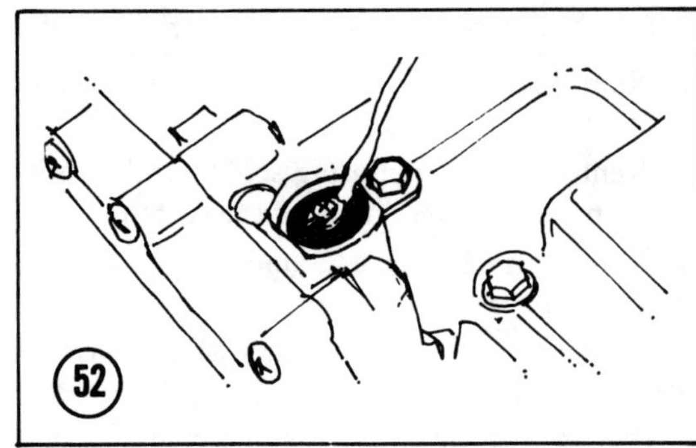

operates the neutral indicator bulb. To remove, disconnect the electrical lead, remove the mounting bolts, and remove the switch. Replace the switch if defective.

The wiring harness is shown in **Figure 53**.

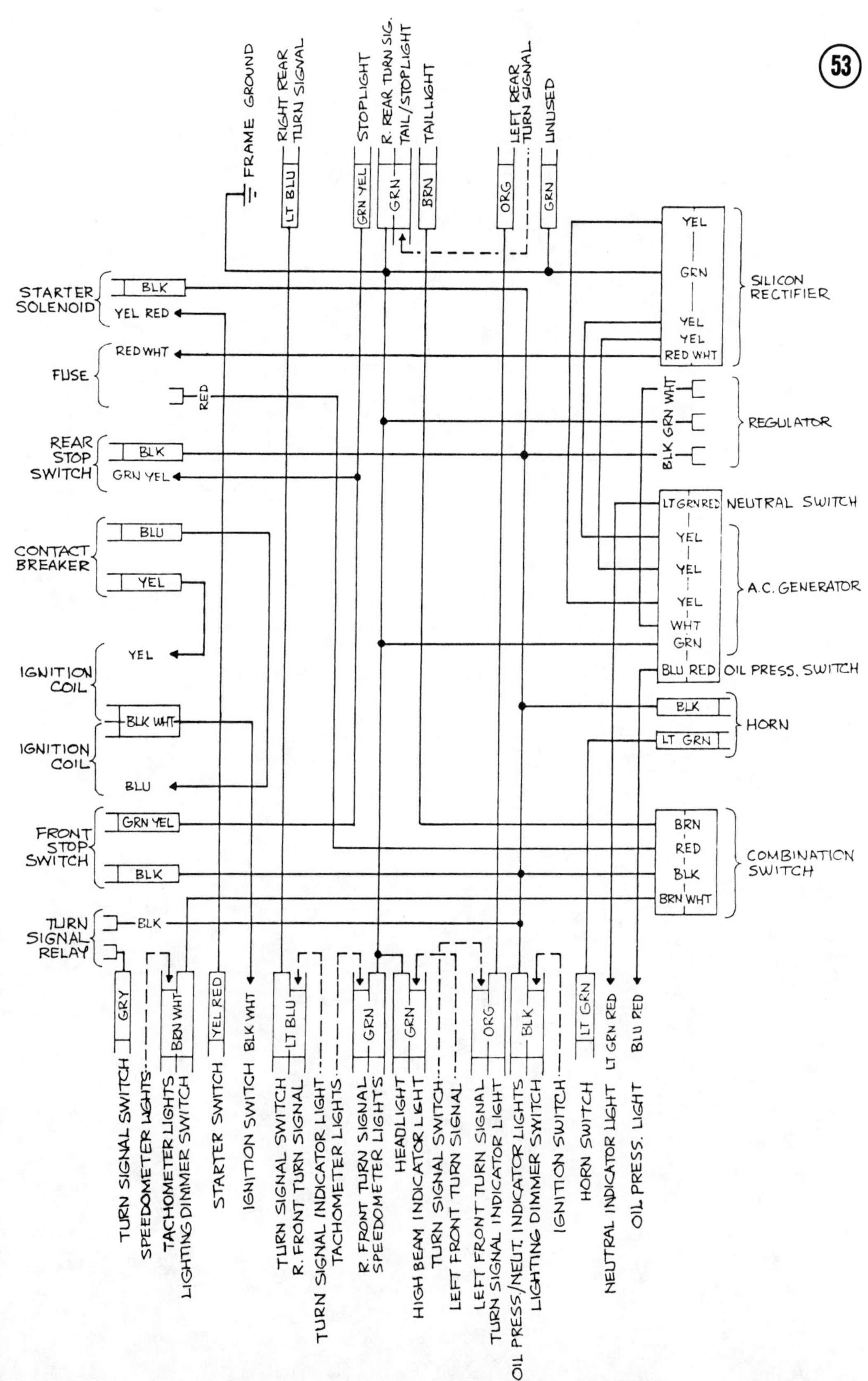
53
FRAME GROUND
RIGHT REAR TURN SIGNAL
STOPLIGHT
R. REAR TURN SIG. TAIL/STOPLIGHT
TAILLIGHT
LEFT REAR TURN SIGNAL
UNUSED
STARTER SOLENOID
FUSE
REAR STOP SWITCH
CONTACT BREAKER
IGNITION COIL
IGNITION COIL
FRONT STOP SWITCH
TURN SIGNAL RELAY
SILICON RECTIFIER
REGULATOR
NEUTRAL SWITCH
A.C. GENERATOR
OIL PRESS. SWITCH
HORN
COMBINATION SWITCH
TURN SIGNAL SWITCH
SPEEDOMETER LIGHTS
TACHOMETER LIGHTS
LIGHTING DIMMER SWITCH
STARTER SWITCH
IGNITION SWITCH
TURN SIGNAL SWITCH
R. FRONT TURN SIGNAL
TURN SIGNAL INDICATOR LIGHT
TACHOMETER LIGHTS
R. FRONT TURN SIGNAL
SPEEDOMETER LIGHTS
HEADLIGHT
HIGH BEAM INDICATOR LIGHT
TURN SIGNAL SWITCH
LEFT FRONT TURN SIGNAL
LEFT FRONT TURN SIGNAL
TURN SIGNAL INDICATOR LIGHT
OIL PRESS/NEUT. INDICATOR LIGHTS
LIGHTING DIMMER SWITCH
IGNITION SWITCH
HORN SWITCH
NEUTRAL INDICATOR LIGHT
OIL PRESS. LIGHT

7

Wiring diagrams for all models appear at the back of the book.

CHAPTER EIGHT

FRONT SUSPENSION AND STEERING

The front suspension is a critical part of the motorcycle for the rider's safety. A loose fork stem, worn steering bearings, or bent fork tubes can cause serious steering and handling problems at high speeds. Chapter Three describes periodic maintenance to minimize trouble.

FORKS
(CB750, CB750 K1-K6)

Removal

Refer to **Figure 1** for details of the front forks.

8

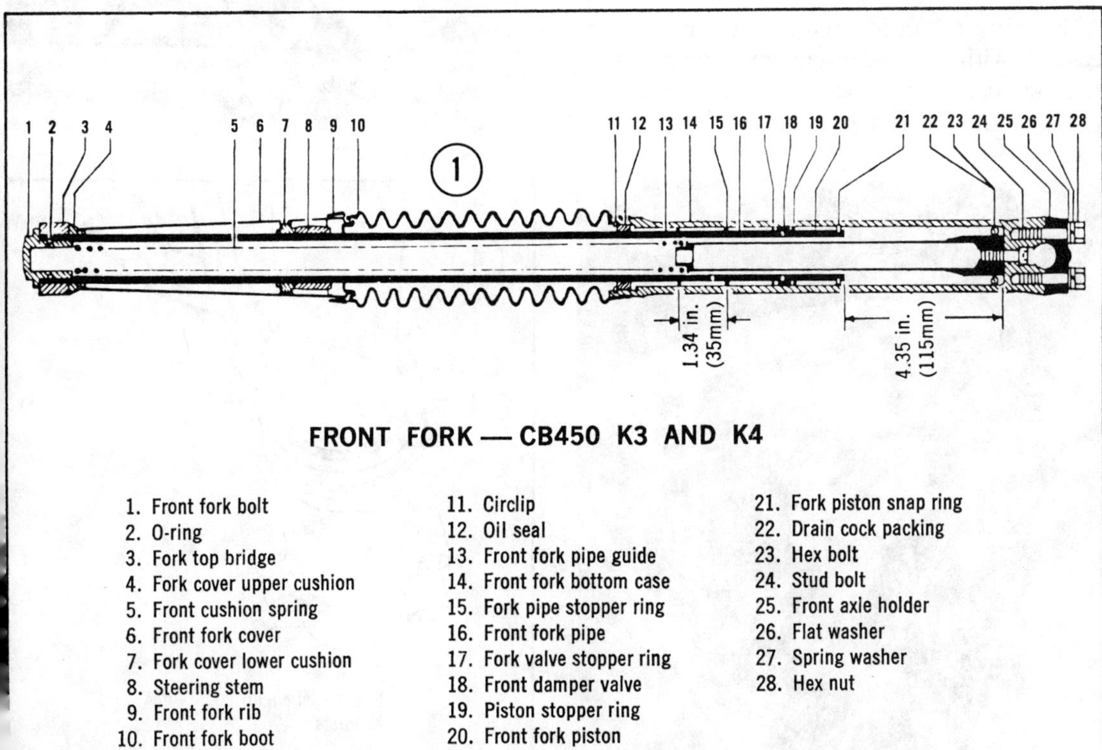

FRONT FORK — CB450 K3 AND K4

1. Front fork bolt
2. O-ring
3. Fork top bridge
4. Fork cover upper cushion
5. Front cushion spring
6. Front fork cover
7. Fork cover lower cushion
8. Steering stem
9. Front fork rib
10. Front fork boot
11. Circlip
12. Oil seal
13. Front fork pipe guide
14. Front fork bottom case
15. Fork pipe stopper ring
16. Front fork pipe
17. Fork valve stopper ring
18. Front damper valve
19. Piston stopper ring
20. Front fork piston
21. Fork piston snap ring
22. Drain cock packing
23. Hex bolt
24. Stud bolt
25. Front axle holder
26. Flat washer
27. Spring washer
28. Hex nut

1. Remove the front wheel according to the instructions in the *Front Wheel* section of Chapter Ten. Drain the oil from the forks as described in Chapter Three under *Periodic Lubrication, Front Fork Oil.*

2. Remove the 3 caliper set bolts and the adjuster nut. See **Figures 2A and 2B**. Then separate the caliper from the left fork.

3. Loosen the fork tube mounting bolts on the top bridge, and the mounting bolts on the steering stem. Then gently pull the fork down and out, as in **Figure 3**.

Disassembly

1. Remove the internal clip (**Figure 4**) with circlip pliers and remove tube from bottom case. Remove the 6mm bolt from the bottom fork case on K4 models.

2. Refer to **Figure 5** and remove snap ring and disassemble the piston and the damper valve.

Inspection

1. Measure piston diameters with a micrometer (**Figure 6**). If its diameter is less than 1.551 in. (39.40mm), the piston should be replaced.

2. Measure the inside diameter of the bottom case (2) with a cylinder gauge (1, **Figure 7**). If the diameter is greater than 1.562 in. (39.68mm), replace the case.

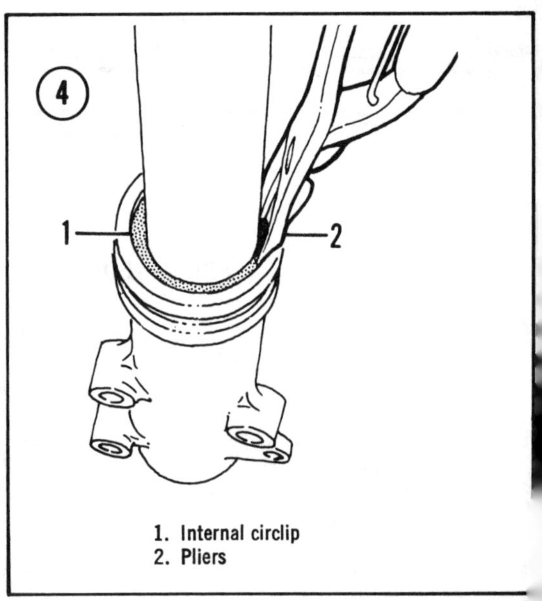

1. Internal circlip
2. Pliers

5

1. Oil seal
2. Fork tube guide
3. Fork tube stopper ring
4. Fork valve stopper ring
5. Damper valve
6. Fork piston
7. Fork piston snap ring

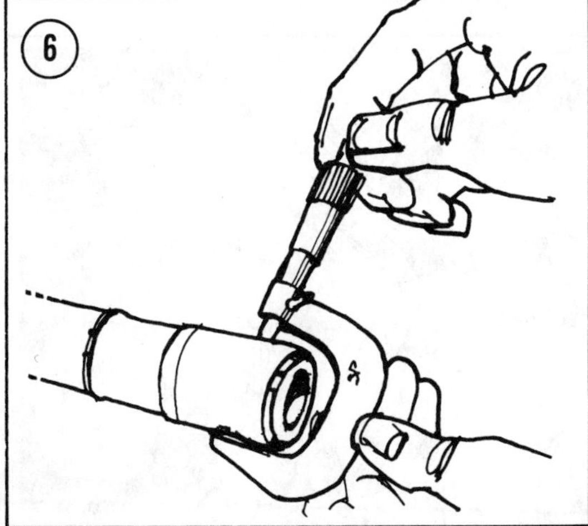

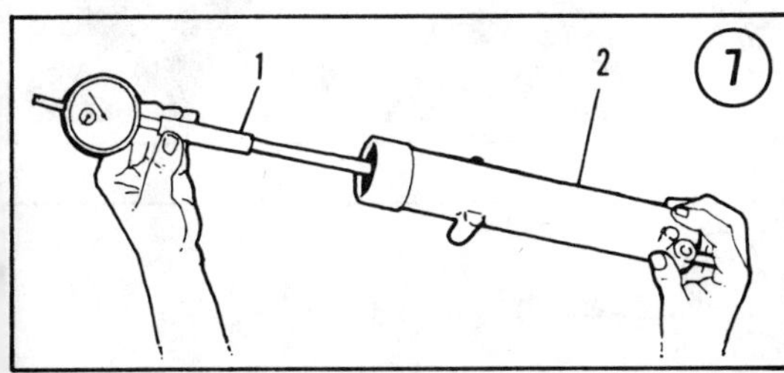

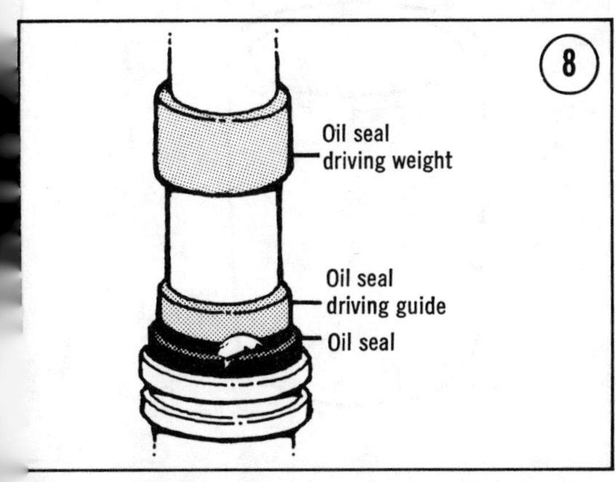

Assembly

1. Clean all parts in solvent. Reassemble the parts in the following order: tube guide, stopper rings, damper valve, piston, and snap ring. See **Figure 5**.

2. Insert the fork tube into the bottom case, and install the oil seal. **Figure 8** shows the special tools needed for the operation. Be careful not to damage the seal.

> NOTE: *In CB750 K1 through K4 models, the outside diameter of the oil seal is 0.8 in. (2mm) greater than in the earlier models, and the circlip diameter is 0.12 in. (3mm) greater. This was to correct the deformation of the seal and consequent oil leakage which occurred in some 750's.*

3. Refer to **Figure 4** and install the circlip.

4. Install the upper cover on the steering stem, above and below the cushion.

Installation

1. Insert the fork tube through the stem. Temporarily tighten with the 10mm set bolt.

2. Fill the forks with oil, as described in the *Front Fork Oil* section of Chapter Three.

3. Tighten the 8mm and 10mm set bolts (refer to **Figure 9**).

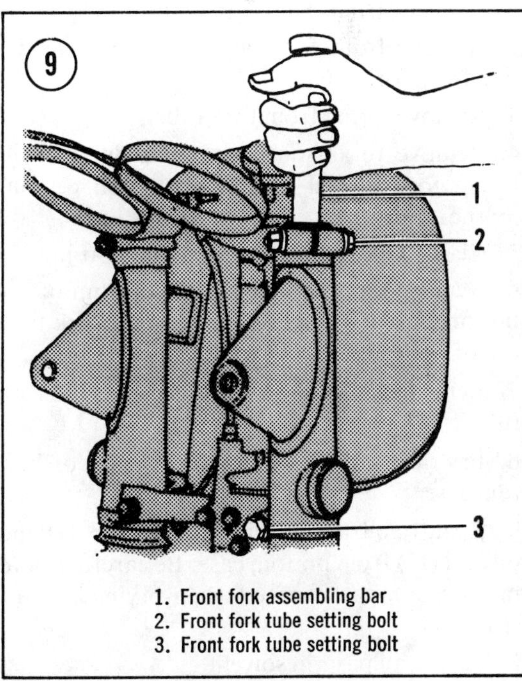

1. Front fork assembling bar
2. Front fork tube setting bolt
3. Front fork tube setting bolt

8

4. Adjust the front brake according to the instructions in Chapter Eleven.

FORK (CB750 K7/8, F AND A)

Removal/Installation

1. Remove front wheel as described under *Front Wheel Disassembly* in Chapter Ten.
2. Remove 2 bolts holding caliper to left fork and lift caliper off. Tie caliper up with wire to relieve tension on brake line.

> NOTE: *Do not touch front brake lever while caliper is off. If you do, the caliper may have to be partially disassembled to retract the brake pads. See* ***Front Brake System*** *in Chapter Eleven for procedure.*

3. Remove the front fender.
4. Loosen the clamp bolts on the upper and lower clamps **(Figure 10)** and slide forks out.
5. Installation is the reverse of these steps. Securely tighten the clamp bolts.

Disassembly/Assembly

Refer to **Figure 11** for this procedure.

1. Hold fork tube in vise with soft jaws. Keep bottom case (slider) lower than top end.
2. Remove front fork bolt (top plug) and O-ring from fork tube.
3. Remove spring from fork tube.
4. Remove fork from vise and pour out oil. Pump fork several times by hand to get out most of the oil.
5. Clamp bottom case in a vise with soft jaws.
6. Remove the Allen bolt at the bottom of the bottom case (17, **Figure 11**) and pull fork tube out of bottom case.
7. Remove parts (4-6, **Figure 11**) from the fork tube.
8. Pry dust seal (9, **Figure 11**) off top of bottom case.
9. Remove oil stopper ring (10, **Figure 11**) and oil seal (11) from bottom case. Be careful not to mar bottom case surface when prying out the seal.
10. Clean all parts in solvent.
11. Measure the fork tube outside diameter at several points where it fits inside the bottom case. Then measure the inside diameter of the bottom case at several points. If a difference of more than 0.001 in. (0.25mm) is noted between any of the outside and inside measurements, either the fork tube or the bottom case should be replaced. If discrepancies are noted, double check by taking the parts to your dealer for remeasurement and determination of the part to be replaced.
12. Measure the length of the spring. Replace if less than 19.5 in. (495mm).

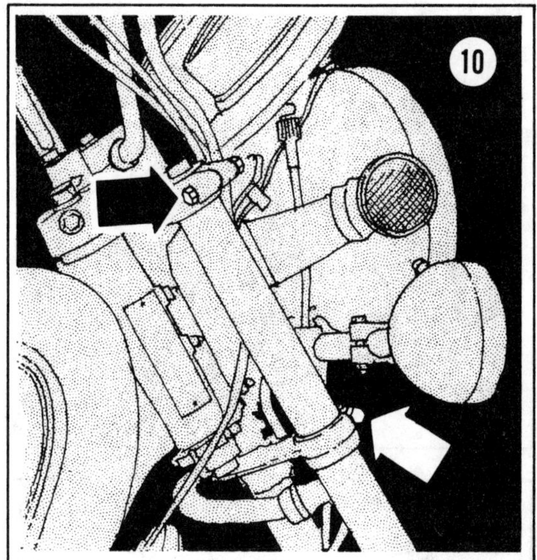

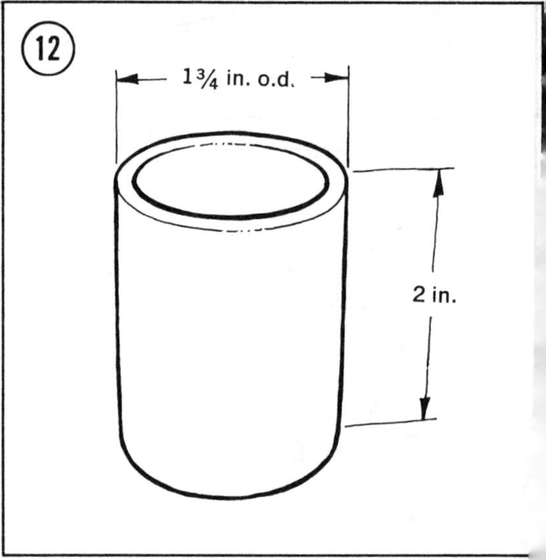

13. Assembly is the reverse of these steps. Use new seals. Install the seal in the bottom case with the seal spring facing down; make sure that it seats squarely and fully in the bore. A special tool can be made from pipe, using the dimensions shown in **Figure 12**.

14. Check and adjust steering play as described in this chapter under *Steering Play*.

STEERING ASSEMBLY

Refer to **Figure 13** for details of the steering assembly.

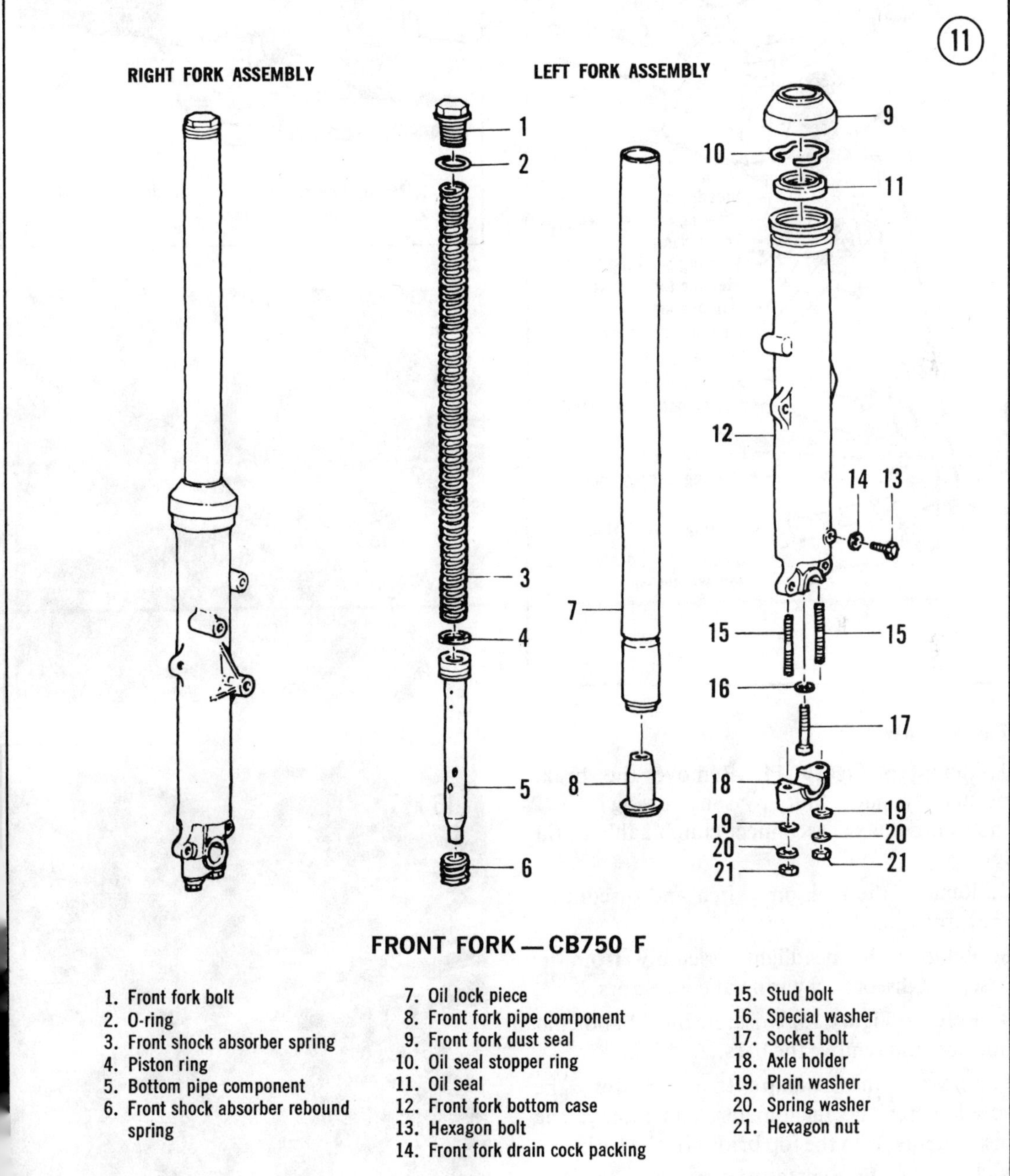

FRONT FORK—CB750 F

1. Front fork bolt
2. O-ring
3. Front shock absorber spring
4. Piston ring
5. Bottom pipe component
6. Front shock absorber rebound spring
7. Oil lock piece
8. Front fork pipe component
9. Front fork dust seal
10. Oil seal stopper ring
11. Oil seal
12. Front fork bottom case
13. Hexagon bolt
14. Front fork drain cock packing
15. Stud bolt
16. Special washer
17. Socket bolt
18. Axle holder
19. Plain washer
20. Spring washer
21. Hexagon nut

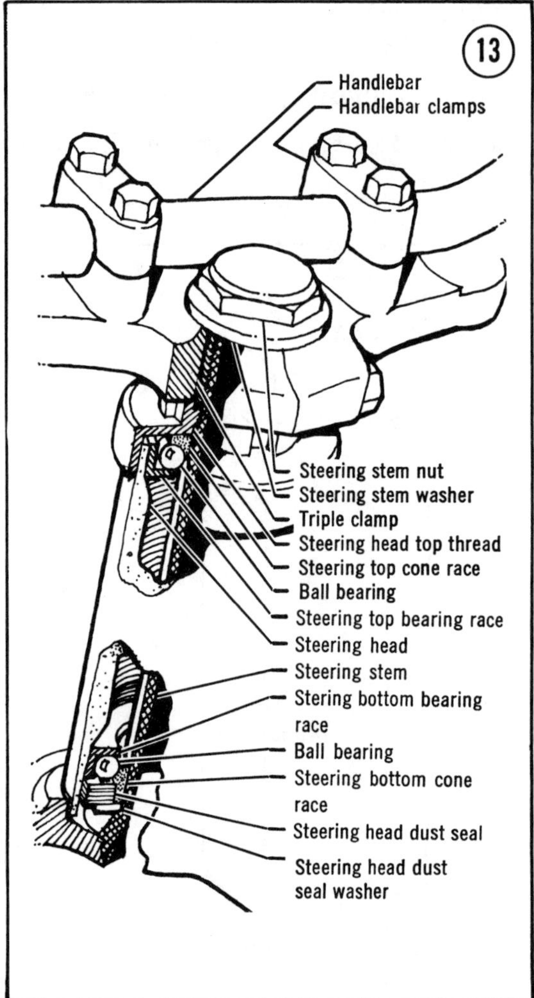

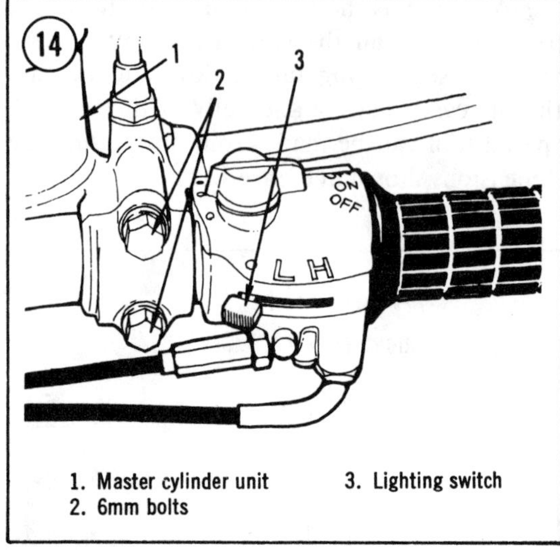

1. Master cylinder unit
2. 6mm bolts
3. Lighting switch

Disassembly

1. Refer to **Figure 14**. Remove the brake master cylinder unit by unscrewing the 2 mounting bolts. Disconnect clutch cable at the lever.

2. Remove the ignition switch and disconnect the throttle cable at the grip.

3. Remove the headlight assembly from its case, and disconnect wiring at connectors.

4. Refer to **Figure 15**. Unscrew the 2 handlebar holders, and remove the bars.

5. Loosen the clamp that secures the speedometer and tachometer, and remove the instruments from the top bridge of the fork.

6. Refer to **Figure 16** and remove the top bridge by loosening the stem nut, 2 top bolts, and the 3 set bolts.

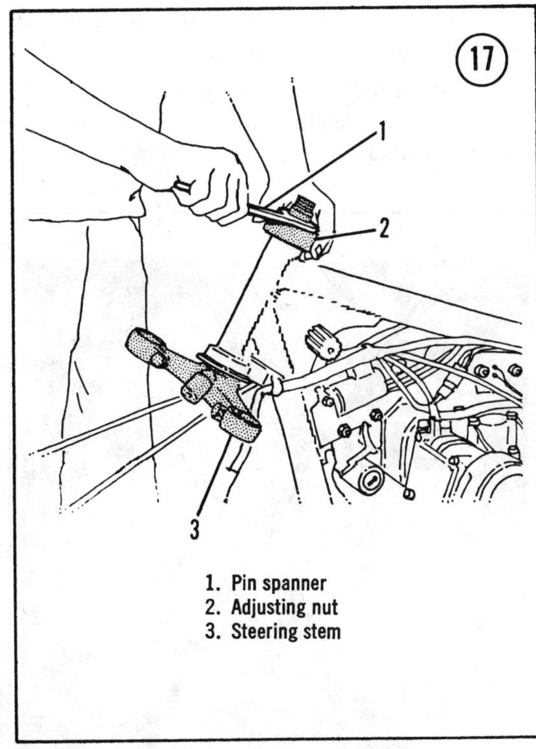

1. Pin spanner
2. Adjusting nut
3. Steering stem

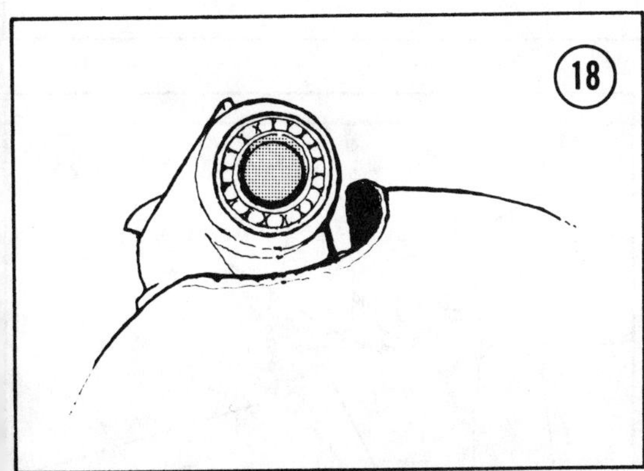

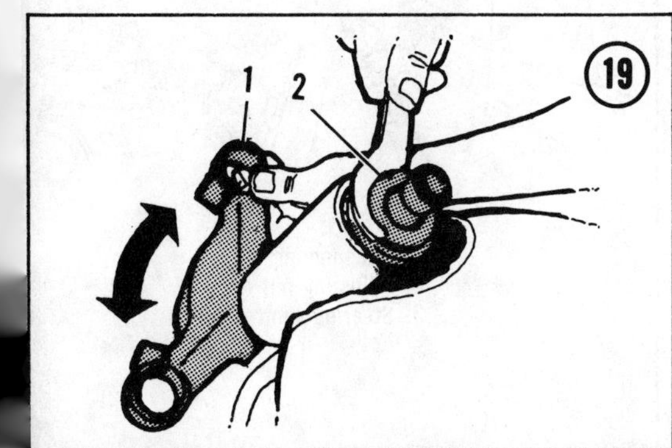

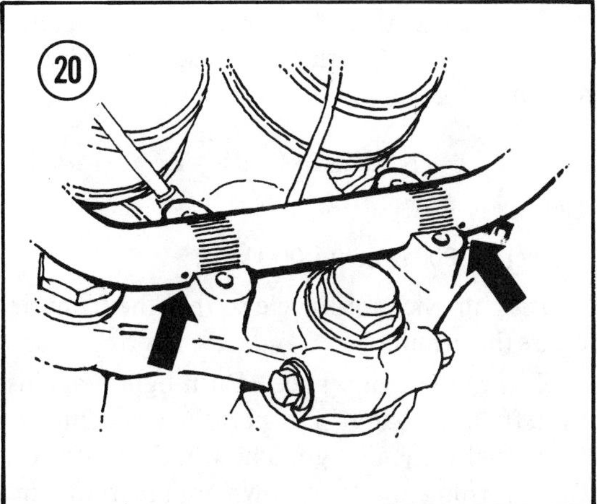

7. Put a block under the front of the engine so that the front wheel is clear of the ground. Remove the front forks as described earlier in this chapter.

8. Remove the steering stem thread. **Figure 17** shows the tool kit wrench that will make the job easier.

9. Pull out the steering stem, being careful not to drop the ball bearings.

8

Inspection

1. Check the handlebars for damage or bends.
2. Inspect the steering stem for distortion or cracks.
3. Check the bearings for wear.

Assembly

1. Liberally grease the steering bearing races. Assemble the bearings, inserting 18 balls on the upper side, and 19 on the lower side. Refer to **Figure 18**.
2. Insert the stem into the head pipe, being careful not to lose any bearing balls.
3. Refer to **Figure 19**. Screw the thread (2) down on the stem (1), so there is no clearance, and assembly turns lightly through an entire arc.
4. Assemble the front suspension.
5. Install the speedometer and tachometer.
6. Mount the handlebar and position it by aligning the punch marks on the bar with those on the holders (**Figure 20**).
7. Connect the headlight wiring and install the light assembly.

8. Connect the throttle cable, clutch cable, and master cylinder, routing the hoses and wires as shown in **Figure 21**.

STEERING PLAY

Check

Every 3,000 miles (5,000 km):

1. Prop up the motorcycle so that the front tire clears the ground.
2. Center the front wheel. Push lightly against the left handlebar grip to start the wheel turning to the right, then let go. The wheel should continue turning under its own momentum until the forks hit their stop.
3. Center the wheel, and push lightly against the right handlebar grip.
4. If, with a light push in either direction, the front wheel will turn all the way to the stop, the steering adjustment is not too tight.
5. Center the front wheel and kneel in front of it. Grasp the bottoms of the 2 front fork slider legs. Try to push them toward the engine. If no play is felt, the steering is not too loose.
6. If the steering adjustment is not correct, readjust it (see *Steering Play Adjustment,* this chapter).

Adjustment

1. Loosen the big steering stem cap nut on top of the top triple clamp.
2. Loosen the steering stem clamp bolt at the rear of the top triple clamp.

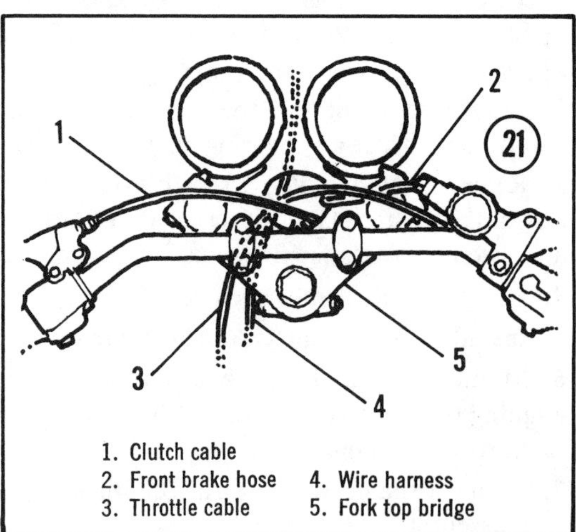

1. Clutch cable
2. Front brake hose
3. Throttle cable
4. Wire harness
5. Fork top bridge

3. Loosen the 2 fork tube clamp bolts on the bottom triple clamp (**Figure 22**).
4. Fit a pin-type wrench to the notched steering stem collar between the top triple clamp and the steering head (**Figure 23**).

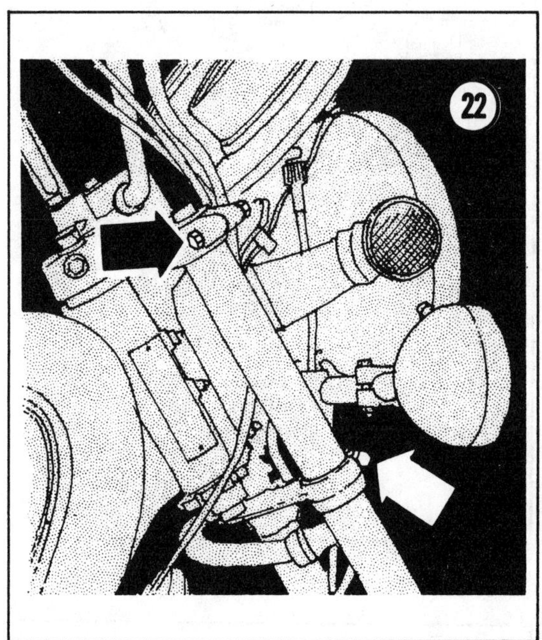

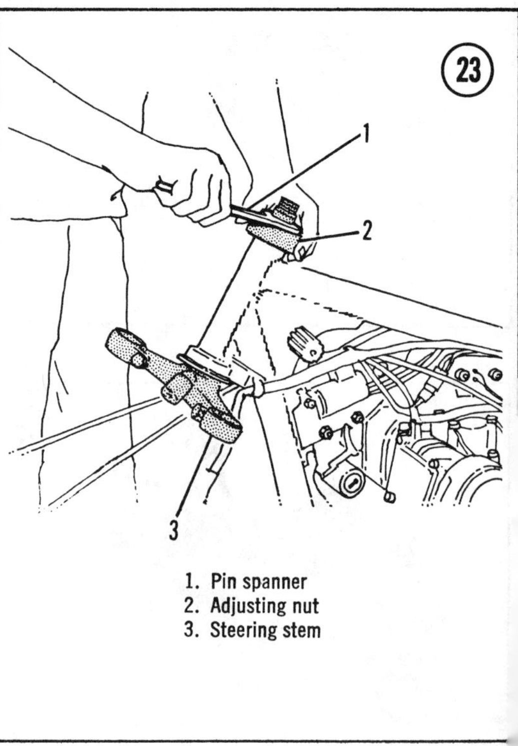

1. Pin spanner
2. Adjusting nut
3. Steering stem

5. Turn the collar clockwise to tighten the steering, or counterclockwise to loosen it.

6. Tighten the steering stem clamp bolt at the rear of the top triple clamp.

7. Torque steering stem clamp bolt at the rear of the top triple clamp to 12-13 ft.-lb. (1.6-1.8 mkg). Check that the 2 fork tube clamp bolts on the top triple clamp are torqued to 12-13 ft.-lb. (1.6-1.8 mkg).

8. Hit each side of the bottom triple clamp from the top and bottom with a rubber mallet to reposition it on fork tubes and relieve strain.

9. Torque the 2 fork tube clamp bolts on the bottom triple clamp to 39-43 ft.-lb. (5.4-5.9 mkg).

10. Recheck steering play (see *Steering Play, Check,* this chapter).

CHAPTER NINE

REAR SUSPENSION

The rear suspension consists of a swing arm, fork, hydraulic shock absorber, and spring. The springs may be pre-loaded for 3 ranges depending on operating conditions. The shocks **(Figure 1)** contain nitrogen gas under pressure and are sealed at the factory. They do not require routine servicing, and disassembly of the damper assembly could be dangerous because of the compressed gas.

REAR SHOCKS

Removal

1. Rest bike on centerstand and set shock on soft setting.
2. Refer to **Figure 2** and remove the nut and bolt from the top and bottom of shock.
3. Pull the unit from the frame.
4. Remove the spring with special Honda tool shown in **Figure 3** or take it to a dealer.

Inspection

1. Measure the free length of the spring with a vernier caliper. See **Figure 4**. If the length is less than 8.11 in. (230mm) for the 750 and 750 K1-K6, or 9.75 in. (244mm) for the F and A models, replace the spring.

2. Check trueness of the spring by placing it o end on a square to calculate the amount of tilt If the tilt is more than 2.5°, the assembl should be replaced.
3. Compress the unit by hand. There should b more resistance on the compression stroke tha on the extension stroke.

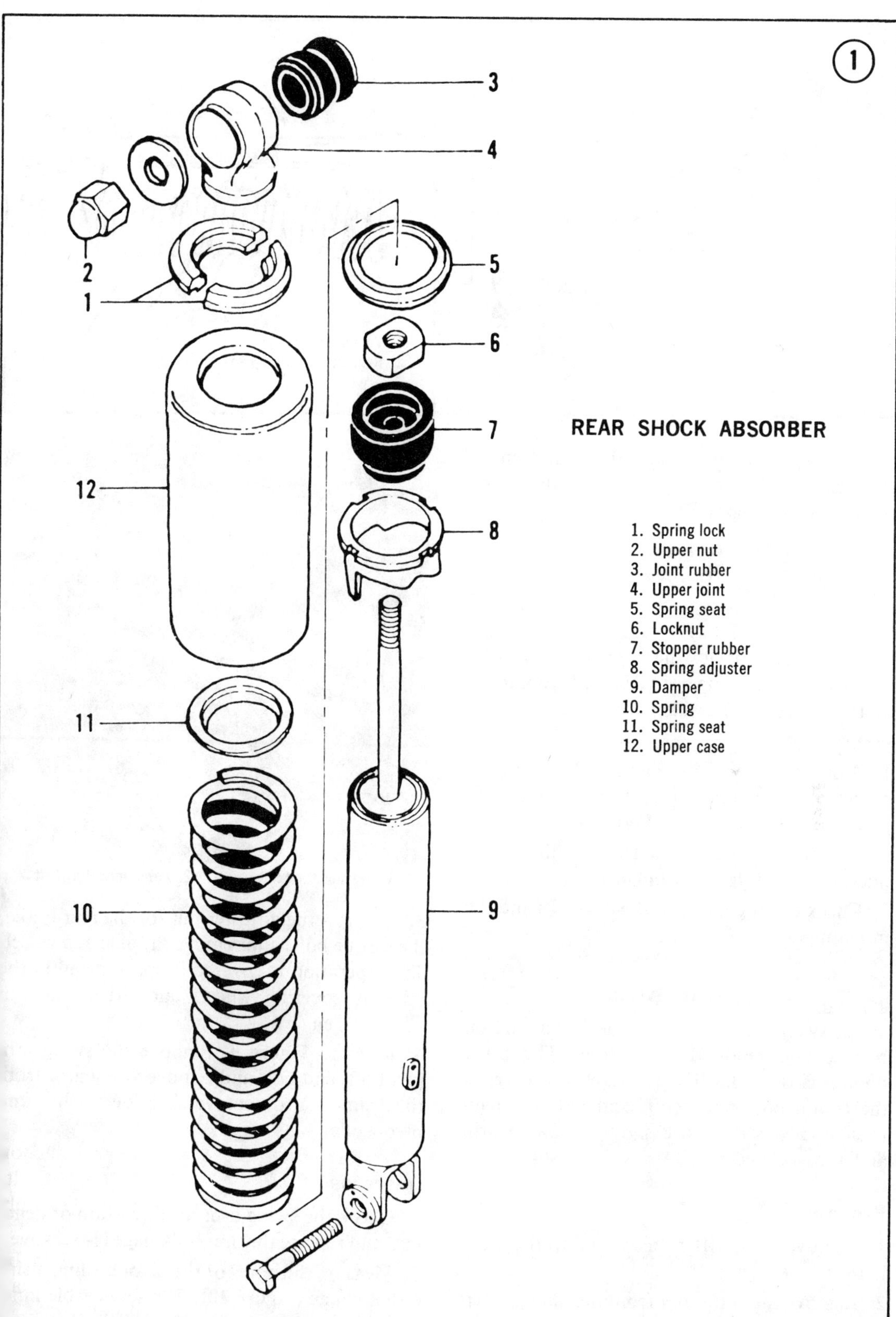

REAR SHOCK ABSORBER

1. Spring lock
2. Upper nut
3. Joint rubber
4. Upper joint
5. Spring seat
6. Locknut
7. Stopper rubber
8. Spring adjuster
9. Damper
10. Spring
11. Spring seat
12. Upper case

9

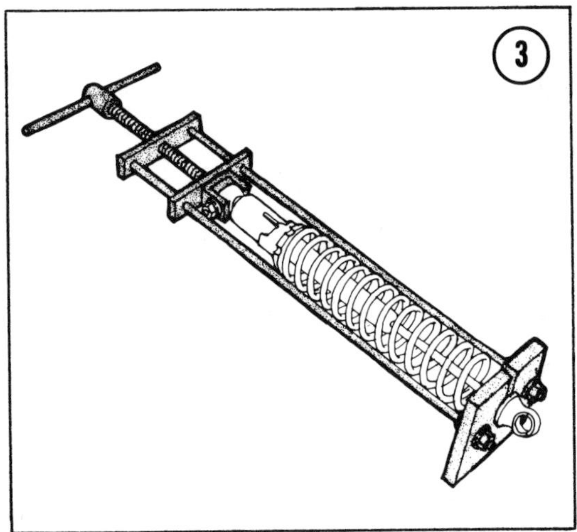

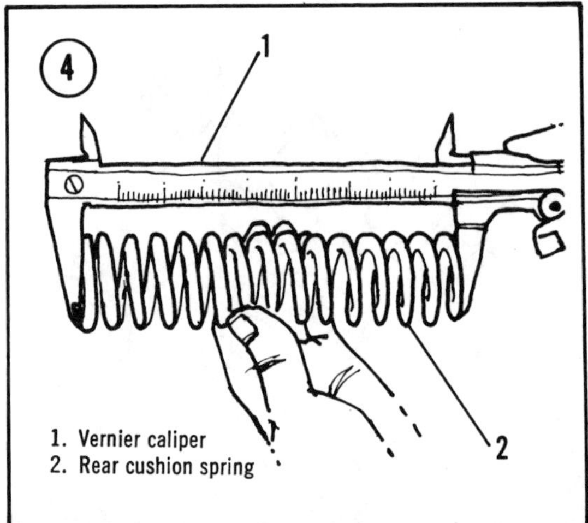

1. Vernier caliper
2. Rear cushion spring

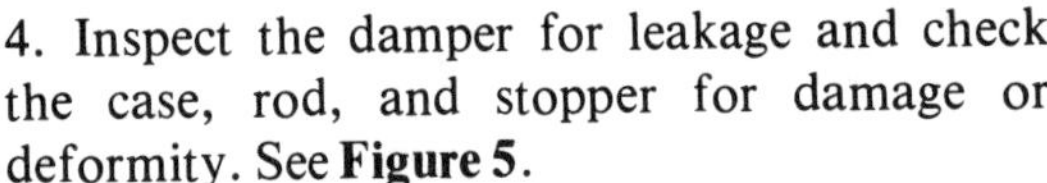

4. Inspect the damper for leakage and check the case, rod, and stopper for damage or deformity. See **Figure 5**.

NOTE: *The damper cannot be rebuilt. It must be replaced as a unit.*

Installation

On K1-K6 models, the dimensions of the stopper and the spring were changed from those on the earlier 750. Parts are not interchangeable between models.

1. Assemble the unit (**Figure 1**) using the special tool to compress the spring and lock it in place with the stopper. See **Figure 3**.
2. Mount the shock on the frame with the cap nuts and bolts (**Figures 5 and 6**).
3. Check the alignment of the 2 shocks and the mounting bolts.

SWING ARM

The swing arm pivots the wheel in an arc on bounce and rebound suspension. The pivot point is close to the drive sprocket, however, so the action does not significantly affect chain tension. **Figures 7 and 8** show the swing arm and its associated parts.

Removal

1. Remove the mufflers according to the steps in the frame section.
2. Remove the cotter pin from the axle, loosen the nut, and remove the drive chain.

1. Upper mounting nut 2. Lower mounting bolt

3. Unscrew the adjuster nut for the rear brake, the torque bolt, and remove the axle and wheel. This operation is covered in more detail in the sections covering wheels and drive chain in Chapter Ten.
4. Refer to **Figure 9**. Remove the swing arm pivot nut and bolt and remove swing arm from the frame. Also remove the side washer and pivot collar.

Inspection

1. Check the swing arm for distortion or bending, and replace the unit if damage is excessive
2. Measure the bores of the pivot bushing using a dial gauge (**Figure 10**). The serviceable inner diameter limit is 0.858 in. (21.8mm).

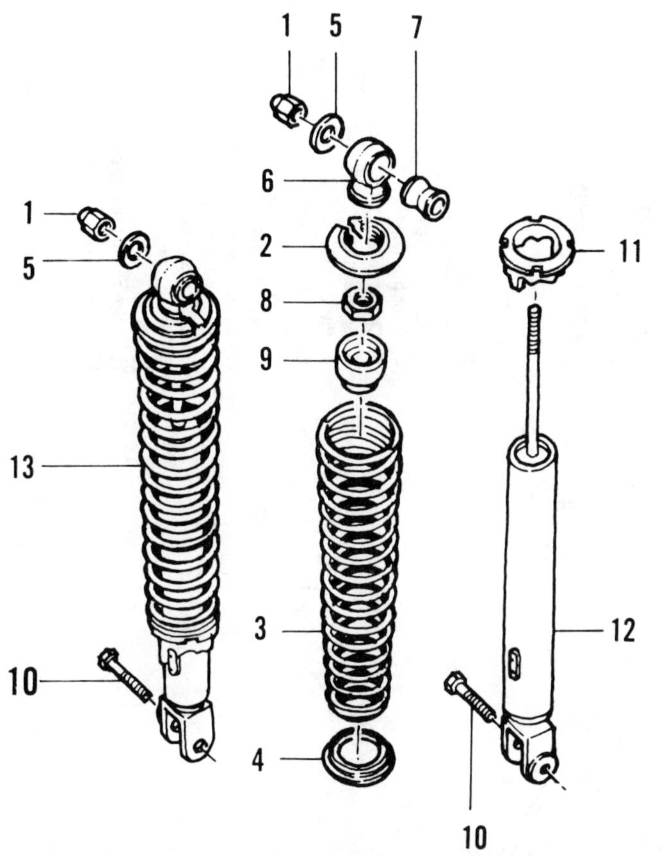

(6)

REAR SHOCK ABSORBER (CB750 F)

1. Rear shock absorber upper nut
2. Spring upper seat
3. Rear shock absorber spring
4. Spring under seat
5. Washer
6. Upper joint component
7. Joint rubber
8. Hexagon nut
9. Stopper rubber
10. Hexagon bolt
11. Spring adjuster
12. Rear shock absorber component
13. Rear shock absorber assembly

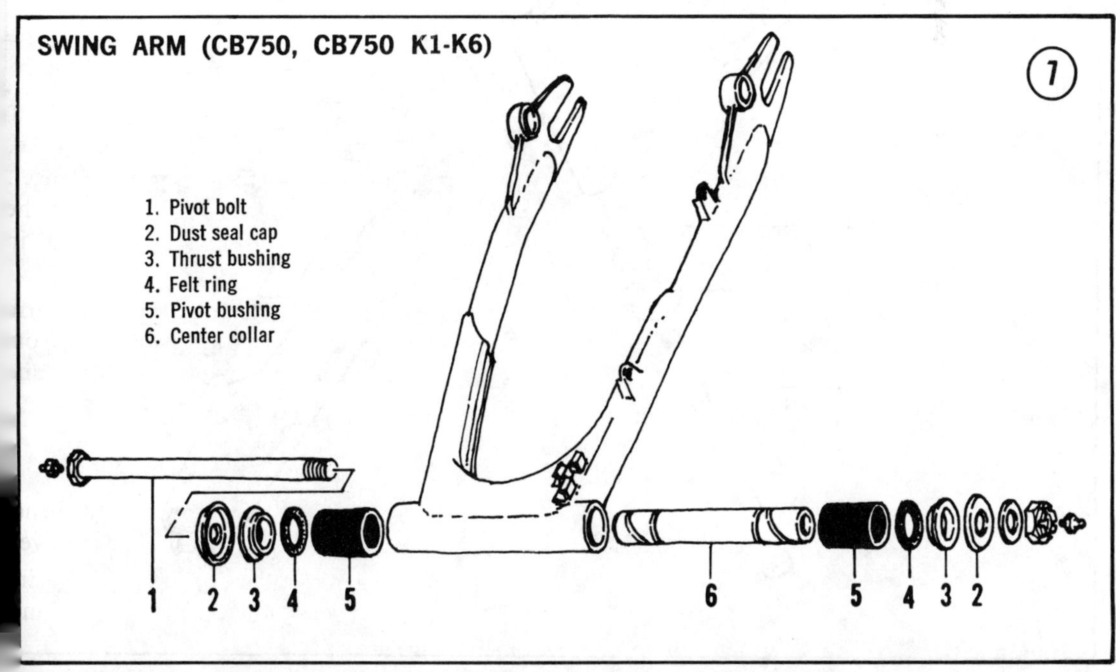

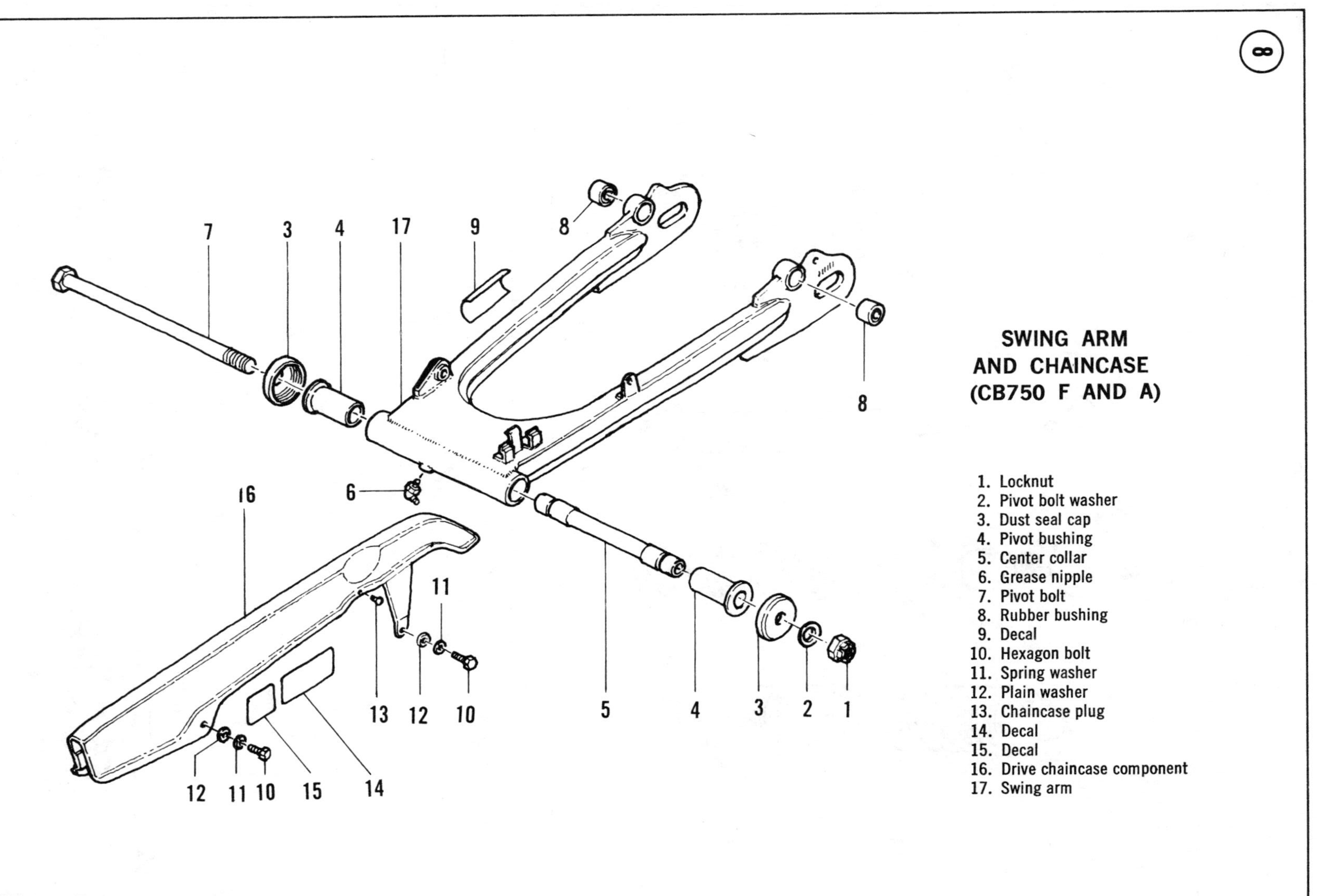
8
SWING ARM
AND CHAINCASE
(CB750 F AND A)
1. Locknut
2. Pivot bolt washer
3. Dust seal cap
4. Pivot bushing
5. Center collar
6. Grease nipple
7. Pivot bolt
8. Rubber bushing
9. Decal
10. Hexagon bolt
11. Spring washer
12. Plain washer
13. Chaincase plug
14. Decal
15. Decal
16. Drive chaincase component
17. Swing arm

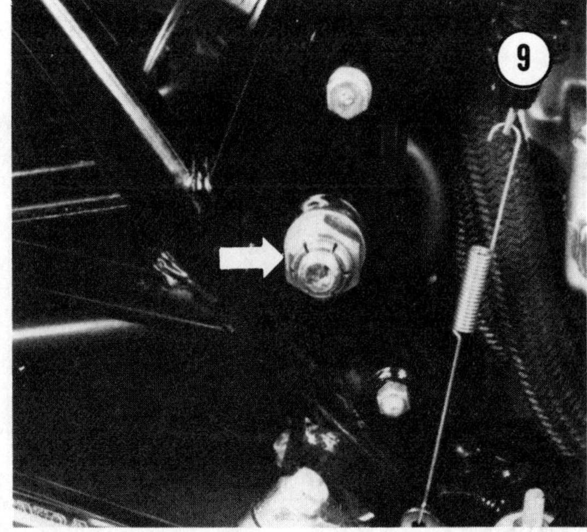

3. Measure the outside diameter of the center collar with a micrometer as shown in the illustration. The outside diameter serviceable limit is 0.8452 in. (21.4mm).

Installation

1. Grease the pivot collar liberally and insert it into the swing arm. Insert the pivot bolt from the right side. While holding the dust caps in place, tighten the nut.
2. Install the rear wheel and drive chain.
3. Adjust the rear brake pedal and drive chain tension. Instructions are in Chapter Three, *Rear Brake Linkage Adjustment,* and *Drive Chain Service,* respectively.

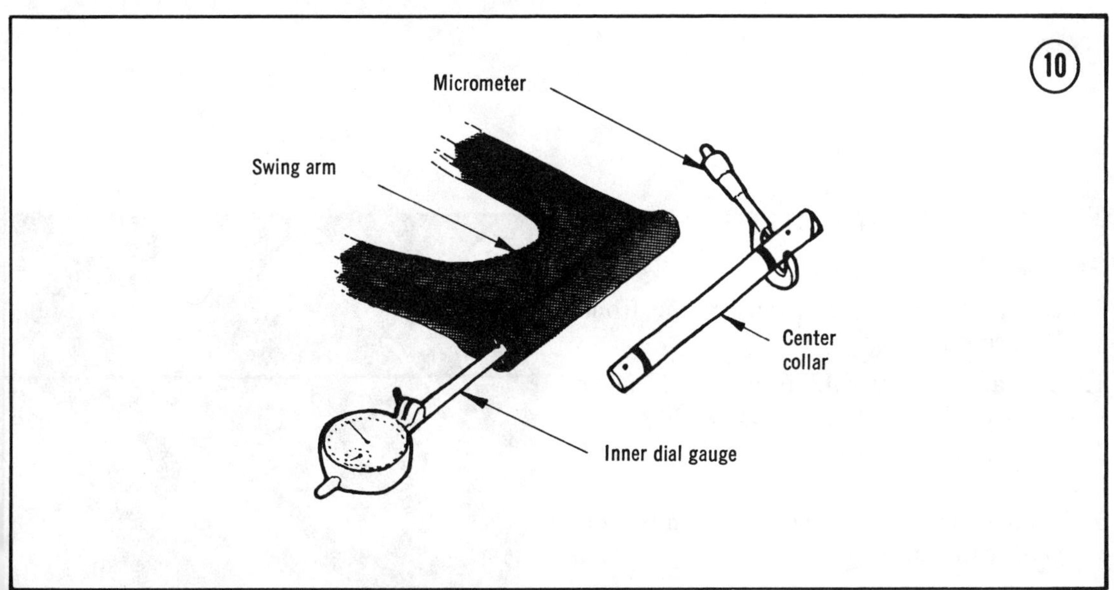

CHAPTER TEN

WHEELS AND FINAL DRIVE

FRONT WHEEL

Removal/Disassembly

Refer to **Figure 1** for details of the front wheel assembly.

1. Place a block under the front of the engine so the wheel is raised clear of the ground.
2. Remove the speedometer cable **(Figure 2)** at the hub.
3. Remove the axle holding nuts. Remove the wheel from the forks.

> NOTE: *Do not work the brake lever when the wheel is off the motorcycle, or the caliper piston will be forced out of the cylinder.*

4. Unscrew the axle nut **(Figure 3)** and remove the axle.
5. Remove the gearbox for the speedometer.
6. On models equipped with lock plates, straighten the lock plates. On all models, unscrew the nuts from the wheel **(Figure 4)** and remove the disc.
7. Remove the bearing retainer from the hub **(Figure 5)** and remove the dust seal from the retainer.
8. Remove the bearing.

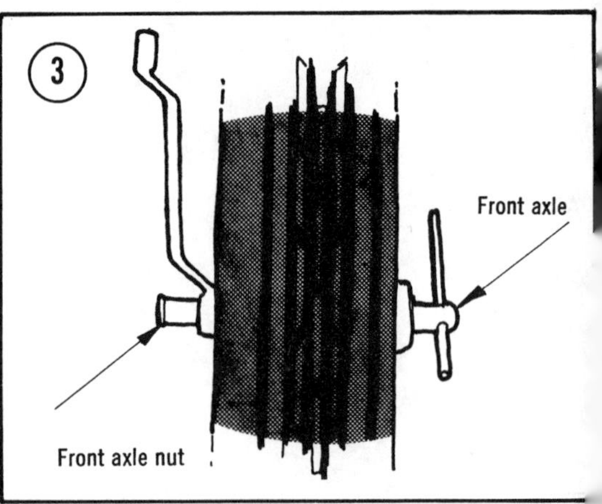

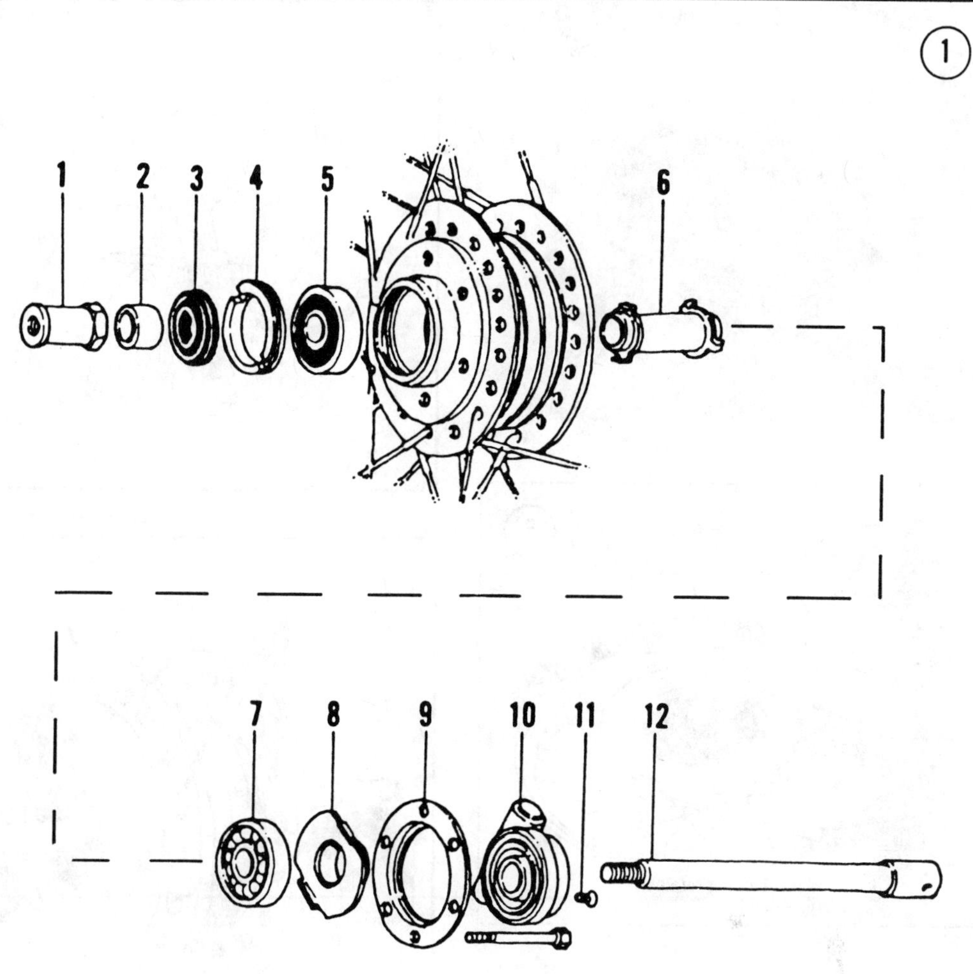

FRONT WHEEL

1. Front axle nut
2. Front wheel collar
3. Dust seal
4. Front wheel bearing retainer
5. Ball bearing
6. Front axle distance collar
7. Ball bearing
8. Gearbox retainer
9. Gearbox retainer cover
10. Speedometer gearbox
11. Oval screw
12. Front axle

4

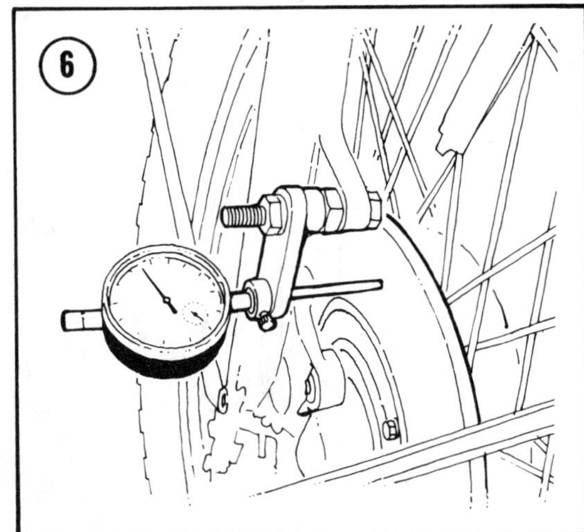
6

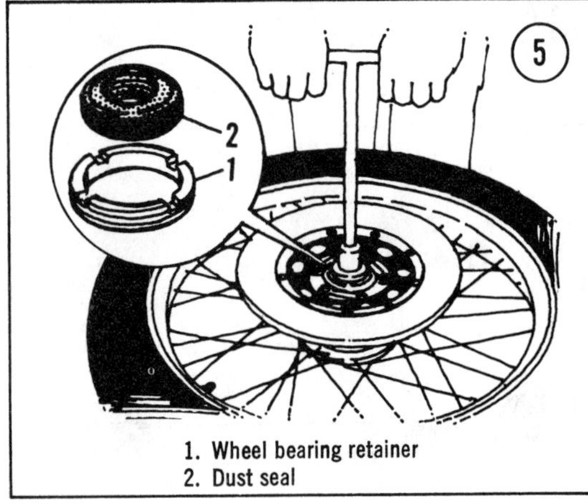

1. Wheel bearing retainer
2. Dust seal

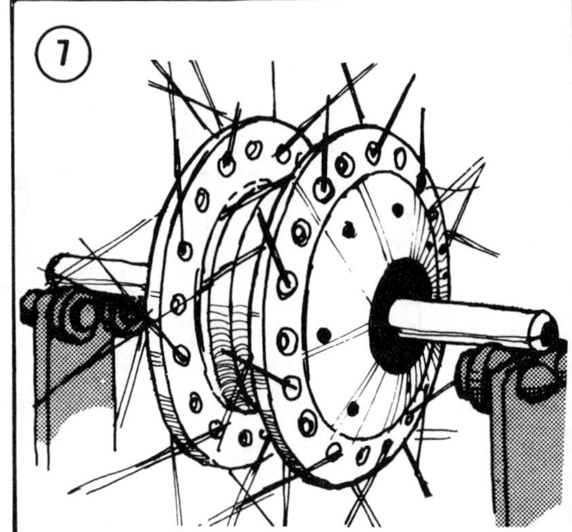
7

NOTE: *Tire removal is only necessary if there is a puncture to be repaired or a new tire is to be installed on the wheel.*

Inspection

1. Measure the flatness of the brake disc with a dial gauge as shown in **Figure 6**. The disc should be placed on a flat surface for this check. If the flatness varies by more than 0.012 in. (0.3mm), the disc should be replaced. If the thickness is less than 0.217 in. (5.5mm), the disc also should be replaced.

2. Measure the runout of the wheel rim using a dial gauge. Mount the wheel on a horizontal shaft so it can turn freely, and measure according to **Figure 7**. Repair or replace the rim if the runout is more than 0.080 in. (2mm).

3. Rotate the bearings by hand and check for roughness (**Figure 8**). If the bearings turn smoothly, they need not be removed. However,

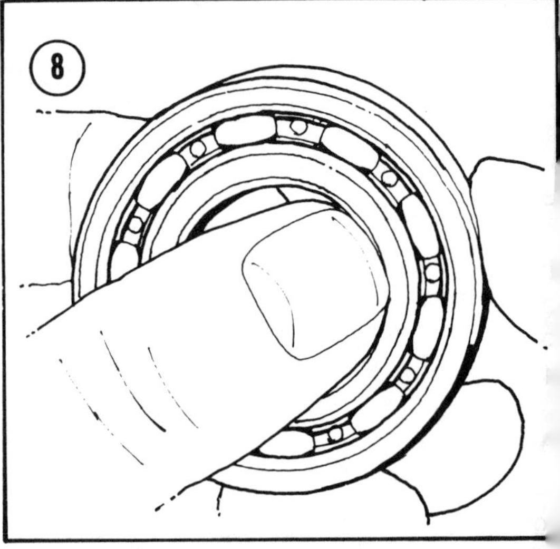
8

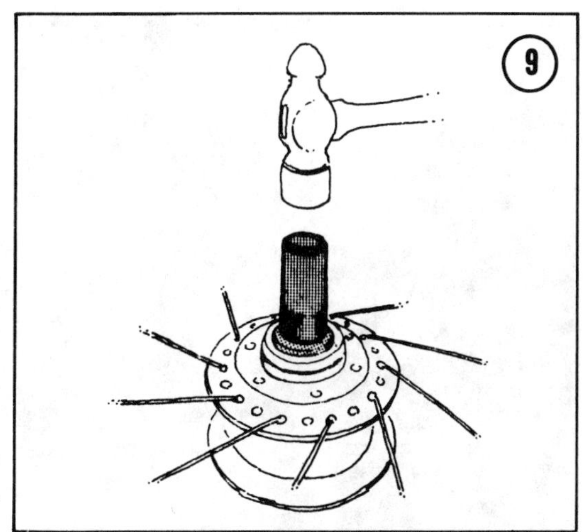

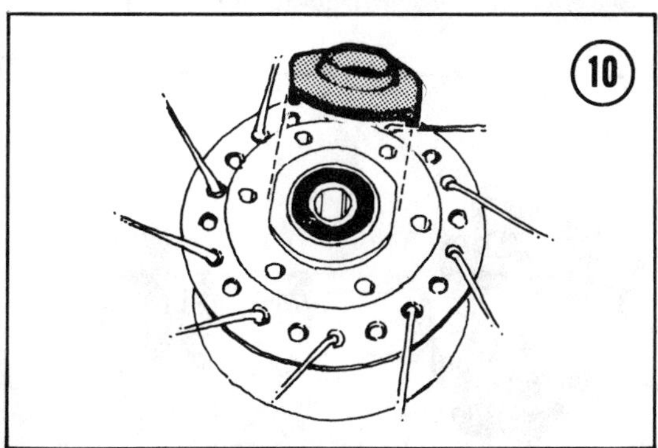

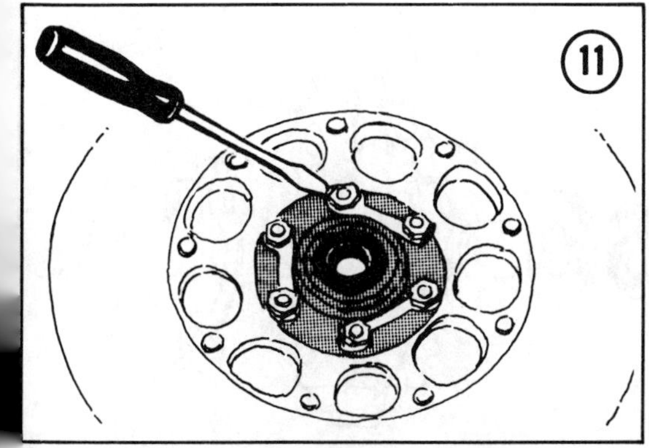

if roughness is apparent, drive the bearings out of the wheel from the inside using a soft drift, or from the outside using a bearing puller.

4. Check axle for wear and straightness.

Assembly/Installation

. Use a bearing driver to install the bearing into the wheel (**Figure 9**).

2. Install the dust seal on the bearing retainer, and mount it into the hub.

3. Align the gearbox retainer (**Figure 10**) to the cutout in the hub, and install it from above.

4. Install the 6 disc mounting bolts (see NOTE) and mount the disc on the opposite side and install the nuts.

> NOTE: *On CB750 K1 through K4 models, the hub is 0.157 in. (4mm) thinner, and the mounting bolts were shortened by the same amount. Using the older, longer bolts on these models will result in the disc loosening during operation.*

When installing the disc models equipped with lock plates, use new lock plates and bend their tabs over against a flat of each nut after the nuts have been tightened (**Figure 11**).

5. Insert the axle through the speedometer gearbox (**Figure 12**) from the right side, and tighten the axle nut.

6. Mount the wheel on the forks, install the axle holders, and tighten the nuts.

7. Connect the speedometer cable to the gearbox (**Figure 13**).

REAR WHEEL

See **Figure 14** (all models except CB750F) for details of the rear wheel and sprocket. See **Figure 15** for CB750F.

Removal/Disassembly

1. Place the motorcycle on the centerstand.
2. Remove the rear brake adjusting nut and rod as shown in **Figure 16** (except CB750F), or perform Steps 1, 2, and 3 of *Rear Disc Brake Caliper* in Chapter Eleven (CB750F).
3. Refer to **Figure 17**. Remove the brake stopper arm lock pin, flat washer, spring washer, and bolt (all except CB750F).
4. Remove the cotter pin from the right side of the axle, and loosen the nut. See **Figure 18**.

14

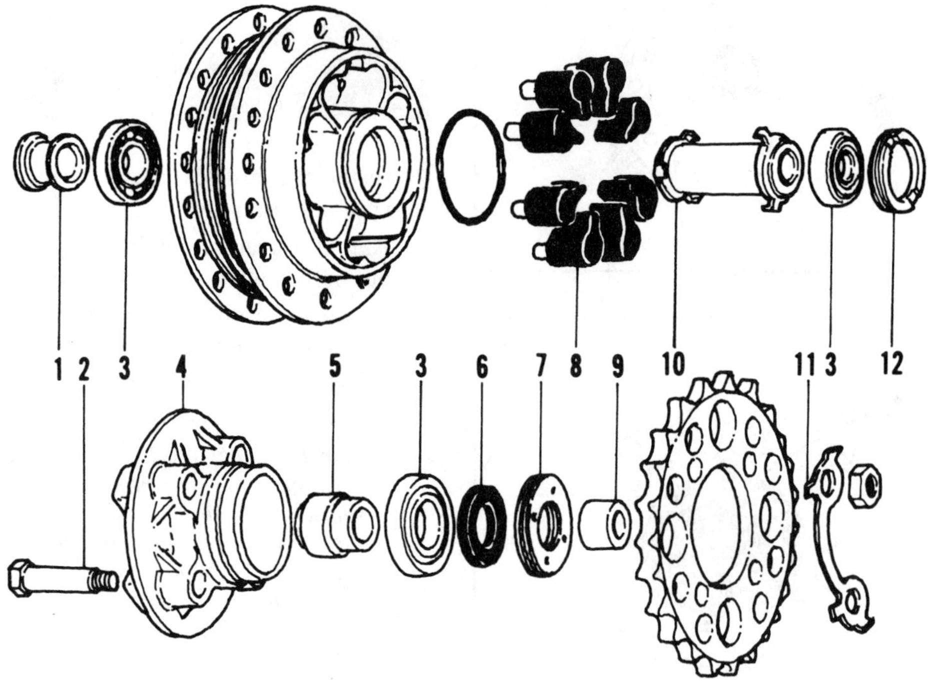

1 2 3 4 5 3 6 7 8 9 10 11 3 12

REAR WHEEL AND SPROCKET (CB750 AND CB750 K1-K6 AND A)

1. Rear brake panel side collar
2. Driven sprocket fixing bolt
3. Ball bearing
4. Final drive flange
5. Axle sleeve
6. Oil seal
7. Bearing retainer
8. Wheel damper
9. Side collar
10. Axle spacer
11. Tongued washer
12. Wheel bearing retainer

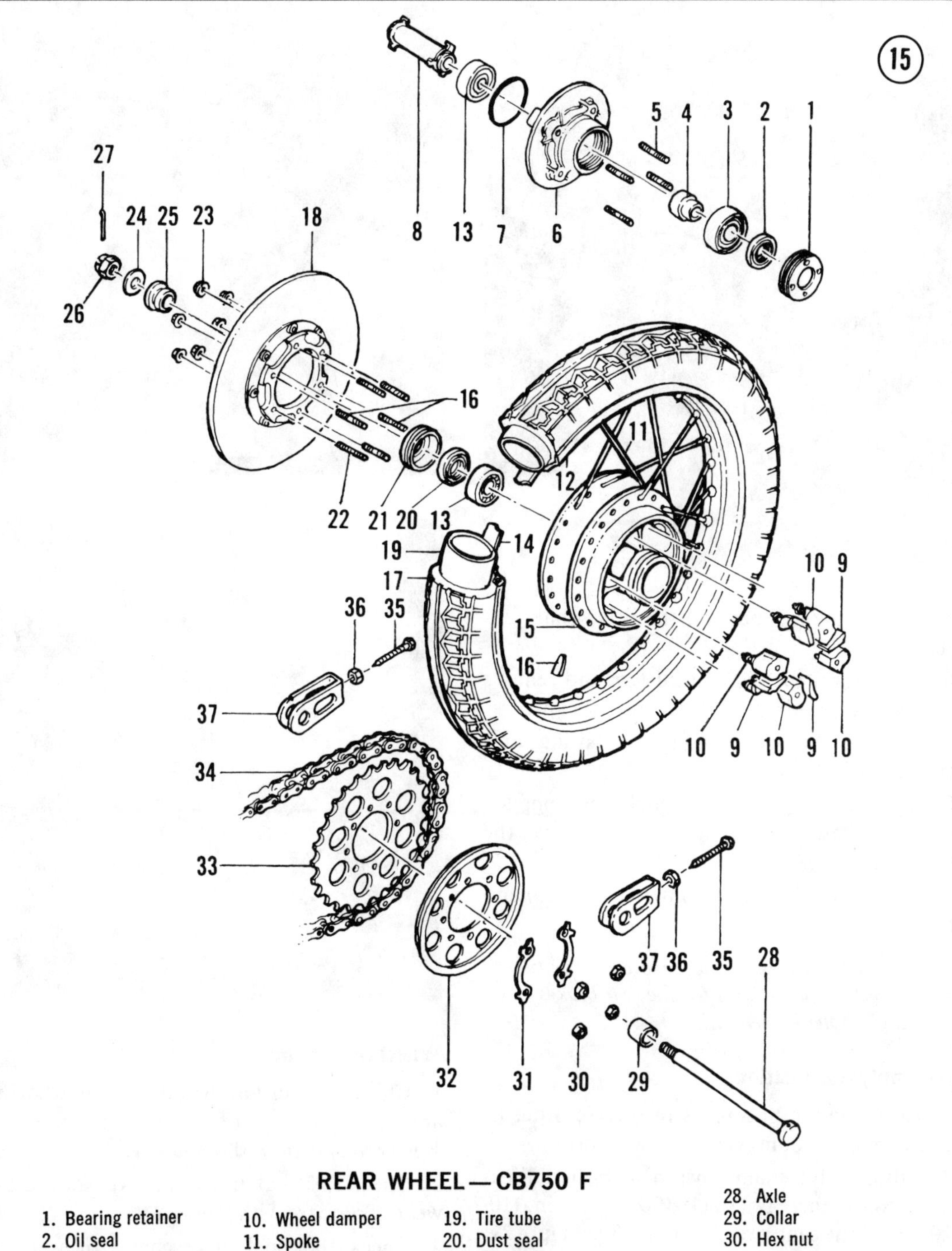

REAR WHEEL—CB750 F

1. Bearing retainer
2. Oil seal
3. Ball bearing
4. Axle sleeve
5. Stud bolt
6. Flange
7. O-ring
8. Rear axle spacer
9. Wheel damper
10. Wheel damper
11. Spoke
12. Wheel rim
13. Ball bearing
14. Tire flap
15. Wheel hub
16. Balancer
17. Tire
18. Brake disc
19. Tire tube
20. Dust seal
21. Rear wheel bearing retainer
22. Stud bolt
23. Hex nut
24. Washer
25. Wheel side collar
26. Wheel axle nut
27. Split pin
28. Axle
29. Collar
30. Hex nut
31. Tongued washer
32. Sprocket side plate
33. Sprocket
34. Drive chain
35. Chain adjusting bolt
36. Hex nut
37. Chain adjuster

5. Loosen the locknuts on the drive chain adjusters.

6. Turn down the chain adjusters and remove the swing arm cap fixing bolts and the caps.

7. Remove the wheel from the swing arm frame.

8. Refer to **Figure 19**. Unlock the tongued washers, unscrew the nuts, and remove the sprocket.

9. Remove the bearing retainer **(Figure 20)** and the bearing.

> NOTE: *Refer to the inspection and overhaul procedures for the rear brakes in Chapter Eleven.*

Assembly/Installation

1. Assemble the hub parts in reverse order of disassembly. Mount wheel on swing arm.

2. Adjust drive chain tension with the adjustment bolt so there is a slack of 0.40-0.80 in. (10-20mm) at the center of the chain. See **Figure 21**. The *Chain* section of this chapter gives more details on the procedure.

3. Adjust free play of the brake pedal according to *Rear Brake Adjustment* in Chapter Eleven.

4. Balance the wheel. See *Wheel Balance* in this chapter.

Wheel Inspection

1. Check runout and wobble of the wheel rim and the condition of the bearing. See *Front Wheel, Inspection,* this chapter.

2. Check the final driven sprocket for excessive wear. Compare with **Figure 22**.

3. Check the final drive chain for wear and stretch. See Chapter Three for routine maintenance and repair under *Drive Chain*.

SPOKES

The spokes support the weight of the motor cycle and rider, and transmit tractive and brak

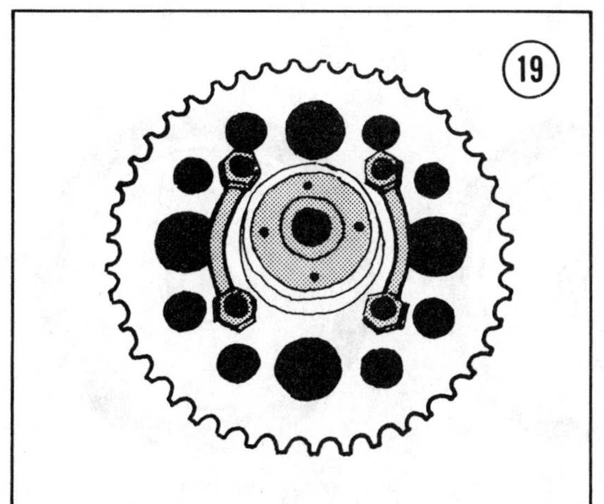

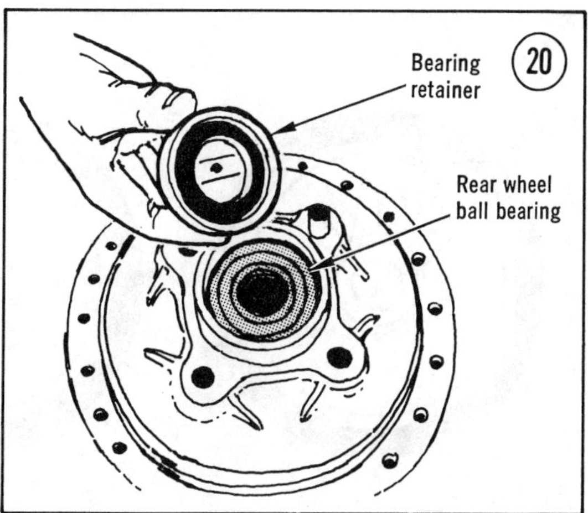

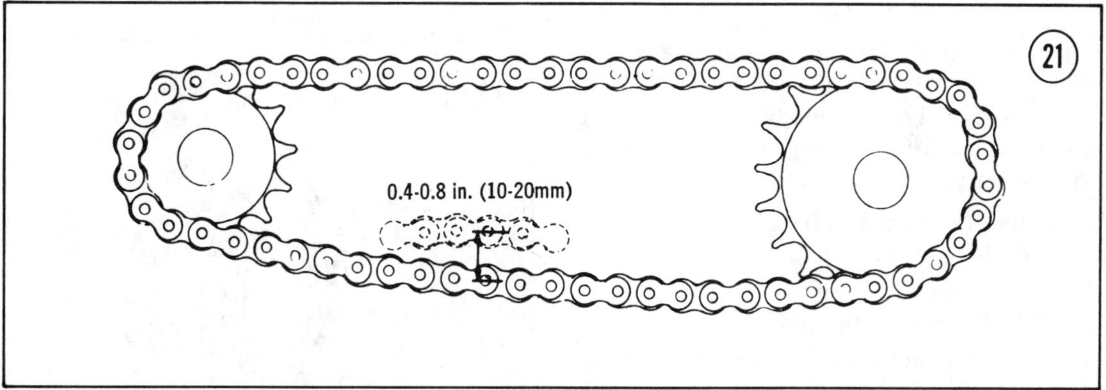

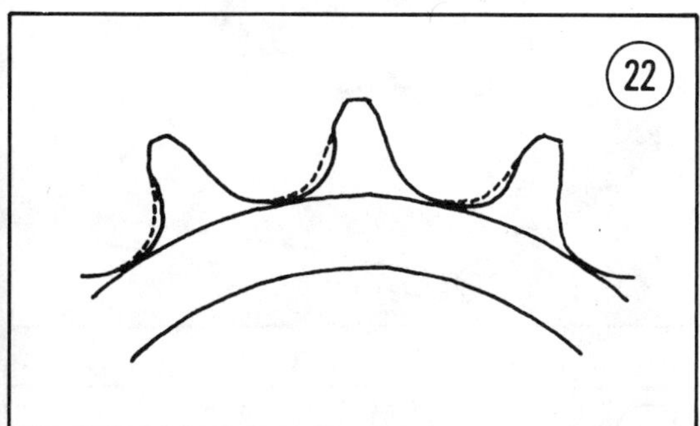

ing forces, as shown in **Figure 23**. Diagram A illustrates action of the spokes as they support the machine. Tractive forces are shown in Diagram B. Braking forces are shown in Diagram C.

Check the spokes periodically for looseness or binding. A bent or otherwise faulty spoke will adversely affect neighboring spokes, and should therefore be replaced immediately. To remove the spoke, completely unscrew the threaded portion, then remove the bent end from the hub.

Spokes tend to loosen as the machine is used. Retighten each spoke one turn, beginning with those on one side of the hub, then those on the other side. Tighten the spokes on a new machine after the first 50 miles of operation, then at 50-mile intervals until they no longer loosen.

If the machine is subjected to particularly severe service, as in off-road or competition riding, check the spokes frequently.

WHEEL BALANCE

An unbalanced wheel results in unsafe riding conditions. Depending on the degree of unbalance and the speed of the motorcycle, the rider may experience anything from a mild vibration to a violent shimmy which may even result in loss of control. Balance weights are applied to the spokes on the light side of the wheel to correct this condition.

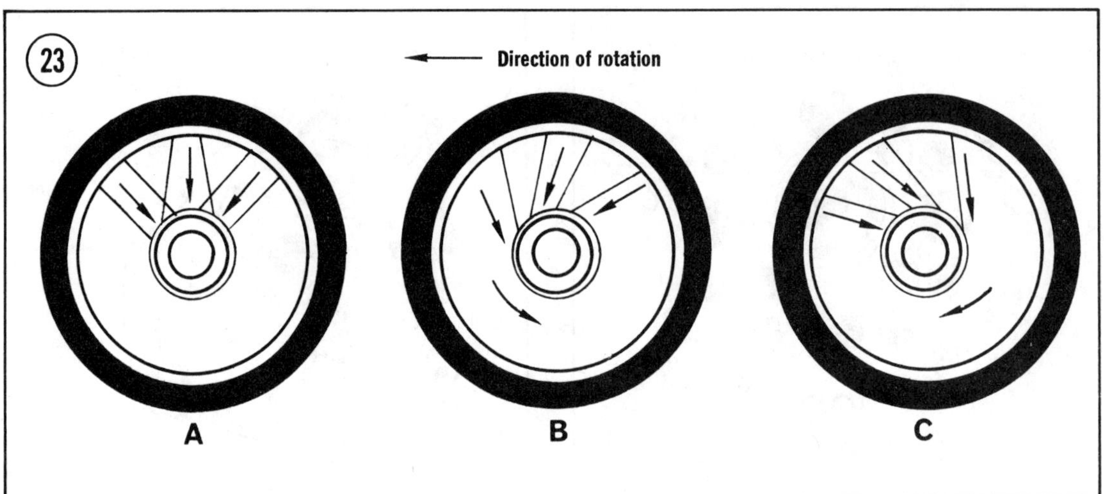

Before you attempt to balance the wheel, check to be sure that the wheel bearings are in good condition and properly lubricated, and that the brakes do not drag, so that the wheel rotates freely.

1. Mount the wheel on a fixture such as the one in **Figure 24** so it can rotate freely.
2. Give the wheel a spin and let it coast to a stop. Mark the tire at the lowest point.
3. Spin the wheel several more times. If the wheel keeps coming to a rest at the same point it is out of balance.
4. Attach a weight to the upper (or light) side of the wheel at the spoke (**Figure 25**). Weights come in 4 sizes: 5, 10, 15, and 20 grams.
5. Experiment with different weights until the wheel, when spun, comes to rest at a different position each time.

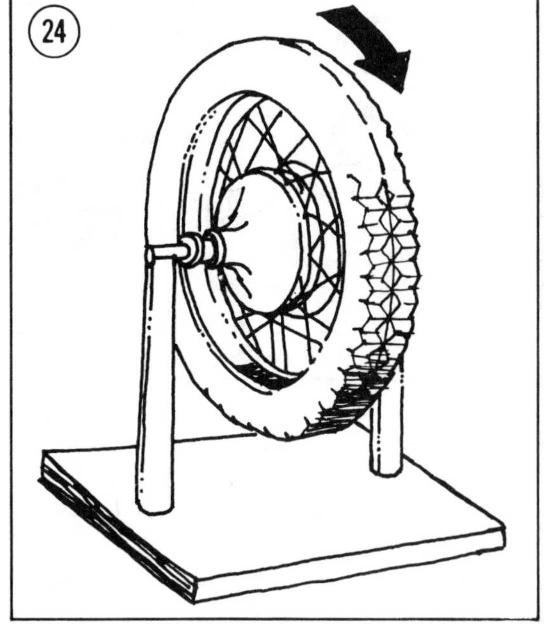

RIM TRUING

1. Prop the motorcycle so the wheel clears the ground.
2. For checking the rear wheel, remove the rear chain from the rear sprocket. For procedures, see *Chain, Removal,* this chapter.
3. Position a dial gauge so that it bears against the side of the rim (**Figure 26**). Turn the wheel slowly, and write down the highest and lowest readings. Subtract the lowest from the highest reading to get axial (side wobble) runout of rim.
4. Position the dial gauge so that it bears against the inner face of the rim near the edge.

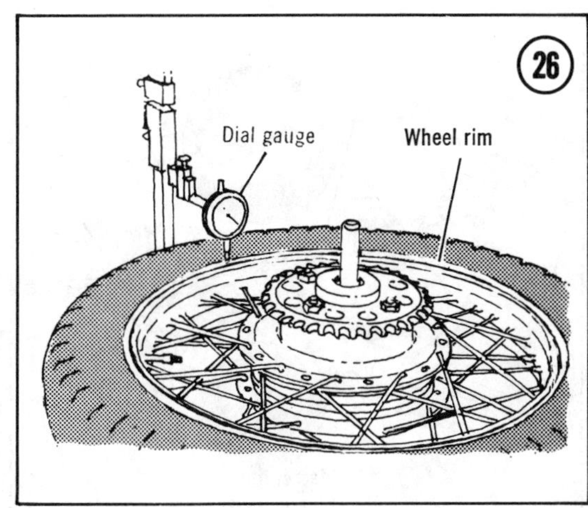

Turn the wheel slowly, and write down the highest and lowest readings. Subtract the lowest from the highest readings to get the radial (up-and-down wobble) runout of the rim.

5. A new wheel has an axial runout of less than 0.04 in. (1.0mm), and a radial runout of less than 0.04 in. (1.0mm).

6. If you measure more than 0.12 in. (3.0mm) of axial runout, or more than 0.08 in. (2.0mm) of radial runout, remove the axle from the wheel and check it for runout. See *Rear Wheel* section, this chapter.

7. If axle runout is within tolerance, adjust spoke tension.

8. If you cannot true the rim with a reasonable amount of spoke tuning as follows, the rim is bent and must be replaced with a new one.

9. Mark the tire with a piece of chalk at the point where runout is greatest.

10. Note whether the reading at the point of greatest runout is a high number or a low number on the dial gauge. If the number is high, the rim is warped toward the side of the wheel being checked with the dial gauge. If low, it is warped toward the far side.

11. Loosen the 2 nearest spokes (½ turn each), on each side of the chalk mark, that are laced to the side of the hub toward which the rim is warped.

12. Tighten the 2 nearest spokes (½ turn each), on each side of the chalk mark, that are laced to the other side of the hub.

13. Check the axial runout again. Continue loosening or tightening those same spokes in the same sequence until the axial runout lies within the acceptable limits.

14. Tap each spoke in the wheel with a wrench, and listen to the sound, to check that you have not tightened or loosened any spoke too much. If considerable tightening of any spoke was required, you may need to remove the tire and grind off the protruding end of the spoke to prevent it from puncturing the tube.

15. If radial runout exceeds the limit, mark the tire with a piece of chalk at the point where the runout is greatest.

16. Note whether the reading at the point of greatest runout is a high number on the dial gauge. If number is high, the rim is stretched away from the hub at that point. If the number is low, the rim is pulled toward the hub at that point.

17. If the number was high, tighten the 2 nearest spokes on each side of the chalk mark ½ turn each. Make another chalk mark on the opposite end of the tire, and loosen the 2 nearest spokes on each side of the new chalk mark ½ turn each.

18. If the dial gauge reading at the point of greatest runout was a low number, loosen the 4 spokes nearest the chalk mark, and tighten 4 spokes at the opposite end of the wheel.

19. Check radial runout again. Continue loosening or tightening those same spokes in the same sequence until the runout lies within 0.040 in. (2.0mm). The same cautions apply as for correcting axial runout.

CHAIN

The CB750 is equipped with one of 2 types of chains, the continuously staked type and the master link type. A special chain breaking tool must be used to separate and join the continuous type chain.

Removal

1. Remove the rear crankcase cover.

2. Break the chain. Depending on the type of link, remove the master link, or follow the instructions with the special tool for cutting a link.

Inspection/Cleaning/Lubrication

See *Drive Chain,* Chapter Three.

Installation

1. Route the chain through the sprockets, and position 2 ends of the rear sprocket for joining.
2. Install the master link, taking care that the retaining clip faces in the direction of rotation, as in **Figure 27**. Use the special tool if the chain is the staked type.
3. Remove the rear axle nut cotter pin, and loosen the nut.
4. Refer to *Drive Chain, Adjustment,* Chapter Three, for adjustment procedure.

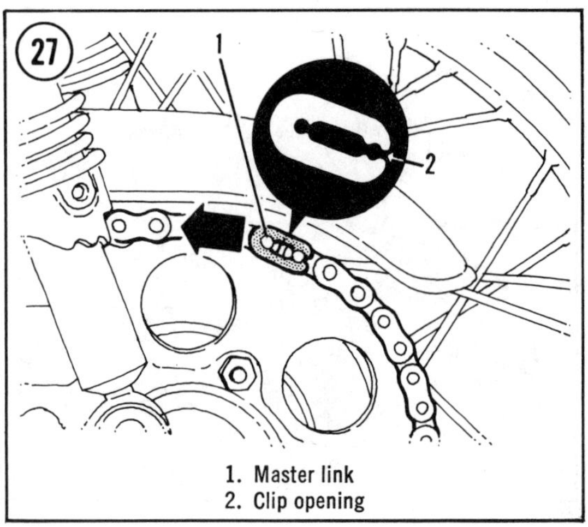

1. Master link
2. Clip opening

TIRE CHANGING AND REPAIR

Removal

1. Remove the valve core to deflate the tire.
2. Press the entire bead on both sides of the tire into the center of the rim.
3. Lubricate the beads with soapy water.
4. Insert the tire iron under the bead next to the valve. Force the bead on the opposite side of the tire into the center of the rim and pry the bead over the rim with the tire iron.
5. Insert a second tire iron next to the first to hold the bead over the rim. Then work around the tire with the first tire iron, prying the bead over the rim (**Figure 28**). Be careful not to pinch the inner tube with the tire irons.
6. Remove the valve from the hole in the rim and remove the tube from the tire. Lift out and lay aside.
7. Stand the tire upright. Insert a tire iron between the second bead and the side of the rim that the first bead was pried over (**Figure 29**). Force the bead on the opposite side from the tire iron into the center of the rim. Pry the second bead off the rim, working around as with the first.

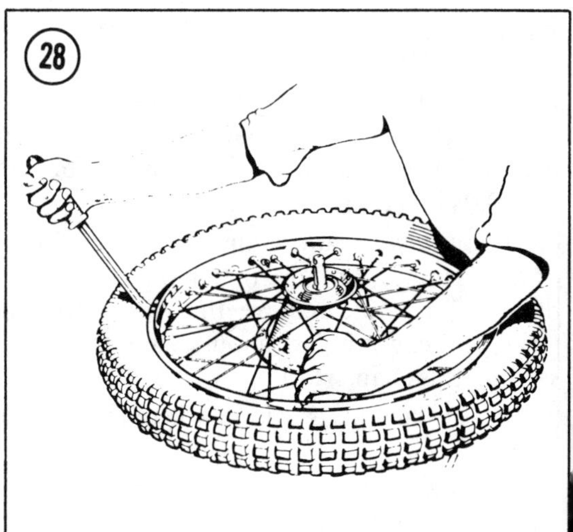

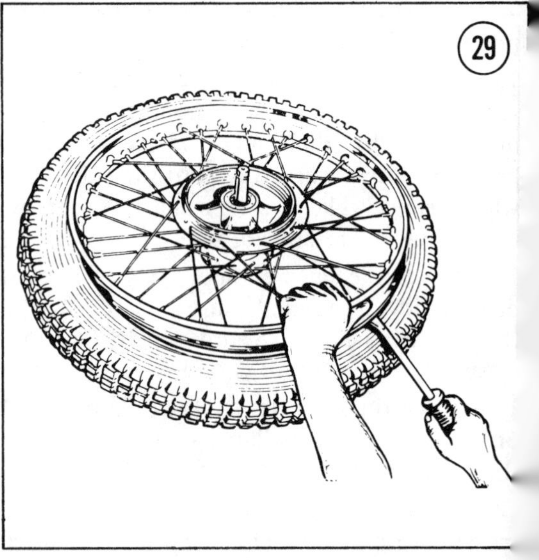

Installation

1. Carefully check the tire for any damage, especially inside.
2. A new tire may have balancing rubbers inside. These are not patches and should not be disturbed. A white spot near the bead indicates a lighter point on the tire. This should be placed next to the valve or midway between the 2 rim locks if they are installed.

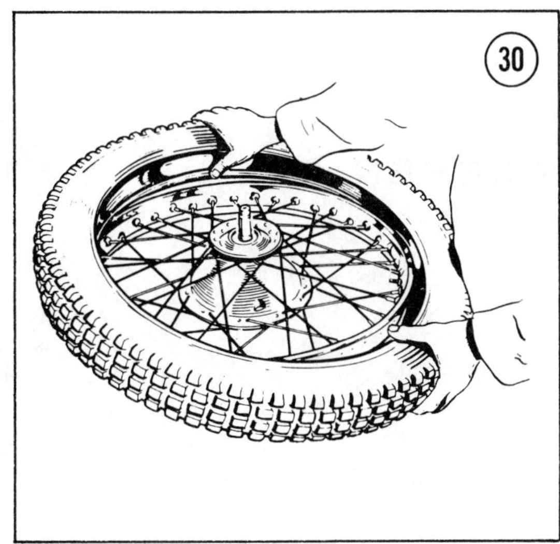

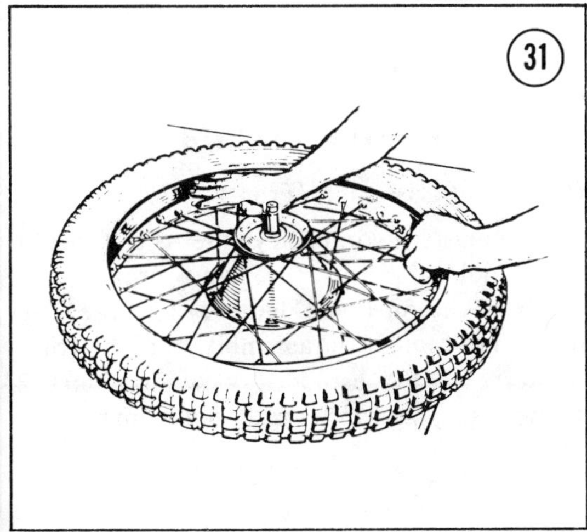

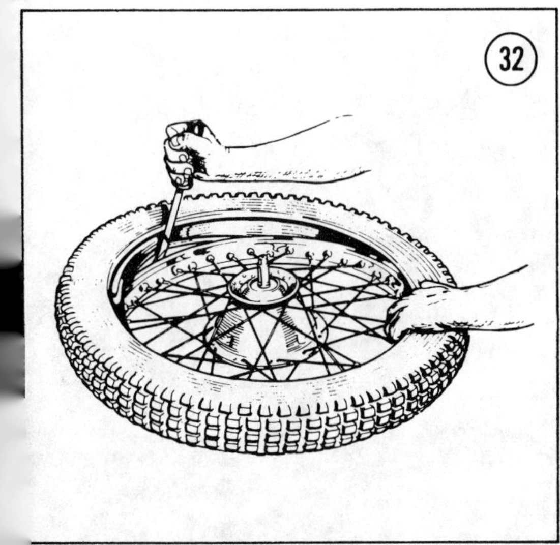

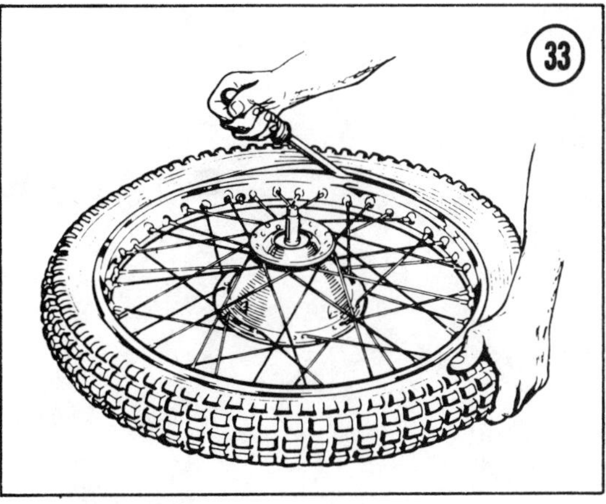

3. Check that the spoke ends do not protrude through the nipples into the center of the rim to puncture the tube. File off any protruding spoke ends.

4. Be sure the rim rubber tape is in place with the rough side toward the rim.

5. Put the core in the tube valve. Put the tube in the tire and inflate just enough to round it out. Too much air will make installing the tire difficult, and too little will increase the chances of pinching the tube with the tire irons.

6. Lubricate the tire beads and rim with soapy water. Pull the tube partly out of the tire at the valve. Squeeze the beads together to hold the tube and insert the valve into the hole in the rim **(Figure 30)**. The lower bead should go into the center of the rim with the upper bead outside it.

7. Press the lower bead into the rim center on each side of the valve, working around the tire in both directions **(Figure 31)**. Use a tire iron for the last few inches of bead **(Figure 32)**.

8. Press the upper bead into the rim opposite the valve. Pry the bead into the rim on both sides of the initial point with a tire iron, working around the rim to the valve **(Figure 33)**.

9. Wiggle the valve to be sure the tube is not trapped under the bead. Set the valve squarely in its hole before screwing on the valve nut to hold it against the rim.

10. Check the bead on both sides of the tire for even fit around the rim. Inflate the tire slowly to seat the beads in the rim. It may be necessary to bounce the tire to complete the seating. Inflate to the required pressure. Balance the wheel as described previously.

CHAPTER ELEVEN

BRAKES

All Honda 750 models except the CB750F have a disc front brake and drum rear brake. The CB750F has disc brake systems, front and rear, with separate controls and master cylinders.

This chapter covers all repair and replacement procedures for all components except the brake discs which are covered under *Front Wheel* and *Rear Wheel* in Chapter Ten.

MASTER CYLINDER

Removal/Disassembly (Front)

1. The master hydraulic cylinder is attached to the handlebars near the front brake lever. Unscrew the oil bolt **(Figure 1)** and the 2 set bolts, then remove the assembly from the grip.
2. Refer to the exploded view in **Figure 2**. Remove stopper washer and boot from body.

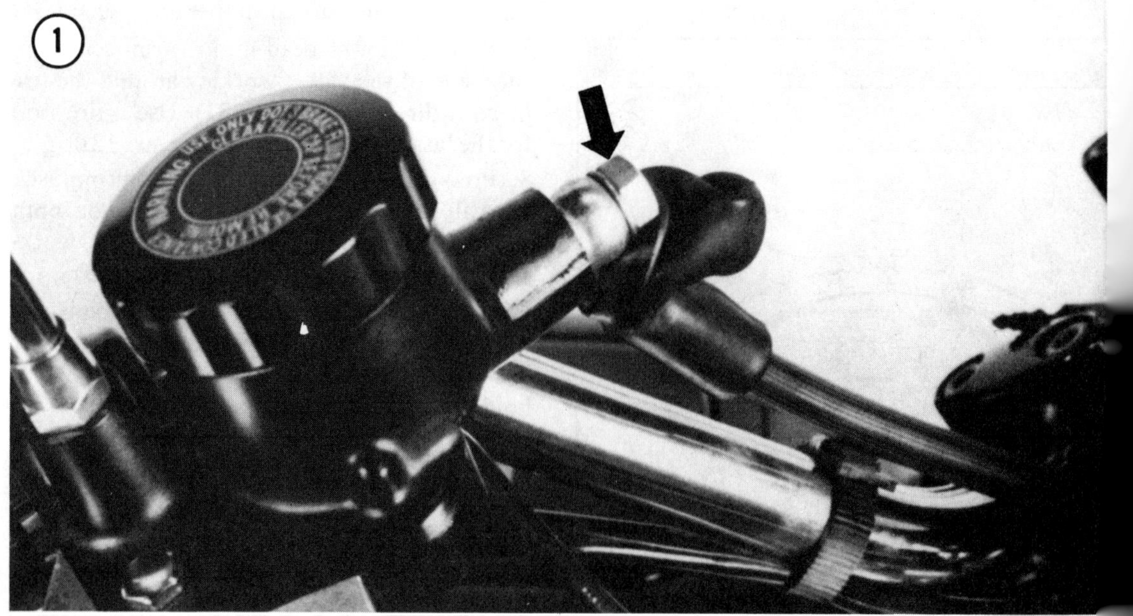

(2)

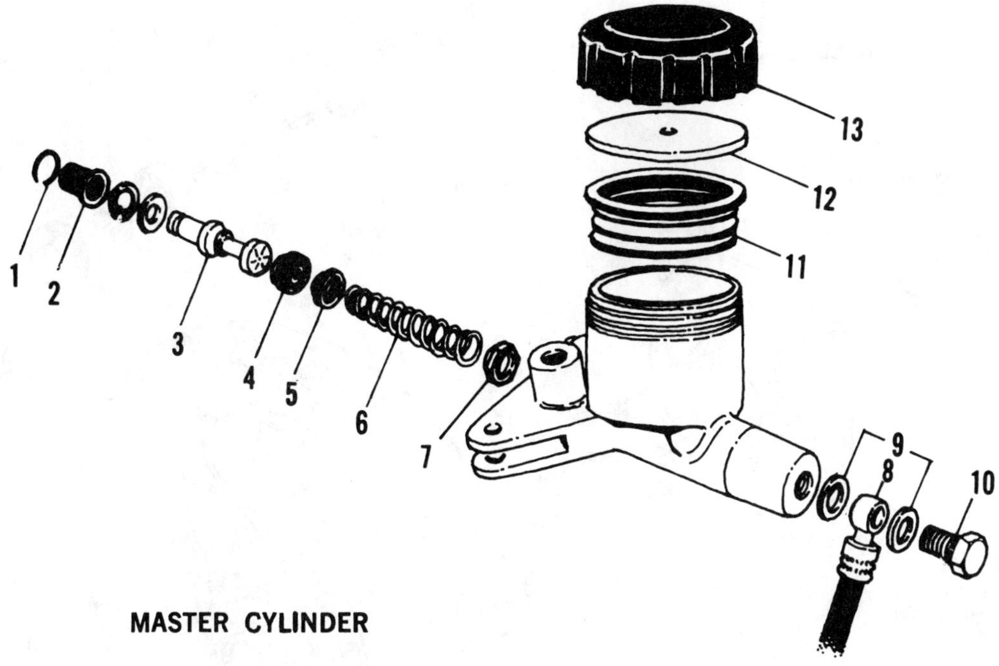

MASTER CYLINDER

1. Stopper washer
2. Boot
3. Piston
4. Secondary cap
5. Primary cap
6. Spring
7. Check valve
8. Front brake hose
9. Oil bolt washer
10. Oil bolt
11. Diaphragm
12. Master cylinder plate
13. Oil cup cap

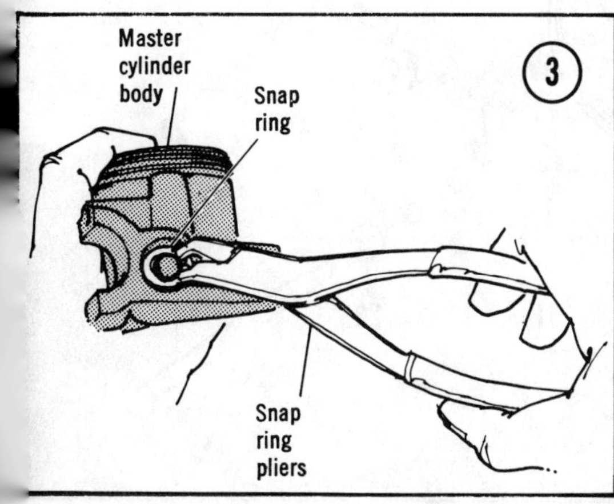

3. Remove the circlip from the body, using circlip pliers as shown in **Figure 3**.

4. Remove the 10.5mm washer, piston, secondary cup, primary cup spring, and check valve shown in **Figure 2**.

Removal/Disassembly (Rear, F Model)

Refer to **Figures 4 and 5** for this procedure. Siphon brake fluid from oil cup before starting.

1. Remove cotter pin, washer, and brake rod pin connecting spindle to brake rod joint.

2. Disconnect hydraulic brake line from master cylinder by unscrewing oil bolt.

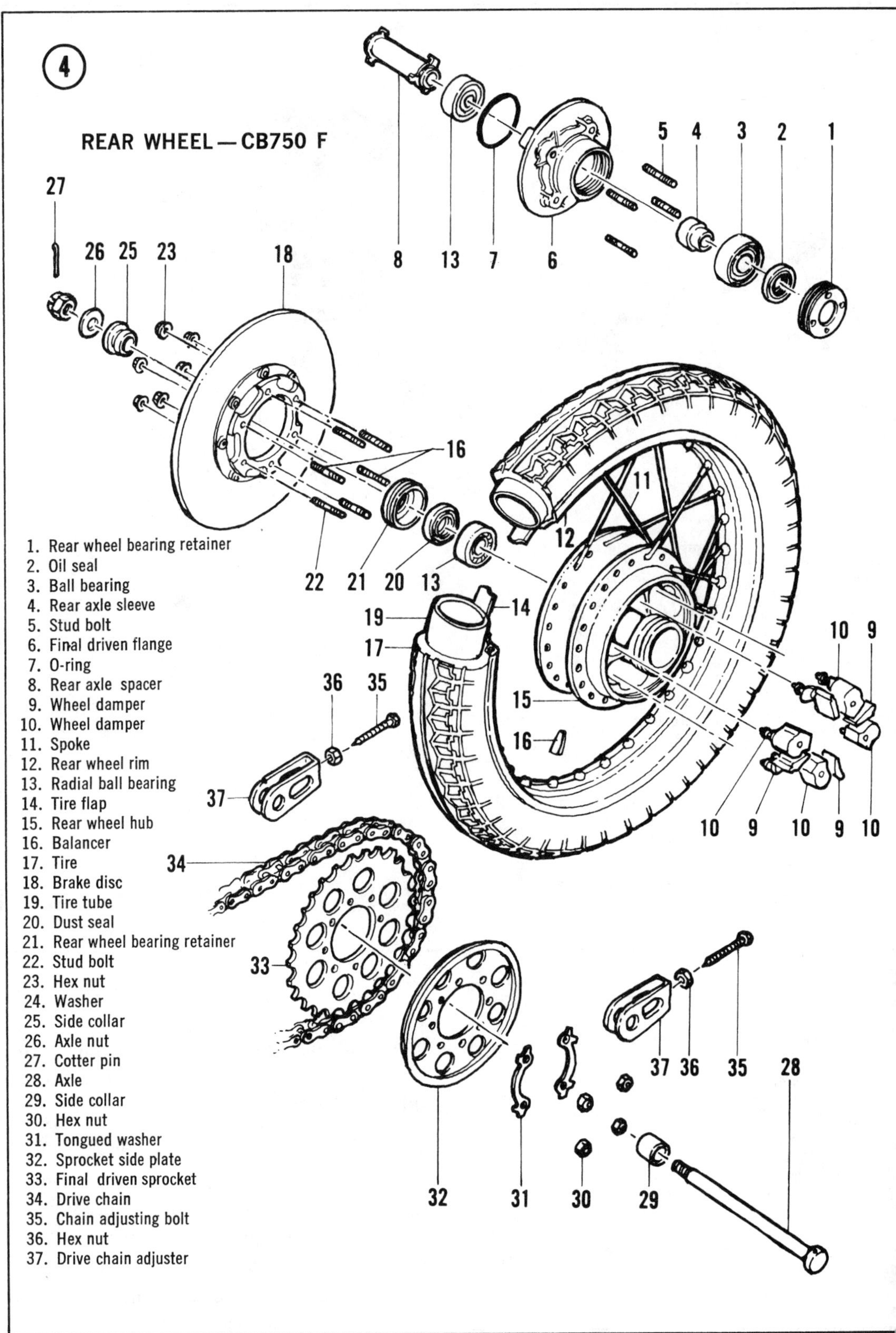
4
REAR WHEEL—CB750 F
27
26 25 23
18
8 13 7 6
5 4 3 2 1
16
11
12
22 21 20 13
19
14
17
36 35
15
10 9
16
37
10 9 10 9 10
34
33
37 36 35 28
32 31 30 29
1. Rear wheel bearing retainer
2. Oil seal
3. Ball bearing
4. Rear axle sleeve
5. Stud bolt
6. Final driven flange
7. O-ring
8. Rear axle spacer
9. Wheel damper
10. Wheel damper
11. Spoke
12. Rear wheel rim
13. Radial ball bearing
14. Tire flap
15. Rear wheel hub
16. Balancer
17. Tire
18. Brake disc
19. Tire tube
20. Dust seal
21. Rear wheel bearing retainer
22. Stud bolt
23. Hex nut
24. Washer
25. Side collar
26. Axle nut
27. Cotter pin
28. Axle
29. Side collar
30. Hex nut
31. Tongued washer
32. Sprocket side plate
33. Final driven sprocket
34. Drive chain
35. Chain adjusting bolt
36. Hex nut
37. Drive chain adjuster

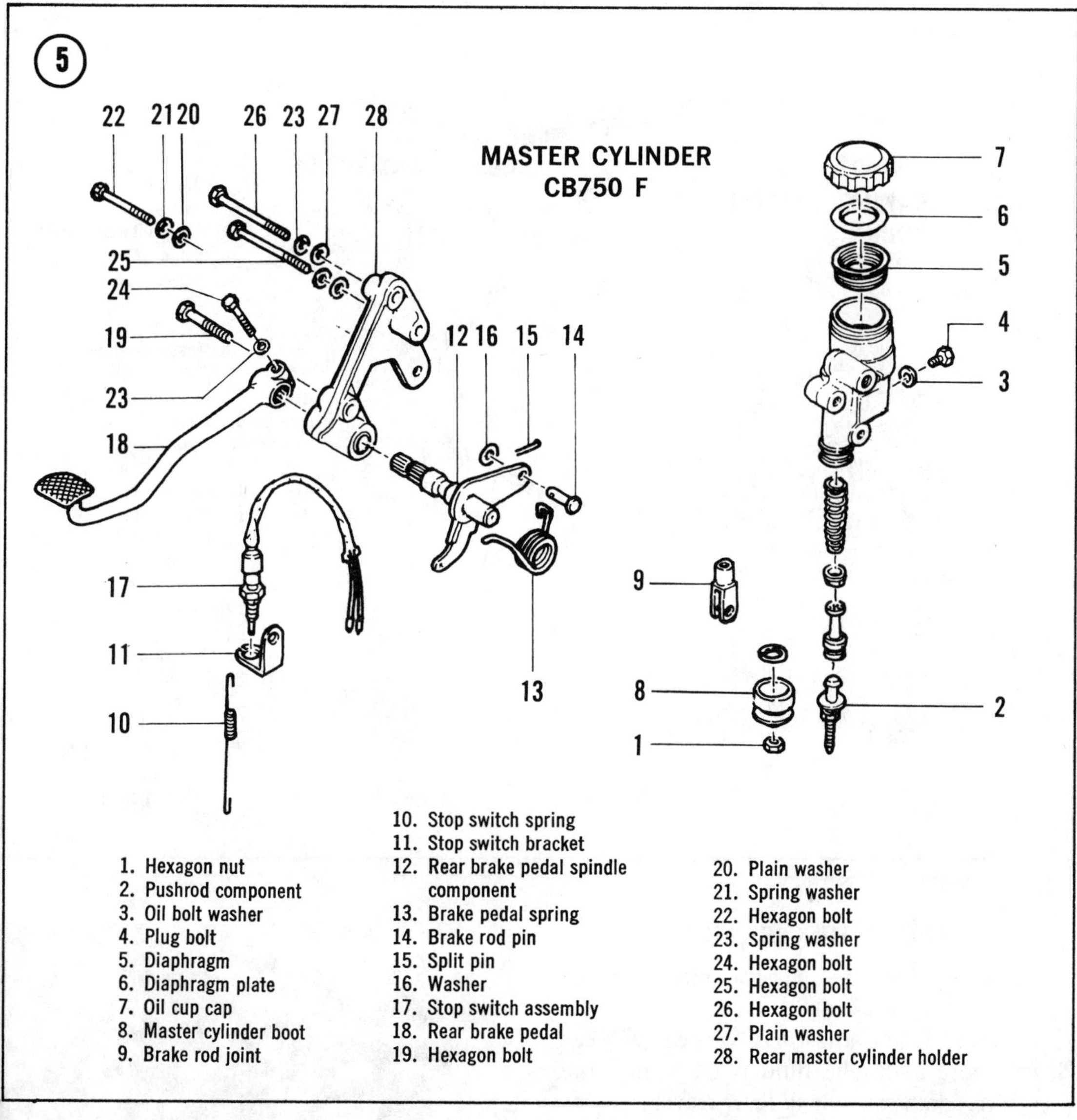

3. Unscrew hex bolts and remove rear master cylinder from rear master cylinder holder.

4. Unscrew and remove brake rod joint from brake pushrod. Remove hex nut and boot from pushrod.

5. Remove circlip, then remove pushrod, piston, cap, and spring from master cylinder.

6. Remove oil cup cap, diaphragm plate, and diaphragm.

nspection

. Clean all parts thoroughly in solvent and dry ith compressed air.

2. Measure the outside diameter of the piston and the inside diameter of the cylinder. If clearance is more than 0.0045 in. (0.115mm), install a new piston kit.

Assembly

1. Assembly is the reverse of disassembly. Make sure all parts are absolutely clean. Assemble master cylinder in a clean, dust-free area.

2. Refill oil cup with brake fluid (DOT 3 only) and bleed the system, following the instructions given in this chapter under *Brake Hydraulic System Bleeding*.

6

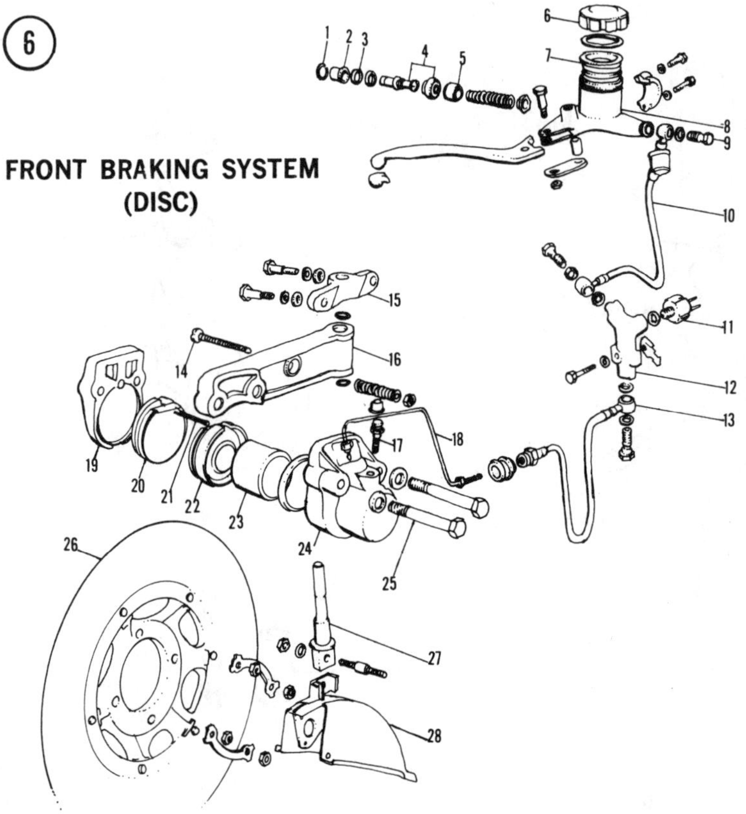

FRONT BRAKING SYSTEM (DISC)

1. Stopper
2. Boot
3. 18mm internal circlip
4. Piston
5. Primary cup
6. Oil cup cap
7. Diaphragm
8. Master cylinder
9. Bolt
10. Front brake hose B
11. Stoplight switch
12. 3-way connector
13. Front brake hose A
14. Caliper adjuster
15. Caliper bracket
16. Caliper holder
17. Bleeder valve
18. Front brake tube
19. Caliper B
20. Pad B
21. 1.6mm cotter pin
22. Pad A
23. Piston
24. Caliper A
25. Caliper securing bolts
26. Front brake disc
27. Caliper holder
28. Disc cover

FRONT DISC BRAKE

Figure 6 shows major components of the hydraulic front disc brake.

The brake is self-adjusting. As the pads wear down, more hydraulic fluid is taken into the system to compensate, and lever travel remains constant.

Brake Pad Replacement

This requires complete disassembly as described in the procedure following.

Disassembly

1. Remove the front wheel and disc according to the instructions in Chapter Ten under *Front Wheel.*

2. Refer to **Figure 7**. Disconnect the front hose by removing the bolt at the joint.

3. Remove the caliper assembly (**Figure 8**) by unscrewing the 3 mounting bolts. Remove the 2

7

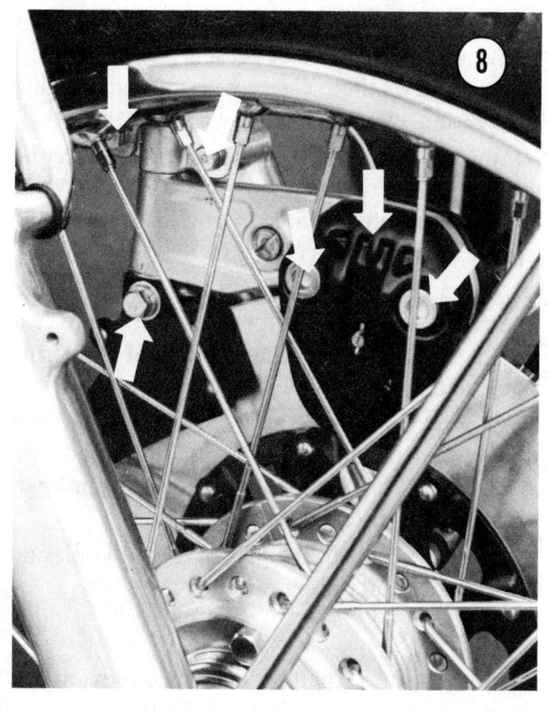

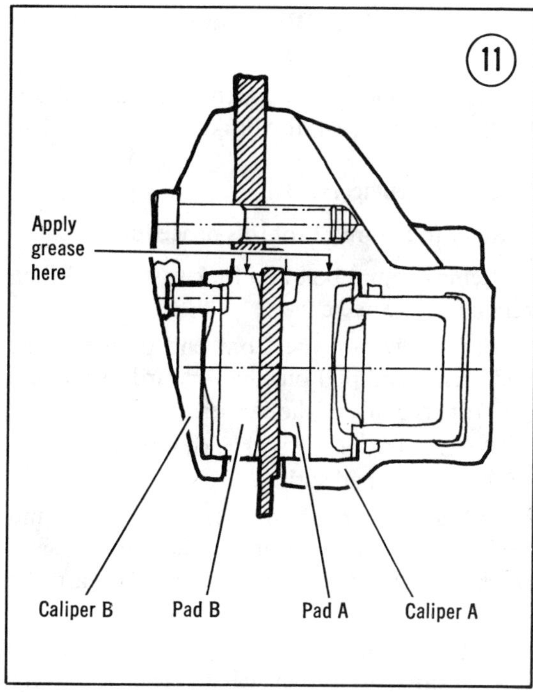

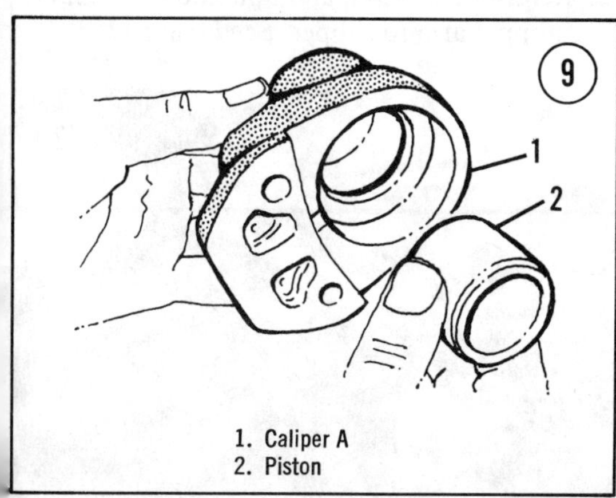

1. Caliper A
2. Piston

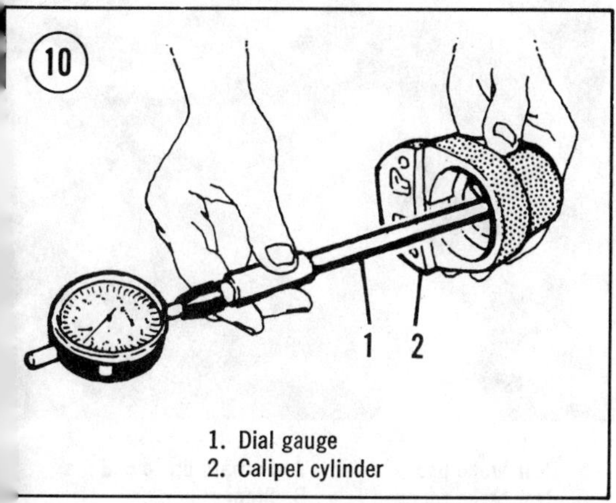

1. Dial gauge
2. Caliper cylinder

set bolts with an Allen wrench, and separate the 2 calipers.

4. Remove pad (A) from caliper (A) and then take out the cylinder and piston, shown in **Figure 9**. Remove pad (B) from caliper (B) by taking out the cotter pin.

Inspection

1. Measure the inner diameter of the caliper cylinder with a dial gauge (**Figure 10**) and the outer diameter of the piston with a micrometer. Compute the clearance by subtraction. If the difference is more than 0.004 in. (0.11mm), the parts should be replaced.

2. Check the caliper piston seal, and replace if it is damaged.

3. Check the hose for damage, and replace if necessary.

Assembly

All parts of the braking system should be absolutely clean before assembly. Assemble in reverse order of disassembly.

Before mounting the pads, apply a small amount of of silicone grease, not molybdenum brake grease, at the points shown in **Figure 11**. Be careful not to get grease on the pad surfaces.

REAR DISC BRAKE (CB750F)

The CB750F is equipped with a hydraulically-operated rear disc brake.

Rear Pad Replacement

Refer to **Figure 12** for this procedure.

1. Remove 5mm bolt and lockwasher and then remove brake pad cover.
2. Press down on the front end of the brake pad spring and pull out the forward brake pad pin from the side of the caliper.
3. Release the brake pad spring and pull out the rear brake pad spring.
4. If rear master cylinder reservoir is full and brake pads are badly worn, siphon about ½ of the brake fluid to avoid overflow. Discard the fluid.
5. Retract caliper pistons by spreading brake pads as far apart as they will go. Then use brake pad spring to pull out brake pads. Carefully note position of the spring and then remove it.
6. Clean replacement pads to remove any preservative that may be present. Use a scraper, if necessary, then clean with a high quality degreasing agent. Wipe dry with a clean cloth.
7. Install the brake pad spring in the second hole from the rear of the new pads (in the same position as noted in Step 5) and insert pads and spring into the caliper.
8. Align the rear holes in the brake pads with the rear hole in the caliper and install the rear brake pad pin. Verify that the end of the spring is located in the notch in the brake pad pin.
9. Apply pressure to the front of the brake pad spring and install the forward brake pad pin. Make sure the forward tang of the spring is seated in the notch in the brake pad pin.
10. Reinstall the brake pad cover with bolt and lockwasher and tighten securely.

Disassembly

1. Remove brake pads as described previously.
2. Remove cotter pin and bolt and nut connecting stopper arm to caliper. See **Figure 12**.

1. Bolt and lockwasher
2. Bleeder valve and cap
3. Brake pad cover
4. Hydraulic brake line
5. Rear brake pad pin
6. Rear brake caliper
7. Forward brake pad pin
8. Stopper arm

3. Disconnect the hydraulic brake line from the caliper by removing the oil bolt and washer.

4. Remove the rear wheel, using the procedure given in Chapter Ten. Remove caliper from axle.

5. Remove the 2 caliper set bolts and separate caliper (A) from caliper (B). Refer to **Figure 13**.

6. Remove the dust cap clips, then remove the dust caps from the calipers. Remove pistons and seals from the cylinders.

Inspection

1. Measure the inside diameter of the cylinders and the outside diameter of the pistons. Replace piston if clearance is more than 0.004 in. (0.11mm).

2. Carefully examine the caliper seals and replace if damaged or doubtful.

Assembly

Clean all parts in solvent and dry with compressed air. All caliper parts must be absolutely clean before reassembly.

1. Install seals in cylinders.

2. Install pistons in cylinders, taking extreme care not to damage seals. Install dust covers with dust cover clips.

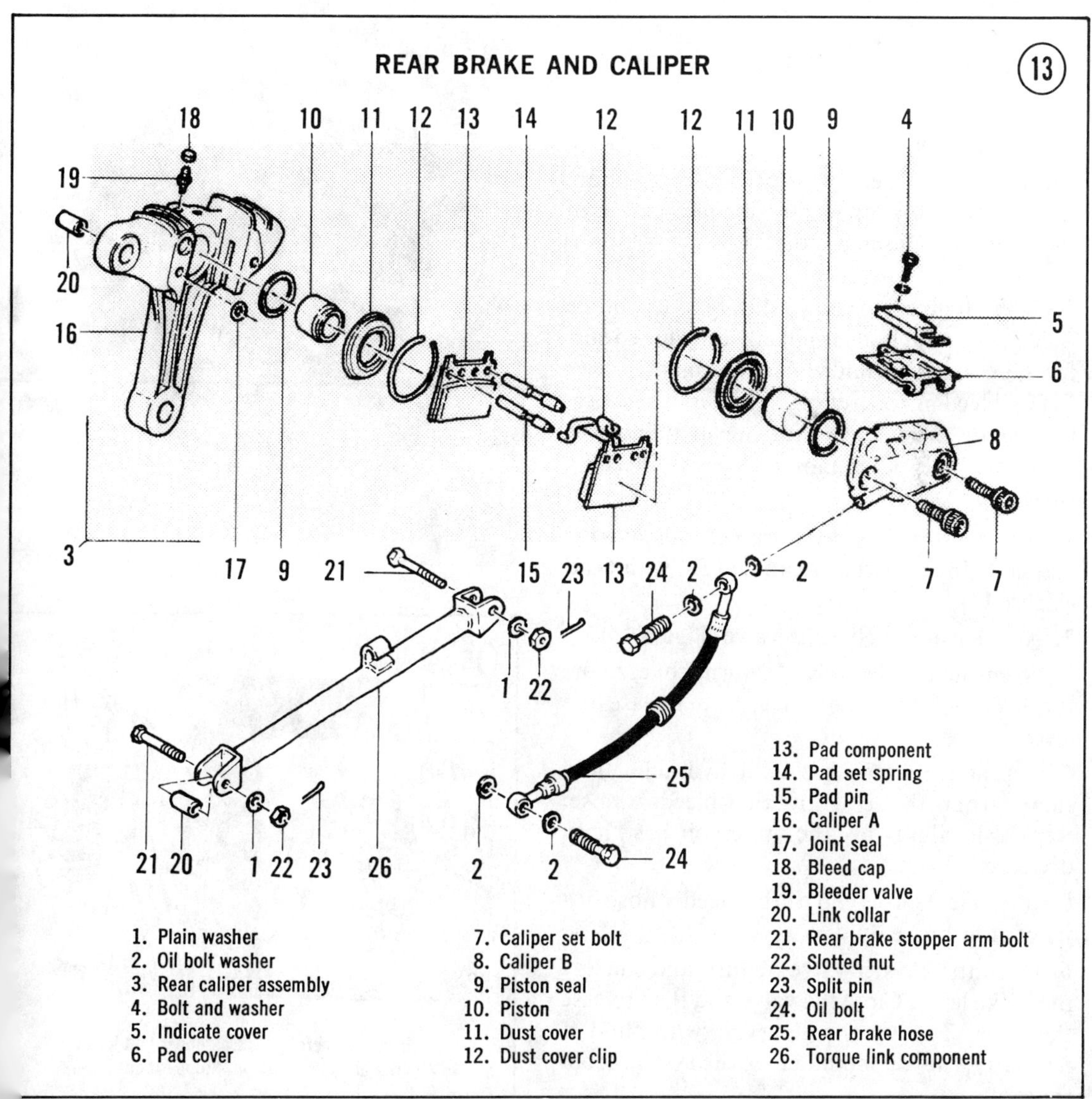

3. Assemble caliper (A) to caliper (B), using the 2 set bolts. Tighten securely. See **Figure 13**.

4. Install caliper on the rear disc and rear axle. Install wheel using the procedure given in Chapter Ten under *Rear Wheel.*

5. Connect stopper arm, using bolt, washers, nut, and cotter pin.

6. Install hydraulic brake line with washer and oil bolt. Tighten securely.

7. Fill rear master cylinder oil reservoir with brake fluid (DOT 3 only). Be careful not to spill fluid on painted surfaces.

8. Attach a bleeder hose to bleeder valve **(Figure 12)** and bleed the system, using the procedure given in this chapter for the brake hydraulic system.

BRAKE HYDRAULIC SYSTEM

Bleeding

Air should be bled from the brake system whenever it has been worked on. In addition, there is probably air in the system if travel of the lever increases markedly, or if the action is spongy.

Use only fresh DOT 3 heavy duty brake fluid. Be careful not to spill any on painted surfaces, because the fluid will leave a mark.

The bleeding operation is easier when performed by 2 persons, with one pumping the lever, and the other monitoring the bleeding valve.

1. If the system has been drained, remove the master cylinder reservoir cap and fill with fluid **(Figure 14)**.

2. Attach a hose to bleeder valve **(Figure 15)**.

3. Open the bleeder valve ½ turn, squeeze the brake lever, close the valve, and release the lever.

4. Repeat the procedure until hydraulic fluid flows from the end of the bleeder hose. Replenish fluid in the reservoir as level decreases.

5. Immerse the free end of the bleeder hose in a jar of clear brake fluid.

6. Open the bleeder valve ½ turn and squeeze the brake lever. Close the valve and then release the lever. Top up the reservoir with fluid if necessary. No air should enter the system from the top.

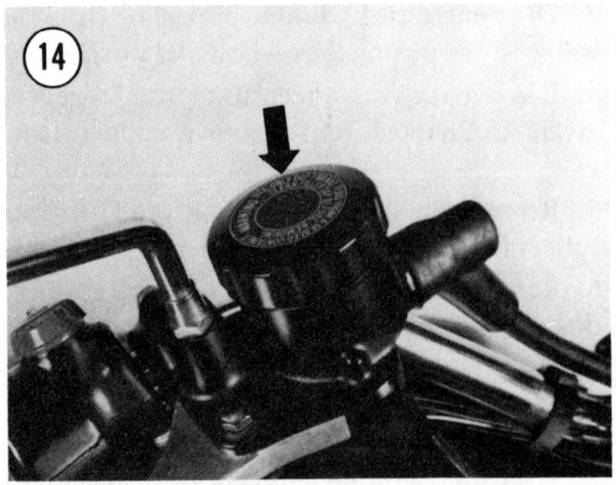

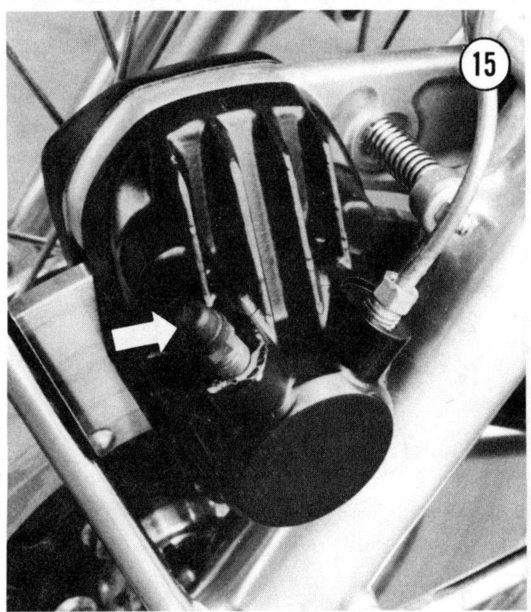

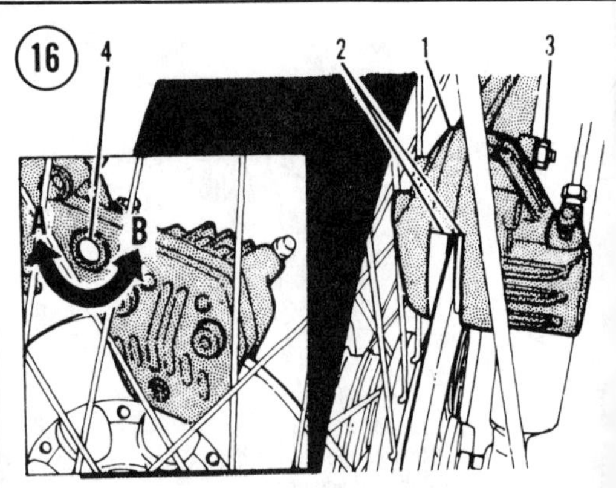

1. Brake calipers
2. Friction pads
3. Stopper bolt locknut
4. Stopper bolt

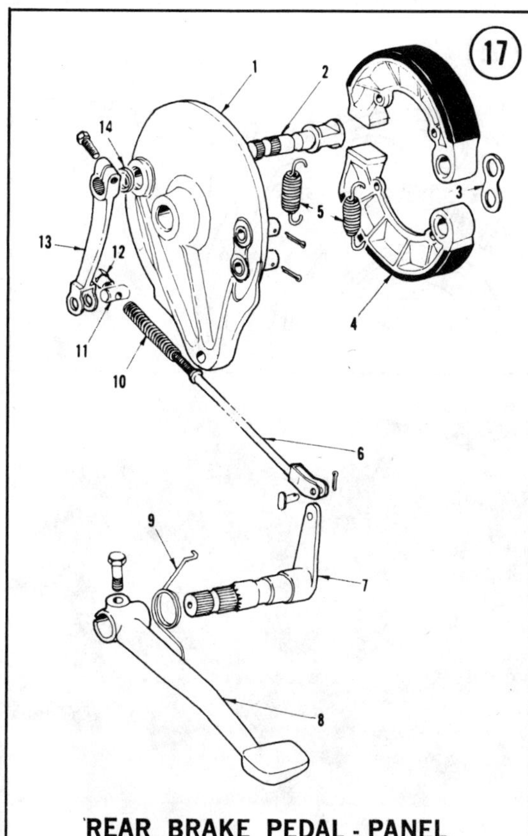

REAR BRAKE PEDAL - PANEL

1. Rear brake panel
2. Rear brake cam
3. Rear brake anchor pin washer
4. Rear brake shoe components
5. Brake shoe spring
6. Rear brake rod components
7. Rear brake spindle components
8. Rear brake pedal
9. Brake pedal spring
10. Rear brake rod spring
11. Rear brake arm joint
12. Rear brake adjusting nut
13. Rear brake arm
14. Brake cover dust seal

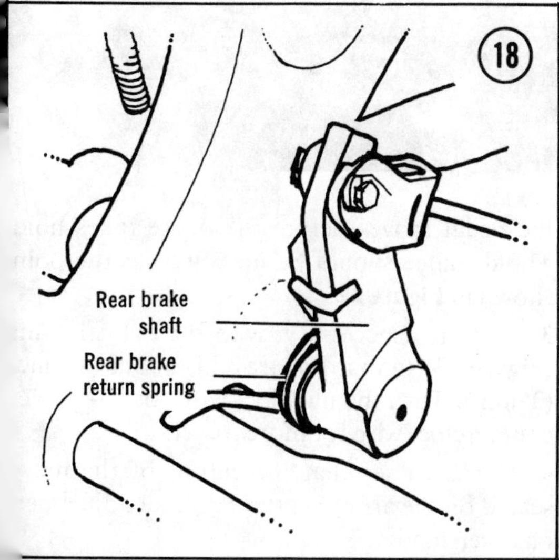

7. Repeat the bleeding operation until no air bubbles come from the tip of the hose.

8. Remove the hose and replace the dust cap. Install the reservoir cap after checking the fluid level one last time.

9. Squeeze the brake lever, and check for pressure leaks and seepage.

BRAKE ADJUSTMENT

1. Raise the front wheel off the ground by inserting a prop under the engine.

2. Loosen the locknut on the stopper bolt. See **Figure 16.**

3. Turn the stopper bolt in direction (A) until the pad contacts the disc. The wheel should drag slightly when it is turned.

4. Rotate the front wheel and slowly back off stopper bolt in direction (B, **Figure 16**), until the wheel turns freely without drag.

5. Back off the stopper bolt ⅛-¼ turn more, and then tighten down locknut.

REAR DRUM BRAKE (CB750, CB750 K1-K8 AND A)

Disassembly

Figure 17 shows details of the rear brake pedal and the linkage.

1. Remove the pedal by unscrewing the mounting bolt and disconnecting stop switch spring.

2. Remove the brake adjuster nut, and pull the rod from the arm.

3. Unhook the brake return spring **(Figure 18)** and remove the shaft.

4. Remove the rear wheel according to the instructions in Chapter Ten.

5. Remove the 2 cotter pins and washer, then pull the shoes from the backing plate. See **Figure 19.**

Inspection

1. Measure the diameter of the drum with a vernier caliper, as shown in **Figure 20.** If the diameter is more than 7.025 in. (183mm), the rear wheel should be replaced. Severe score marks, or grooves, in the drum also indicate wheel replacement.

11

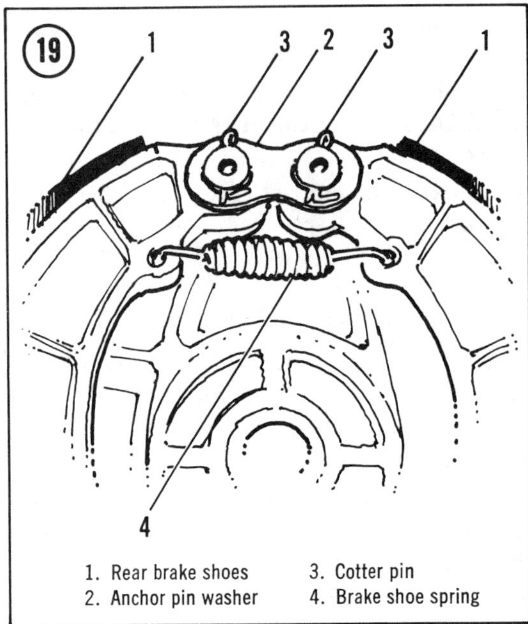

1. Rear brake shoes
2. Anchor pin washer
3. Cotter pin
4. Brake shoe spring

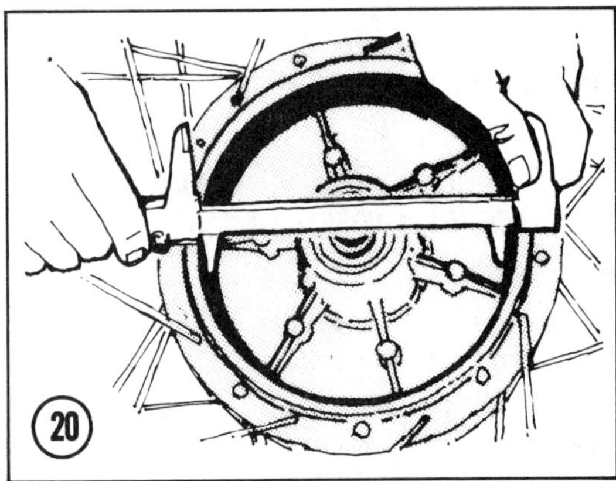

2. Measure shoe thickness with a vernier caliper (**Figure 21**). If the reading is less than 0.08 in. (2mm), the part should be replaced. If the lining is worn unevenly, the shoe also should be replaced.

Assembly

Assemble in reverse order of disassembly, referring to the exploded view (**Figure 17**).

Adjustment

1. Place the motorcycle on the centerstand to lift the rear wheel clear of the ground.
2. Check free travel of the brake pedal by rotating the rear wheel and noting the distance

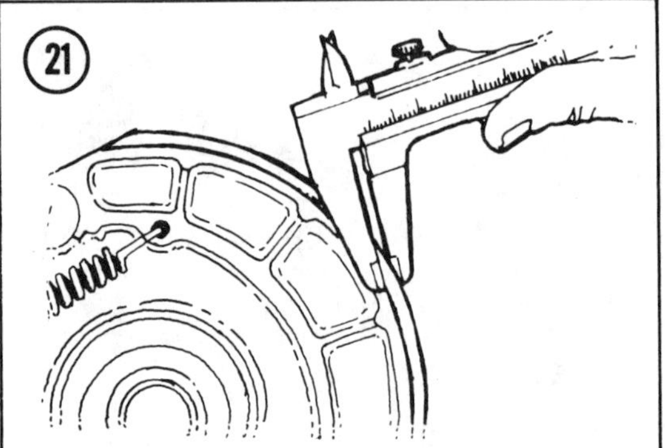

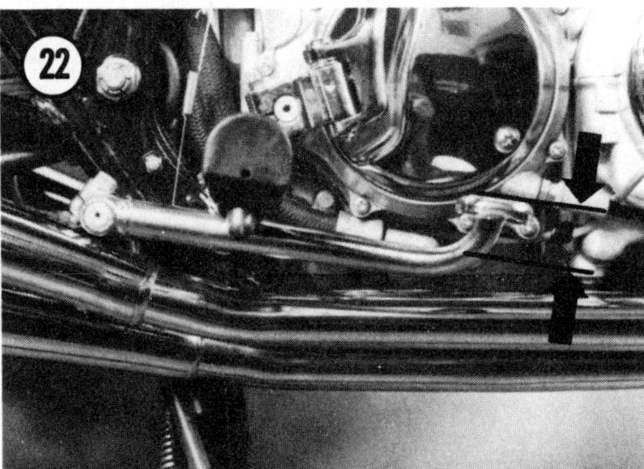

the pedal moves before the brake takes hold The distance should be measured at the poin shown in **Figure 22**.

3. Adjust, if necessary, with the adjusting nu (**Figure 23**) so that free travel is about one inc (25mm). Turn the nut clockwise for less travel counterclockwise for more travel.
4. Check to see that the cutout of the nut seated on the arm pin after the final adjustme has been made.

INDEX

A

B

C

12

D

E

F

H

I

K

L

M

N

O

P

R

S

T

V

W

12

CB750K0 (1969-1970)

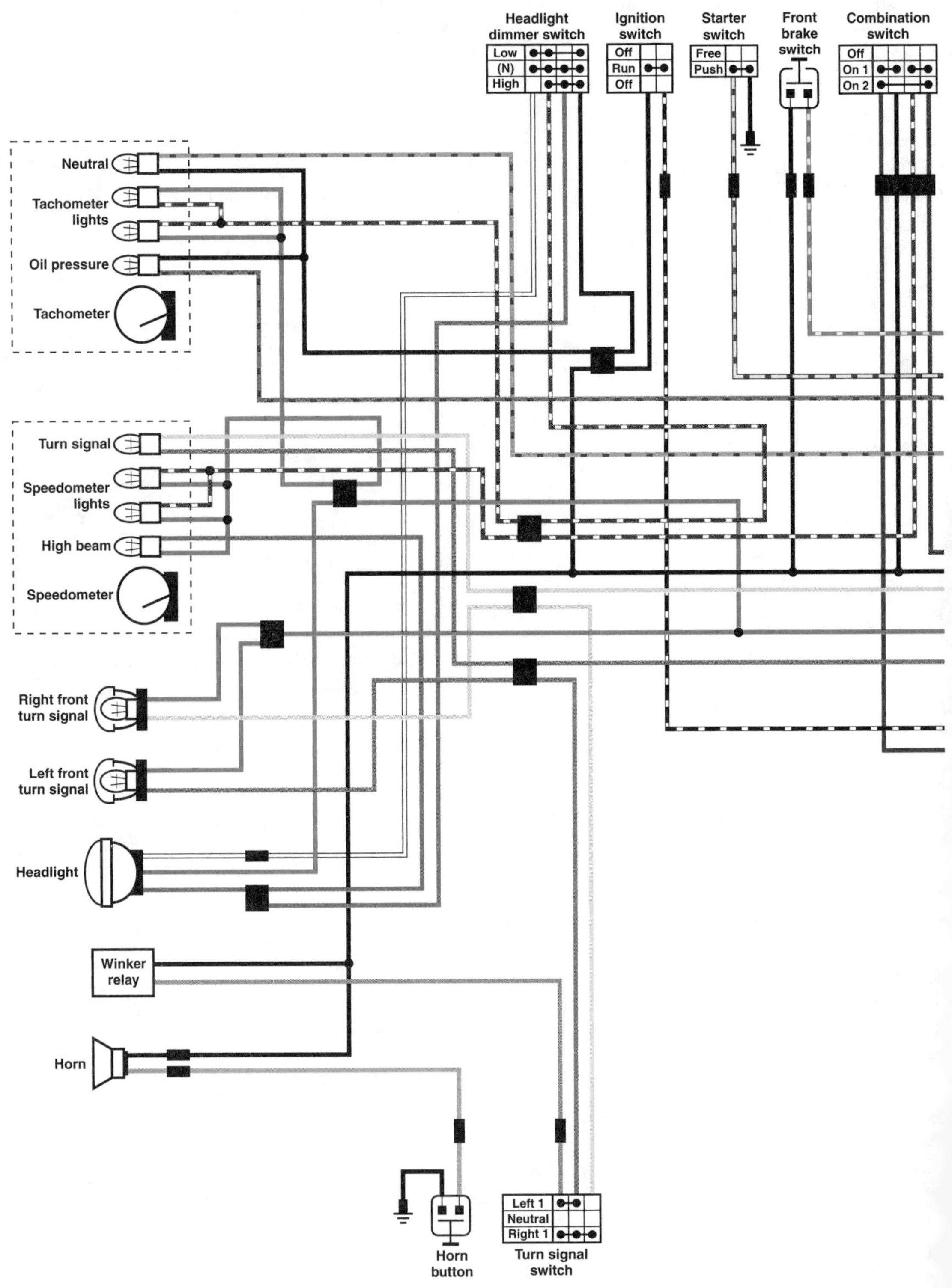

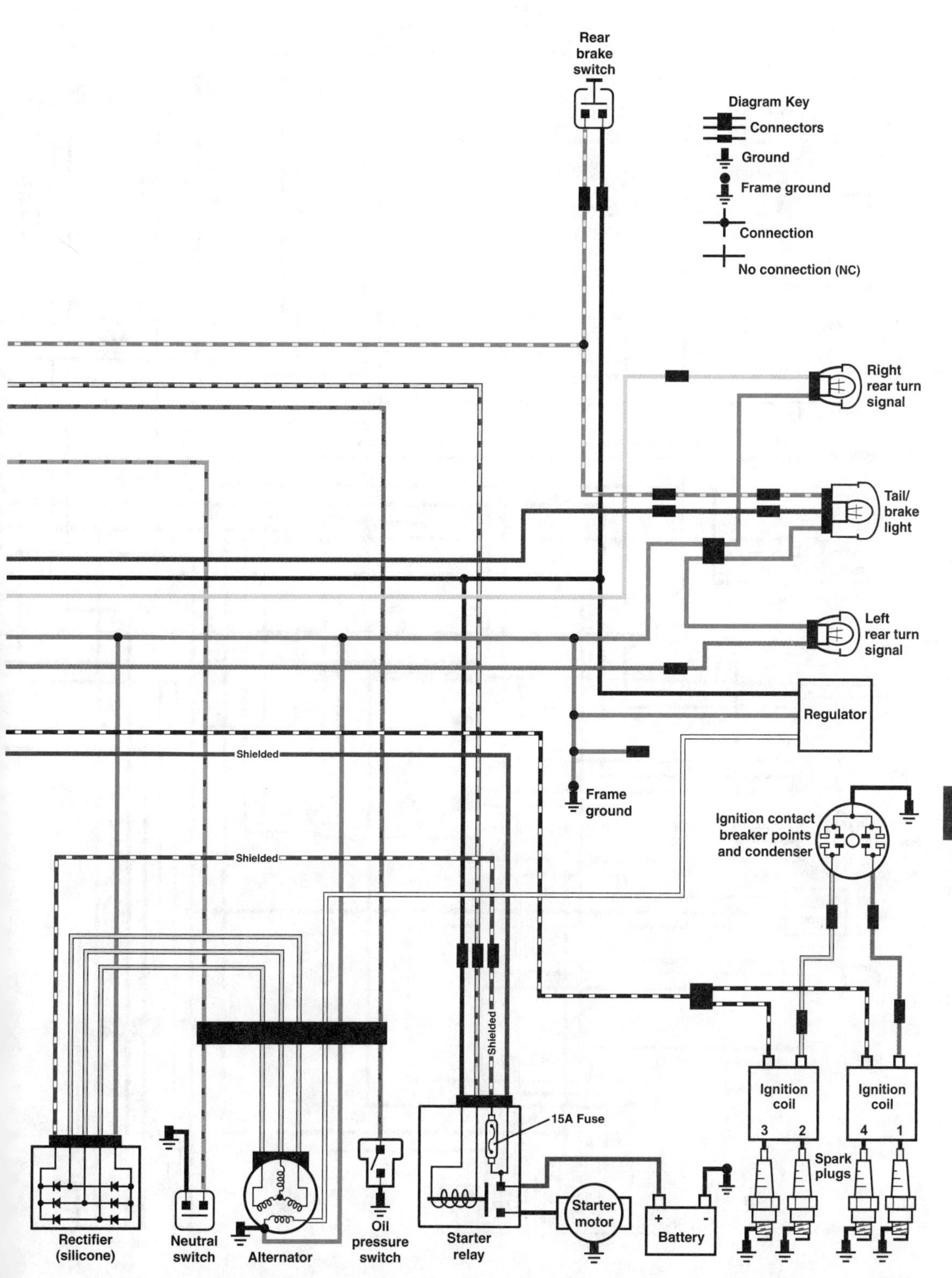
Rear brake switch
Diagram Key
Connectors
Ground
Frame ground
Connection
No connection (NC)
Right rear turn signal
Tail/ brake light
Left rear turn signal
Regulator
Shielded
Frame ground
Ignition contact breaker points and condenser
Shielded
Shielded
15A Fuse
Ignition coil
Ignition coil
3
2
4
1
Spark plugs
Rectifier (silicone)
Neutral switch
Alternator
Oil pressure switch
Starter relay
Starter motor
+
-
Battery

CB750K1-K5 (1970-1975)

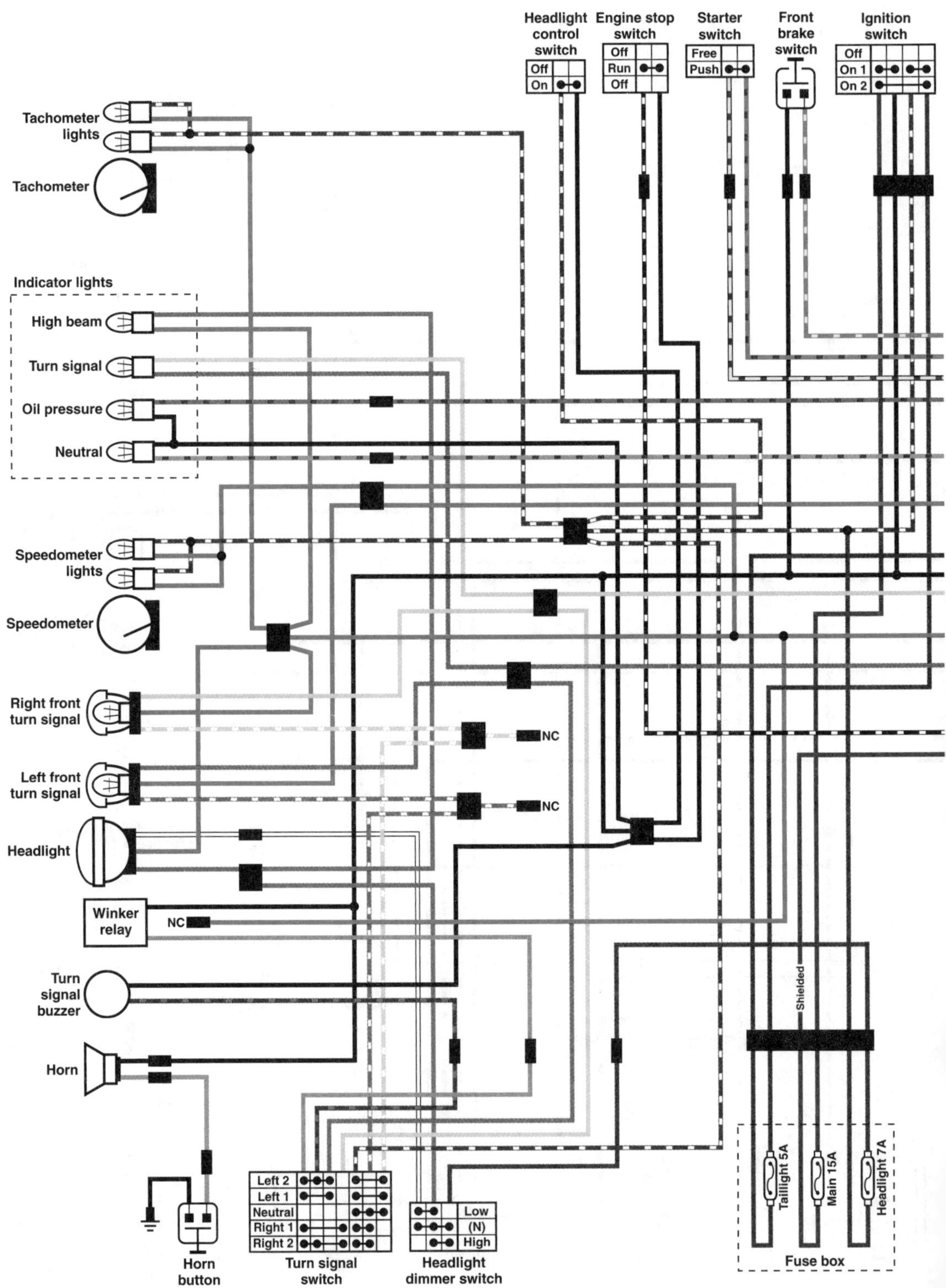

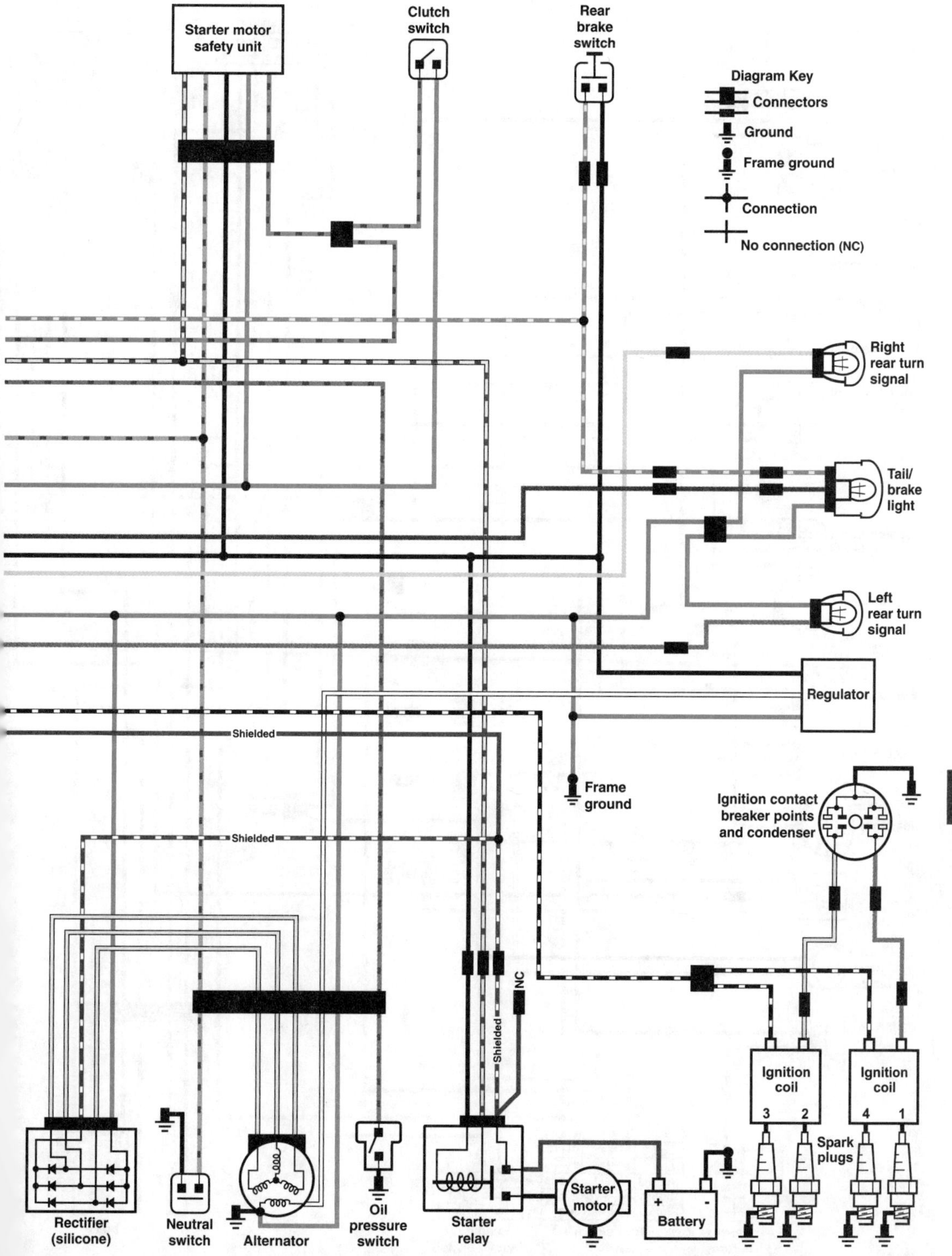

Starter motor safety unit

Clutch switch

Rear brake switch

Diagram Key

Connectors

Ground

Frame ground

Connection

No connection (NC)

Right rear turn signal

Tail/ brake light

Left rear turn signal

Regulator

Shielded

Frame ground

Ignition contact breaker points and condenser

Shielded

NC

Shielded

Ignition coil

3 2

Ignition coil

4 1

Spark plugs

Rectifier (silicone)

Neutral switch

Alternator

Oil pressure switch

Starter relay

Starter motor

+ -

Battery

CB750K6 (1976)

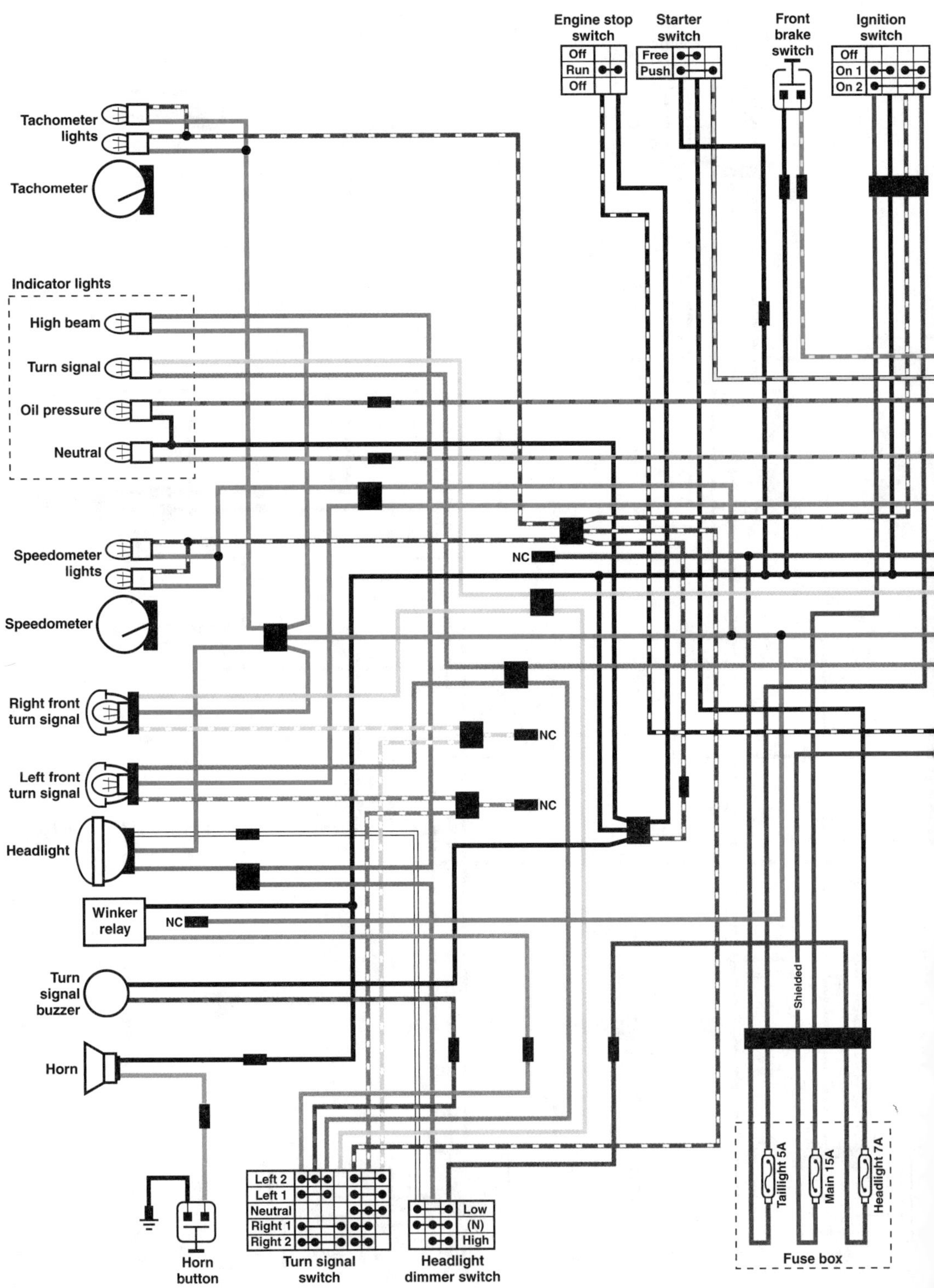

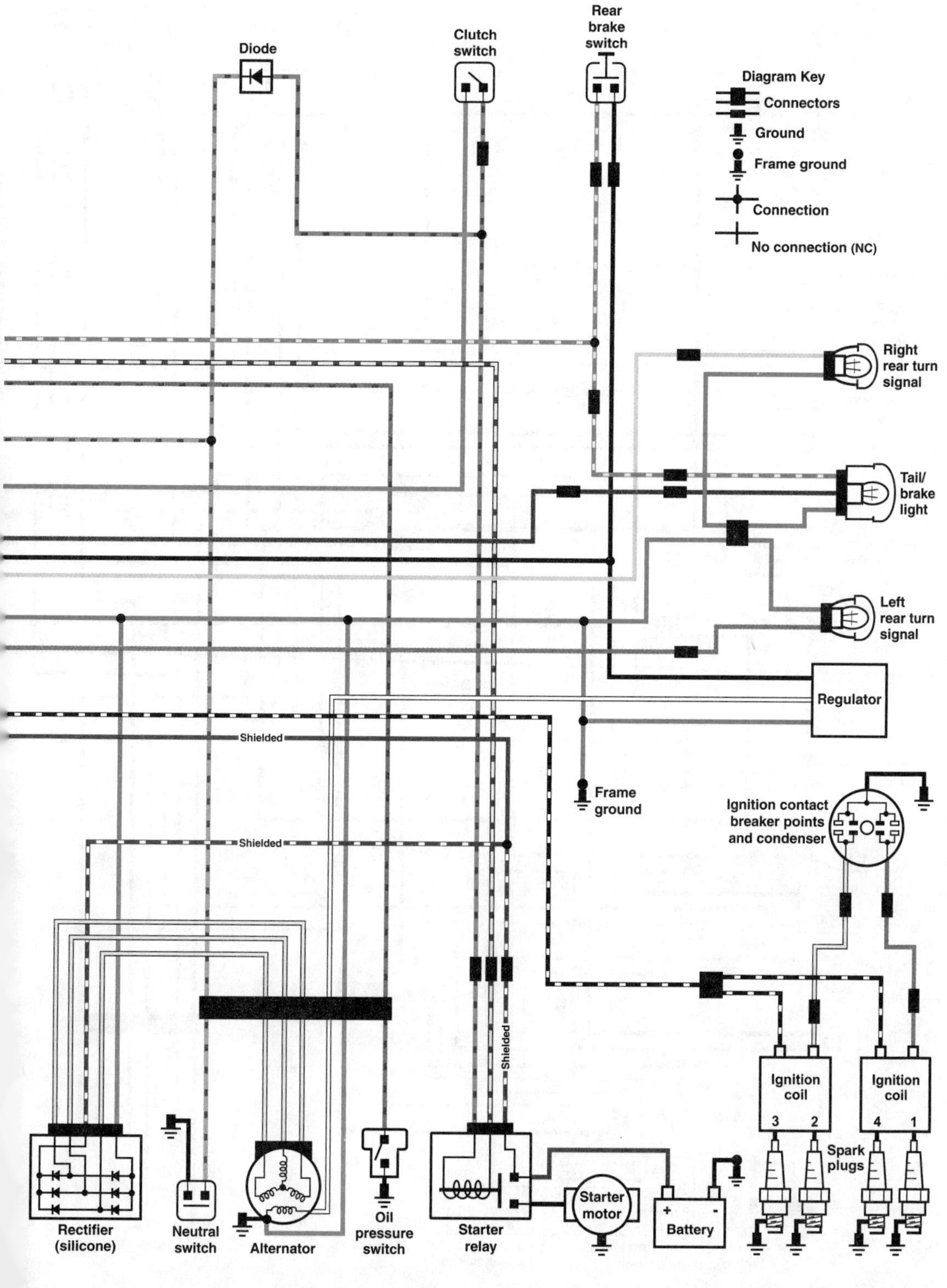

Diode

Clutch switch

Rear brake switch

Diagram Key

Connectors

Ground

Frame ground

Connection

No connection (NC)

Right rear turn signal

Tail/ brake light

Left rear turn signal

Regulator

Shielded

Frame ground

Ignition contact breaker points and condenser

Shielded

Shielded

Ignition coil

3 2

Ignition coil

4 1

Spark plugs

Rectifier (silicone)

Neutral switch

Alternator

Oil pressure switch

Starter relay

Starter motor

\+ -

Battery

CB750K7 (1977)

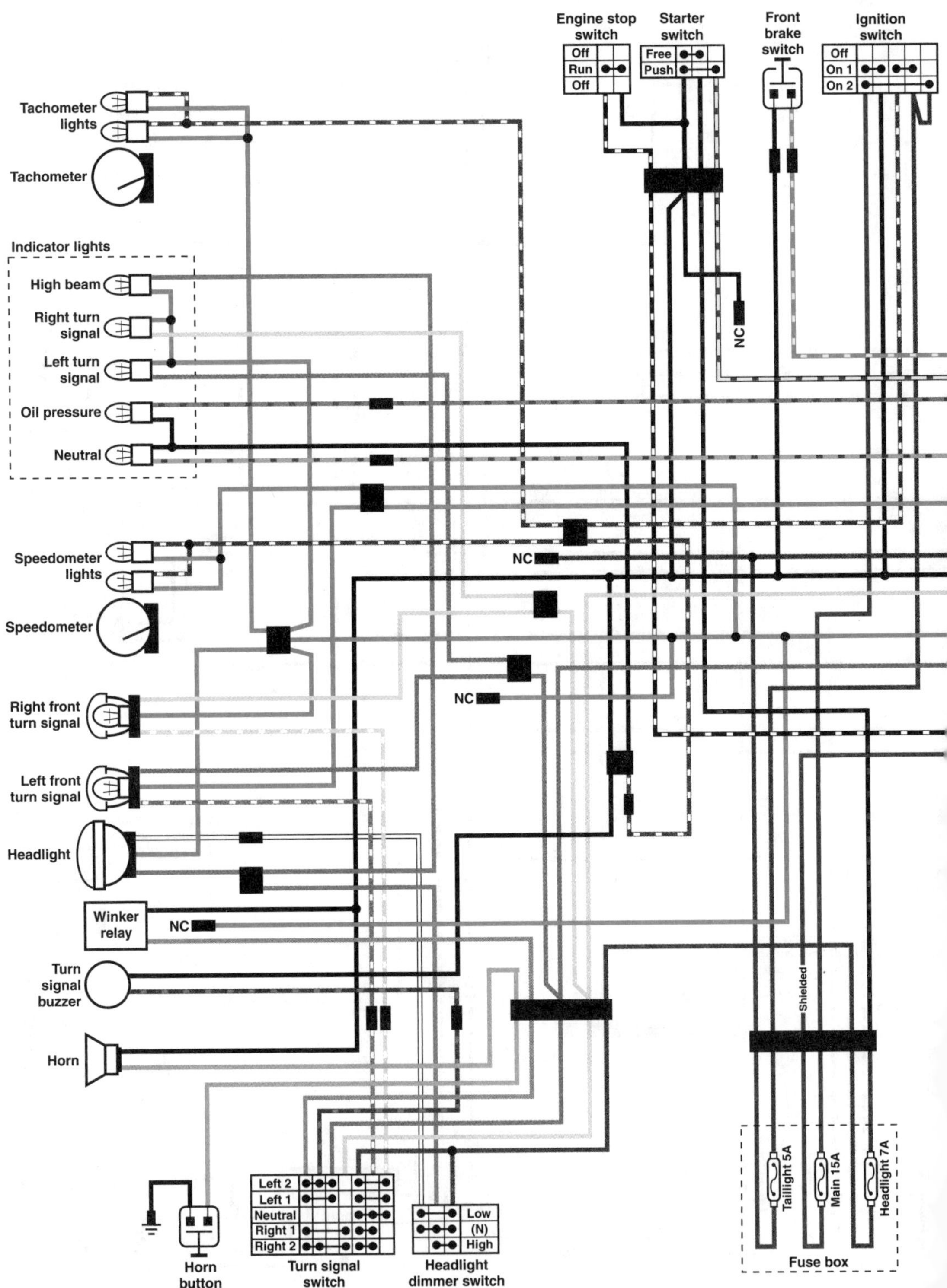

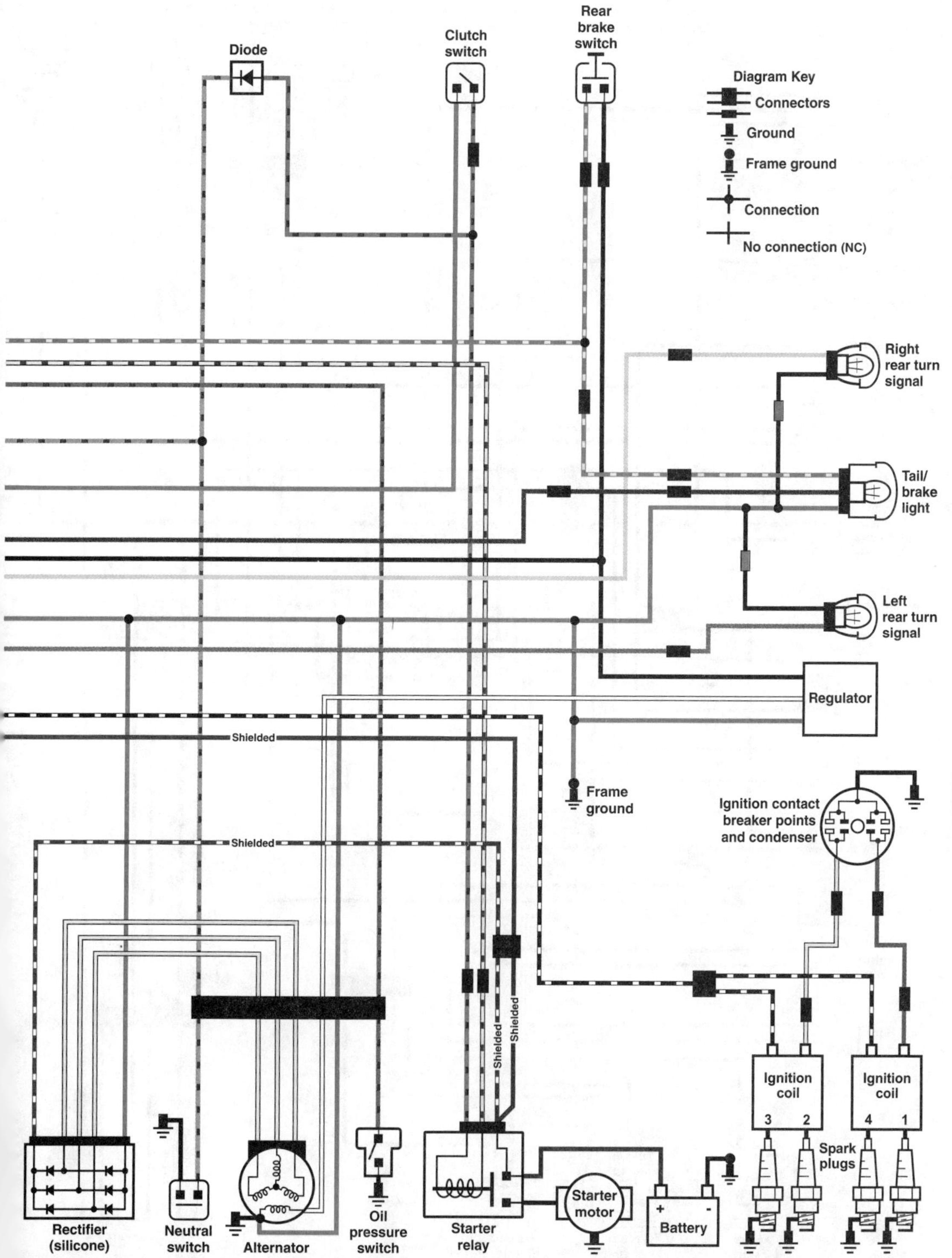

Diode

Clutch switch

Rear brake switch

Diagram Key
Connectors
Ground
Frame ground
Connection
No connection (NC)

Right rear turn signal

Tail/ brake light

Left rear turn signal

Regulator

Shielded

Frame ground

Ignition contact breaker points and condenser

Shielded

Shielded

Shielded

Ignition coil
3 2

Ignition coil
4 1

Spark plugs

Rectifier (silicone)

Neutral switch

Alternator

Oil pressure switch

Starter relay

Starter motor

+ -
Battery

CB750K8 (1978)

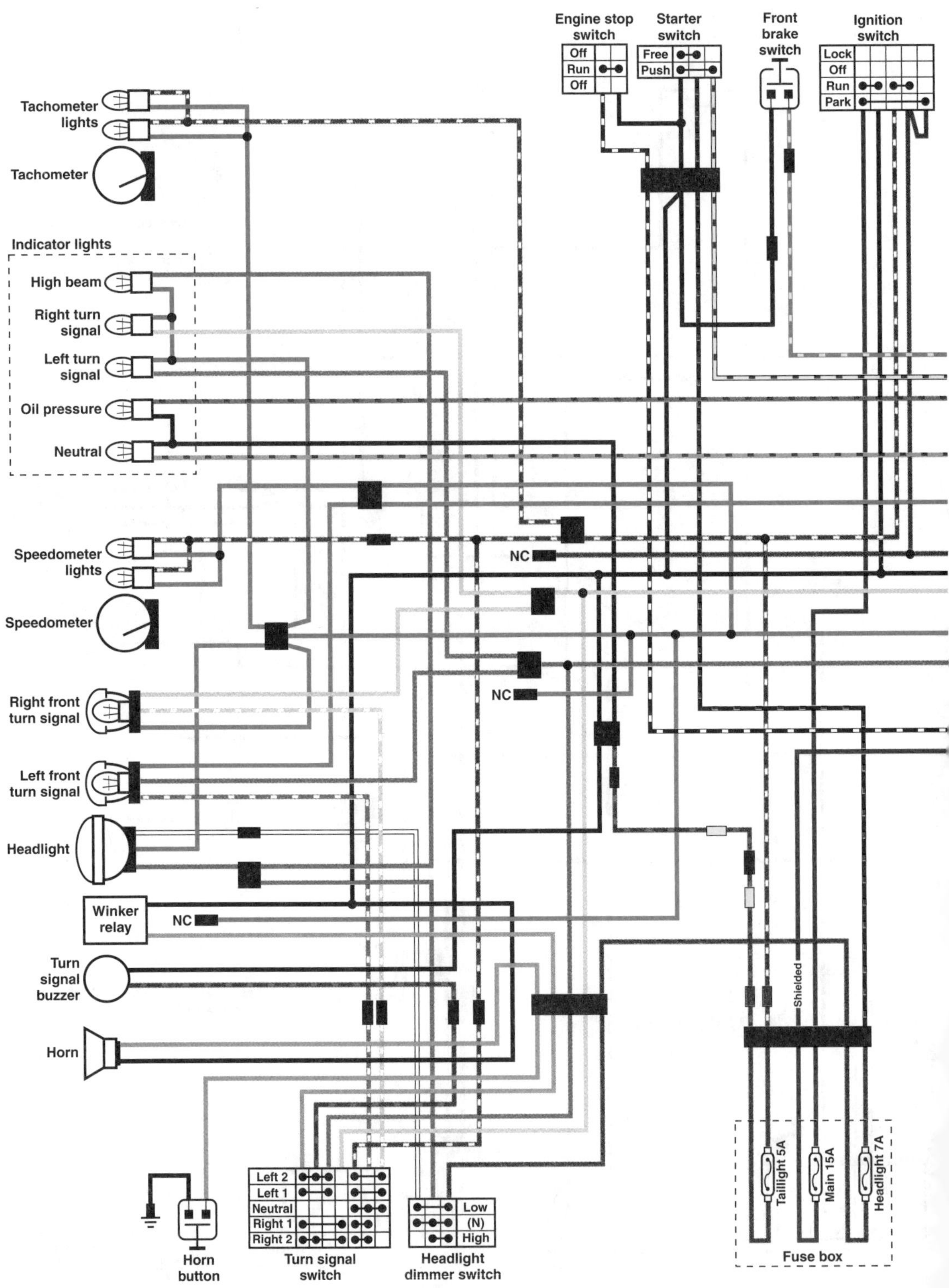

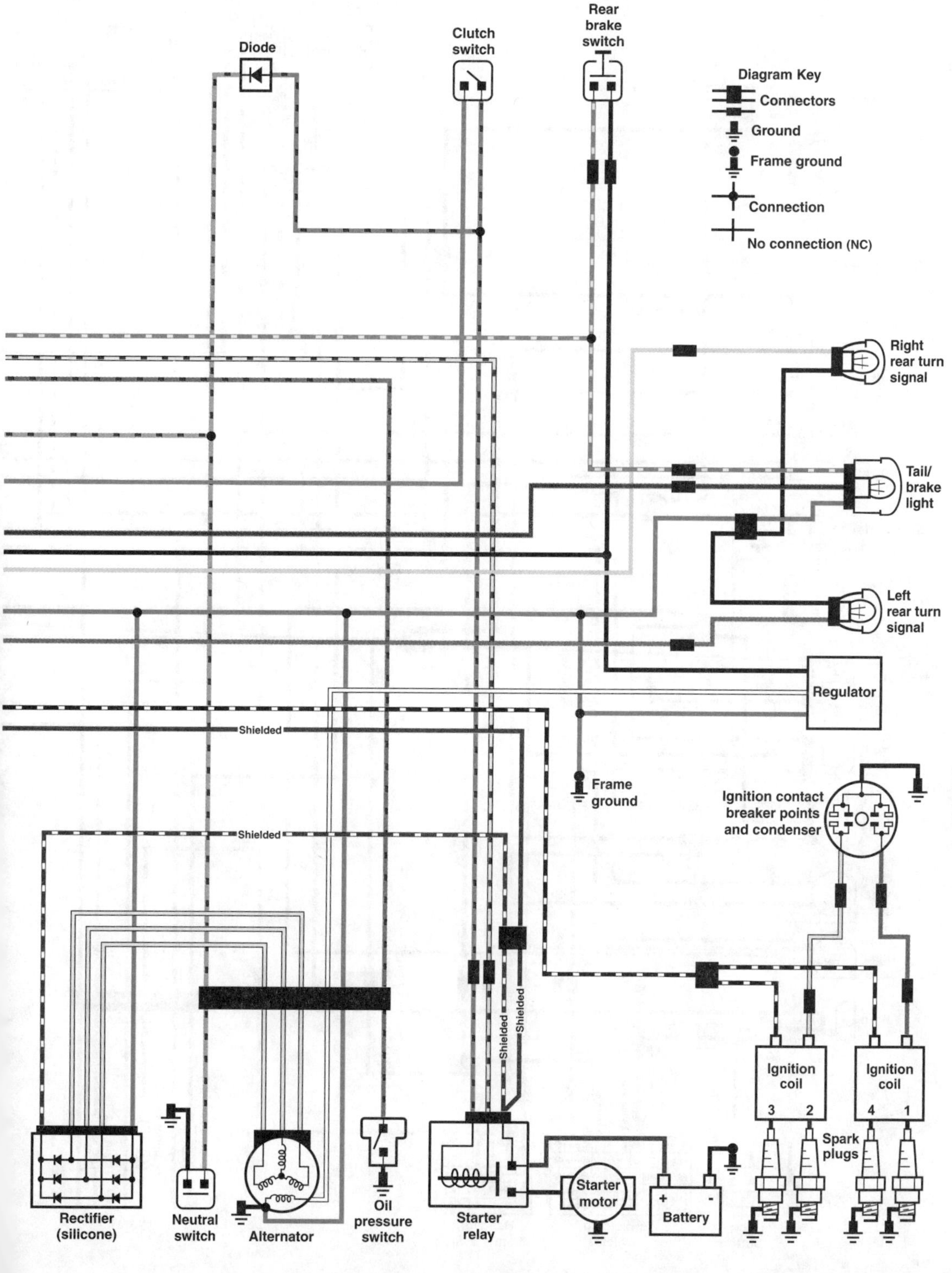

Rear brake switch

Clutch switch

Diode

Diagram Key

Connectors

Ground

Frame ground

Connection

No connection (NC)

Right rear turn signal

Tail/ brake light

Left rear turn signal

Regulator

Shielded

Frame ground

Ignition contact breaker points and condenser

Shielded

Shielded

Shielded

Ignition coil

3 2

Ignition coil

4 1

Spark plugs

Rectifier (silicone)

Neutral switch

Alternator

Oil pressure switch

Starter relay

Starter motor

Battery

+ -

CB750F (1975-1976)

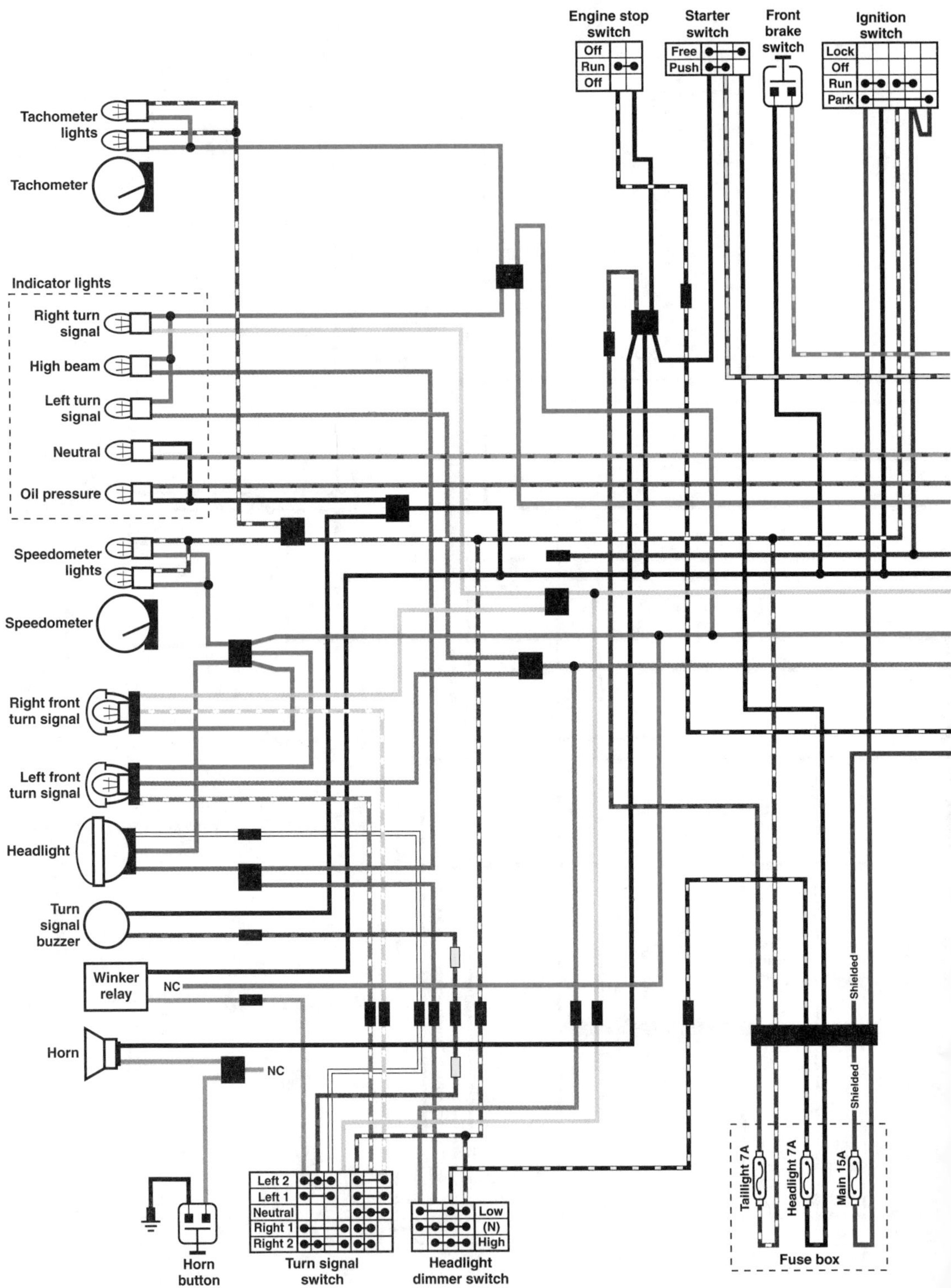

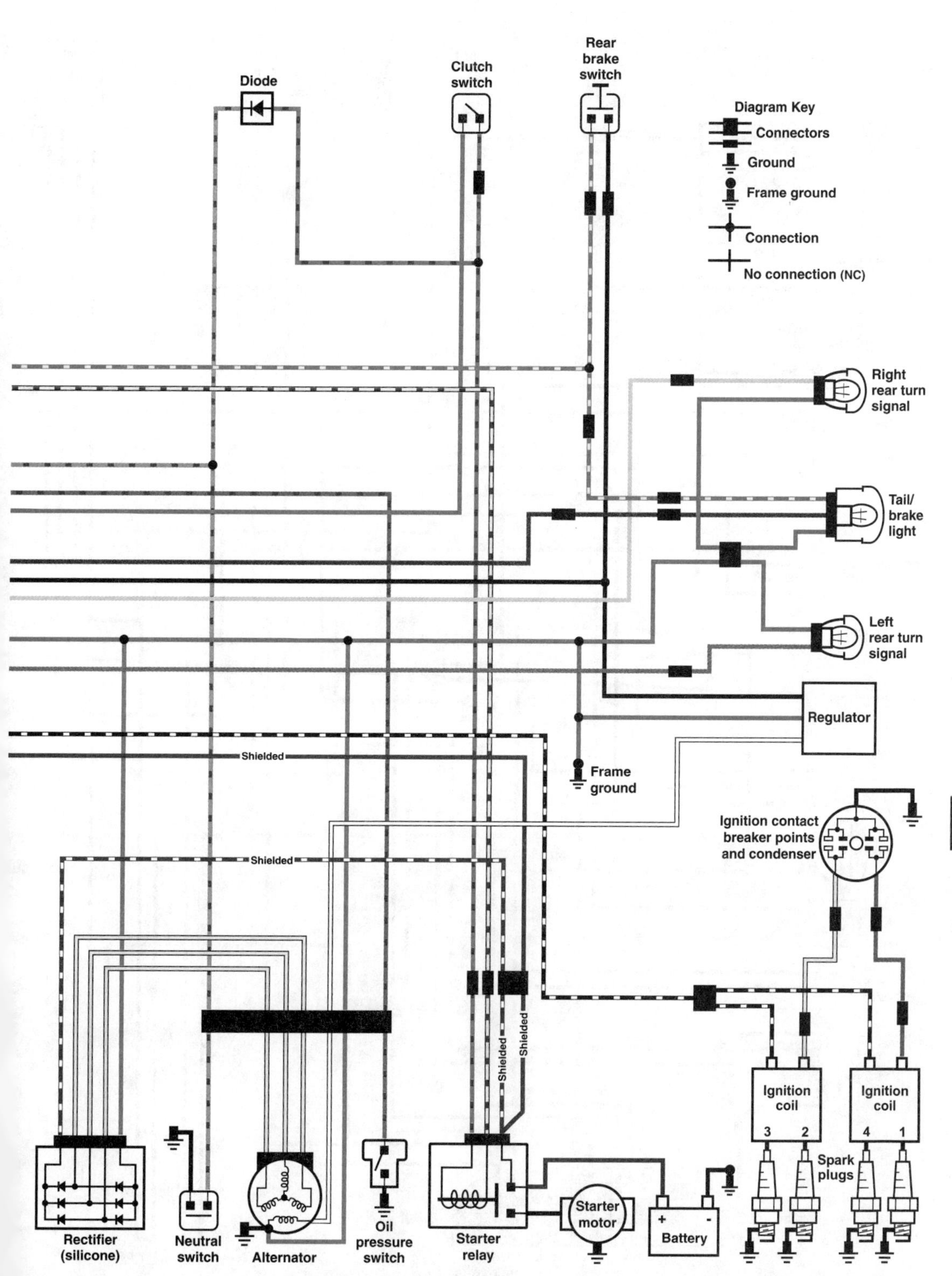
Diode
Clutch switch
Rear brake switch
Diagram Key
Connectors
Ground
Frame ground
Connection
No connection (NC)
Right rear turn signal
Tail/ brake light
Left rear turn signal
Regulator
Frame ground
Shielded
Shielded
Ignition contact breaker points and condenser
Shielded
Shielded
Ignition coil
Ignition coil
3
2
4
1
Spark plugs
Rectifier (silicone)
Neutral switch
Alternator
Oil pressure switch
Starter relay
Starter motor
+
-
Battery

CB750F (1977-1978)

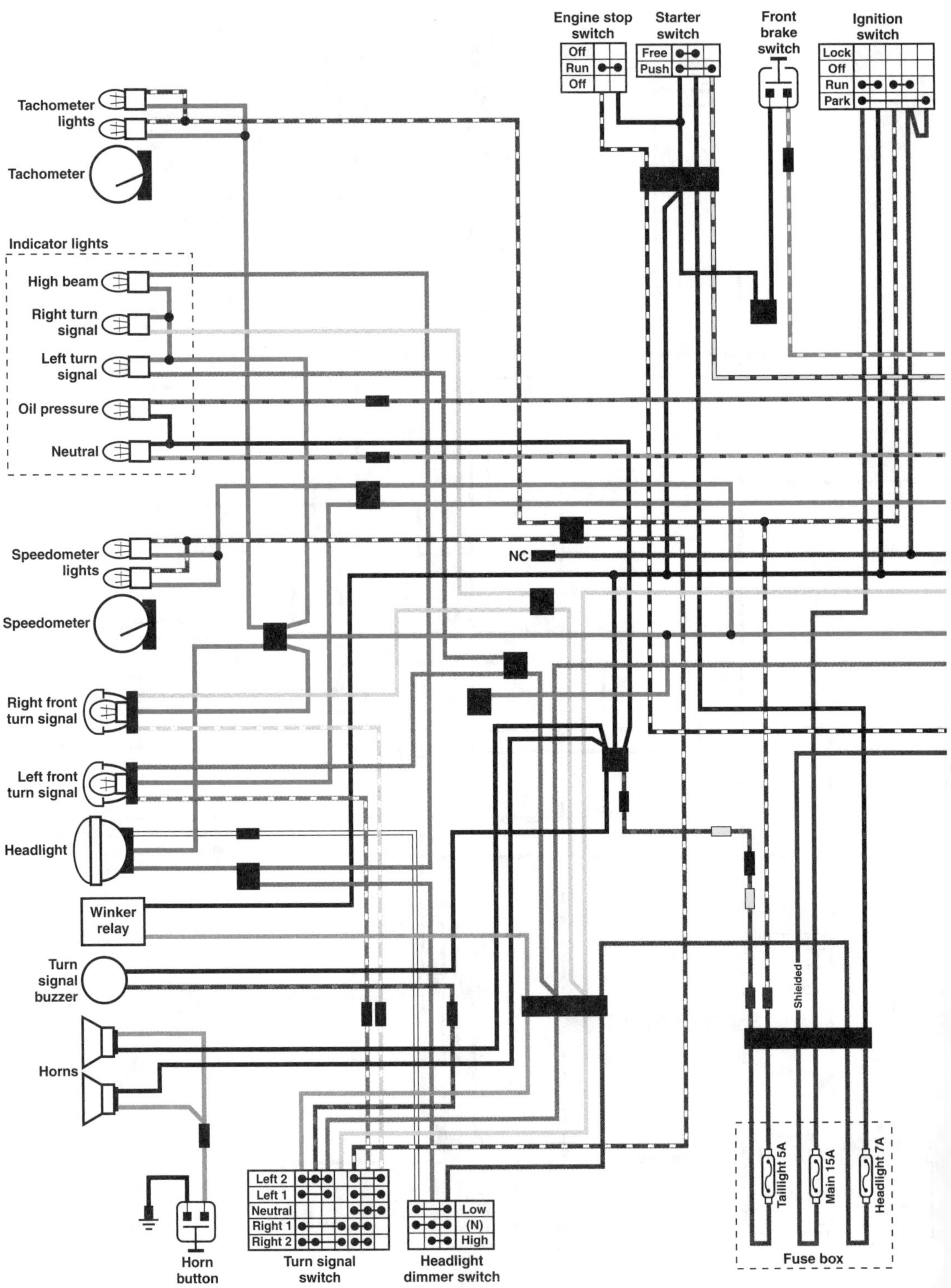

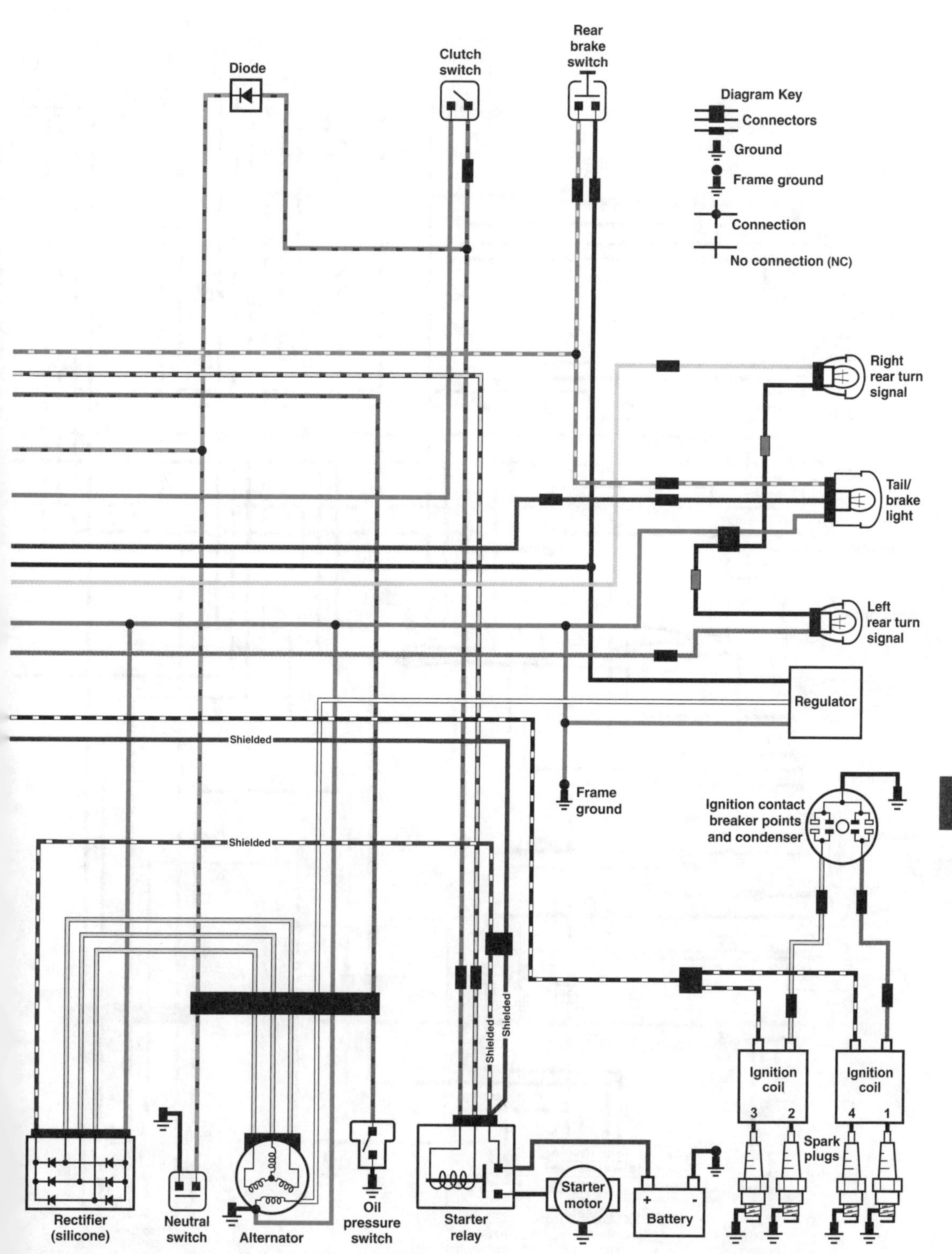
Diode
Clutch switch
Rear brake switch
Diagram Key
Connectors
Ground
Frame ground
Connection
No connection (NC)
Right rear turn signal
Tail/ brake light
Left rear turn signal
Regulator
Shielded
Shielded
Frame ground
Ignition contact breaker points and condenser
Shielded
Shielded
Ignition coil
3 2
Ignition coil
4 1
Spark plugs
Rectifier (silicone)
Neutral switch
Alternator
Oil pressure switch
Starter relay
Starter motor
+ -
Battery

CB750A (1976)

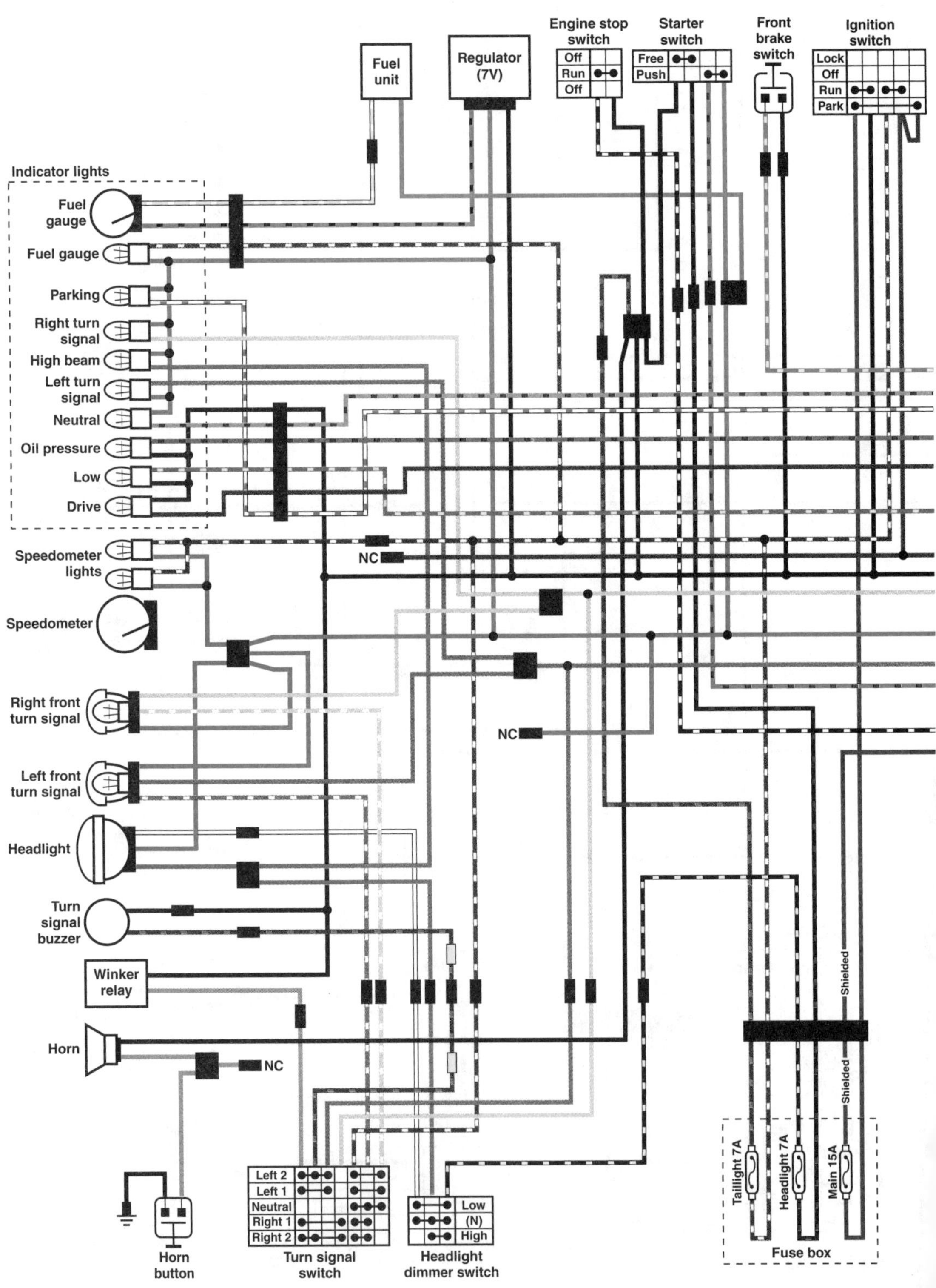

Fuel unit
Regulator (7V)
Engine stop switch
Off
Run
Off
Starter switch
Free
Push
Front brake switch
Ignition switch
Lock
Off
Run
Park
Indicator lights
Fuel gauge
Fuel gauge
Parking
Right turn signal
High beam
Left turn signal
Neutral
Oil pressure
Low
Drive
Speedometer lights
NC
Speedometer
Right front turn signal
NC
Left front turn signal
Headlight
Turn signal buzzer
Winker relay
Shielded
Horn
NC
Shielded
Taillight 7A
Headlight 7A
Main 15A
Fuse box
Left 2
Left 1
Neutral
Right 1
Right 2
Turn signal switch
Low
(N)
High
Headlight dimmer switch
Horn button

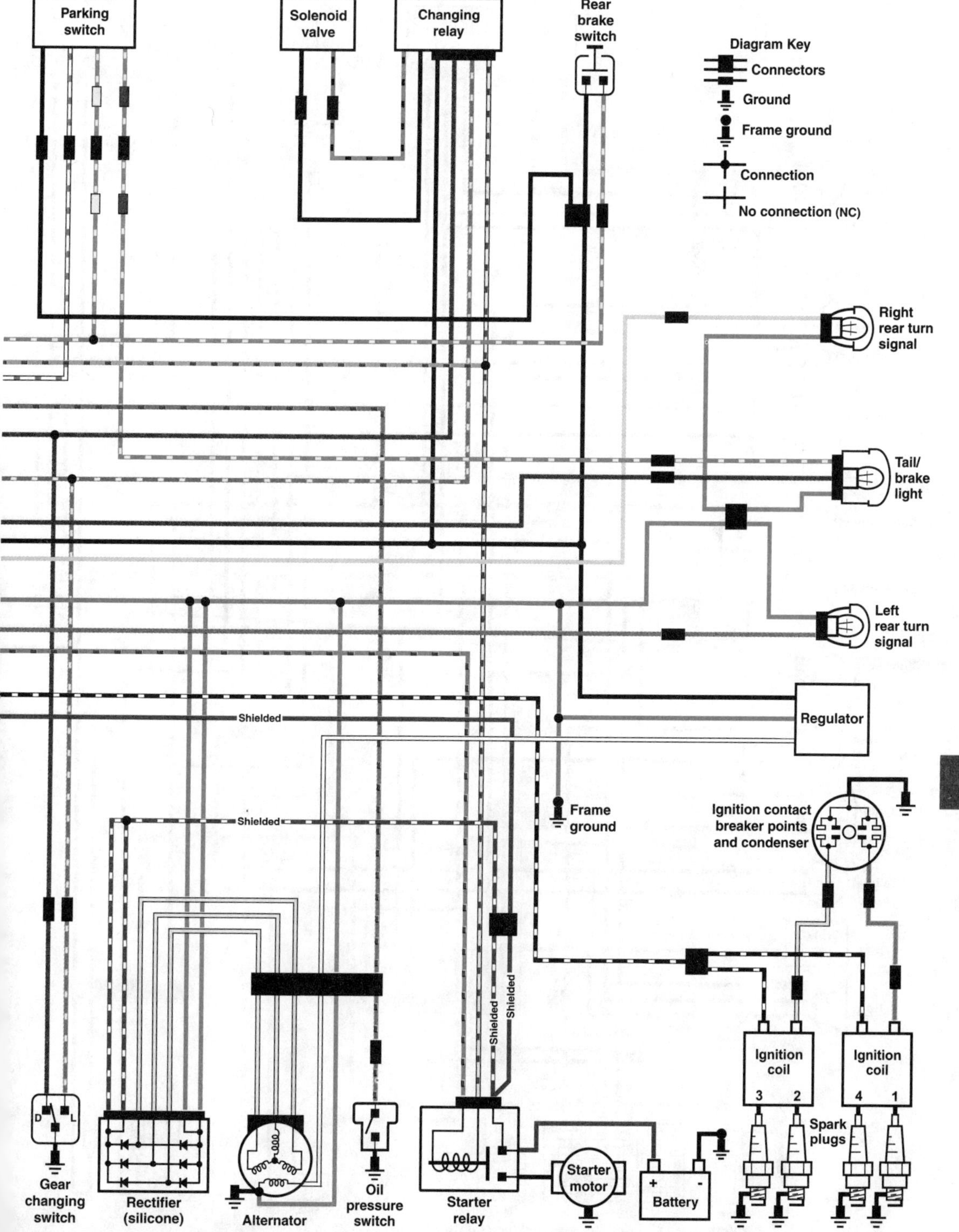
Parking switch
Solenoid valve
Changing relay
Rear brake switch
Diagram Key
Connectors
Ground
Frame ground
Connection
No connection (NC)
Right rear turn signal
Tail/ brake light
Left rear turn signal
Regulator
Shielded
Shielded
Frame ground
Ignition contact breaker points and condenser
Shielded
Shielded
Ignition coil
Ignition coil
3
2
4
1
Spark plugs
D
L
Gear changing switch
Rectifier (silicone)
Alternator
Oil pressure switch
Starter relay
Starter motor
+
-
Battery

CB750A (1977-1978)

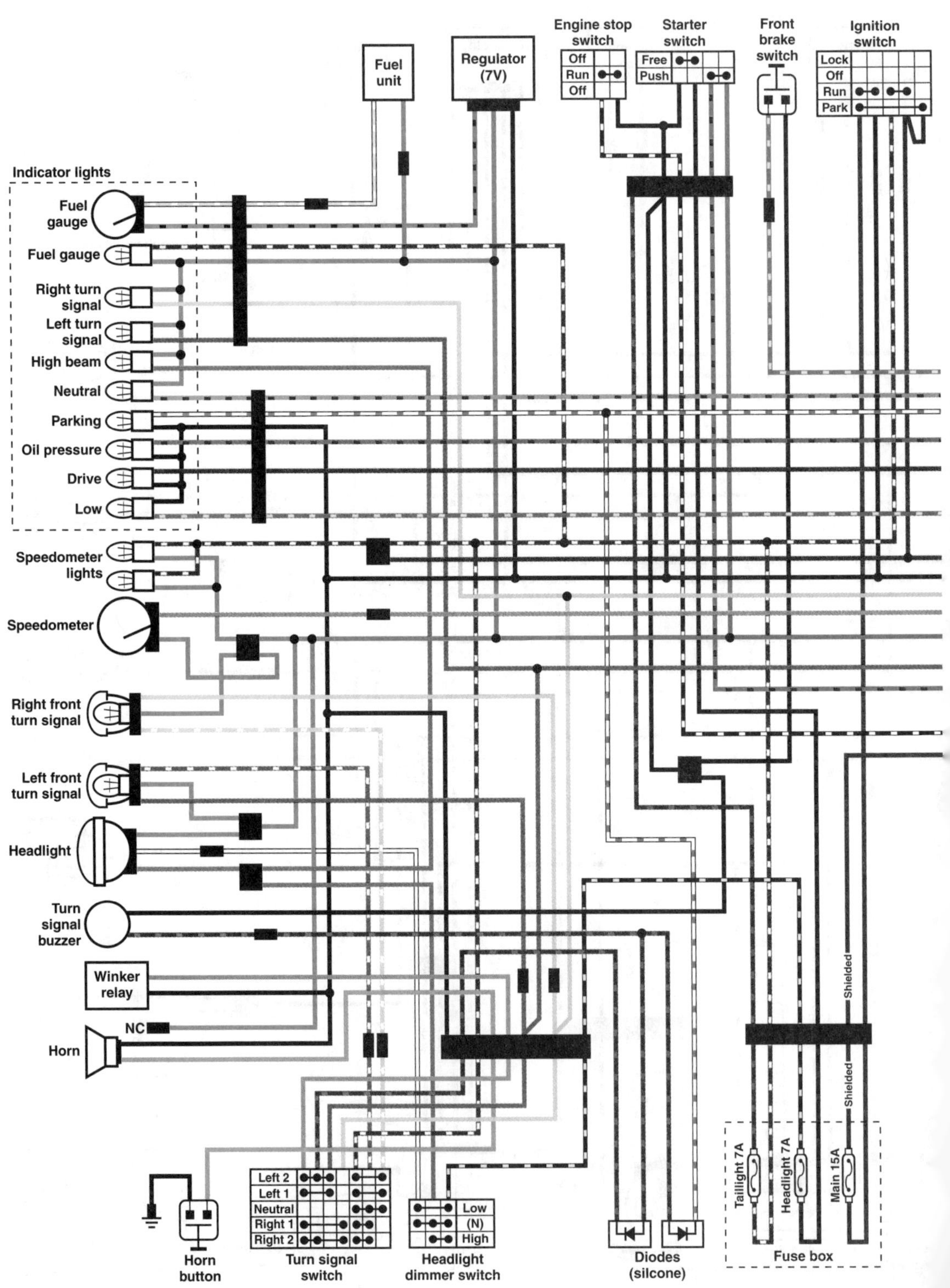

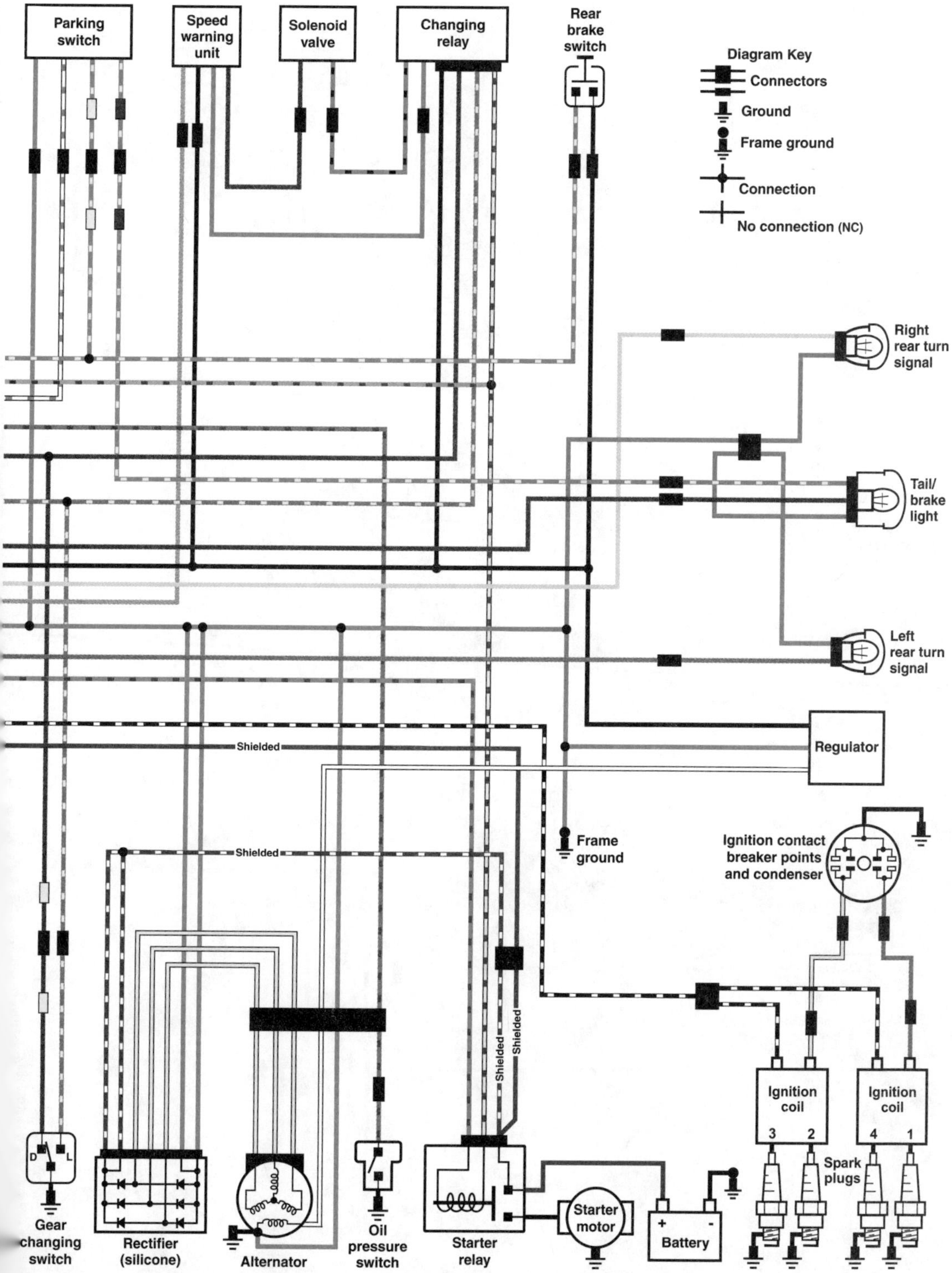

Parking switch

Speed warning unit

Solenoid valve

Changing relay

Rear brake switch

Diagram Key

Connectors

Ground

Frame ground

Connection

No connection (NC)

Right rear turn signal

Tail/ brake light

Left rear turn signal

Regulator

Shielded

Shielded

Frame ground

Ignition contact breaker points and condenser

Shielded

Shielded

Ignition coil

3 2

Ignition coil

4 1

Spark plugs

Gear changing switch

D L

Rectifier (silicone)

Alternator

Oil pressure switch

Starter relay

Starter motor

Battery

+ -

NOTES

NOTES

NOTES

MAINTENANCE LOG

Date	Miles	Type of Service